Bounce Back!

A Wellbeing and Resilience Program
2nd edition

With online IWB activities

Years **K–2**
Classroom Resources

Helen McGrath and Toni Noble

Pearson Australia
(a division of Pearson Australia Group Pty Ltd)
20 Thackray Road, Port Melbourne, Victoria 3207
PO Box 460, Port Melbourne, Victoria 3207
www.pearson.com.au

Sydney, Melbourne, Brisbane, Perth, Adelaide
and associated companies around the world

Copyright © Helen McGrath and Toni Noble 2011
First published 2011 by Pearson Australia
2014   2013   2012   2011
10 9 8 7 6 5 4 3 2 1

Reproduction and communication for educational purposes
The Australian *Copyright Act 1968* (the Act) allows a maximum of one chapter or 10% of the pages of this work, whichever is the greater, to be reproduced and/or communicated by any educational institution for its educational purposes provided that that educational institution (or the body that administers it) has given a remuneration notice to Copyright Agency Limited (CAL) under the Act. For details of the CAL licence for educational institutions contact Copyright Agency Limited (www.copyright.com.au).

Reproduction and communication for other purposes
Except as permitted under the Act (for example any fair dealing for the purposes of study, research, criticism or review), no part of this book may be reproduced, stored in a retrieval system, communicated or transmitted in any form or by any means without prior written permission. All enquiries should be made to the publisher at the address above.

This book is not to be treated as a blackline master; that is, any photocopying beyond fair dealing requires prior written permission.

Commissioning Editor: Sabine Bolick
Project Editor: Andrea Davison
Editor: Anne McKenna
Designer: Anita Adams
Copyright & Pictures Editor: Marg Barber
Production Controller: Claire Henry
Cover Design: Justin Lim
Illustrators: Técha Noble and Bruce Rankin
Printed in Malaysia (CTP-VVP)

National Library of Australia Cataloguing-in-Publication entry
Author: McGrath, Helen.
Title: Bounce back! : years k - 2 : a wellbeing and resilience
program / by Helen McGrath & Toni Noble; illustrated by Técha Noble.
Edition: 2nd ed.
ISBN: 9781442534629(pbk.)
Notes: Includes bibliographical references.
Subjects: Resilience (Personality trait) in children.
Other Authors/Contributors: Noble, Toni. Noble, Técha.
Dewey Number: 370.153
Pearson Australia Group Pty Ltd   ABN 40 004 245 943

Acknowledgements
We thank the following for their contributions to our text book:

AMPD: All Music Publishing & Distribution Pty. Ltd.,

Every effort has been made to trace and acknowledge copyright. However, should any infringement have occurred, the publishers tender their apologies and invite copyright owners to contact them.

Disclaimer/s
The selection of internet addresses (URLs) provided for this book was valid at the time of publication and was chosen as being appropriate for use as a primary education research tool. However, due to the dynamic nature of the internet, some addresses may have changed, may have ceased to exist since publication, or may inadvertently link to sites with content that could be considered offensive or inappropriate. While the authors and publisher regret any inconvenience this may cause readers, no responsibility for any such changes or unforeseeable errors can be accepted by either the authors or the publisher.

Contents

Introduction iv

Unit 1: Core values 1

Unit 2: People bouncing back 34

Unit 3: Courage 50

Unit 4: Looking on the bright side 70

Unit 5: Emotions 86

Unit 6: Relationships 118

Unit 7: Humour 143

Unit 8: No bullying 161

Unit 9: STAR! (Success) 180

Introduction

Welcome to *Bounce Back! A Wellbeing and Resilience Program*. This program contains resource materials and strategies to teach young people the social–emotional learning skills that underpin wellbeing and resilience. The program consists of three books as well as online resources. In this **Classroom Resources** book, there are nine curriculum units suitable for Years K–2 or lower primary students. The **Handbook** outlines the theory, rationale and research that underpin *Bounce Back!* and describes in detail the key teaching strategies and resources for its delivery.

This *Years K–2* book is suitable for students in the first three years of primary schooling, i.e. students aged approximately five to seven years.

The two other books in the series are:
- *Years 3 & 4*, which is suitable for students in the third and fourth years of primary schooling, i.e. students aged approximately eight to ten years
- *Years 5–8*, which is suitable for students in the fifth and sixth years of primary schooling and the first two years of junior secondary, i.e. students aged approximately 10 to 14 years.

The key concepts that are taught in the nine curriculum units are summarised below. Each unit begins with explanations of each of the key concepts and is followed by a rich curriculum to teach these key concepts. All units include Circle Time; cooperative learning; use of children's literature, songs and music, games and activities (many for the interactive whiteboard or classroom computers); visual and performing arts; construction and a wide range of engaging learning activities, many supported by blackline masters.

Unit 1: Core values

- Honesty
- Fairness (including social justice)
- Responsibility
- Support (being kind; showing care and compassion)
- Cooperation
- Acceptance of differences (accepting, respecting, living with and finding the positive side of differences in others)
- Respect (for the rights and feelings of others; self-respect, e.g. cybersafe behaviour and protective behaviours)
- Friendliness and inclusion (being friendly and socially responsible; including others in games, activities and conversations)

Introduction

Unit 2: People bouncing back

- The ways in which nature bounces back (e.g. bush regeneration and skin repair)
- Well-known people who have bounced back after hard times or hardship
- The BOUNCE acronym and ways to teach it
- Using helpful thinking that calms you down and reflects reality
- Recognising that neither you nor other people are perfect
- Focusing on the positives and using humour as a way of coping
- Normalising instead of personalising

Unit 3: Courage

- Understanding that if there is no fear, there is no courage
- Learning to discriminate between everyday courage, heroism (acting bravely to help someone else), thrill seeking, professional risk taking and foolhardiness
- Recognising that everyday courage can be either physical (e.g. diving into a pool), psychological (e.g. asking someone to come and stay) or moral (e.g. supporting someone who is being treated unfairly despite the risk of losing friends or being criticised)
- Understanding that fear is relative—what makes one person scared or nervous may not make another person scared or nervous
- Developing the skills and perceptions that lead to being more courageous in many areas of one's life

Unit 4: Looking on the bright side

- Using positive tracking, i.e. the skill of focusing on the positive aspects of a negative situation, however small they may be
- Positive conversion of negative events and mistakes into opportunities and learning experiences
- Accepting that bad times are temporary and don't have to spoil other parts of your life
- Developing an optimistic explanatory style when faced with setbacks or difficulties by understanding that setbacks:
    – are only temporary ('things will get better')
    – happen to other people too ('not just me')
    – are limited to the immediate incident(s) ('just this')
- Expressing gratitude by being thankful for the good things that happen and taking time to express thanks and show appreciation towards others
- Finding hope in difficult times
- Being open-minded and flexible when solving problems and having confidence in your own ability to solve problems and take positive actions

Unit 5: Emotions

- Understanding that very few events are good or bad in themselves and that how you think about something strongly influences how you feel about it
- Recognising, enjoying and recalling your own positive emotions and the events that promote these positive feelings
- Learning how to change a bad mood into a good mood
- Amplifying positive emotions by sharing positive experiences with others
- Recognising and managing negative emotions such as anger, sadness, worry, disappointment and embarrassment, and understanding that choices can be made about how to manage these emotions and what actions to take

- Recognising the feelings and intentions of others
- Responding with empathy to the feelings of others
- Using positive self-talk and low-key emotional language

Unit 6: Relationships

- Developing social skills for making and keeping friends
- Developing social skills for getting along well with others and being accepted
- Developing skills for managing disagreements well

Unit 7: Humour

- Understanding that humour can help with coping in hard times as well as with supporting others
- Differentiating between humour that helps and humour that harms, stereotypes, trivialises or denies
- Participating with classmates in humorous actvities through Giggle Gym sessions (brief daily humorous activities that can be used as a stress break in class)

Unit 8: No bullying

- Understanding terms such as *bullying* and *cyberbullying* and helping students discriminate between bullying and other kinds of anti-social behaviour
- Understanding the difference between asking for support, acting responsibly to support someone else and 'dobbing'
- Developing skills for responding adaptively to being bullied or put down, for example:
  - accepting that if you have 'self-respect' then you 'self-protect'
  - 'saving face'
  - asking for support/help
  - verbal and non-verbal assertiveness
- Developing skills for understanding and managing negative peer pressure
- Developing skills for discouraging bullying and offering bystander support

Unit 9: STAR! (Success)

- Helping students to identify and confirm their own relative intellectual and character strengths
- Understanding that strengths can be developed and limitations improved through effort
- Understanding that success is mostly a result of effort and persistence (but ability contributes too)
- Developing skills of self-discipline and self-management (e.g. willpower, effort, time management and organisational skills)
- Developing skills and attitudes for achieving goals (e.g. setting goals, identifying different pathways to goal achievement, making a plan with small steps, taking sensible risks, persisting in the face of obstacles, problem solving and being resourceful when things are challenging or when something goes wrong)
- Challenging students to use their initiative and hence understand the real-life 'rocky up-and-down' process of goal achievement
- Encouraging a sense of meaning and purpose through doing things for others

Introduction

Supplementary online unit: Elasticity

This unit is available online at www.pearsonplaces.com.au/bounceback.aspx.
- Investigating and experimenting with elastic forces
- Springs: how they work and their uses.

Glossary of icons

The following icons are used to indicate the types of activities in all curriculum units.

Circle Time is used to introduce each key concept. There are guidelines for running Circle Time on pages 84 to 88 in the **Handbook**.

Picture books, poems and other literature are used extensively throughout all curriculum units. The best books to teach *Bounce Back!* concepts are also often the best books to achieve literacy outcomes. Rich activities to teach the *Bounce Back!* concepts using the recommended children's literature are suggested. Add your own literacy activities to achieve both literacy and social–emotional learning outcomes. See pages 95 to 96 of the **Handbook** for literature and *Bounce Back!* discussion prompts.

Follow-up activities develop students' deep understanding of the *Bounce Back!* concepts.

Songs and music are used throughout the units. Some are *Bounce Back!* songs written to familiar tunes. Others are engaging, age-appropriate songs to teach the *Bounce Back!* concepts, most with animations and lyrics available online at www.pearsonplaces.com.au/bounceback.aspx.

Role-plays and the use of puppets and props to act out good and bad ways to bounce back are featured throughout the program.

Games are used in all units, especially to consolidate the learning of key concepts.

Every unit has individual blackline master worksheet activities, e-activities, e-games and e-tools that can be downloaded from www.pearsonplaces.com.au/bounceback.aspx. The e-activities, e-tools and e-games can be used for whole-class instruction on the intereactive whiteboard (IWB) or for individual, pair or small-group work on classroom computers. Each unit has a detailed list of all the resources used in the program, with ideas on how to find books, poems, songs, websites, weblinks and films. The Elasticity unit, assessments and information for parents are also available online.

vii

Unit 1

Core values

Key points

Values are easy to say, but often hard to do.
A value is a statement of something you believe is important to do. Nobody is perfect, but you can try to put your values into practice and do what you believe is the right thing, even though you may not always succeed.

It is important to be honest.
Being honest means telling the truth, not stealing, giving things back when they belong to someone else and owning up when you have done the wrong thing.

It is important to be fair.
Being fair means following the rules and not cheating; returning favours and kindnesses; and helping others to get a fair deal, i.e. have justice, food, shelter, medical treatment and schooling.

It is important to be responsible.
Being responsible means not letting people down, and doing what you agree to do without having to be told all the time. It also means doing your chores, trying to be on time so that you don't upset other people's plans, being sensible, and helping those who need it, such as younger children or animals.

It is important to care about and support others and be kind.
Supporting and caring about other people means helping when they need it, being kind and thoughtful, giving encouragement, listening when they have a problem, and being patient with them when they find it hard to do something.

It is important to cooperate.
Cooperating means working together to achieve something that you both want. It requires sharing ideas and resources, listening, encouraging each other, letting everyone have a say, doing your share of the work, and making decisions that are fair to everyone.

It is OK to be different.
Everyone is different and that's OK. If you feel OK about differences in people, then you get to know people who are different, you include them in games and conversations, you don't tease or exclude them and you see the fact that everyone is different as a good thing. You enjoy the differences and you learn to just put up with those differences you may not like.

It is important to be friendly.
Being friendly means being kind and welcoming to others and including others even if they are not your friends or they are people who are hard for you to like. This means looking in their eyes and smiling, saying hello and talking to them, finding something funny to laugh about together, being kind to them and inviting them to join in games and conversations. Being friendly towards strangers is not a good thing to do until you are very sure they are safe people.

It is important to show respect to others.
Respecting other people means treating others as you want them to treat you. It means you have to stop and think about the feelings and rights of others. Respect involves being polite and using good manners, not insulting or hurting others, not getting in the way of others when they are trying to do something, looking after shared property and the property of others, asking permission to use things that belong to someone else, and speaking in a polite tone of voice.

It is important to respect yourself.
Self-respect is when you like and accept yourself. You believe that you matter and should be treated well by others. If you have self-respect then you also self-protect, i.e. you take care of yourself and keep yourself from harm. If you self-respect, you speak up when someone doesn't treat you respectfully.

Bounce Back! Classroom Resources Years K–2

Circle Time: Honesty 4
Picture books 4
   Pinocchio
   David Gets in Trouble
   Franklin Fibs
   It Wasn't Me! Learning About Honesty
   That's Mine, Horace
   I Always, Always Get My Way
   Give That Back, Jack! A Cautionary Tale
   Don't Tell Lies, Lucy! A Cautionary Tale
e-activities 5
Drama 5
   Good fairy/wizard and bad fairy/wizard ....

Circle Time: Not cheating (being honest and fair) 6

Circle Time: Being fair 6
Picture books 7
   The Lion and the Mouse
   The Little Red Hen
   It's Your Turn, Roger
   The Giant Child
   For Every Child
Song 8
   'Two Little Boys'

Circle Time: Being responsible 8
Picture books 8
   Outside Over There
   Horton Hatches the Egg
   Little Toot
   Bradley's Call for Help

Circle Time: Caring about and supporting others and showing kindness 8
Class discussion or inquiry-based learning 9
   Guide dogs support people
Picture books 9
   Dogger
   Have You Filled a Bucket Today? A Guide to Daily Happiness for Kids
Game 10
   Snowman
Activity 10
   Alien!

Circle Time: Teacher support 11

Circle Time: Supporting people we don't know (a combination of kindness and fairness) 11
Picture books 11
   Wilfrid Gordon McDonald Partridge
   Room on the Broom
   Max
   Goodnight Harry
Game 12
   People who help us

Circle Time: Family support 12
Picture books 13
   The Kissing Hand
   Love You Forever

Circle Time: Kindness to animals 13
Picture books 14
   Little Lost Bat
   The Cat with No Name

Circle Time: Cooperation 14
Songs 15
   'I'd Like to Teach the World to Sing'
   'It's a Small World'
   'We All Sing with the Same Voice'
   'Cooperation Makes it Happen'
   'The Sharing Song'
   'I Can't Get No Cooperation'
Picture books 15
   We Share Everything!
   The Bad Tempered Ladybird
   Pepo and Lolo and the Red Apple
   Sharing a Shell
   Share Said the Rooster
   Ten Things I Can Do to Help My World
   Never Ever Before
Team cooperative activities 16
   Beat the clock
   Safe island
   Class vegetable soup
   Class keep-it-up
   Lions fly
   Change places
   Cat and mouse
   Whisper game
   Memory cards
   Cooperative ball pass
   Cooperative clap ball
   Clap race
Cooperative activities with a partner 18
   Cooperative tower
   Cooperative building
   Cooperative drawing
   Cooperative cooking
   Red elbow
   Peg sorting race
   Alphabet cooperation

Circle Time: It's OK to be different 19
Activities 19
   Favourite photo
   Class statistics
Picture books 19
   Guess the Baby
   The Ugly Duckling
   Wombat Divine
   The Best Beak in Boonaroo Bay
   Green Eggs and Ham

Unit 1

Core values

Susan Laughs
Too Loud Lily
Our Stripy Baby
Baby Boomsticks
The Very Blue Thingamajig
It's OK to Be Different
Whoever You Are
Grandpa and Ah Gong
Henry and Amy
Activity 22
  Toys and difference

Circle Time: We can think differently. 22
Song. 23
  'What We Like'
Activities 23
  Movers and shakers
  We can draw differently
  Guess who's different?
  How are we the same?
  Same and different
  Celebrating diversity
Picture books 24
  Everybody Bakes Bread
  Everybody Brings Noodles
  Everybody Cooks Rice
  Everybody Serves Soup

Circle Time: Including others. 24
Picture books 25
  Rhino Neil
  This Is Our House

Circle Time: Being friendly. 25
Picture book 26
  Say Hello
Songs. 26
  'Bonjour Mes Amis'
  'Hello'
  'The Hello Song'
  'Hello Song'
  'Greetings!'

Circle Time: Smiling is contagious 27
Picture book 27
  The Gotcha Smile
Songs. 27
  'Smiling Is Contagious'
Poem 28
  'A Smile Is Just a Frown Turned Upside Down'
Activity 28
  Friendly greetings!

Circle Time: Respect 28
Poem 29
  'What Do You Suppose?'
Song. 29
  'Two Fat Gentlemen'

Game 29
  May I?
Picture books 30
  The Elephant and the Bad Baby
  Max and the Magic Word
  I Won't Say Please!
  Tissue Please!
  Excuse Me!
  Dirty Bertie
  Smelly Bertie
  Don't Be Greedy, Graham
  Greedy Grumpy Hippo
  Do Unto Otters: A Book About Manners
Activity 31
  A class 'good manners' book or a flipbook
Drama. 31
  Acting out good manners

Circle Time: Respect and self-respect . . . 31
Picture books 32
  I Can Be Safe
  Roonie B. Moonie: Lost and Alone

Consolidation: Core values 32
Activities 32
  Movers and shakers
  Other activities
  Reflections
Games 33
  Bingo strips
  Other games

Resources 33

3

Circle Time: Honesty

Start with the story of Pinocchio or any of the following books: *I Always, Always Get My Way*; *David Gets in Trouble*; *Franklin Fibs*; *It Wasn't Me!*; or *That's Mine, Horace* (see below).

Ask students to each tell a partner one thing about their family or pets that is true and one thing that is a fib. Their partner's task is to guess which statement is true and which is a fib. Then they swap roles.

Back in the circle, ask:
- How did it feel to be told a lie? How did it feel to tell the lie? Talk about what it means to be honest (see Key points, page 1).
- Ask each student in turn to give an example of someone being honest or dishonest and see if the other students can say which one it is.
- How do you feel when someone tells you a lie? Takes something of yours? Doesn't own up to what they have done? How do people treat you after they find out you have been dishonest?
- Can you tell when someone is telling you a lie?
- Talk about why it is important to be honest. Why is it important to tell the truth?
  (Being honest is fair and respects the rights of others. People can trust you; if people can trust you, they like you more and want you as a friend. You feel like you are a decent person so you like yourself more. Your parents are proud of you. It would be terrible if we had to distrust and be suspicious of everyone we met—no one would feel safe.)
- What happens to people who tell fibs or take things that belong to other people?
  (People don't trust them any more; if something else is stolen they are the first to be blamed. They don't feel good about themselves and don't like themselves much. People don't want to be their friends. They get a bad reputation because people expect them to do it again.)

Picture books

Pinocchio
There are many storybook versions of the fairytale *Pinocchio*, written by Italian author Carlo Collodi (1826–1890), and you probably have one in your library. There are also simple Italian versions for use in LOTE. Geppetto is a woodcutter who creates a wooden puppet called Pinocchio. A fairy grants his wish that the puppet become a human boy. Whenever Pinocchio tells a lie his nose grows longer but finally he learns to be honest.

→ Follow up with any of these:
- Turn the story into a drama activity. In pairs, students make a paper plate puppet (see **Handbook**, page 100) with a long nose like Pinocchio and a puppet with a normal-sized nose. When they are telling the fib they hold up the Pinocchio puppet and the other student holds the 'normal' puppet.
- Give students the challenge of making a Pinocchio puppet with a nose that can extend. This could also be a fun activity for older buddies to do with their younger buddies (as part of a buddy system within the school).
- Show one of the following films of the story: *Pinocchio* (1940, remastered in 2009)—in this Disney animated version a character called Jiminy Cricket acts as Pinocchio's conscience; *The Adventures of Pinocchio* (1996).

David Gets in Trouble
This is a simple and humorous book about honesty and responsibility. The story is about a little boy learning to move from not doing it, not meaning to do it, forgetting, not being his fault to being sorry.

Franklin Fibs
Franklin lies about his achievements but learns about honesty.

It Wasn't Me! Learning About Honesty
This is a simple cartoon-style book about why it can be hard to be honest, how a lie is usually a lot worse than whatever you did wrong in the first place, how lies get bigger and bigger and how people end up looking silly when others find out about their lie.

That's Mine, Horace
Horace, a little leopard, takes a truck that he finds in the schoolyard and refuses to give it to Walter, who claims it is his. When his teacher asks if the truck is Walter's, Horace denies it. When his mother asks about it, Horace says it is a gift from Walter. The adults make him feel worse by telling him that that they know he is an honest person. He sleeps poorly as a result of his feelings of guilt and next day he feels too ill to go to school. A get-well card from Walter helps to resolve the situation gently.

I Always, Always Get My Way
Emmy, aged three, is the youngest of three children in the family. Whenever anything goes wrong, even when she is clearly involved and often started things, she never admits that it's her fault and usually tries to blame things on one of the older children. Her behaviour is always explained away by a comment about how young she is and Emmy soon learns to use this as an excuse. Eventually, Emmy realises that she can't get away with her behaviour forever and that her actions do eventually have consequences. The story is written in humorous rhyme.

Give That Back, Jack! A Cautionary Tale
This is an exaggerated funny story in which the main character behaves badly and suffers dire consequences (similar to *The Boy Who Cried Wolf*). Jack thinks he can take anything he wants and often takes things belonging to his friends and doesn't give them back. But when he goes on a class trip to the zoo, the consequences for doing so are very unpleasant as he gets eaten by a snake.

Don't Tell Lies, Lucy! A Cautionary Tale
This is another cautionary tale by the same author as *Give That Back, Jack!* about Lucy, who tells lies and as a result, gets carried away by a giant wave.

Activities

Students can make a class book (see **Handbook**, page 97) about honesty (or a digital class story with each student making a page on honesty) and complete **BLM 1.1: Honesty Cartoons**. Students can also make their own versions of the pictures with both an honest and a dishonest response to choose from. These can be either hand-drawn or created using digital story software, such as Kid Pix. They can complete each other's activities or compile them in a class book in which the honest response is highlighted.

Drama

Good fairy/wizard and bad fairy/wizard
For these stories you need paper plate puppets (see **Handbook**, page 99) made from a magazine photo stuck onto a paper plate and held by a craft stick. Alternatively, cut out a crescent-shaped mouth and place it on a stick. The actors hold the mouth part of the mask over their own mouth but use their own eyes and nose. The same can be done with just a picture of eyes. You will need two girl puppets, three boy puppets and a parent puppet.

Use the good fairy/wizard and bad fairy/wizard strategy with the play. You will need the props for this (see **Handbook**, page 90). Make one good fairy or wizard puppet, and one bad fairy or wizard puppet.

- Anna takes Jake's ball when it is left somewhere. When Jake asks her if she has taken it she says 'No'. The good fairy asks Anna, 'Is that honest? Will people want to be your friend if you are dishonest? Do you feel bad about being dishonest? Will you feel better if you tell the truth and give it back?' The bad fairy says, 'No one will find out. Who cares about Jake? Just do what's good for you.' Anna thinks for a while and gives it back.
- Maria spills her drink on the carpet after her parent has told her not to put it on the carpet. When her parent sees it, Maria says, 'Jane did it'. The good wizard asks Maria, 'Is that honest? Will your parent be able to trust you to tell the truth? Do you feel bad about being dishonest? Will you feel better if you tell the truth?' The bad wizard says, 'No one will find out. Who cares anyway? Just do what's good for you.' Maria thinks for a while and then she tells her parent she did it and she's sorry.
- Sam takes his older brother Carl's cap and loses it. Carl is upset because he can't find it anywhere. The good fairy asks Sam, 'Is that honest? How do you think Carl is feeling? Do you feel bad? Would you feel better if you told the truth?' The bad fairy says, 'No one will find out. Who cares about Carl? Just do what's good for you.' Sam thinks for a while and then tells Carl he took it and he will replace it.

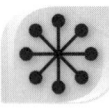

Circle Time: **Not cheating (being honest and fair)**

Start by playing a simple board game or a game of boxes or noughts and crosses on the board with a student. While you do this, cheat in an obvious way (e.g. throw the dice twice to get a better score or have a go when it's not your turn). You don't have to finish the game. Stop and say, 'Some of you seem upset? Why?' Then explain that you pretended to cheat to make the point about the importance of not cheating. Cheating is both dishonest and unfair. Talk about what cheating means. Ask each student to tell about a way in which someone could cheat in a game. Use examples of games the students play such as cards, Concentration, board games and ball games. Ask:

- Has anyone ever seen someone cheat (no names)? Make a list of all the ways in which people can cheat. Why do we dislike cheating? How does it make us feel? Do we want to play with and be friends with someone who cheats? Why not? (We can't trust them. It takes the fairness and the fun out of the game. We expect that they will cheat again next time.)
- What happens to someone who cheats? (They don't feel good about themselves and don't like themselves much. They can't find anyone to play with or be friends with. They get a bad reputation because people expect them to do it again.)

→ Follow up: Students can work with a partner to write and illustrate a story or compile sentences about a character who cheats in a game. You could also use puppet plays here with different kinds of games (see **Handbook**, pages 99 to 101, for ideas on puppets).

Circle Time: **Being fair**

Take in small treats such as stickers, marbles or pencils and some bowls to put them in. Set up an unfair situation. Organise students into groups of three and distribute the treats

Unit 1

Core values

unfairly by giving some groups a lot and some hardly any. Tell students not to touch the treats until you tell them to. Ask:

- Some of you seem upset—why? Discuss the concept of unfairness and explain that you deliberately set up an unfair situation to make the point that it is important to be fair. Ask students for ideas on how the items could be shared so that everyone got a fair deal. Redistribute the treats.
- How did it feel to be treated unfairly? Talk about what 'being fair' means. Selected students can talk about a time when they thought something that happened to them or to someone else wasn't fair.

Picture books

The 'Animal asks' e-tool (see **Handbook,** page 89) can also be used with eight selected critical prompts that can be applied to one or more of these books.

The Lion and the Mouse
In this fable by Aesop, a mouse is caught by a lion; to avoid being eaten he offers to help the lion at a later point. The lion thinks the idea of a mouse helping a lion is hilarious, but he lets him go. Not long after, the lion is trapped in a hunter's net and only the mouse can save him by gnawing through the ropes. The mouse honours his promise.
→ Ask: How was the mouse fair? Students can make lion and mouse masks and act out the story. See **Handbook,** page 99, for how to make masks.

The Little Red Hen
The Little Red Hen asks for help with making her bread, starting by sowing the wheat seeds right through to baking it. None of the other animals will help her, so ultimately they do not get any bread.
→ Ask: Was this fair? Students can act out the story or sequence the key parts of it. They could write a letter from the other animals to the Little Red Hen or from the Little Red Hen to the other animals.
→ Follow up by having students make a class digital story (see **Handbook,** page 97) of *The Little Red Hen* using small animal figures and drawings.

It's Your Turn, Roger
Roger, a young pig, refuses to take his turn at setting the table but eventually learns about being fair.

The Giant Child
A 'giant' child gets lost and ends up in a village where the villagers don't believe he is really a child and make him work hard for his food. The children in the village realise that, despite his size, he is only a child and help him with the work. Eventually the adult villagers realise they have inadvertently been cruel and decide they will never make any child work too hard again.
→ Link the story with the rights of a child to be protected against cruelty and to be properly looked after. Talk about how many children around the world have to work like adults. Ask students to write and draw about their typical day and then compare it with the typical day of very young children in poorer countries who have to work in mines, weaving carpets or selling souvenirs.

For Every Child
This book features 14 rights chosen from the United Nations Convention on the Rights of the Child, with each of the rights described in simple, evocative text.

Song

'Two Little Boys'
This is a song recorded by Rolf Harris about two little boys who are friends and share their toys and help each other. Later on they serve together in a war and again one friend helps the other.
→ Ask students what can be learnt about 'being fair' from the song (which also links with loyalty in friendships).

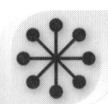

Circle Time: Being responsible

Read one or more of the books below to the class as a starting point. Ask: What do we mean by 'being responsible'? (See Key points, page 1.) How did these characters act responsibly? Ask each student one way in which they are responsible at home. (They can be relied upon to do a chore, mind a brother or sister for a few minutes, put away toys, feed a pet, be ready to go to school on time, etc.)

→ Follow up by sending a note home and asking parents to name one thing their child is responsible for and can be relied upon to do well. Make a class graph and follow up with sentences/report writing.

Picture books

Outside Over There
Ida is supposed to be minding her baby sister but she isn't doing a very good job and some goblins come and take the baby away. Ida realises that she has to make up for her irresponsibility by getting her sister back from the goblins.

Horton Hatches the Egg
Horton is left egg-sitting at the request of a bird who doesn't return. He follows through, doing the responsible thing and stays there as he promised.

Little Toot
Little Toot is a tugboat who mucks around and is irresponsible until the crunch comes and he must be responsible in a storm.

Bradley's Call for Help
When Bradley discovers that he can't wake his mum up, he rings 000 and saves the day.
→ Consider:
◎ adopting a nearby tree and, as a class, responsibly caring for it
◎ having a class pet, plant or garden and responsibly caring for it.

Circle Time: Caring about and supporting others and showing kindness

Talk about what we mean by supporting others. Use the 'Smiley ball' strategy (see **Handbook**, page 92) and ask each student how they could support people in one of the following situations:
◎ when someone in the class is feeling sick, loses their pencil case or forgets their lunch money

Unit 1

Core values

- when someone's pet dies, grandparent is ill or parent has to be in hospital for a while
- when a friend has to go in the swimming pool but they feel scared
- when a classmate is having trouble understanding their maths or reading
- when a brother or sister comes home from school after having a bad day because they got into trouble with a teacher
- when a classmate is worried because their parent who doesn't live with them wants them to stay at their house more often and they don't want to
- when a smaller child is alone and crying in the playground
- when a classmate is feeling embarrassed because they couldn't read aloud in class very well
- when a friend is upset because their parents had a argument, lost a job or have to move
- when a classmate has no one to play with, is feeling left out or isn't invited to a party.

Encourage students to give responses such as:
- *We could listen to them.*
- *We could remind them of previous successes.*
- *We could invite them to play.*
- *We could stay with them.*
- *We could tell them we understand their feelings.*
- *We could cheer them up.*
- *We could help them solve the problem.*
- *We could not laugh at them.*

Students can also take turns to talk about when a classmate helped them or was kind and caring. Follow up with **BLM 1.2: Our Classroom Is a 'Lift-up' Zone**.

You could also select eight of the above questions to be used with the 'Animal asks' e-tool (see **Handbook**, page 89).

Class discussion or inquiry-based learning

Guide dogs support people

Start with students using 'Lightning writing' (see **Handbook**, page 91) about guide dogs. Then talk about the support they give to people who are blind. They can discuss:
- the kinds of dogs that are trained (mainly labrador retrievers)
- the concept of 'puppy raisers', i.e. people who care for and train the dogs when they are puppies. How would it feel to give the puppies back after a year?

→ Follow up with drawings and a simple sentence about how the guide dogs help people. You may be able to get a member of the Guide Dogs Association or a puppy raiser to visit your school with their dog.

For further information, refer to the websites listed in the Resources online at Pearson Places.

Picture books

Dogger

David is very attached to Dogger, his stuffed dog. Dogger gets lost and David is very upset. Dogger turns up for sale at the local fete but David doesn't have enough money to buy him. His older sister, Bella, is kind and supportive and helps him to get Dogger back. His whole family is supportive.

→ When reading the story to the class, stop at the point where David realises he doesn't have enough money and the little girl who has purchased Dogger at the fete won't give him up. Have pairs of students take turns to talk about how they would help David and what he could do. Read on and then discuss how Bella was kind and supportive. Students can illustrate their favourite part of the story and include the words from that page, using the same colours as the book.

Have You Filled a Bucket Today? A Guide to Daily Happiness for Kids
This book encourages children to show kindness, appreciation, gratitude and love on a daily basis. Children are told that they carry an invisible bucket in which they keep their feelings about themselves. When their bucket is full they feel happy and when it's empty they feel sad. Showing kindness, affection and appreciation to others can help them to fill their own bucket.

→ Follow up by encouraging students to perform acts of kindness, write about them and then place them in their own 'bucket'. Each student could have a folder with a picture of a bucket on the cover, a bucket made from cardboard, a toy bucket or their own digital 'bucket' on the computer.

There are many websites that describe other activities to accompany this book—just search for the name of the book. Link this book with the 'Appreciation station' in Unit 4: Looking on the bright side (page 80).

Game

Snowman

This game emphasises supporting others and cooperating and can be played as a whole-class activity. You will need a small beanbag for every player. If you don't have beanbags, you can use anything that will stay on the students' heads fairly securely when they are standing still, but will tend to fall off when they move. The aim of the game is for the class as a whole to score five points before the Snowman gets five points.

- One student stands with his or her back to the group. This person is the Snowman.
- Every student (except for the Snowman) places their beanbag on their head. They must not hold it in place.
- The teacher gives the class instructions about how to move (e.g. walk one step, hop twice, do a star jump).
- If anyone's beanbag falls off their head while they are following the instructions, they cannot bend down and pick it up themselves. The only way for them to get their beanbag back (and get back into the game) is for another member of the group to stop, pick it up and hand it to them. This, of course, means that the helper risks losing their own beanbag!
- At varying intervals the Snowman turns around unexpectedly and says 'Freeze'. At this command everyone must immediately stop. If, at that very moment, every person in the group has their beanbag on their head, the group gets a point. If not, the Snowman gets a point.

Activities

Alien!

Ask students to imagine that two new students have enrolled in their class, a boy and a girl. They are both from another planet, are only half a metre high, and their body temperature is always five degrees higher than the normal human temperature. They communicate only by sign language that no one understands. Make models of the aliens—encourage the students to be creative in making their aliens look different to people. For each pair of students you will need: butcher's paper marked with a length of half a metre, paint or markers, fabric pieces, glue, recycled materials, pipe-cleaners, googly eyes (from craft shops).

Discuss how these alien students would feel and how they could be supported. Before the discussion, students could pair up to think about their answers to the following questions:
- How would they be feeling?
- What kinds of extra support would these new students need?
- What other information would the class need about the students to be able to help them?
- What could the class do to help them settle in?
- What classroom procedures could we change to support them?
- What changes could be made in our room?

Students can write sentences and draw what has been discussed. You could also use this activity with the focus on a new student who is 2.5 metres tall, is always cold and has to move for one minute after every ten minutes of sitting still.

Support a sick classmate

If a student in the class is away ill for a prolonged time, consider making a giant class get-well card for them, with each student making and attaching a small lift-up flap on the card (see **Handbook**, page 97). Each student writes their name on their flap, and a get-well message inside. The teacher writes a special message as well.

Circle Time: **Teacher support**

Talk about how teachers care for and support students at school. Students take turns to tell about a time when a teacher helped them, or was kind and caring towards them. (listened to them when they felt sad; showed them how to do something; took care of them when they were sick; showed them where to go when they were lost)

→ Follow up by having all students contribute illustrations and sentences to a class poster, class book or digital class book (see **Handbook**, page 97) entitled *Teachers Care for Kids: Talk to One Today!*

Circle Time: **Supporting people we don't know (a combination of kindness and fairness)**

Start by reading *Wilfrid Gordon McDonald Partridge* (see below). Talk about groups that care for people who need help or may not be able to support themselves. Ask: Do you know the names of any of these organisations? What do they do? In the discussion, draw out the theme of care and support for others, even if they are not in your family.

Picture books

Wilfrid Gordon McDonald Partridge
Wilfrid is a small boy who lives next door to an aged care facility. He discovers that his favourite person there has lost her memory. He feels so upset about this that he takes in lots of items to help jog her memory.
→ Follow up with students:
- finding out two facts about a charitable organisation by asking parents or using the Internet and library (this could also be the basis of inquiry-based learning)

- writing and drawing about one caring thing they do for grandparents or another older person
- bringing an item from home that signifies something they have shared with their grandparent or a special older person in their life, e.g. a book they have shared, a game they have played together, a photo.
- visiting a nearby facility for the elderly so that students can spend some time with residents (and practise their conversation skills at the same time). They could play a board game or a card game with the residents or do a jigsaw together.
- sending drawings, photographs and get-well messages to children in the local children's hospital (after checking with the hospital administration).
  Other ideas for this book can be found in Unit 9: STAR! (Success), page 180.

Room on the Broom

This rhyming story begins with a witch and her cat flying through the sky on her broomstick. When the witch is forced to retrieve her hat which has been blown to the ground, they encounter a dog who asks if there's room on the broom for him. They welcome him onto the broom and take off. And so the story continues with different things falling off, the witch having to land to hunt for them and a different animal asking to join them on the broom. Eventually there are too many on the broom and it breaks. When the broom-less witch becomes the target of a dragon wanting 'witch and chips' for tea, the animals that she has treated with kindness defend her in their own unique ways.

Max

Max is a super-baby striving to grow up in a household of superheroes. Although Max already wears his superhero costume, he is reluctant to take on the role of superhero and develop his flying skills until he has to use them to save a baby bird.

Goodnight Harry

Harry, a soft toy elephant, can't get to sleep. He tries lots of things to get to sleep (reading a bedtime story, tidying the room, doing exercises) but nothing works until his friends help him by looking out at the night sky and then snuggling up together. Finally Harry can fall fast asleep.

Game

People who help us

Students make an ABC book of people who help us. For example:
- ambulance driver
- dentist
- doctor
- fire officer
- lifeguard
- nurse
- police officer
- teacher.

Circle Time: Family support

Start by having students complete **BLM 1.3: Who Helps Me in My Family?** Students bring their sheet to the circle. They take turns to give an example of how they are cared for and helped by a member of their family and how they help and care for others in their family. Talk about family loyalty and ask why it is important to not tell others the secrets of people in your family. Why is it important not to say nasty things to others about members of your family?

Unit 1

Core values

→ To follow up, students can write a letter to a member or members of their family saying how they appreciate the ways in which they help and support them. They can address an envelope and post the letter home.

Picture books

The Kissing Hand

Chester Raccoon is very nervous about his first day at school. To help him feel less worried, his mother kisses his palm just as they arrive at school and tells him to put his hand to his cheek if he feels lonely at school to remind him that she is always caring about him.
→ To follow up:
◎ Ask: Would this help Chester feel less nervous?
◎ Discuss raccoons. They are nocturnal so does Chester go to night school?

Love You Forever

In this simple, repetitive and moving story a mother sings to her sleeping baby that she will love him forever. She continues to sing the same song when her baby becomes a painful two-year-old, a messy nine-year-old, an annoying teenager and a young adult. Eventually the boy becomes a man and sings the song to his ailing mother and his newborn daughter.

Circle Time: **Kindness to animals**

Start by singing 'Little Cottage in the Woods' (also called 'In a Cabin in the Woods'). This familiar action song is about a person who saves a rabbit from a hunter. The actions are:
◎ draw a house in the air
◎ use binoculars
◎ cross arms over self in fear
◎ raise both arms in the air
◎ raise shotgun and sight
◎ beckon
◎ stroke rabbit.

Use it to introduce the notion of helping, caring and supporting animals. Then students take it in turns to say one way in which they have cared for a pet or any other animal.
→ Follow up with students:
◎ acting out one way to care for a pet while the class tries to guess what the pet is
◎ drawing pictures of their favourite kind of pet or animal and writing sentences about it
◎ writing brochures about how to care for their favourite kind of pet
◎ making a class graph of the pets in the class
◎ making a book in the shape of either a cat or a dog. Use the cat and dog pattern on **BLM 1.4: Kindness to Animals.** Use the sentence 'This is how we can care for and help a cat/dog'.

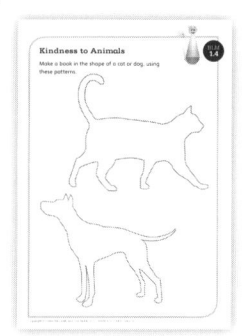

Picture books

Little Lost Bat

When a baby Mexican free-tailed bat is born, his mother cares for him deep inside a cave where millions of bats live. The baby bat hangs upside down clinging to the ceiling by his thumb claws; below, thousands of hungry beetles wait to catch and eat any little bats that fall. One night he waits, as usual, for his mother to return from her daily hunting trip but she never comes back. After three days of waiting, he is adopted and cared for by another new mother bat whose own baby has died.

→ Follow up with a class discussion or inquiry-based learning project on either bats or human adoption.

The Cat with No Name

A young city cat with no name and no home is kept alive by the kindness of people at different ethnic restaurants in the city who feed him leftovers. Each person greets the cat in their own language. The cat slowly moves further out of the city in search of 'proper' food for a cat and reaches a home with a garden and kind children who want to care for him.

→ Follow up with a discussion or inquiry-based project on:
- Why do cats or dogs sometimes end up with no home?
- What organisations take care of lost or injured animals?

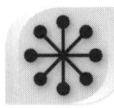

Circle Time: **Cooperation**

At the start of the day, tell students that just for one morning, no one has to put up their hand to speak—they should just call out instead. Tell them that you might not speak to them when they call out and that no one is going to cooperate. Alternatively, you could play a classroom game (e.g. Buzz) or outdoor game (e.g. Streets and Lanes) with no rules. In Circle Time after lunch, talk about what happened when the class did not cooperate to follow rules that help everyone work well together. Talk about what cooperation means. Students take it in turns to give an example from their own lives of people cooperating or working together. For example:
- having a meal (one cooks, one prepares, one sets the table, one clears up and one washes up or stacks the dishwasher)
- getting ready for school (trying to be ready on time, packing your school bag, helping people carry things to the car).

Talk about the kinds of skills you need to be able to cooperate well. For example:
- work together
- share materials
- share ideas
- take turns
- share the work
- listen to each other
- help each other
- encourage each other
- no put-downs
- sort out disagreements in a friendly way.

→ Follow up with students:
- working with a partner to make a poster about these skills for cooperating
- completing **BLM 1.5: Communities and Teams**
- singing songs about world harmony and cooperation (see following).

Unit 1

Core values

Songs

'I'd Like to Teach the World to Sing'
'It's a Small World'
'We All Sing With the Same Voice'
'Cooperation Makes it Happen' (*Sesame Street*)
'The Sharing Song'
'I Can't Get No Cooperation' (*Sesame Street*)

Picture books

We Share Everything!
Amanda and Jeremiah, who are in their first year of school, are always fighting over whose turn it is to use something. Their teacher keeps telling them to share so they take her advice to the extreme and end up sharing clothes and shoes as well. Chaos reigns in the classroom! This is a humorous way to introduce the subject of sharing, cooperation and conflict management.
→ Follow up by having students make a list of things they share at school and home.

The Bad Tempered Ladybird
In this story by Eric Carle, a bad-tempered ladybird won't work cooperatively with other ladybirds to share the aphids they all like to eat. She gets into arguments with many other larger animals but eventually returns to the other ladybirds and learns to share.
→ Follow up with students:
- Drawing what the ladybird is doing at 12 o'clock, 2 o'clock, 4 o'clock etc.
- Carrying out a survey (with graphs) on which part of the story each student liked best
- Acting out the story with a ladybird puppet.

Pepo and Lolo and the Red Apple
Pepo the pig and Lolo the chicken work together to get an apple from a branch that is too high for either of them to reach.

Sharing a Shell
The tiny hermit crab loves his new shell and does not want to share it, even though an anemone and a bristle worm would like to move in with him. However, life in the rock pool is more challenging than the hermit crab expected and he finds that his new housemates can be very useful at times.
→ Hermit crabs make good classroom pets, and crabs and other marine creatures that live in shells make an interesting topic for inquiry-based learning.

Share Said the Rooster
This book contains five simple stories about Billy and Ben, little men who will not share anything, whether it's a sticky bun, a pair of blue boots or an apple. But when Billy and Ben go out in a row boat, they find that it is dangerous not to share and cooperate. This book offers opportunities for discussing sharing, cooperating and negotiating.

Ten Things I Can Do to Help My World
This book offers ten things that children can do to help protect the Earth, e.g. turn off the television when not watching it, walk to school, turn off the lights when leaving a room and grow plants from seed.
→ To follow up, students could choose one thing they can try to do for a week and keep a diary about their efforts. Discuss how they might encourage their family to participate.

Never Ever Before
This book pays homage to the surrealist and abstract painters of the 20th century and focuses on how shapes can create emotion. The story features three types of characters, each represented by shapes of different sizes—Smalls, Big and Talls. Big lives in the land of Smalls and enjoys watching them play and being blown about by the breeze. He is too big to leave the ground himself but he shelters the Smalls when the breeze is gusty and strong. Then the Talls are born but even the tiniest breeze blows them over so Big offers them a place to lean. Sometimes the Talls cooperate so they can lift Big off the ground. A strong wind arrives and blows the smallest Smalls away. The Talls, anchored to Big, are able to reach out and rescue the Smalls. They all fly off, joined cooperatively together.
→ Discuss how the illustrator changes the mood of the story using only shapes. Follow up by having students make a shape story.

Team cooperative activities

Before each of the cooperative activities listed below, review the cooperative skills discussed in Circle Time (see **Handbook**, page 84). After each activity, review how well specific skills were used by the class. Also, look for (and comment on) students who are focusing, cooperating well and trying hard to achieve the class goal.

Beat the clock
Use a timer or the 'Timer' e-tool and see if the whole class can cooperate to beat the clock when:
- packing up
- moving to the mat
- starting work
- lining up to come into class
- lining up in order of the number or letter each student is given (on a small card or piece of paper) or in alphabetical order according the words they are given.

Make a chart and keep a visual record of their times. This activity also links to Unit 9: STAR! (Success) on page 180, time management and setting goals.

Safe island
Mark a circular area of the yard as a 'safe island', making a boundary for it with a rope or markings on the ground. The area should be large enough for all students to stand in it closely together without being too squashed. Alternatively, use a square or circular mat in the classroom. Tell the students to pretend it is an island and that all around it is the sea that contains sharks. Explain that they are going to practise cooperating to swim to the island. In turn each child pretends to 'jump' off a line, 'swim' to the island and 'climb' onto it. As they arrive, the students who are already on the island should make room for them. None of their bodies should touch the 'water' when they are on the island. Then make the island smaller and repeat the activity.

Class vegetable soup
Make vegetable soup as a class (you may need an extra adult to help). Before you start, ask, 'Which is the most important vegetable in vegetable soup?' Students will all give a different answer but then finally say that no one vegetable is the most important. It wouldn't be vegetable soup if many different vegetables didn't cooperate together. This is like us—no one is more important than anyone else. We all have a contribution to make. This could also be used as an activity prior to Circle Time.

Class keep-it-up
The class cooperates to keep four balloons in the air so that none hits the ground. What is the class's best time for keeping them in the air? Can they beat that next time? Use the 'Timer' e-tool.

Lions fly

This is a version of musical chairs so you need one less chair than students plus teacher. The teacher is the first leader. Students start by sitting on the chairs and the teacher stands up. Make several statements (e.g. about animals) that are true (e.g. Cats have whiskers) and then an occasional statement that isn't true (e.g. Lions fly). If an untrue statement is said, all students must change seats with someone else, as does the leader. The person who doesn't get to a seat stands and becomes the next leader. Stress that for this game to be successful everyone must follow the rules and not use put-downs.

Change places

This is another version of musical chairs so you need one less chair than students plus teacher. Have students sit on the chairs in a circle while the teacher stands up. Give every student in the class a card with one of five feelings written on it. Make sure they can read and understand it. Have five cards with each feeling placed in a container. The teacher is the first leader and stands in the middle of the circle. He/she draws a card out of the container and acts out or mimes the feeling on the card. All the students who have that feeling card must change seats with someone else as does the leader. The person who doesn't get to a seat stands in the middle and becomes the next leader. This process is repeated several times. Stress that for this game to be successful, everyone must follow the rules and not use put-downs.

Cat and mouse

You need five balls of one colour (cats) and one ball of another colour (mouse). Students sit in a circle and pass the 'cats' around in any direction, but they cannot hold them for longer than two seconds. The mouse can only be passed to one person at a time in a clockwise direction. The aim is for the class to ensure that no one ever has a cat and the mouse at the same time. Stress that everyone must follow the rules.

Whisper game

Play the 'Whisper game' (see **Handbook**, page 92) with three teams and eight words in each set of cards to choose from. Words on the cards are:

- share
- work
- together
- listen
- help
- encourage
- turns
- friendly.

Memory cards

Play the 'Memory cards' e-game (see **Handbook**, page 91) with the words listed above and more.

Cooperative ball pass

This is played in groups of six with six small balls. The group chants 'one, two, three' and on 'three' they all pass their ball to the person on their left and receive the ball being passed to them.

Cooperative clap ball

You will need a medium-sized ball. Students stand in a circle. One person throws it to another who then throws it to someone else and so on. Whenever the ball is thrown, everyone claps once. When it is caught, everyone stamps once. See how quickly and accurately the class can do this.

Clap race

Sit in a circle. Start a clap that passes from person to person around the circle (domino-style). Practise to see how fast it can travel (use a stopwatch to time it).

Cooperative activities with a partner

Debrief after the activities by asking students questions such as:
- How did your partner help you?
- What did you have to share to do this well?
- What was one good thing your partner did to help the two of you do this well? What is one good thing you did?

Take photos and make a slide show of students undertaking these activities and underneath write:
- We cooperate because we care about each other.
- We did this together.

Publish the photos in the school newsletter.

Cooperative tower
You will need wooden blocks of different sizes. The aim is to have as many blocks in your tower as possible. Students work with a partner to use different sized blocks to build the tallest tower they can. They start by agreeing on which block to use as their base block. Only that base block can touch the table or floor. Then the students take turns to place one extra block on the tower each time. They keep a record of how many blocks they were able to put on their tower before it fell over. They set a goal to cooperate to add at least one more block than last time when they build their next tower together.

Cooperative building
Students work with a partner to make something specific from building bricks (e.g. a tall red tower, a green and yellow house).

Cooperative drawing
Students work with a partner to make one drawing between them (not two separate drawings on the same page) on a theme, such as a farm or the beach.

Cooperative cooking
Students undertake a cooking activity with a partner under the supervision of an adult helper or older peer buddy. Recipes that could be used include:
- pikelets/drop scones
- rocky road
- chocolate crackles
- gingerbread people.

Red elbow
Play this game in pairs. You need an even number of players so students can cooperate in pairs. The leader calls out a colour and a body part (e.g. blue knee) and each pair has to find a way for both of them together to place their knee on something that is blue. You may like to give the whole class a point each time all pairs have successfully followed the instruction within 60 seconds. The class can try to get ten points.

Peg sorting race
You will need three ice-cream containers and 60 spring pegs: 20 each of blue, green and red. Each pair plays at a different time, so you won't need more than one set. Use a stopwatch to see how long each pair takes to correctly select colours and peg all the red ones on one ice-cream container, the green ones on another and so on. Alternatively, see if they can finish within a specified time (be generous!).

Alphabet cooperation
Each group of three students needs a large sheet of paper to paste things on and old magazines. Nominate a letter of the alphabet (or a blend), then give students 20 minutes

Unit 1

Core values

to find as many pictures as they can that begin with the letter/s, cut them out, paste them on their named sheet and write the word (that the letter/s came from) underneath. In each group, one can be the cutter, one the paster and one the writeer.

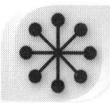

Circle Time: It's OK to be different

Take in one red apple and one green apple. Ask students to describe the properties of each. Then peel them and make the point that although the apples have different coloured skins they are the same inside, i.e they both have pips, flesh and juice and are good to eat. Talk about how we are all different and that is a good thing. Students take it in turns to say one way in which they think they are different from other students in the class. Stress that it is not good if people use other people's difference as a reason to exclude them, tease them or treat them as though they were less important and less valuable.

Discuss the ways in which we are different from others and they are different from us:
- different things they like
- different ideas about things
- different personalities (how we behave)
- different cultural backgrounds
- different strengths and weaknesses
- different kinds of families
- different ways of doing things.

Activities

Favourite photo
Read the book *Guess the Baby* or *Baby Boomsticks* (see below). Invite parents to email a baby photo of their child (or lend one that you can scan) and make a slide show of students' photographs entitled, 'We are all different'. Then ask students to try to guess which baby photos belong to which classmates. Show five a day. Use the slide show again and ask several students each day to talk about their photo, say what they are doing and who else, if anyone, is in it.

Class statistics
Put together class pictographs based on questions about differences such as:
- What do people in this class think is the best pet?
- How many people have brown/black/blond/red hair in this class?
- How many people have blue/green/brown eyes in this class?
- Where were students in this class born?
- Where were the parents of the students in this class born?
- What are the favourite ice-cream flavours, TV shows and books of people in this class?

Picture books

Guess the Baby
The students in Mr Judd's class have to guess who belongs to each person's baby photo. Even the teacher's photo is included. The humorous message is that everyone is different and everyone changes and has to grow up. This book could also be used in Unit 2: People bouncing back (page 34).

The Ugly Duckling

Read or tell the story of the ugly duckling. Ask: Why were the other ducklings so mean to the ugly duckling? Were they being fair? Were they accepting difference? Be careful of the ending of this story in which the other ducks accept him because he really is a beautiful swan, not a 'different' duckling as they thought. Stress that the ducklings would have been kinder if they had accepted the ugly duckling for what he was, not for what he turned out to be. Students can take turns interviewing different characters in the story. Start by being the first interviewer so you can model the process.

→ Follow up by:
- singing 'Six Little Ducks' as a class
- making a paper plate mask. On one side of the paper plate can be a drawing of the ugly duckling. On the other side can be a drawing of the beautiful swan. They can also make masks (see **Handbook**, page 99) for each animal or character and act out the story. See **BLM 1.6: The Ugly Ducking**.

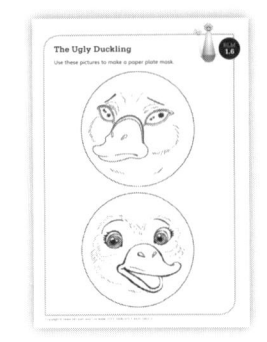

Wombat Divine

The animals (all Australian) are planning their nativity play. Wombat is very excited at the idea of playing a part but they can't work out what role he can play. He's too big to be Mary and too short to be a king. His friends finally work out how to make the best of his strengths in the play and everyone is delighted.

Talk about how everyone has different strengths and how everyone has something to offer and can be included. See Unit 6: Relationships (page 118) for more ideas on how to use this book.

The Best Beak in Boonaroo Bay

All the birds are arguing about who has the best beak. Pelican tries to sort it out by setting a series of tests for all the birds, but each bird is good at only one of the tests because their beak is best suited to that test. Eventually they realise that all their beaks are different and valuable for certain purposes but there is no beak that is the best.

Link the book with the notion that we all have different strengths. This book can also be used for Unit 9: STAR! (Success) on page 180, which looks at different strengths. Follow up with students completing **BLM 1.7: People Hunt—Difference**.

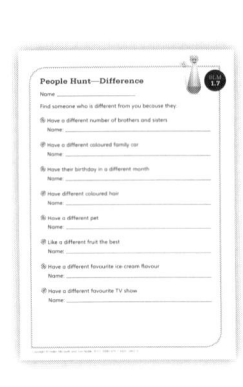

Green Eggs and Ham

This is a simple repetitive story of a character who follows another character around asking him to try some green eggs and ham. The second character resists until the very end of the book. When he tries them, they taste just as good as any other eggs and ham. They just happen to look different.

→ Beforehand, prepare three boiled eggs—one with a white shell, one with a brown shell and one with a green shell (boil with green food dye in the water). Before reading the story, ask the students which egg they think looks different and which one looks nice or yucky. Ask why they think this. Then peel the eggs and show the class what colour they are inside—all are the same colour even though they are different on the outside. You could also consider making green scrambled eggs as a class.

Susan Laughs

This book is about a little girl called Susan doing many different things. On the last page, the reader is shown that Susan is also in a wheelchair but still does all the things that any other child would do. Halfway through the book, ask students to chat with a partner and then, as a pair, predict what the story might be about.

- → Follow up with:
- Pairs of students making a chart of all the things Susan can do. Ask: Are there any things that Susan can't do? In what ways is Susan the same as you? In what ways is she different?
- Saying: Look closely at the drawings—what are some of the things that Susan needs help with? (e.g. dancing on Grandpa's feet)
- Asking: If Susan were in our class, what are some ways we could support her?
- Talking about how some children have disabilities such as difficulties with hearing, seeing or, like Susan, moving. Make the point that these children are children first and have some things they can do well and some things they need help with, just like everyone else.
- Drawing a map of the classroom that shows the physical layout (seats, equipment, board, etc.). Give each group of students a copy of the map as well as a map of the classroom without the furniture drawn in. Ask students to draw on the blank map to show how everything could be placed so Susan could easily move about in her wheelchair and be included.

Too Loud Lily

Everyone in Lily's family says Lily (a young hippo) is too loud, enthusiastic and over-exuberant. But when Miss Loopiola comes to Lily's school to teach music and drama, Lily finds that being loud is just what is needed.

This is a book about valuing differences and can also be used in Unit 9: STAR! (Success) on page 180.

Our Stripy Baby

When Zara's new baby brother arrives, it is something of a shock. Everyone in Zara's social world has colourful spots, but Zack is different—he has stripes. Zara is initially disappointed because Zack doesn't seem like a normal baby and she envies her friend who has a spotty little brother. She works through her distress and is unable to resist the gorgeous little baby who smiles, blows kisses and always wants hugs.
→ Links can be made with having a sibling with special needs.

Baby Boomsticks

A very tiny mother and father have a giant baby (Boomsticks) and although they are thrilled and proud of him, the people in their village are worried that he will hurt their own tiny children. He has to play alone and away from the other children and becomes sad and lonely. One day, there is a flood in the village and Baby Boomsticks is able to rescue everyone in the village by carrying them on his giant shoulders and back. The villagers begin to accept and include him and work out ways in which the children can safely play with him.

Ask students to look at the illustrations to identify the ways that the villagers work out for Boomsticks to play with the other children.

The Very Blue Thingamajig

A newly hatched thingamajig is very blue and very plain compared to the other thingamajigs. They all sneer at him and exclude him because he is so different. Then, on Sunday he wakes up with one 'twisty twirly tail'. On Monday he wakes up with 'one twisty twirly tail and a pair of yellow waxy wings'. On Tuesday he wakes up with 'one twisty twirly tail, a pair of yellow waxy wings and an odd number of red hideously hard horns' and so on. On each new day a turn-back picture opens up to show what new characteristic has arrived overnight. By the following Sunday he is an amazing-looking thingamajig indeed! The other thingamajigs again scorn and exclude him but he discovers that there is a girl thingamajig who says, 'How delightfully different you are!'

This book can also be used with Unit 8: No bullying (page 161). Discuss with the students how the very blue thingamajig would feel when he is excluded and mocked.

It's OK to Be Different
Australian author Todd Parr uses child-like smiling stick figures, bold, brilliant colour and simple text to give the message that it's important to be yourself and that being different to others is fine. For example, it's OK to:
- be adopted
- need some help
- be a different colour
- wear glasses
- dance by yourself.

Whoever You Are
In this simple book, many characters from different countries and ethnic groups affirm that they are different but they are also the same in that they all smile, love, hurt and laugh.

Grandpa and Ah Gong
Read this story to the class as an introduction to cultural differences. A young girl's Asian grandfather comes to stay. Her Australian grandfather lives with her and the two grandfathers clash in terms of what they consider is 'normal' and what they think should happen. There is an eventual resolution of their differences.

Henry and Amy
See Unit 2: People bouncing back (page 47) for a summary of the story of Henry and Amy and follow-up activities.

Activity

Toys and difference
This activity allows you to challenge stereotypes and to encourage both girls and boys to be themselves, rather than just conforming to a gender role. Ask students to each bring in a toy from home, not necessarily one of their own. Then use hoops or large sheets of paper to sort the toys into as many groups as students can suggest, for example:
- large/small toys
- toys that move/don't move.

Ask each student to come out, choose a toy and group it by putting it into the appropriate hoop. Then ask them to decide whether it is a toy for a girl, a toy for a boy or a toy for all children. Ask them why they think it is a toy for a girl, boy or all children. Gently challenge any stereotypical thinking by saying, 'Can anyone think of a reason why this toy might be for all children?' Address any put-downs that occur by saying, 'Let's remember that everyone has a right to their own opinion. Your opinion is not the only one that there is.'

→ Follow up with sentence writing (e.g. *We looked at a lot of toys. We saw that all toys are for all children, not just for a boy or a girl.*).[1]

Circle Time: We can think differently

Select a topic such as picnics, Christmas, swimming, football, staying at a friend's place overnight or doing maths. Ask the students to take turns to make a comment about the topic. Draw out the similarities and differences in their comments. At the end of the circle, talk about why people had different ideas. Stress that we can think differently about the same thing and that is OK. Our view is just different, not better or worse. Talk about how sometimes our thinking about something can change after hearing what

[1] Adapted from Reid-Nguyen 1999, *Think Global: Global Perspectives in the Lower Primary Classroom*, Curriculum Corporation

Unit 1

Core values

other people have to say about it, but sometimes we feel even stronger about what we thought in the first place.
→ Follow up with:
◎ writing sentences about the different ideas they had
◎ singing the song below. Beforehand, ask each student to write down or draw one thing they like that has two syllables (e.g. chicken, pasta, salad, roast beef, hot chips, lamb chops, ice-cream). Then sing the song many times using different students' preferences.

Song

'What We Like'[1]

(To the tune of 'Frere Jacques')

I like pizza (*sung by one student*)

I like pizza (*sung by the same student*)

So do we (*students who also like pizza stand up and sing*)

So do we (*repeat*)

Some of us like pizza (*same*)

Some of us like pizza (*same*)

Sit down please (*whole class*)

Sit down please (*whole class*)

Activities

Movers and shakers

Use 'Movers and shakers' (see **Handbook**, page 91) with difference questions such as these:
◎ if you have been on a speed boat (pretend to drive the speed boat, staying on the spot)
◎ if you have a dog (sit like a dog and pant)
◎ if you have lived in another country (move hands in Bollywood-style dancing)
◎ if you have ridden a horse (pretend to ride a horse)
◎ if you speak another language (use your hand to speak)
◎ if you have a baby at home (pretend to rock a baby in your arms)
◎ if you have been to an aquarium (move hands together like a fish swimming).

We can draw differently

Each student completes a drawing of a specified scene such as:
◎ a happy picture
◎ a sad picture
◎ an animal picture
◎ a beach picture.

Then they get together with two other students and talk about what is the same and different about their drawings. Then they tell the class about one thing that was different about what they drew and the different colours they used in their drawings.

Guess who's different?

This activity focuses on getting to know others in the class and the ways in which they are different. Students first think of as many things as they can about themselves that are different from everyone else in the class. Then on the outside of a lift-up flap (see **Handbook**, page 97) they write one thing that they think no one else will know about them. Underneath the flap they write their name. For example, 'Guess who was born in Mauritius?' (on the outside), 'Shelley' (underneath).

How are we the same?
With a partner, students can identify two ways in which they are the same and two ways in which they are different. Then they change partners and repeat the exercise twice. They use **BLM 1.8: How Are We the Same and Different?** to record their answers as one pair. Ask pairs to read out what they have written. You can also do this as a whole-class exercise in which two students come to the front and think of two ways they are the same and different.

Same and different
Students work with a partner to cut out pictures from a magazine that show people who are the same as they are and different from them. Ask each pair to also say one way in which they are 'the same as' the people in the pictures they choose and one way they are 'different to' them.

Celebrating diversity
Using the cultural diversity of your classroom as a starting point, discuss with students the ways in which all cultures are different but also the same. For example, most cultures:
- have bread as a staple part of their diet but they have different kinds of bread. This discussion can be followed by a visit to a bakery to see (and hopefully taste) various kinds of bread.
- have festivals and celebrations. Celebrate some that relate to your students.
- play ball games. Find out about one or two and play them.

Set up a parent-supported cooking activity for students in which they cook foods from other cultures. Stress that one of the values of difference is that it allows all of us to have a greater variety of experiences.

Picture books

The Pearson series *How Australians Eat* or one or more of the following picture books by Norah Dooley and Peter Thornton could also be used here:

Everybody Bakes Bread

Everybody Brings Noodles

Everybody Cooks Rice

Everybody Serves Soup

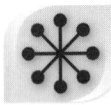

Circle Time: Including others

Start with one of the picture books below or with a brief drama activity in which five or six students pretend to play a game that two students (one at a time) want to join in with but are told to go away. Pick well-liked students to be the rejected children. Repeat the enactment several times. Ask the actors how it felt to be excluded. Use the term 'excluded' a lot in preparation for discussions on bullying at later year levels.

Say: Everybody gets left out sometimes. How does it feel to be left out and not have anyone to play with? How does it feel when people tell you that you can't play with them? Students can volunteer to tell about a time when they felt left out or had nobody to play with and what they felt like. Students suggest ways in which others could be invited into a game if they looked lonely. For example:
- call out 'Do you want to play with us?'

- go over to them and start talking, then just start playing
- ask them to do something to help the game, such as getting the ball when it has gone out. Then they can just join in.

Re-play the dramatic scenarios from the start of the lesson, but this time with students being accepting and including all others. Follow up each enactment with a discussion of one or two things they did well and one way they could improve to help that person be included in their group.

Picture books

Rhino Neil
All the other animals in the safari zoo are warned to stay away from the huge Rhino Neil with his large horns, so he becomes quite lonely and excluded. It is only when Tuscany the elephant arrives at the zoo that Rhino Neil at last finds a friend.

This Is Our House
George has a house made from a big cardboard box and won't let anyone else in the playground come in, finding all sorts of reasons to exclude people. When George leaves his house for a moment, the other children take it over and exclude him. He changes his mind and announces that the house is now OK for everyone to be part of, including him.

Circle Time: Being friendly

Before the activity, make a number of cards with the following phrases written on them:
- helping someone to clean up
- smiling at someone when you see them in the playground
- stopping to say hi when you see a classmate at the shops
- making and sending a get-well card
- having a chat with someone from your sports team that you don't know very well when you sit next to them on the bus
- ignoring a classmate when you see them at the movies with their family
- telling someone they played well in a game
- making fun of someone when they miss a shot
- telling a classmate to go away when they wander over to your group's game
- inviting a classmate to play in your group because their friend is away that day
- telling a classmate a funny joke you have just heard.

Start with students passing a gentle 'friendly wrist squeeze' around the circle one at a time, accompanied by a smile and eye contact. Talk about friendliness and what it means. Students take it in turns to tell about a time when someone was friendly to them or they were friendly to someone else. Emphasise that if you are friendly then you are more likely to make friends and also like yourself more.

Ask: What do people do to show they are being friendly? (See Key points, page 1.) Briefly mention the 'Friendly' Olympics in Australia in Sydney 2000. Talk about how people in Sydney and the volunteers who helped out were friendly to interstate and international visitors (they smiled at them, helped them with directions, had a chat with them, shared a laugh and said hello when they saw them). Alternatively, refer to a recent school event with families where people were friendly.

Place the cards in the centre of the circle. Have students take turns to select a card and say whether it is a friendly thing to do or not.

→ Follow up with students:
- making a collage of people being friendly, using magazine pictures
- making 'friendly' badges (see **Handbook**, page 101). They can be given at the end of each day or week for acts of friendliness. The recipient can wear the badge for a week. Alternatively, use a certificate or a cardboard disc on a cord that goes around the child's neck
- making a class poster or digital story (with photos of the students acting out the ideas) about the friendly things they could do in the class, for example:
  - write to a classmate if they are away sick for a while and then welcome them back
  - talk to someone who seems lonely and include them in games
  - say hello and smile at someone they don't know very well (but reinforce the need to be self-protective with strangers and not smile at them, talk to them or help them if they ask).

Picture book

Say Hello

A lonely dog comes across some children playing. He quickly finds a way to join in their game. They are all having so much fun with their different ball games that they don't notice the lonely little boy standing off to the side. No one invites him to play. Eventually the dog goes over to him and drops the ball at his feet, inviting him to play. This is a simple story with very few words and the pictures are mainly black and white with colour highlights. It encourages social assertiveness, empathy and inclusion. Inside the back cover is the word 'hello' in more than 30 languages.

The message of the book is two-fold: It is sensible to be proactive (i.e. 'say hello') and try to join in but it is also kind to include others.'

Songs

'Bonjour Mes Amis'

'Hello'

'The Hello Song'

'Hello Song'

'Greetings!'

(To the tune of 'Humoresque in G Flat Major' by Antonin Dvorak. You may know it as the humorous song called 'Passengers Will Please Refrain'.)

When we see someone we know

We smile and say a big hello

Friendliness is such a simple thing

If everyone could find a way

To be more friendly every day

Think of all the good times that would bring

Unit 1

Core values

Circle Time: Smiling is contagious

Begin by talking about the concept of 'contagious'. Ask each student to tell about a time when they or someone they know 'caught' an illness from someone else (e.g. chickenpox, a cold, the flu).

Ask: What can we do to stop germs? (wash your hands properly; cover your mouth when you cough; don't put your mouth where someone else's mouth has been) The class can sing the song 'Cover Your Mouth and Turn Your Head'.

Talk to students about why smiling is so important. Highlight the importance of smiling as a way of being friendly, but also as a sign of confidence and approachability. People are more likely to see 'smilers' as potential safe friends who can be trusted and are not mean.

This song can also be linked to the notion of infectious diseases. Review the meaning of 'contagious'. Talk about how behaviour can be contagious too, i.e. other people can see you do something nice and decide to do it too. Students can sing the song 'Smiling Is Contagious' (see below) using a smiling mask with a picture of a broad smile (see **Handbook**, page 99). They hold it over their lower face while they sing this song.

Picture book

The Gotcha Smile
Clarine finds it hard to make friends when she first goes to school but her grandfather teaches her how to flash a 'gotcha smile', which always gets a smile back.

Song

'Smiling Is Contagious'
(To the tune of 'Ten Green Bottles')

> Smiling is contagious
> You catch it like the flu
> If you smile at someone
> They start smiling too
> If you say hello as well
> They'll say hello to you
> Being kind and friendly
> Is what we like to do

→ Follow up with:
- Taking a photo of students smiling and writing underneath it 'Smiling is contagious. You catch it like the flu'.
- Students working in pairs and taking turns to count how often they see their partner smile over a set period of time (e.g. before lunch or during the whole school day). Add up the two counts for the pair and then write 'Together we smiled ... times today' under a drawing of a big smile or under a photo of them both smiling.

Poem

'A Smile Is Just a Frown Turned Upside Down'

A smile
Is just a frown
Is just a frown
Turned upside down
So if
You feel a frown
Just make your frown
Turn upside down.

Students make a mask (see **Handbook**, page 99) from a paper plate or from cardboard; they give the mask a moveable mouth attached with a split pin so that the 'smile' can become a 'frown' if it is turned upside down. Then they can sing the song or recite it as a poem.

Activity

Friendly greetings!

Each day, announce what the new greeting word is. Students shake hands using the greeting and try to use it as much as they can all day. On the next day, choose a different greeting. Remind them to smile and look into the person's eyes. Here are some starters, but your choices should reflect the cultural diversity in your classroom:

- *buongiorno* or *ciao* (Italian)
- *bonjour* (French)
- *guten tag* (German)
- *konnichiwa* (Japanese)
- *marhaba* (Arabic)
- *yassou* (Greek)
- *chao em* (Vietnamese)
- *ni hao* (Chinese).

Circle Time: Respect

Pass out a small treat (e.g. a sticker or a pencil) to each student and count how many of them say 'thank you'. Tell them the results but don't mention specific students.

Ask: Why is it good to say thank you? (It makes the other person feel respected and appreciated.) Students take turns to tell about a time when they have said thank you. Talk about why people say thank you and why it is a good thing to do.

Ask: How does it feel when you do something for someone and they don't say thank you? Talk about what we mean by respecting someone (see Key points, page 1). Then talk about good manners. Students take turns to tell one example of good manners.

→ Follow up with students:
- making a class graph of the thank you investigation at the start
- learning the poem below about good manners. Act out the poem and then include another version where a 'bird sat on my nose and said "Please excuse me, I thought you were a tree"'. Students can draw these silly scenes, i.e. a bee or a bird on a person's nose, and write underneath, 'I beg your pardon' or 'Please excuse me'.
- making a bee. For each student, you will need half a polystyrene ball. Cut a slit on each side of the ball. The student slots in two cardboard wings and colours in the bee's stripes with a black felt pen. Thread hat elastic through the ball (below the wings) so each student can wear their bee on their nose.

Unit 1

Core values

Poem

'What Do You Suppose?'

What do you suppose?

A bee sat on my nose!

And what do you think?

He gave me a wink

and said, 'I beg your pardon,

I thought you were the garden'.

Song

'Two Fat Gentlemen'

(Students use their thumbs as the gentlemen.)

Two fat gentlemen met in the lane

Bowed so politely, bowed once again

How do you do?

How do you do?

How do you do, again?

Game

May I?

Ask the students why we have 'good manners'. Highlight the need to respect the rights and feelings of others. Respect is thinking about what is thoughtful and good for other people. Talk about some of the typical good and bad manners, such as saying 'please', 'thank you' and 'excuse me'; covering your mouth when you cough; using a handkerchief; not talking with your mouth full. To reinforce the use of good manners, play the 'May I?' game. Firstly, talk to the students about when it is good manners and respectful to say 'May I?' and 'Thank you'.

There are four to ten students in each group. You will need:
- space! (e.g. a multi-purpose room, gym, oval or asphalt area)
- chalk (or string or ribbon) to mark the starting and finishing lines
- action cards with one of the following nouns written on each card—frog, bird, fish, giant, kangaroo, lollipop
- number cards, with a number from 1 to 10 written on each card
- two containers, one for the action cards and one for the number cards.

Students line up at the starting line. The teacher (or another student) pulls out one action card and one number card for each player in turn, and then tells them what to do, for example, 'Chen, you can take two frogs'. Chen then has to say, 'May I?' The teacher replies, 'Yes'. Then Chen has to say 'Thank you'. Then Chen takes two steps, i.e. two frog movements. If any player forgets to say 'May I' or 'Thank you', they must go right back to the starting line. The aim is to be the player who reaches the finishing line first.

These are the actions to be used with each action card:
- Bird: raise one knee and take a large step forward. At the same time flap both arms and make a bird noise with each step.
- Fish: make breaststroke movements and open and shut your mouth like a fish. At the same time, while wiggling and shimmying your whole body, take one large step.

- Frog: tuck both hands under your armpits (left hand under left armpit and so on). Squat down, say 'Ribbet' and jump once.
- Giant: take a very, very long step forward with both arms held out at the side and curved to indicate a large sized body. Say 'Fee fi fo fum' with each step.
- Kangaroo: hold both hands up in front at chest level like paws. Take a large bouncing jump using both feet. At the same time say 'boing'.
- Lollipop: take a tiny heel-to-toe step.

Picture books

The Elephant and the Bad Baby
An elephant takes a delighted baby for a ride on his back through the town where the baby accepts offers of cakes and pastries but never says 'please' or 'thank you'. Eventually the elephant reminds the 'bad baby' about using good manners.
→ Students talk about all the ways in which babies show that they aren't yet old enough to learn consideration for other people. Students contrast this with how they use good manners now at their current age. Then students draw one way in which babies have no manners and write a sentence under each drawing (e.g. Babies use their fingers to eat). Make a class book (see **Handbook**, page 97) or wall display of their drawings.

Max and the Magic Word
Max is a young dog who becomes angry when he can't get his friends to give him what he wants and to share with him. He finally realises that saying 'please' will solve his problems.

I Won't Say Please!
Queen Bee issues commands but never says 'please'. Finally her staff refuses to help her unless she starts using good manners and she has to change her behaviour.

Tissue Please!
At school, dance rehearsal and home, Frog and his friends all simply sniff when their noses run, until Frog's parents show him how much better it is to use a tissue.

Excuse Me!
Frog really likes to burp but he never says 'Excuse me'. He seems unaware of how much he is distressing his friends with his bad manners. Finally, he is banished from the town to a settlement further away where less well-mannered frogs burp all the time and he realises how bad his manners have been. He returns to his town and from then on always says 'Excuse me' if he accidentally burps.

Dirty Bertie
Bertie has shockingly dirty habits. Whenever he does anything dirty his family pulls him up. But there's one habit Bertie won't give up—picking his nose. Bertie doesn't change his behaviour, but the book is engaging and is a starting point for a discussion about good manners and what offends other people.

Smelly Bertie
Bertie is a bit smelly as a result of constantly breaking wind. He makes his mum cross, embarrasses his dad, upsets his gran and offends his sister. But Bertie also points out that everyone in the household does it, not just him. The only difference is that they pretend it was the cat or create a diversion to cover it up. There is no simple resolution in the book, but it will make students giggle and can lead into a discussion about good manners and what offends other people.

Unit 1

Core values

Don't Be Greedy, Graham
In this exaggerated cautionary tale, students discover why it's bad to be greedy. Graham is so greedy that he takes food from his friends and upsets them, but he suffers from stomach-ache and is finally carried off by a pack of runaway pigs.

Greedy Grumpy Hippo
Hippo fills his picnic basket with sandwiches, apples, bananas, strawberries, yoghurt, carrots, cheese, orange juice and boiled eggs. He has no intention of sharing it with anyone else because today Hippo is greedy and grumpy.

Do Unto Otters: A Book About Manners
Mr Rabbit's new neighbours are Otters and he is a bit nervous about how they will get along together. The book highlights how to be a good friend and neighbour by following the 'Golden Rule' when Mr Owl advises him to treat otters the same way that he would like them to treat him.

Activity

A class 'good manners' book or a flipbook
Discuss good manners and how manners are about being polite and respecting other people's rights and feelings. Students can make a 'good manners' flipbook (see **Handbook**, page 98). The sentence can be: 'When I am showing good manners I ...' Students can also make a class book (see **Handbook**, page 97) about good manners at school and home and the manners that are polite in both places.

Drama

Acting out good manners
Students act out scenarios to show how to use good manners in specific situations.
- Your grandmother has just played a board game with you and you enjoyed it. What good manners rule should you use here?
- You sneeze without warning and you are very close to two other people. What good manners rule should you use here?
- You accidentally step on someone's toes when you are trying to get to your seat in a movie theatre. What good manners rule should you use here?
- You go to someone's house to play and you are just about to leave. What good manners rule should you use here?

Circle Time: Respect and self-respect

Introduce the concept of self-respect. Ask students how they think someone who has self-respect behaves. Read the book *I Can Be Safe* (see over). Ask each student one of the following kinds of question:
- You matter, so what could you do to keep yourself safe from harm when you go to the beach?
- You matter, so what could you do to keep yourself safe from harm when you are walking to and from school?
- You matter, so how could you eat well so that you stay healthy?
- You matter, so what could you do to keep fit and healthy?
- You matter, so what could you do if someone sends you nasty emails?

- You matter, so what could you do if someone pushes you over and tries to hurt you in the playground?
- You matter, so what could you do if someone keeps telling others not to play with you?

The 'Animal asks' e-tool (see **Handbook**, page 89) could be used with these questions.

Picture books

I Can Be Safe
This book clearly explains for students the key things to remember about safety in different situations such as playing in dangerous places, road safety, safety in sports and activities, if a stranger approaches them, or if someone touches them inappropriately. There is a strong focus on encouraging them to find and talk to a trusted adult if they feel unsafe.

→ In discussing this book, elicit cybersafety suggestions as well. (don't tell people your email address or password; talk to your parent or teacher if someone sends you a nasty email, phone or text message; don't click on pop-ups; don't reply to anyone who sends you an email but is not someone you know)

→ Follow up with activities and ideas about cybersafety from the ACMA website (see the Resources list on Pearson Places).

Roonie B. Moonie: Lost and Alone
Roonie B. Moonie, a young bee, gets lost. He is approached by a stranger who offers to help him, but it doesn't feel safe. Roonie remembers what his mother has taught him so he looks for someone more trustworthy. He asks a nearby mother ladybug to use her mobile phone to call his mother and is able to recite his phone number for her.

Consolidation: Core values

Use one or more of the following ideas to give students feedback on their use of the core values.
- Students make a variety of flowers, leaves and hearts from cardboard. Each time a student in the class tells you that someone was kind or thoughtful to them, write the information on a flower, leaf or heart and add it to a string across the room. This could also be created on a computer.
- Students cut out strips of coloured paper to use in paper chains. These are stored. Whenever a student acts in a friendly way, write it on a strip of paper and add it to 'our classroom friendly chain'.
- Use a camera to keep photographic records of students putting any of the core values into practice.

Activities

Movers and shakers
Use 'Movers and shakers' (see **Handbook**, page 91) with directions such as:
- Pretend to eat with a knife and fork if you have ever been responsible and set the table for a family meal.
- Pretend to write if you ever have made a special card for someone to make them feel cared about.
- Pretend to hammer in a nail if you have made a present for someone to be kind to them.

Unit 1

Core values

- Give yourself a pat on the back if you ever included someone in a game who was alone.
- Shake someone's hand if you have ever shared your toys with someone.
- Cup your hand behind your left ear if you have ever listened carefully to your partner when you were working together.
- Pretend to put toys away in a big basket if you are responsible and do this before bedtime every night.

Other activities
The following activities reinforce the key concepts in this unit:
- 'Missing words' e-activity
- **BLM 1.9: Crossword**.

Reflections
Use the 'Reflections' e-tool (see **Handbook**, page 92), which has these eight reflection questions.
- Why do we have rules in games?
- How could you show kindness and support for someone who was feeling sick at school?
- What should you do if you lost someone's ball after they let you borrow it?
- How could you support someone who was worried about their lost pet?
- Why is it good to take turns and share?
- How could you help a new student in our class who was a bit shy?
- What should you do when you sneeze?
- What should you do if you have to interrupt a teacher with an urgent message?

Games

Bingo strips
Use some of these words to play 'Bingo strips' (see **Handbook**, page 89).

care	honest	manners
different	hurt	respect
fair	include	rules
good	kind	safe
hello	lie	

Other games
The following games reinforce the key concepts in this unit:
- 'Memory cards' e-game (see **Handbook**, page 91)
- 'Cross-offs' e-game (see **Handbook**, page 89). The secret message is 'We care about other people'.
- 'Secret word' e-game (see **Handbook**, page 92). The secret word is 'Honest'.

Resources

A complete list of resources (including references for books, poems, films, websites and weblinks for songs) is available on Pearson Places.

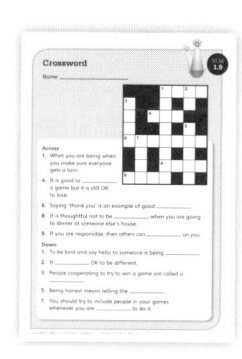

33

Unit 2

People bouncing back

Key points

Everybody feels sad and worried sometimes, not just you.
You are not the only person who sometimes feels left out, sad or worried. Everyone feels like this sometimes.

People can bounce back like balls bounce back.
A ball can bounce back up again when it hits the ground. It doesn't stay squashed. Like a ball, you can bounce back too when you have an unhappy, worrying or sad time in your life. Then you will feel better again.

Bad feelings and unhappy times always go away again.
Unhappy times and bad feelings always go away again. Things always get better but not always straight away. Unit 4: Looking on the bright side also addresses this point.

Other people can help you feel better if you talk to them.
When you have a problem or feel unhappy or worried, talk to someone who cares about you. They can help you do a reality check to see if you have got things right. Nothing is so awful that you can't talk about it to someone you trust. It is brave to talk to someone about your troubles.

Unhelpful thinking makes you feel more upset.
The way you think about what happens to you helps influence your feelings. If you use helpful thinking you will have happier feelings and feel better. Helpful thinking means not jumping to conclusions, checking your facts and not believing the worst picture.
Unit 5: Emotions also addresses this point.

Nobody is perfect. Mistakes can help you to learn.
There is no such thing as a perfect person. Everyone makes mistakes, forgets things, fails at some things and is thoughtless at times. It is normal. We are all people just doing our best, and we all have our weaknesses.

Concentrate on the good things in an unhappy situation.
Concentrate on the good things in an unhappy situation, no matter how small they are. This will help you feel stronger and more hopeful. Unit 4: Looking on the bright side also addresses this point.

Having a laugh helps you to feel better.
Try to find any part of an unhappy situation that is a little bit funny. This will help you to feel more relaxed and more hopeful. Laughing is good for you. Unit 7: Humour also addresses this point.

Change happens a lot in everyone's life. It's normal.
We all experience many changes in our life and some of these can be difficult or challenging. Examples of changes that most people experience are: growing up, starting primary school, going to camp for the first time, the birth of a new baby in your family and changing friends. Other kinds of changes include: being unwell, moving house, changing school, losing a pet or family member, having a friend or someone we care about move away or parents separating.

Sometimes there is nothing you can do to change a situation and you just have to put up with it.
Sometimes you have to just accept something if you can't do anything about it. But try to see if there's anything you can do about it first.

One bad thing doesn't spoil everything else.
Bad times usually only happen in one part of your life. They do not have to spoil all the other things in your life. Unhappy times are like a small hole in a jumper. It is only a hole and the rest of the jumper is OK.
Unit 4: Looking on the bright side also addresses this point.

Unit 2

People bouncing back

Circle Time: Everyone has unhappy times sometimes, not just you **36**
Picture books 36
   Good Days Bad Days
   Alexander and the Terrible, Horrible, No Good, Very Bad Day
   Smudge's Grumpy Day
   Franklin's Bad Day
Activities 37

Circle Time: Change happens a lot in everyone's life **37**
Picture books 37
   Fiona the Pig's Big Day
   I Am Too Absolutely Small for School
   I Don't Want to Go to School
   I Don't Want to Go to School
   I Don't Want to Go to School: Helping Children Cope with Separation Anxiety
   First Day
   Wemberly Worried

Circle Time: Moving house and/or moving to a new school **38**
Picture books 39
   First Day Jitters
   Alexander Who's Not (Do You Hear Me? I Mean It!) Going to Move
   Augustine

Circle Time: Growing up and bouncing back **39**
Picture book 39
   Eight

Circle Time: Losing someone or a pet you love **40**
Picture books 40
   Dan's Grandpa
   Little Bear's Grandad
   Moonshadow
   Harry and Hopper

Circle Time: Family changes **40**
Picture books 41
   Brand New Baby
   Two Homes
   A Day with Dad
   Sam's Sunday Dad

Circle Time: Other people can help you feel better if you talk to them **42**
Picture books 42
   A Terrible Thing Happened
   Lilly's Purple Plastic Purse
Science and technology activity 42
   Make a bounce-backer

Songs 43
   'We Can Bounce Back'
   'I'm a Bouncy Person'

Circle Time: Bouncing back from being sick or injured **43**
Activities 44
   Lightning writing
   Investigation: plants can bounce back
Picture book 44
   Bounce Around Tigger
Song 45
   'Tigger's Song'
Activities 45

Circle Time: Unhelpful thinking makes you feel more upset **45**
Picture books 45
   Koala Lou
   Chicken Licken
   The Terrible Plop
   Baby Bear Goes Camping
   The Grump

Circle Time: Nobody is perfect **46**
Picture books 46
   Gordon's Got a Snookie
   The Ugliest Dog in the World
   Henry and Amy

Circle Time: Learning from mistakes and problems **47**
Activity 47
   Make a class book

Consolidation: People bouncing back **47**
Activities 47
   Self-assessment
   Cut-up sentences
   Other activities
   Reflections
Games 48
   Bingo strips
   Snap
   Other games
Activities for consolidating understanding of the BOUNCE! acronym 49
Game 49
   BOUNCE ping pong ball

Resources **49**

Circle Time: Everyone has unhappy times sometimes, not just you

Read the book *Good Days Bad Days* (see below). A key message is that everyone has ups and downs in their life. Ask each student to tell about one not-so-happy time they have had recently. Talk about how sometimes things happen that you don't like and these things make you feel bad for a while. Stress that even though you may think these things only happen to you, they happen to everyone. Talk about how every family has good days and bad days too. Ask: Can you remember a day in your family when everything was perfect? Can you remember a day in your family when lots of things seemed to go wrong?

Picture books

Good Days Bad Days
This simple book contains lots of detailed pictures and very little text. It depicts an average family having a variety of days, some good and some not so good. It focuses on opposite types of days, e.g. sunny days and rainy days, slow days and fast days, work days and fun days, hot days and cold days. It is a good stimulus for discussion and helps students to see that you can have a bad day, but then a new day comes and it can be quite a different sort of day. It also reminds them that bad days, sad days, rainy days and boring days are as normal as good days, happy days, sunny days and fun days.

Alexander and the Terrible, Horrible, No Good, Very Bad Day
Alexander wakes up to the start of a 'terrible' day and it's all downhill after that! Everything goes wrong. Some things are simply bad luck and others are a result of his own actions. At the end of this humorous story, the author 'normalises' having bad times in your life every now and then.

→ Follow up with any of these activities:
- Students can act out the bad things that happened to Alexander.
- Write on cards the bad things that happened to Alexander. Use two hoops or pieces of paper and ask students to categorise the bad things into the those due to bad luck and those due to the things that Alexander did.
- Ask about each bad thing: How could he have felt better about this? (e.g. he could accept that not getting anything in the cereal box was just bad luck) Each time you talk about the things that happened in Alexander's bad day, ask if anyone has had something similar happen to them.
- Ask: Have you ever had a day like this? Students can write a story about 'My bad day'.
- Students can also predict what kind of day Alexander will have next. (probably a good one because bad times don't last and things get better quickly)

Smudge's Grumpy Day
Smudge, a little mouse, is having a bad day. She hurts her toe, fights with her friend Stripe (a raccoon) and gets grumpier and grumpier as the day progresses. She runs off and sulks but the situation is saved by Stripe's caring and his understanding that everyone gets grumpy and has a bad day sometimes.

Franklin's Bad Day
Nothing goes right for Franklin, the young turtle in this series, and it makes him very angry. He ends up kicking over his toys and getting into trouble. Eventually he becomes aware that he is having a bad day because he is sad and angry about his friend Otter moving away. He decides to make a scrapbook of the things they did together. He sends it to Otter with a 'Please write' note and a dozen stamped, addressed envelopes.

Unit 2

People bouncing back

Activities

- Ask: Have you ever had a bad day because you were feeling sad or worried or angry?
- Students can make a turtle puppet (see **Handbook**, pages 99 to 101) or use the Tashi/Timba puppets on **BLM 5.8: Tortoise Puppets** and act out the story.
- Students draw one of their unhappy times and then write underneath: 'My unhappy feelings went away again' and draw a smiley face.
- Students make their own version of the *Good Days Bad Days* book using three of the contrasting days.
- Students make a scrapbook about their good days.
- Students draw two stick figures to represent themselves, then add two dialogue balloons. The first one tells of a good day and the second one tells of a not-so-good day.
- Introduce the students to the BOUNCE! acronym using the BOUNCE! e-tool and/or **BLM 2.1: BOUNCE!**

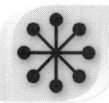

BOUNCE!
When you feel unhappy, you can BOUNCE back again and feel better

Bad feelings always go away again.
Other people can help you feel better if you talk to them.
Unhelpful thinking makes you feel more upset. Think again.
Nobody is perfect. Mistakes help you learn.
Concentrate on the good things and have a laugh.
Everybody feels sad and worried sometimes, not just you.

Circle Time: Change happens a lot in everyone's life

Read one of the books listed below about starting school, as the basis for a discussion about the joys and challenges of starting school for the first time. This lesson is more relevant for students who have started school in the past year or two, to show that everyone finds good things and hard things about coping with change.

Ask each student in turn to throw a dice. If they get an even number, they say one of the good things about when they started school. If they throw an odd number, they say one of the things that they found hard or scary when they started school. For younger students, have two ping pong balls in a container for them to draw from instead of using a dice. On one ping pong ball place a sticker that says 'a good thing' and one that says 'a hard thing'. You could also ask if anyone has a younger brother, sister, cousin or neighbour who will be starting school soon. What advice will they give them about how to enjoy starting school and some of the hard things about starting school? (For example, you should say hello to the other students and tell them your name so you can make friends.)

→ Follow up: Students could write simple sentences about their first few days at school, saying one good thing and one hard thing.

Picture books

Fiona the Pig's Big Day
Fiona doesn't have a problem with separation anxiety on her first day at school and she thoroughly enjoys herself. Her parents, on the other hand, suffer a sleepless night and an anxious day worrying about how she will cope.

I Am Too Absolutely Small for School
Lola is worried about starting school and comes up with all kinds of reasons why she doesn't need to go (e.g. she doesn't have the time). Charlie comes up with lots of positive reasons for going to school (e.g. she will learn to read bedtime stories, write to Father Christmas and count biscuits) and little by little Charlie is able to convince her to go to school. Once she arrives, she finds a friend and all is well.

I Don't Want to Go to School
Simon, a rabbit, is apprehensive about going to school until he recognises what a great time he can have drawing, playing at recess, eating a yummy lunch and playing drums. After a day of enjoying himself at school, he is reluctant to go home when his mother collects him.

I Don't Want to Go to School
Kate does not want to go to school but in helping her new friend, Li, she overcomes her fears and soon discovers that school is not the scary place she imagines it to be.

I Don't Want to Go to School: Helping Children Cope with Separation Anxiety
Honey Maloo, a little honey bee, is about to start school but she fears being apart from her mother. She tries everything to avoid going to school, from pretending to be sick to sneaking off the school bus, but she has to go. Her mother, her teacher, the music teacher and new friends help her to discover that school can be fun. The focus of this book is on separation anxiety and it conveys the message that students can still enjoy school even if they miss their family while they are there.

First Day
The story follows six children on their first day at school. They all experience a combination of excitement and nervousness that focuses on different issues around starting school, such as being able to find a friend, tying your own shoelaces, sitting still and counting. They all cope in their own ways.

Wemberly Worried
This book is described in more detail in Unit 5: Emotions (see page 110), but can also be used to focus on starting school.

Circle Time: Moving house and/or moving to a new school

Describe a time in your own life where you had to deal with a major change such as moving house or starting a new job. Focus on both the hard parts and the positive aspects of the change. Read one of the books listed below. Use the 'Partner retell' strategy (see **Handbook**, page 91) and ask students to tell each other about whether they or anyone they know has moved to a new place to live or moved to a new school. When they return and report to the circle, draw out as many positives in what each pair says about their own experiences as you can (I had my own room in our new house; my new school had a good oval to play on; I made new friends) but also highlight at least one thing they mention that caused them to feel apprehensive or which they found difficult to do (I had to leave my friends; I couldn't find my things in the packing boxes).

→ Follow up: Students draw a stick figure to represent themselves, then add a dialogue balloon in which they write about the best way to bounce back if you move somewhere else or start at a new school. You could use this pre-printed sentence stem in each dialogue balloon: 'One thing you can do to bounce back if you move to a new house/school is ….' Prompt students to think about actions such as emailing to stay in touch with their friends if they change schools, looking for the good things about the new house/apartment they move to, putting labels on their packing boxes so they can easily find things, etc.

Unit 2

People bouncing back

Picture books

First Day Jitters
Sarah Jane Hartwell is scared about her upcoming first day at a new school and she is not keen to go. She doesn't know anyone there and imagines the worst. She goes to school where she is befriended by Mrs Burton, who helps her settle in. The surprise ending will delight younger students (Sarah Jane is actually one of the teachers!).
→ Discuss how teachers might be feeling when they have a job at a new school and what they might say to themselves or do to help them to bounce back. How might some of their feelings be similar to those that students have?

Alexander Who's Not (Do You Hear Me? I Mean It!) Going to Move
Alexander's parents announce that they are moving to another state because of his father's work. Alexander is outraged and becomes upset at the idea of leaving his friends and all the things he is familiar with. He eventually comes to terms with the move and even starts to see the possibilities in it.
→ Discuss what helped Alexander to bounce back.

Augustine
Augustine, a shy young penguin who was named by her parents after the artist Pierre-Auguste Renoir, finds it hard to move with her family from the South Pole to the North Pole. She misses her friends, her grandparents and her old bedroom and everything looks different. When it's time to go to her new school, Augustine becomes very apprehensive but uses her pencils to ' break the ice' with her new classmates and draws her journey using 'penguinised' versions of van Gogh, Munch, Picasso and other artists.
→ Discuss Augustine's way of bouncing back and getting to know the new students. Ask: Do you have a strength that would help you to get to know people if you moved to a new school?

Circle Time: Growing up and bouncing back

Ask students to bring in a soft toy that was (or still is) important to them so that they have them on the day you read the book *Eight* (see below). After you have read the story, ask each student to introduce their toy and say how it has helped them to be strong, feel safe and feel better. Discuss what other soft toys they had when they were little. What has happened to these toys? Do their older/current soft toys still have a role to play in their lives? Have they outgrown them?

Picture book

Eight
Timmy and Eight, his toy octopus, have been together since babyhood and have done everything together, including going to preschool. Eight is left behind after a family picnic and Timmy is distraught because he thinks he can't cope without his beloved toy. A bedraggled Eight is eventually found and cleaned up but by then Timmy has realised that he can now cope on his own.

Circle Time: Losing someone or a pet you love

Read one of the books listed below. Ask students to raise their hand if they have lost a loved family member or pet. Ask each student who raised their hand to briefly say who they have lost and why they loved them. Ask students to raise their hand if a family member had died before they were born. Ask selected students to say who it was and why they would have liked to have met them. Make the point that even though we sometimes lose pets and people that we love, they are still with us in our hearts and we can think about how much we still love them by remembering happy times.

→ Follow up: Students can illustrate a happy memory of someone (or a pet) they loved whom they have lost and write a brief sentence about them. These can be scanned into the computer and then shown as a slide show.

Picture books

Dan's Grandpa
Sally Morgan, a descendant of the Palku people, has written this story about Dan and his grandpa and their very special relationship. Grandpa has always promised Dan that no matter what happens, he'll always be there. When Grandpa dies, his pet cockatoo flies away but then returns as a special messenger from Grandpa who helps Dan to cope with the loss and move on. Animals play an important role in the lives of Aboriginal people and one belief is that when you are in trouble an animal will come to support you for as long as you need them.

Little Bear's Grandad
Little Bear has a very special relationship with Grandad and visits him every week to have tea with him and hear one of his stories. Grandad falls ill and is taken to hospital. When he visits Grandad, Little Bear tells him a story about their special times together. Grandad dies but the family copes with his death in a positive and moving way.

Moonshadow
Moonshadow, a young swan, is flying south for the first time, with his grandfather leading the flock on their great journey. A terrible storm strikes and not all the swans make it through but, although grief-stricken, Moonshadow finds the strength to go on.

Harry and Hopper
Harry and his dog Hopper have a deep bond but it ends sooner than expected when the dog dies. Harry has difficulty coping with his first experience of grief and loss but finally uses the memory of his good times with Hopper to move on.

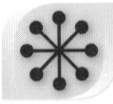

Circle Time: Family changes

The key point in this session is that change happens a lot in everyone's life and that's normal.

Version 1
Read *Brand New Baby* (see below) and then ask students whose family has had a new baby to say one good thing and one not-so-good thing about having the baby in the house. Consider asking a parent with a fairly new baby or small infant to bring them in and introduce them to the class. Students can prepare questions to ask the parent about the baby, watch for expressions and behaviours that tell them how the baby might be feeling or what they might need, and take photographs.

→ Follow up: Students could write about or draw the baby or put together a display of photographs. This helps students to learn abut empathy and 'reading' the feelings and needs of others.

Version 2
Read one of the other books below about families who are separated. Make the point that when parents separate there is nothing that children can do to change that situation for lots of different reasons, such as:
- adults in your family have made their decisions and that's what adults have to do
- judges may have made decisions about who lives where
- one parent may live a long way away and it is harder for them to see their children as much as they would like to.

However, they can do things to feel better about it and be happier. Ask each student one of the following questions:
- What might be a good thing about having two homes?
- What might be a good thing about having a step-parent?
- What might be a good thing about seeing one of your parents only on weekends or holidays?
- What might a child want to take to both houses if their parents were separated?
- How could a child stay in touch with the parent whose house they weren't living in?

You could also ask students about their experiences with knowing or being part of a blended family when one or both of their parents has re-partnered and they must deal with changes such as:
- getting along with a step-parent
- getting to know and getting along with step-siblings
- forming a relationship with a half-sibling with whom they may not live.

→ Follow up: Students could work with a partner to make a poster that affirms that parents still love and care about their children even if they can no longer live together and that they think of their children all the time, no matter which parent they are with or where they are.

Picture books

Brand New Baby
This is a gentle and realistic portrayal of family life and the birth of a new sibling, Walter. The story opens with Mum heavily pregnant. Dad manages the household while Mum is in hospital and he helps the two small children adjust to the new arrival. The older children aren't particularly impressed and find Walter a bit boring. The story focuses on adjusting to change and new routines.

Two Homes
This is a matter-of-fact book with limited text in which a young boy describes how he lives in two homes, one with his mother and one with his father. He shows the reader what his room looks like in each home, where he hangs up his coat in each home, his favourite chair in each home, the kitchen in each home and so on. He also tells how his friends visit him in both homes and his mummy rings him at his daddy's. The book reinforces the fact that he is loved by both parents no matter where he is or where they are.

A Day with Dad
Tim's parents are separated but his father comes to visit for the day. Tim is very excited and they go to the movies, eat pizza and go to the library. Tim is very proud to introduce everyone to his dad. This story normalises a child's positive relationship with a non-custodial parent.

Sam's Sunday Dad
Sam's parents are separated. Every day Sam has something he wants to tell his dad, but he has to save it all up till he sees his dad on weekend visits. This is an optimistic look at a young boy's acceptance of the fact that he can't see his dad as often as he would like.

→ Talk about how sometimes we cannot see or be with a person we care about. Discuss the feelings we might have in response to that. Point out that sometimes we just have to accept things that we can't change and still try to get on with our lives and be happy, just like Sam does. Ask students to give examples of things they just have to put up with even if they don't like it because they can't do anything to change things.

Circle Time: Other people can help you feel better if you talk to them

Read *A Terrible Thing Happened* (see below). Ask: What could the terrible thing have been? Why does talking about a problem to someone we trust help us feel better? (the other person has had more experience; they can help you do a reality check to see if you have got things right; they can see things about a situation that you can't; they can give you some ideas about how you can solve the problem or feel better; it feels better if someone knows about the problem and cares) Ask: Have you ever felt bad about something and then felt better after you have talked to someone about it?

→ Follow up: Students make a list of the trusted people in their life that they would talk to if they had a problem. They also complete **BLM 2.2: Talking to People Who Can Help Us**.

Picture books

A Terrible Thing Happened
In this simple story, we never find out what the terrible thing that happened to the young bear actually was. For a long time, he feels sad and worried and has bad feelings because of the 'terrible thing'. Eventually he talks to his teacher about the 'terrible thing' and gradually he starts to feel less distressed about it.

Lilly's Purple Plastic Purse
Lilly is an exuberant little mouse whose life is pretty good. She loves school and especially her very 'cool' teacher Mr Slinger. Lilly is also very fond of fashion and so she is very excited when she receives a purple plastic purse from her grandmother. It plays music when opened and contains sunglasses studded with rhinestones. She takes it to school but eventually Mr Slinger takes the purse away after Lilly refuses to stop showing it off and disturbing the class. Lilly is hurt, angry and embarrassed and she draws a terrible picture of Mr Slinger and puts it into his book bag. When she gets home, she talks to her parents and they help her to cope with what has happened and make amends. The book links nicely with the concepts that 'Bad times don't last' and 'Other people can help if you talk to them'. You could also make links with classroom rules and cooperation.

Science and technology activity

Make a bounce-backer
Getting every student to make a 'bounce-backer' will help them to learn in a concrete way the principles of bouncing back (see **Handbook**, page 94, for instructions). Talk about how their bounce-backer always returns to where it was, even if you try to push it over.

Tell students that people can be like that too—sometimes they get pushed around by life, but if they try they can go back to where they were, i.e. 'bounce back'.

Songs

'We Can Bounce Back'
(To the tune of 'Frere Jacques')

We can bounce back
We can bounce back
When we're sad
When we're sad
Find someone to talk to
Think about the good things
Then feel glad
Then feel glad

We can bounce back
We can bounce back
When we're sad
When we're sad
Have a little laugh
Remember things get better
Then feel glad
Then feel glad

We can bounce back
We can bounce back
When we're mad
When we're mad
Have a little exercise
Think about the best way
Then feel glad
Then feel glad.

'I'm a Bouncy Person'
(To the tune of 'I'm a Little Teapot')

I'm a bouncy person
I bounce back
When I feel unhappy
And my world is black
When I feel down-hearted
I don't crack
I stay hopeful
And bounce back!

Sing the songs above and/or make a BOUNCE! bookmark using the template on **BLM 2.3: BOUNCE! Bookmark**.

Circle Time: Bouncing back from being sick or injured

Ask students to think about a time when they were sick and then bounced back and got well again. Then ask them to talk about any injuries that they or members of their family have had. Make the link between bouncing back emotionally and other kinds of 'bouncing back' (recovery to almost the same state), such as recovering from an illness or injuries. Ask: How do we bounce back after we have been sick or injured? What do we do that helps us bounce back? Who helps us bounce back? (A student in the class may have someone in their family who will not recover from injury or illness—if so, you can talk about how people mostly bounce back, but not always, and children nearly always bounce back.)

→ Follow up with any of these:
◎ Talk with the class about how our hair and fingernails bounce back and grow again after being cut. Students can draw their hair or fingernails in various stages to show how fast they grow (hair grows about 1 to 1.5 cm per month).
◎ Link with a 'people who help us' theme (also see Unit 1: Core values and Unit 3: Courage). Students can draw a simple flow chart, i.e. an incident in four frames from the time they get a cut, break or graze to the time when it has healed again. They write underneath 'Our skin can bounce back when it has been cut'. Stress that our skin takes longer to recover from serious cuts.
◎ Students can make 'get well' cards on the computer using Kid Pix or another publishing program and give them to anyone in their family who is sick or injured. Talk about why kind actions, such as giving a card, help someone to bounce back and feel better again. See how to make a giant class get well card in Unit 1: Core values, page 11.

Activities

Lightning writing
(See **Handbook**, page 91.) Students write what they know about how plants grow and what they need to grow.

Investigation: plants can bounce back
This activity can be used with procedural writing. Ask students to predict what would make a plant bounce back if it wasn't growing well. Record their predictions.

Take three healthy impatiens plants (because they wilt and recover quite dramatically). Set up these three conditions:
◎ water and light: regularly spray and water one plant and keep it in filtered sunlight
◎ no water: leave one plant in filtered sunlight but do not water
◎ no light: water plant but leave it in the dark.

At the end of ten days, compare the conditions of the three plants. Then water the plant that was not watered. Put the third one into filtered light. What happens? Which plants bounce back? Does one bounce back quickly and the other slowly? What does that tell us about what plants need?

Picture book

Bounce Around Tigger
The message in the story is that we can bounce back after we lose energy if we take the right actions. In the story, Tigger loses his bounce. Tigger and his friends go looking for his bounce but can't find it. Finally Christopher Robin realises that Tigger is just tired and hungry so he makes Tigger have a snack and a snooze and he gets his bounce (energy) back.
→ Follow up with:
◎ Ask students what makes them lose their bounce. Discuss how they can lose their bounce if they don't have enough good food, exercise and sleep.
◎ They can draw the foods that give them good 'bounce' and draw themselves having a good night's sleep. They could also draw on a clock face the times when they need to eat, and when they need to go to sleep and get up if they are to retain their 'bounce'.
◎ Mention that some orphaned children in poor countries are fed but waste away because they do not have enough caretakers to give them love and affection. Ask students who gives *them* hugs and cuddles to give them the energy to grow in their hearts and bounce back.

Unit 2

People bouncing back

Song

'Tigger's Song'

Activities

- Consider watching *The Tigger Movie* on DVD.
- Make tiger masks from the template on **BLM 2.4: Tiger Mask**.

Circle Time: Unhelpful thinking makes you feel more upset

Read the book *Koala Lou* to begin, then follow up with *Chicken Licken* (see below).

Use the 'Smiley ball' strategy (see **Handbook**, page 92). Students take it in turns to answer one of the questions below. If they give the incorrect answer (which is 'Yes') then ask someone else 'Is there another way to think about this that is more helpful and makes you feel better?'

- If someone couldn't come over to play at your house when you asked them to, would that mean they didn't like you? (No, it probably means they are busy or not allowed. I should ask them again another time.)
- If you spelt a word wrong, would that mean you are a bad speller? (No, it means that I need to learn that word. There are many other words I can spell correctly.)
- If you met someone who didn't want to play with you, does that mean you are not a nice person? (No. There is nobody who is liked by every person they meet.)
- If a teacher is cross with you, does that mean they hate you? (No, it means that I have probably broken a rule or misbehaved and the teacher is worried.)
- If someone is not as good at reading as someone else in the class, does that mean they are a bad reader and will always be a bad reader? (No, it means that they have more learning to do. There are things they are better at than other people. They will be a better reader when they have had some more time to practise.)
- If you are worried about your mother having a car accident, does that mean she will have one? (No, it means that you keep thinking about it so it seems real. She will not have a car accident just because you are worried she will.)

Picture books

Koala Lou

As her mother had more children and less time, Koala Lou thought her mother no longer loved her. So Koala Lou decided to win the gum-tree-climbing event in the Bush Olympics to win back her mother's love, but only comes second. When she eventually returns home her mother is waiting to show how much she loves Koala Lou. The message is that it is important to do a reality check and look for evidence; don't just assume that you know what another person feels or thinks. Koala Lou used unhelpful thinking and jumped to conclusions.

→ Talk about how sometimes we think about things that worry us in ways that aren't helpful.

Chicken Licken

Read one of the many versions of *Chicken Licken*, *Chicken Little* or *Henny Penny*. Chicken Licken exaggerates a simple event into a catastrophe, and thinks the sky is falling in. He has

45

no evidence that the sky is falling in but his unhelpful thinking makes everyone worried. This kind of thinking leads to all the animals being tricked by the fox. Students can act out the story and ham it up to show how unhelpful this kind of thinking is.

The Terrible Plop

This is a humorous rhyming reworking of the story of Chicken Little, who thought a falling leaf meant that the sky was falling. Six little rabbits having a picnic hear (but do not see) the loud plop of an apple falling into the river, and panic. They run away in fear and their panic is contagious. They frighten all the animals they meet, who then pass on the message about 'the terrible plop'. Nobody stops to check the facts. Their unhelpful thinking (they jumped to conclusions and didn't check their facts) made things worse for everyone.

Baby Bear Goes Camping

Papa Bear and Mama Bear take Baby Bear on his first camping trip. Lying in bed in his tent that night, Baby Bear feels very scared when he sees shadows on his tent and hears strange noises. He jumps to the conclusion that he is in danger but then, when he checks his facts, he discovers that the shadows and noises belong to his new friends, who have come to say good night.

→ Ask: Has anyone ever been in bed and heard scary noises but then discovered it was just a possum on the roof or a bush brushing against the window?

The Grump

Early one morning a little boy is woken up by what he calls 'the Grump', a very scary monster. He carefully follows the Grump's footsteps and discovers that the Grump has eaten most of the leftover birthday cake from his party. He follows a strange rumbling sound and discovers that the Grump is really his father, fast asleep on the sofa. He started by jumping to conclusions but then he checked his facts.

Circle Time: Nobody is perfect

Ask students to put up their hands if they are perfect. Then use the 'Think–ink–pair–share' strategy (see **Handbook**, page 92) and ask them to talk about what they think 'perfect' means. (making no mistakes; having no weaknesses; doing nothing wrong) Ask pairs to say what they talked about. Ask: Do you know any perfect people? Students take it in turns to say one way in which they are not perfect. (bodily imperfections; schoolwork weaknesses; loss of temper; being messy; being thoughtless) After each contribution the whole class can say in unison, 'That's OK because nobody is perfect'. Stress that nobody is perfect even if they seem to be. Everybody makes mistakes because mistakes help us to learn. Everybody has something about them that is not quite right (e.g. something they are not good at, physical imperfections such as not seeing well and so on). Make the point that another reason why nobody can be perfect is because there are so many different and good ways to look, act and behave and no one can say which is the best way.

Picture books

Gordon's Got a Snookie

The animals in the zoo are so excited that Gordon, a silverback gorilla, is coming to live at their zoo. When Gordon arrives he is very impressive but he has a security blanket (a 'snookie'). The animals laugh at him; the hyena laughs so hard that he ends up being taken to hospital. How can Gordon live up to his strong image if he needs a security blanket? But he does of course! Nobody is perfect.

Unit 2

People bouncing back

The Ugliest Dog in the World
This is the story of a young girl who loves her dog, which is far from perfect, as everyone points out to her. The point is that we can love and care for others when they are not perfect because nobody is perfect.

→ After reading to the class, ask students to draw their pet and list all its imperfections. If they do not have one, they can think about one they know of or used to have or they can think of a category of pet (e.g. dogs) and in what ways that animal isn't perfect. This book is also used in Unit 6: Relationships.

Henry and Amy
Amy seems perfect because she does everything right, but she isn't very artistic and she doesn't have many good ideas. She becomes friends with Henry, who gets lots of things wrong but he has some wonderful ideas and is very artistic. Neither of them is perfect and they learn to appreciate the strengths the other person has. For more ideas on how to use this book, see Unit 6: Relationships.

Circle Time: Learning from mistakes and problems

Share with the class a mistake you have made that helped you to learn something, e.g. when you tried a new recipe or made something from a pattern or instructions. Talk about how everyone makes mistakes and that making mistakes is normal and necessary. You cannot learn without making mistakes.

Ask students to take turns to talk about a time when they made a mistake or got something wrong but learned something from it. Encourage them not to over-focus on schoolwork mistakes. Did they feel stronger and more confident after learning from that mistake?

→ Follow up: Students write and illustrate a one-page story of a mistake they made that helped them to learn something. They can use this format:
- The mistake I made was…
- What I learned from making that mistake was…

Activity

Make a class book
Make a class book or a class digital story book (see **Handbook**, page 97) or a wall display of the students' one-page stories about a mistake they have made and what they learnt from it (see above).

Consolidation: People bouncing back

Activities

Self-assessment
Students complete a self-assessment of how well they bounce back by using **BLM 2.5: How Well Do You Bounce Back?**

Cut-up sentences
(See **Handbook**, page 89.) Cut these sentences into individual words and place each cut-up sentence into an envelope. Make enough sets

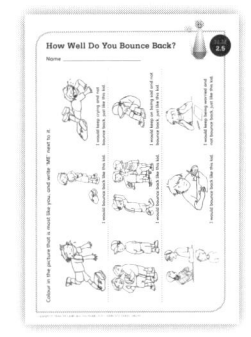

47

for each pair of students to have one set of six envelopes. Each pair reconstructs the six sentences.
- Bad feelings go away again and things get better.
- Other people can help you to feel better if you talk to them.
- Your thinking can change your feelings.
- Nobody is perfect. Mistakes help you learn things.
- Think about the good things and have a laugh.
- Everybody feels sad and worried sometimes.

Other activities

The following activities reinforce the key concepts in this unit:
- Complete (as a class or in pairs) the 'Missing words' e-activity.
- Complete **BLM 2.6: Crossword**.

Reflections

Use these questions with either the 'Animal asks' e-tool (see **Handbook**, page 89) or the 'Reflections' e-tool (see **Handbook**, page 92).
- How could someone stop themselves from thinking about sad or worrying things when they go to bed?
- Tell about a time when you had hurt feelings. How did you make yourself feel better?
- Who are you most likely to talk to when you are worried about something?
- Have you ever worried about something that might happen but it never did?
- How can other people help you when you are worried?
- What does it mean when we say that bad feelings go away again?
- Why is it important to check your facts when you are worried or upset about something?
- Nobody is perfect. How are you not perfect?

Games

Bingo strips

Use some of these words to play 'Bingo strips' (see **Handbook**, page 89).

back	facts	normal
bounce	feelings	other
can	good	perfect
change	helpful	people
check	laugh	talk
down	mistakes	upset
everyone	nobody	

Snap

Use **BLM 2.7: BOUNCE! Cards** to make six cards. Photocopy one page onto light cardboard for each student. Students colour in their sheet, cut out the cards and join their collection with that of another student to make a set of twelve cards to play Snap with.

Other games

The following games reinforce the key concepts in this unit:
- Complete the 'Cross-offs' e-game (see **Handbook**, page 89). The secret message is 'Everyone feels unhappy sometimes, not just you'.
- Play the 'Memory cards' e-game (see **Handbook**, page 91).

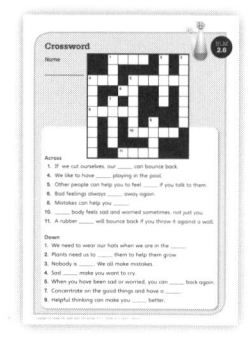

Unit 2

People bouncing back

Activities for consolidating understanding of the BOUNCE! acronym

The following activities will help students master the BOUNCE! statements.
- Regularly use the 'BOUNCE!' acronym e-tool to provide students with an opportunity to practise the six key statements.
- Make giant BOUNCE! letters in the air, from sandpaper (they could make their own sandpaper using paper, glue and sand in a shaker), from play dough or baked bread dough or on the computer.

Game

BOUNCE ping pong ball

The game is played in two teams. You will need:
- twelve ping-pong balls—six of one colour (for one team) and six of a different colour (for the other team) in two ice-cream containers
- two egg-carton strips with six sections—cut a twelve-egg carton in half lengthwise; paint one strip the same colour as the first six ping-pong balls and the other strip the same colour as the other balls.

The aim is to be the first team to fill all of the six BOUNCE 'slots'. This is done by correctly making the statements that go with each letter of BOUNCE.
- Write one letter of BOUNCE on the outside of each of the six egg-carton sections and also on the sets of six balls.
- Divide the class into two teams and give them a colour name that reflects the colour of the balls and egg-carton sections.
- Place each team's 'set' of six BOUNCE balls in a separate ice-cream container.
- In turn, pull out one ball at a time and ask a student in that team to tell you what the letter stands for. If they are correct, place the ball in the corresponding section in the team's egg-carton strip. Make sure that you don't pull out the same letter for one team that the previous team has just had.

Resources

A complete list of resources (including references for books, poems, films, websites and weblinks for songs) is available on Pearson Places.

Unit 3

Courage

Key points

What is courage?
Courage means feeling frightened about doing something scary or difficult (because you might get hurt, you might fail or get rejected, etc.) but being brave and doing it anyway. Deciding to do the brave thing sometimes happens very quickly, but sometimes you have to think about it for a while before you decide to be brave.

When you show 'everyday courage', you are being brave.
Everyday courage is when you have to do something ordinary but it makes you feel a bit scared or anxious. This might be trying to do something new at school when you are not sure whether you can do it. It might be saying 'No, I don't want to' when someone else wants you to do something stupid or mean.

Help yourself to be brave.
Some 'tough self-talk' is needed when you want to be brave. 'Tough talk' is when you say things to yourself such as 'Just do it' or 'This is important; you have to do it' or 'I know I can do this if I try'.

Everyone has fears.
Everyone gets frightened. When you feel scared it is because you feel unsafe—you realise that there might be some danger. Don't ignore unsafe feelings. Tell someone you trust if you are feeling unsafe. They can help you work out if there is any real danger. Sometimes you need to be brave and face your fear.

Everyone feels nervous too.
A fear is when there really is something dangerous. Being anxious is when there *might* be something dangerous. Another word for 'anxious' is 'nervous'. You feel anxious when you think about something scary that could happen to you but hasn't yet (and probably won't). There are more activities about being anxious in Unit 5: Emotions (page 86).

Everyone has different fears and worries.
We are all scared of some things. We are all brave about other things. But we might not be scared and brave about the same things as other people we know. One person may be very scared of going to the top of tall buildings, but may not be scared of talking in front of the class. On the other hand, someone else might be very frightened of speaking in front of the class but doesn't feel scared about going to the top of a tall building.

Different things will seem scary and difficult at different ages.
Some things that took courage to do when you were little may now be easy for you to do. Things that take a lot of courage for you to do now will be a lot easier and less scary as you get older.

Being a hero is another kind of courage.
When someone is a hero it means that they do something brave and risk their own safety so that somebody else can be safe. Not very many people are in situations where they can be a hero. Sometimes it is foolish to try to save someone else if you do not have the skills or resources to do it with and the danger level is very high. It could end up with both of you being hurt. Think carefully. The best way to help them might be to get help.

Being foolish is not the same as being brave.
Being foolish is doing something scary and unnecessary that could seriously hurt you or someone else. It is a dangerous and silly form of courage because: the person is doing it to impress someone else or because they feel pressured to do it; what they will gain from it is not worth the risk they are taking; they haven't learned the skills to do it; they could get seriously hurt.

Unit 3

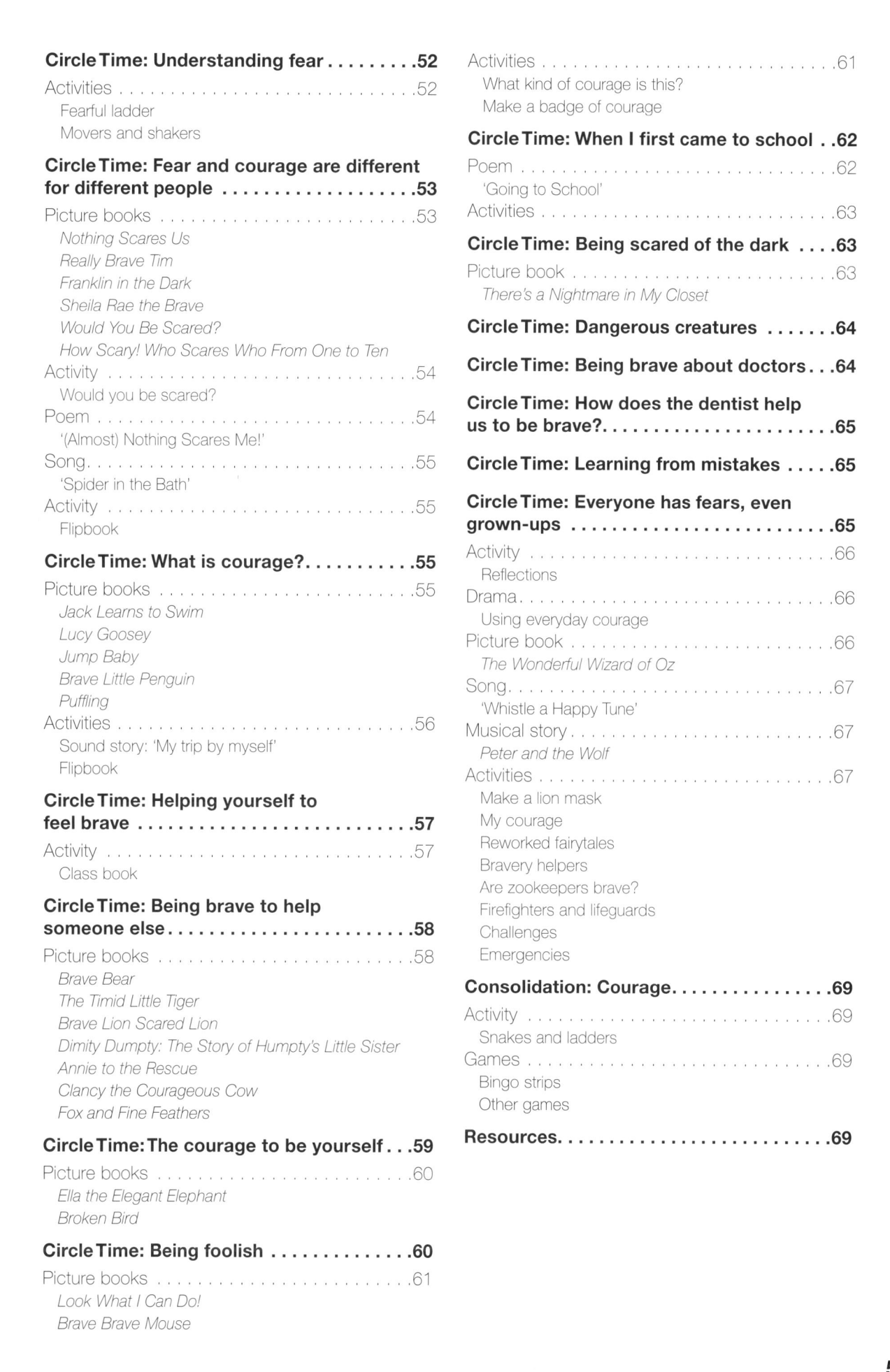

Courage

Circle Time: Understanding fear 52
Activities 52
   Fearful ladder
   Movers and shakers

Circle Time: Fear and courage are different for different people 53
Picture books 53
   Nothing Scares Us
   Really Brave Tim
   Franklin in the Dark
   Sheila Rae the Brave
   Would You Be Scared?
   How Scary! Who Scares Who From One to Ten
Activity 54
   Would you be scared?
Poem 54
   '(Almost) Nothing Scares Me!'
Song 55
   'Spider in the Bath'
Activity 55
   Flipbook

Circle Time: What is courage? 55
Picture books 55
   Jack Learns to Swim
   Lucy Goosey
   Jump Baby
   Brave Little Penguin
   Puffling
Activities 56
   Sound story: 'My trip by myself'
   Flipbook

Circle Time: Helping yourself to feel brave 57
Activity 57
   Class book

Circle Time: Being brave to help someone else 58
Picture books 58
   Brave Bear
   The Timid Little Tiger
   Brave Lion Scared Lion
   Dimity Dumpty: The Story of Humpty's Little Sister
   Annie to the Rescue
   Clancy the Courageous Cow
   Fox and Fine Feathers

Circle Time: The courage to be yourself . . .59
Picture books 60
   Ella the Elegant Elephant
   Broken Bird

Circle Time: Being foolish 60
Picture books 61
   Look What I Can Do!
   Brave Brave Mouse

Activities 61
   What kind of courage is this?
   Make a badge of courage

Circle Time: When I first came to school . .62
Poem 62
   'Going to School'
Activities 63

Circle Time: Being scared of the dark 63
Picture book 63
   There's a Nightmare in My Closet

Circle Time: Dangerous creatures 64

Circle Time: Being brave about doctors . . .64

Circle Time: How does the dentist help us to be brave? 65

Circle Time: Learning from mistakes 65

Circle Time: Everyone has fears, even grown-ups 65
Activity 66
   Reflections
Drama 66
   Using everyday courage
Picture book 66
   The Wonderful Wizard of Oz
Song 67
   'Whistle a Happy Tune'
Musical story 67
   Peter and the Wolf
Activities 67
   Make a lion mask
   My courage
   Reworked fairytales
   Bravery helpers
   Are zookeepers brave?
   Firefighters and lifeguards
   Challenges
   Emergencies

Consolidation: Courage 69
Activity 69
   Snakes and ladders
Games 69
   Bingo strips
   Other games

Resources 69

51

Circle Time: Understanding fear

Make one A3 photocopy of the picture of the scared wombat on **BLM 5.3: Animal Pictures** in Unit 5: Emotions. Alternatively, scan the picture into your computer and display it on the IWB.

Introduce the topic of fear by showing the picture and asking students to come out and point to the different parts of the body that change when the wombat feels scared. (butterflies in the stomach; trembling knees; sweaty palms; shaky voice; heart beating faster; goosebumps; red face; lump in throat; headache; needing to go to the toilet)

Ask the students to show with their body what happens when they feel scared. Then read out each of the following sentences and ask them to use their bodies to show how scared they would be in each situation.
- A spider climbs up the arm of your chair.
- You have to talk at assembly to the whole school.
- You invite a classmate you don't know very well to come to your home.
- You go to stay with your relatives by yourself while your parents are away.

Then ask: How do people show that they are frightened? Students take turns to say one way their body feels or they behave when they are scared. Emphasise that being scared is useful because fear warns us of things that might be unsafe or could harm us. Feeling fear makes our body ready to run away or fight. That's what makes our body feel funny when we are scared. Ask students to tell about any time when they felt scared and unsafe and how the feeling was helpful because it stopped them from being hurt. Stress that sometimes when we feel scared there is no real danger. It is a 'false alarm'. We might just be scared of making a mistake, or of looking silly. We might be scared of something that can't really hurt us (e.g. a moth) because we don't know whether or not it is really dangerous. As we get older we are scared of fewer things because we get better at knowing what really is dangerous. Conclude by stressing that fear is useful but that sometimes what we think is scary really isn't dangerous and sometimes we have to face our fear and try to be brave.

→ Follow up by having students write and draw about what used to scare them but does not any more. (I used to be scared of birds but now I'm not and I have a pet bird. I used to be scared of the waves but now I'm not and I ride the waves on my boogie board.) Students could also trace around their bodies and label the parts that show fear.

Activities

Fearful ladder

Photocopy **BLM 3.1: Fearful Ladder** onto card and have students order the words and pictures from 'low fear' to 'high fear' (D: worried, B: nervous, C: scared, A: terrified). Students colour them and paste them onto the ladder with 'worried' at the bottom. Ask: Why is it important to use the right word for how you are feeling? (so you don't overreact and make things worse for yourself) It is harder to be brave if you use a word that is too strong such as 'terrified'.
→ Follow up with a writing activity based around the four words.

Movers and shakers
(See **Handbook**, page 91.) Use statements such as these:
- Jump on the spot if you have ever been frightened by a spider.
- Do a star jump if you would like to be a sky diver who jumps out of planes with a parachute.

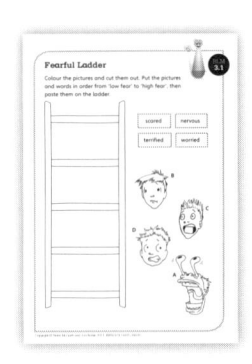

Unit 3

Courage

- Put your hands on your head if you have ever been nervous about acting, singing or dancing in public but you did it anyway.
- Put both your arms up in the air if you have ever put your hand up to answer a question even though you were not sure the answer you were going to give was correct.
- Pat yourself on the back if you found it scary when you were learning to ride a bike, swim or read but you did it anyway.

Circle Time: Fear and courage are different for different people

Read the book *Nothing Scares Us* to the class (see below). Students can then use the 'Think–ink–pair–share' strategy (see **Handbook**, page 92) to find one thing they are both scared of, and one thing for each of them that one is scared of but not the other. Ask for selected responses.

→ Follow up with the pairs of students making a mobile (see **Handbook**, page 99) using drawings to show all the things they are both a bit scared of (one colour) and the things that only one of them is a bit scared of (another colour).

Picture books

Nothing Scares Us
The two children in this story are good friends but for a long time each keeps their secret fear hidden from the other. He is scared of spiders. She is scared of a monster in a TV show. Eventually they share their fears with each other and realise that it is not embarrassing to be scared of certain things and that a friend can still like and admire you even if there are some things that scare you.

Really Brave Tim
This is another book that links with the idea that fear and courage are relative and that what scares one doesn't scare another. Several friends are talking about scary things and each tells an exaggerated tale of how brave they are in dealing with being scared of the dark, the water and heights. But not Tim, because he isn't brave at all when it comes to the dark, the water and heights. But he is the only one who isn't frightened of spiders and there's one in the cubby house where they are all sitting.
→ Follow up with students completing the following sentence several times: 'I am not scared of… but I am a bit scared of…'

Franklin in the Dark
Franklin, a young turtle, is pretty brave about a lot of things but he is really scared of small dark places and this means that he is too frightened to crawl into his shell, especially at night, even when his mother offers him a night light. Franklin does a 'reality check' with other animals about what scares them and how they cope with it. He finds that they all have one thing that they don't feel brave about, and in each case, it's something Franklin isn't scared of at all. He feels reassured.

Sheila Rae the Brave
Sheila Rae is a small mouse who continually reminds her younger sister Louise in a rather boastful way that she, Sheila Rae, is not afraid of anything! But when she gets herself lost, Sheila Rae is very scared and starts to panic. Only Louise is level-headed enough to get them back home again. Finally Sheila Rae announces that they are both very brave.

Would You Be Scared?
This book presents illustrated situations that might make some people scared and asks whether you would be scared. Many of the situations presented are the normal ones that children experience, such as going past a fierce dog, going upstairs alone when it's dark, being stuck in the top of a tree or being yelled at by an adult. Others are humorously whimsical, such as wrestling with a crocodile.

How Scary! Who Scares Who From One to Ten
Two characters talk about the things that are scary using one to ten.

Activity

Would you be scared?

John Oakley's book *Would You Be Scared?* (see below) is a good starting point for this activity. If you can't find the book, use some of the situations described below in the synopsis and add a few more of your own. Ask: Which situations are real? Which are imaginary? Talk about things that are a bit scary for a lot of people (e.g. seeing snakes in the wild, climbing a tall ladder, having a spider in the same room, going on a roller coaster, going to the top of a very tall building, staying at camp, being dumped by a big wave, speaking at assembly, performing in public). The picture book *How Scary!* (see above) can also be used here.

- List the different events in the story and ask, 'Would you be scared?' Ask students to go to different sections of the room according to how scared they would feel in each situation (see the 'Four corners' strategy, **Handbook**, page 89, but use three corners):
  – not scared (blue corner)
  – a bit scared (yellow corner)
  – very scared (red corner).
- Make 'People graphs' followed by pictographs. Prepare three large sheets of paper by writing YES, NO, NOT SURE on them. Place these at the front of the room or in an area with more space. Use examples of scary things, ask 'Would you be scared?' and encourage the students to line up behind the statement that is true for them. With each line-up, count the number of students in each line.
- Students make a class version of *Would You Be Scared?* with pairs of students contributing both typical scenarios and silly ones. This could also be made as a digital story for the school library.
- Read *How Scary!* to the class and follow up with pairs making their own number books of scary things.

Poem

'(Almost) Nothing Scares Me!'

I wouldn't be afraid of a lion or a vampire

I would fight a dragon or a dinosaur for free

I wouldn't run away from an earthquake or volcano

But cockroaches absolutely terrify me!

(By Helen McGrath & Toni Noble in the style of Judith Viorst)

Read the poem to the class.
→ Follow up by asking students to illustrate the poem. They could then change the last line to relate to something that scares *them*. Older students can write their own four-line version, substituting and rhyming where appropriate.

Unit 3

Courage

Song

'Spider in the Bath'
Students will enjoy singing this song about this typical scary thing.

Activity

Flipbook
Students make a flipbook called 'What we think is scary!' (see **Handbook**, page 98).

Circle Time: What is courage?

Use the 'Lightning writing' strategy (see **Handbook**, page 91) to start the discussion or use one of the books listed below. Ask students what we mean by courage, highlighting through their responses that it is about facing fear rather than not having any. Stress that everyone gets frightened or scared of different things and that this is normal. Introduce the idea of everyday courage (see Key points, page 50). Talk about what makes it hard to be brave. Stress that everyone finds it hard to be brave. Students take turns to talk about a time when they were scared but still did the brave thing. Talk about the word 'avoiding' and what it means. Introduce the idea that avoiding a scary thing is often the worst thing you can do, especially if it is something you have to do at school or is about getting on with other people. Ask students to write what they know about people being brave.

Picture books

The following picture books focus on being brave when you need to do or try something new or difficult.

Jack Learns to Swim
Jack, a young platypus, wants to venture out into the river with his mother and sister, but he is scared of the water. His ongoing response to offers of help is that he's fine even though he isn't fine at all. When he finally gets the courage to try to swim he is swept away by the current. A turtle rescues him and explains that having courage is a good thing but that he also needs support to learn how to swim properly if he is to stay safe. He lets his older sister Alice shows him how to swim and safely navigate the swirling waters. Discuss why children sometimes pretend 'it's fine' when they really need help.

Lucy Goosey
Lucy, a little goose, is too scared to fly south with the flock and continually worries about 'what if…' (she gets lost, tired, etc.). She refuses to join them and they leave her behind. But her mother comes back and helps her to find the courage to undertake the journey.

Jump Baby
Mother possum, big sister possum and baby possum are eating their 'breakfast' (at night!) at the top of a very high walnut tree. Mother and big sister move around confidently but baby is scared and he wants to stay close to his mother. When mother and big sister jump to the peach tree, baby is left behind. They entreat him to try to jump but he freezes. He finally finds the courage to have a go.

Brave Little Penguin
Little Penguin and Papa Penguin live together in the Antarctic. Papa Penguin sets out to fish for their food, telling Little Penguin he will be back before dark. Little Penguin feels

worried and sad but then decides to be brave by finding things to think about and enjoy in his imagination and take his mind off his worries.
→ Follow-up activities could include inquiry-based learning about penguins.

Puffling
Little Puffling feels safe living in the family burrow with his parents but he knows that one day he will have to begin life on his own. His parents gently prepare him for the time when he will need to be strong enough and brave enough to waddle off to the sea and become independent.

Activities

Sound story: 'My trip by myself'
Create a sound story about fear and courage, i.e. a story told entirely in sound effects. The sound effects are performed by different groups or the whole class. Use a story about being a bit scared to go on a plane as an unaccompanied minor to visit a relative in a different state. Link this with 'Transport'. Ask if anyone has gone on such a trip and to talk about their experiences. At first, rehearse the story with sounds and actions, and then perform it entirely in sounds with teacher prompts. Brainstorm ideas for sound effects. Some suggestions are:
- waking up (rooster crowing plus alarm bell then yawning)
- feeling relaxed (ordinary slow heartbeats—perhaps on a drum)
- remembering that today is the day you will be going on a plane by yourself; you are both excited and scared (rapid heartbeats interspersed with excitement noises)
- having breakfast (toaster pops, milk pours, cereal crunching, orange juice gurgles)
- having a shower (and perhaps going to the toilet—just the flush sound!)
- brushing teeth and gargling
- packing
- travelling in the car to the airport (keys jangling, car door slamming, car travelling noises and then car stopping sounds)
- airport sounds (laughter, chatter, announcements)
- kissing goodbye
- taking a deep breath and then walking onto the plane
- plane taking off (increased heartbeat)
- having fun on the plane (eating chips, drinking, drawing, chatting to the flight attendant)
- sounds of the plane stopping
- greetings from relative ('ahhh' sounds and more kissing)
- feeling pleased with how brave you were (clapping).

→ Students can follow up the sound story by drawing or writing it or acting it out with more than just sound effects. They can focus on words that express their fearful feelings and the self-talk they can use to overcome the fear and act bravely.

Flipbook
Each student makes a flipbook (see **Handbook**, page 98) using the sentences: 'I was brave when I....' 'I was scared when ....' Some situations students could use include:
- trying to do something hard by yourself
- having a go at something new
- getting up and going on again after falling over
- speaking up in class or performing in front of an audience
- doing something you haven't done before
- having a go at something you aren't sure you can do or couldn't do last time
- standing up for yourself and your rights

Unit 3

Courage

- standing up for others who are being mistreated
- admitting when you are wrong, when you have made a mistake or when you did something naughty
- telling a teacher or parent when you have a problem you need help with
- saying 'No, I don't want to' when asked to be mean to someone else
- going to the doctor, hospital or dentist.

Circle Time: **Helping yourself to feel brave**

Use the 'Smiley ball' strategy (see **Handbook**, page 92) to ask the following questions. You could also use the 'Animal asks' e-tool (see **Handbook**, page 89) here instead of the smiley ball.
- When have you had to be brave at home?
- When have you had to be brave at school?
- When have you had to be brave at the doctor's?
- When have you had to be brave at the dentist's?
- How can you be brave if you have hurt yourself? It's OK to cry but if you are brave, you try to stop crying as soon as possible.
- What things can you do to make yourself feel more brave?
- What things can you say to make yourself feel more brave?

Discuss how you can help yourself feel braver when you feel scared. For example:
- Think about the good things that will happen if you can do this bravely.
- Remind yourself of the times when you have been brave before.
- Stay calm and say to yourself, 'This is not so bad'.
- Remind yourself that people never or hardly ever get hurt doing this.
- Talk 'tough talk' to yourself, e.g. 'Just do it!' or 'I can do this. It will be OK'.
- Go slowly and take it one step at a time.
- Don't exaggerate the danger to yourself.
- Ask someone else to tell you whether it is really dangerous or not. Get a reality check.
- Think of something funny or happy to take your mind off it.
- Take something with you that makes you feel braver, such as a toy, a favourite thing or a photo.

Stress that there *is* possible danger in many situations. Do not allow 'false bravado' on the part of some students to take over so that others feel that it is not acceptable to talk about being scared. Encourage students to offer other suggestions for 'tough talk'.

Activity

Class book
Make a class book (see **Handbook**, page 97) with each student contributing a page on one of the following:
- The most scared I have ever felt was…
- The bravest I have ever been was…
- I would be brave if… would you?

Circle Time: Being brave to help someone else

Read *Brave Bear* (see below) to the class. Ask: What did the little bear do? What was the challenge for the little bear? What kind of character was the little bear? What would you do if you saw someone fall over in the playground? Brainstorm words to describe the little bear. (kind, gentle, courageous) Ask:

- How did the bear feel looking up at the tall tree? Have there been times when you felt like this?
- Why has the illustrator drawn the perspective from the top of the tree looking down?
- Who is someone you could ask for help?
- What is a hero? (someone who feels scared but acts bravely to help someone else)
- Can you name a hero you have heard about? Was the brave bear a hero? What gave him the strength to be brave? (kindness and care for another)

Stress that very few people ever have to be heroes. Also stress that if you don't have the skills to save someone, you could be putting yourself and them in worse danger. Often the best way to be a hero when you are young is to warn someone that there is danger or tell a grown-up who can help.

→ Follow up with any of these:
- Read *Willy the Wimp* (see Unit 8: No bullying, page 174). Was Willy a hero? What helped him to be brave and help someone else? (love for Milly and learning some skills so he would feel more competent)
- Students can work together as a class to make a tree from a branch and, using a teddy bear, a little bird and a nest, take turns to retell *Brave Bear*. They can tell or write the story from the bird's point of view as well.
- Cut out leaf shapes on which each student can draw or write one thing that they need courage for. On the other side of the leaf they can write the names of 'people who can help me to be brave'. The leaves can be attached to the 'brave bear' tree.
- Give each student a big sheet of art paper. On one side of the paper, they draw: 'What is scary for Brave Bear to do but he still does it anyway?' On the other side, they draw: 'What is one thing that is scary for me to do but I still have a go?' This can be made into a class book on courage or a class digital story (see **Handbook**, page 97).
- Students can make the text into a song, using instruments that relate to the bear's feelings. Record the song and make a listening post so students can read along and listen to the book.

Picture books

Brave Bear

This story has a simple message about finding the courage to be kind. The story is about a young bear who encounters a baby bird that has fallen out of its nest. The baby bird asks the bear to help him by returning him to his nest. Bear agrees to help him and returns the bird to the nest high up in the tree even though the bear is scared of its height and is not sure that he can do it.

→ Ask students what kind of 'tough talk' he might have used to help him be brave so that he could help someone else.

The Timid Little Tiger

A little tiger cub finds it hard to be brave until one day his mother gets ill and he has to run in the dark to get the doctor to save her life.

Unit 3

Courage

Brave Lion Scared Lion
Jake believes that he is the brave lion cub in the family and often shows off by doing daring activities. In contrast, his twin brother Jasper is seen as timid and scared. Both have been told by their mother to stay away from the river because of the crocodiles. But Jake wants to show how tough he is so he foolishly goes down to the river, only to get himself in serious trouble with the crocodiles. He freezes in fear and it is Jasper who rescues him in a moment of courage.

Dimity Dumpty: The Story of Humpty's Little Sister
Although Humpty Dumpty's little sister is too shy to be part of her family's circus act, she finds courage when her brother needs her help after an accident. The details of the Dumpty family and their life in the circus are delightful and there is a new twist on why Humpty was on the wall from which he falls.

Annie to the Rescue
Annie always tries to be brave, even when getting her hair washed or when she falls over. When Callisto the cat gets stuck up a tree, Annie climbs up to save him. But then Callisto gets down by himself and Annie becomes stuck. She finds the courage to slowly climb down again (although it's partly to avoid looking scared in front of her younger brother).

Clancy the Courageous Cow
Clancy is part of a herd of Belted Galloway cows but, unlike the others, he is totally black. The other cows treat him like an outcast. He tries different ways to give himself a white patch, but nothing works. However, being totally black means that he can sneak unnoticed into the rich pastures of the fat Herefords next door. He gets stronger and fatter, until he's big enough to win the Cow Wrestling Contest and win grazing rights for all the members of his herd.

Fox and Fine Feathers
This could be seen as a contemporary Australian fable. The forest is a dangerous place for ground birds such as lyrebirds, coucals, pittas and nightjars as they are easy prey for predators such as foxes. The birds with brighter feathers are more at risk. In this story, four different kinds of ground birds play together on the forest floor and don't immediately notice a fox sneaking up on them. He is focused on the three more colourful birds, who have become quite absorbed in their colourful dancing, but he doesn't see the greyish-brown nightjar who is standing back a little because he lacks the colour to join in. Realising that the fox hasn't seen him, the nightjar act as a decoy and draws the fox away from his friends. Students will enjoy trying to find the pictures of the camouflaged nightjar.
→ Follow up with inquiry-based learning on camouflage, foxes or these Australian birds.

Circle Time: The courage to be yourself

You could use the 'Animal asks' e-tool here (see **Handbook**, page 89). Read *Ella the Elegant Elephant* (see below). Make links to the 'It's OK to be different' value in Unit 1: Core values (page 19). Ask students in turn one of these questions:
- What do we mean by saying 'be yourself'? (having your own ideas and preferences and sticking to them even if they are different to other people's)
- Should you listen to what others say you should do? (not if they are telling you to do something different to what you like to do or think is right; listen to others if they are giving you good advice about getting along with people or doing well in your schoolwork)
- Why was the hat so important to Ella?
- Why was Ella brave? (She didn't give in and dress how others said she should.)
- Has anyone made fun of you before? How did you feel? How did you respond to being made fun of? Were you able to still be yourself?

- Why is it hard sometimes to be brave enough to keep being yourself?
- How does Ella feel about making new friends?
- How does Ella help herself feel better?

→ Follow up:
- Read *Broken Bird* (see below).
- Students could design and make their own 'unique' hats and have a hat parade.

Picture books

Ella the Elegant Elephant

Ella, the shyest and littlest elephant in the village, is very nervous about starting school and making new friends. When she receives a beautiful red hat that belonged to her grandmother, it becomes her lucky charm. Although she gets teased about her hat and called 'Ella the Elegant Elephant', she has the courage to keep wearing it. When Belinda, the classmate who has mocked her the most, slips on the safety wall that surrounds the schoolyard, Ella tries to rescue her and fortunately, her lucky hat acts as a parachute, and saves them both from a very nasty fall.

Broken Bird

Broken Bird is born with only one wing and life is difficult. His brothers tease him, steal all the best worms and sneeringly tell him he will never fly. One day he decides to explore the world from the ground and he sets off courageously on his adventures.

Circle Time: Being foolish

Read or show the book *Look What I Can Do!* (see over). Ask: Have you ever seen anyone doing something foolish that could hurt them? Define 'foolish' as being brave but in a stupid way because:
- you are doing it just because you want to impress someone else
- it is not worth it in terms of the possible negative outcomes and what you get from it, i.e. not very much that is worthwhile
- you haven't learned the skills to do it
- you could get seriously hurt.

Stress that people who do risky things such as sky diving have usually learnt how to do it well. Although there is still some risk, they enjoy it so much and have such skills that they don't think it is foolish.

Ask: Why do you think some people do foolish things, such as diving into shallow water or riding their bike in a dangerous way? (to show off to their friends; to make people think they are brave; because they don't realise how dangerous it really is; because others put pressure on them to do it so they will be part of the group) Stress that you have to think very carefully before you decide to do something that might be very foolish. Also stress the idea of not being a 'sheep' (see Unit 8: No bullying, page 170). Think for yourself; don't just follow what others are doing. Remind students that 'When in doubt, don't!', but stress that this saying is only relevant to dangerous things, not everyday small things that need to be done.

→ Follow up with:
- students working with a partner to draw a picture of someone doing something foolish with a warning message
- students making a poster about being foolish that stresses all the dangerous foolish things that people shouldn't do

Unit 3

Courage

◎ reading *Brave Brave Mouse* (see below) to show a character who decides against acting with foolish courage because he hasn't got the right skills and experience to be able to tackle a certain challenge yet. Students could make a list of the things that require some bravery that they should not be doing now but may be able to do later when they have grown more and leant more.

Picture books

Look What I Can Do!
This classic book has very little text but interesting pictures. Two foolish animals compete with each other to show off by doing sillier and more dangerous things until ultimately they end up nearly drowning.

Brave Brave Mouse
Little Mouse is anxious about many things, but with the support of his loving family and a little inner voice (that speaks in rhyme) he learns to be brave when faced with challenges such as a babysitter, the swimming pool, new kinds of food, going to the dentist or scary shadows in the night. When his playmates at the park dare him to foolishly go on the big play equipment, he decides he can still choose to say 'no' to some challenges because they are too dangerous for him at the time.

Activities

What kind of courage is this? 
◎ Students work in pairs to each cut out the pictures on copies of **BLM 3.2: What Kind of Courage Is This?** and, with two copies of each picture, play Memory, Snap or Fish.
◎ Cut out the pictures on the BLMs and sort them into 'being brave', 'being brave to help someone else' and 'being foolish'. The pictures could also be used with role-plays: place the pictures in a lucky-dip bag and ask pairs of students to plan and act out the picture they select; other students try to guess what is being acted and say whether it is 'courage', 'bravery to help someone else' or 'foolishness'. Students can colour the 'everyday bravery' ones in green ('go for it'), the 'being foolish' ones in red ('stop!') and 'being brave to help someone else' in orange ('think first!') and then make a class mobile.
◎ Use the 'Memory cards' e-game (see **Handbook**, page 91) with the whole class or with students playing in pairs.

Make a badge of courage
For each pair of students you will need:
◎ cardboard
◎ sticky tape, glue, scissors, hole puncher and felt pens to share
◎ coloured wool
◎ foil

In pairs, the class makes a number of badges of courage using different materials and artwork. Use the templates on **BLM 3.3: Badge of Courage**. Photocopy the big shapes on card. Photocopy the small shapes on coloured paper. Write four jobs (see below) on cards and place in a lucky-dip container. Each student draws two cards and the cards tell them what jobs to do:

- 1st job:
  - choose a shape for your badge
  - cut out the big badge
  - cut out the small badge of the same shape
- 2nd job:
  - cover the big shape with foil
- 3rd job:
  - write 'showed courage' at bottom of small badge
  - leave space for a name at top of small badge
  - decorate small badge
- 4th job:
  - glue the small badge to the big badge
  - use a hole puncher to put a hole at top of the big badge
  - thread wool through the hole to hang the badge around the neck

When a student is nominated for an act of courage by a classmate or a teacher, they receive one of the badges with their name on it and a copy of **BLM 3.4: Certificate of Courage**. The certificate can provide a brief summary of what they did. For example, 'Callum acted with courage when he went in the spelling contest because he was nervous and he wasn't sure he would be able to spell all the words'. Remember to focus on acts of everyday courage.

Circle Time: When I first came to school

This teaches the key point that everyone has fears and feels nervous sometimes. To start, read the poem below. The topic of starting school is also dealt with in Unit 2: People bouncing back (page 37) and some of the books listed there could be used here.

Ask: What did you feel nervous about when you first came to school? Students take turns to talk about one thing they were nervous about. How was school different to preschool?

Poem

'Going to school'

If I DO go to school:

Will they let me go to the toilet if I really need to go?

What if we have a spelling test with words that I don't know?

Will my teacher remember my name and think that I'm OK?

Or will she just forget me until the end of the day?

And what if I lose my lunch or it gets squashed in my bag?

And if I spill the paint pot, where will I go for a rag?

What if the rest of my class knows exactly what to do?

While I can't even work out how to tie my shoe?

Will the other kids let me play in their games? Will I be all alone?

And if I'm missing my mummy, will they let me use the phone?

And if they let me use it, will I remember what number to call?

And will the principal make me sit right outside in the hall?

Unit 3

Courage

What if the book I'm reading is too hard for a kid like me?

Will they make me go back to preschool and play beneath a tree?

Will I get into lots of trouble? Will I know where I have to go?

Will my sister remember to take me home? Will big kids stand on my toe?

I was really getting excited about finally going to school

But maybe my mum should go instead. At least she knows the rules!

Helen McGrath & Toni Noble, in the style of Judith Viorst

Activities

- Students make a labelled class mural, with each student drawing the biggest worry they had about their first day of school.
- Students write a personal story called 'My worries about school'. Stress that many of our worries are groundless but understandable. Encourage the students to also write about what they did to feel braver.
- Make a class book entitled 'How we were brave when we first came to school'. Each student contributes a drawing about their biggest worry about school and a statement about how they managed to be brave.
- Prepare a worksheet on which students complete these sentences:
  - When I first came to school I was a bit scared about…
  - I was brave about it because I…
  - One thing I was worried about that didn't happen was….

  Then they write 'This is a picture of me being brave'.

Circle Time: Being scared of the dark

Read *There's a Nightmare in My Closet*. Ask anyone who has had a night-light of some kind in their house to put up their hand (count and make this into a class graph later on). Stress how many people have a night-light or leave a light on at night. Discuss why most people feel more frightened at night than in the daytime. Repeatedly mention that our night-time fears are usually our imagination or have a rational explanation, e.g. possums on the roof or trees moving.

→ Follow up with students drawing a night picture of their house or room and drawing and writing about all the things they do to feel braver at night. (have a night-light; sleep with the dog or a sister or brother in their room; cuddle a teddy; have a special rug; read a book before they go to sleep; get a hug; think of nice things)

Picture book

There's a Nightmare in My Closet

This classic book helps students to normalise their irrational fear of the dark. A young boy used to be afraid of the dark but then he decided to face his fear. The 'monster' that is in his closet comes out to sit at the foot of the boy's bed. He is very cute and cuddly with big friendly eyes and a non-threatening appearance. The boy threatens to shoot the monster with his toy gun and the monster starts to cry. So the boy tucks him into bed and closes the closet door because it seems that the monster is also afraid of the dark and pleased to be able to sleep with someone. The story ends with the creature and the boy asleep, as another cute and cuddly monster peeks out of the wardrobe door.

Circle Time: **Dangerous creatures**

Start by showing some pictures of dangerous creatures such as stinging jellyfish, snakes, scorpions and redback spiders. Discuss how some creatures are dangerous because they can seriously hurt you. It is useful to feel a bit scared when you see them, but not useful to overreact and exaggerate the danger. Students take turns to name one dangerous creature they have seen and say why it is dangerous. Be a bit careful here, as the more anxiety-prone students will panic if they think there is a dangerous creature at every turn or if there is a high likelihood of encountering one. Emphasise that we rarely see any of these scary things, hardly anyone gets hurt by them and there are antidotes/treatments for them. The aim is to be careful when we do encounter them.

→ Follow up with students making a class poster about dangerous creatures, why they are dangerous and how best to avoid them. Use drawings, pictures from nature magazines and other sorts of magazines, and internet pictures.

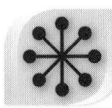

Circle Time: **Being brave about doctors**

A good introduction to this topic is a visit by a doctor or to a hospital. You could also ask students to bring in any x-rays, old plaster casts or photos of themselves in hospital or in plaster, and ask others to guess what happened. One aspect of being brave is enduring pain and discomfort without too many tears. Talk about being brave when you have been hurt, are sick, or have to undergo preventive medical treatment. Students take turns to talk about a time when they have been hurt and how they handled feeling scared and upset about their pain and discomfort. Mention stitches, injections, broken bones, hospitalisation, taking unpleasant medicine, cuts or grazes that bleed and hurt, and bruises. Ask selected students how they dealt with their fear and tried to be brave. Stress that pain always gets worse if you give in to fear. Stress these two rules:

- It is OK to feel upset when you are first hurt but not OK to make too big a deal about it. Don't keep crying. Be brave and use 'tough talk' to yourself, e.g. 'I will be OK'; 'I'll feel better very soon'; 'This is uncomfortable and I don't like it but it will make me better'.
- If something unpleasant has to happen to keep you healthy, then you shouldn't cry. Instead you should use brave 'tough talk' and remind yourself that it is what you have to do to stay healthy and well and look after yourself, e.g. 'I can do this'; 'This will keep me healthy and well'; 'It won't last very long'; 'I can think of something good to take my mind off this'.

→ Follow up with any of these:
- Students can draw about a time when they experienced some pain or discomfort. Stress that this is normal and everyone experiences it.
- Link this activity with an understanding of people who help us keep safe and healthy, such as doctors, dentists, nurses, ambulance workers (paramedics), family, teachers and after-school carers.
- Students can make a collage from magazine pictures showing the many ways people help us when we are hurt or sick.

Circle Time: How does the dentist help us to be brave?

Talk about dentists and ask students if they have been to the dentist and what happened there. Only ask every second student, as this topic can get a bit repetitive. Ask about the work that dentists do and how they help us. Why do we sometimes need to be brave at the dentist? Students can then brainstorm some ways the dentist helps us to be brave. (the dentist: is friendly and says hello; uses our name; has things in the surgery to help us be brave, such as a fish tank; has toys and books to play with in the waiting room; has pictures on the ceiling; has a DVD to watch; tells us what is going to happen so that we know what to expect) Ask the students to look for these things when they go to the dentist.

→ Follow up with:
- Students making posters with the message 'Dentists help us be healthy'. They can draw the dentist's surgery, showing ways the dentist helps them be brave.
- A class excursion to a local dentist or a visit from a dentist.

Circle Time: Learning from mistakes

Ask students to raise their hand if they have heard the old saying about learning to ride a bike: 'If you fall off, get up and get straight on again.' Make links with other kinds of 'falls' in life, e.g. when things go wrong at school, when you lose something, when you make a mistake.

Ask students to take turns to tell about a time when they were learning to do something and they had a fall or made a big mistake. (when they were learning to swim and went under the water; when they accidentally deleted a computer file; when they burnt themselves when they were cooking; when they fell off a bike)

→ Follow up with students drawing a two-frame picture sequence of someone falling off a bike and then getting back up, with a helpful thought balloon such as: 'I just have to get back on and try again. I can use tough talk.'

Circle Time: Everyone has fears, even grown-ups

Prior to the lesson, have students interview their family members about a time when they had to be brave. Send a note home, explaining that you have defined 'being brave' as doing something that is a bit scary or difficult. For example, a parent might talk about when they had to go for a job interview, give a presentation at work, go somewhere where they didn't know anyone, start a new job or ring a difficult client. What did they do to be brave? What 'tough talk' did they use to help overcome their fear?

In Circle Time, ask students to take turns to share what they found out. Stress that most of the events they have been told about by their family are things that are just a normal part of life. Ask what things were mentioned a lot by them about how to be brave, and make a list of them.

→ Make a follow-up class summary.

Activity

Reflections

Use the 'Reflections' e-tool (see **Handbook**, page 92) or the 'Animal asks' e-tool (see **Handbook**, page 89) with questions such as these:
- Have you ever hurt yourself? How were you brave?
- Tell about a time when something new was scary. What helped you to be brave?
- What is something you used to find scary but now you don't?
- Have you ever seen an animal being brave? What did the animal do?
- Have you ever had to have an injection? How did you manage to be brave?
- Have you seen anyone do something dangerous and foolish just to show off?
- What could help someone be brave if they had to give a talk?
- Have you ever stayed at someone else's house overnight? How were you brave?

You could use six of the courage pictures on **BLM 3.2: What Kind of Courage Is This?** instead of the questions. Ask about each picture: 'Do you think this would be scary? Why?'

Drama

Using everyday courage

Drama or puppets can be used to act out situations where everyday courage is used to overcome fear. Use the 'Freeze frame' and 'Good fairy/bad fairy' strategies (see **Handbook**, pages 80 and 90). The good fairy whispers messages of bravery and 'tough talk', and the bad fairy encourages the puppet to avoid the situation or exaggerate their fear. Here are some situations to use:
- You see older students saying mean things to someone in your class. You want to ask them to stop but you are scared they will say mean things to you too.
- You are a slow runner but you are expected to enter the races for your age at the school sports. You are scared of making a fool of yourself.
- You have to give a class talk on a hobby and you are scared that you will forget what you want to say.
- You want to join in a game that other kids are playing at lunch time but you are scared that they will tell you to go away.
- You have to go in a boat and you are scared of falling overboard because you can't swim.
- You want to ask someone to come and play at your house but you feel scared and shy about asking.

Picture book

The Wonderful Wizard of Oz

Watch or read the story of the Wizard of Oz. What helps to make the cowardly lion brave? The wizard is really a ventriloquist and believes in illusion or bluff. He gives the cowardly lion a green Bravery Potion to drink. Because the lion now thinks he is brave, he *is* brave. Ask: What do we learn from this story?
- Other people can help you feel brave if you talk to them.
- Saying brave words to yourself can also help you feel brave.
- Sometimes you have to 'fake it till you make it'!
- If you think you can be brave, then you can!
→ Follow up with the class singing 'If I Only Had the Nerve' from *The Wizard of Oz* film.

Unit 3

Courage

Song

'Whistle a Happy Tune'

There is a link to a video clip of Grover from *Sesame Street* singing this song on Pearson Places. In the interests of preventing predictable problems connected to the second line, you could change the first verse to:

Whenever I'm feeling scared

I hold my head up high

I tell myself I'm strong

Look fear right in the eye

I'm OK.

Musical story

Peter and the Wolf

Read the story of *Peter and the Wolf* and then play the music. There is also a narrated version available on CD. Ask the usual questions that are posed about the story and the music. Pose these additional questions:

- Peter was brave when he tried to save the duck and catch the wolf. Was he a hero? He had people to help him be brave. Who were they? How did they help him to feel brave when he was scared?
- How was the music used to express being scared?
- How was the music used to express being brave?
  Students can use music and sound effects to express fear and courage.

Activities

Make a lion mask

For each student you will need:
- a white paper plate
- old magazines and paste to share
- brown tissue paper
- hat elastic and a stapler.

Cut out eyes and nose from the centre of the plate. Students find yellow- and orange-coloured pictures in the magazines and tear up small squares of paper to paste on their mask. They use strips of brown tissue paper for the mane and make the mouth and whiskers out of the tissue paper (see right).

My courage

Involve parents with this activity. Students keep a journal in which they write down times when they are brave. They also keep a section where they fill in the following many times: My (mum/dad/sister/brother/grandfather/grandmother/aunt) said I was brave when I…

Reworked fairytales

Read any fairytale where there is danger to the characters (e.g. 'Red Riding Hood', 'Hansel and Gretel', 'The Three Little Pigs'). Then read it a second time and ask students to put up their hand whenever a character has to be brave or where there is something they could have done to keep themselves safe (even though they didn't do it in the story).

Bravery helpers

Talk about the people and things that help us feel brave when we are scared. Ask:
- Is it easier to be brave with others to help you? Why?
- How do our favourite pets or toys or teddy bears help us to feel braver?

Find some photographs of meerkats in an animal book or on the Internet to show the students. Read out the story on **BLM 3.5: Meerkats Are Braver Together Than Alone**, with students reading along with you if they can. Then they complete the BLM.

Are zookeepers brave?

Discuss the different animals that zookeepers feed and point out that many zoo animals can be very dangerous. Zookeepers have rules, training, helpers and equipment so that they find it easier to be brave. Make a list on the board. Discuss the following safety rules that many zookeepers follow so they can work safely with dangerous animals. Make links with safety rules about managing pets.
- Keep dangerous animals separated from you when you put down food.
- Sedate animals before you transport them.
- Do not put your hand too close to the animal's mouth.
- Do not try to take food away from the animals when they are eating.
- Work in pairs.

Students can draw a zookeeper feeding a dangerous animal.

Firefighters and lifeguards

Talk about firefighters and lifeguards. They find it easier to be brave because they have rules, helpers, training, experience and helpful equipment. They are brave because they overcome fear and do not let it beat them, not because they don't have any fear. Students complete **BLM 3.6: How Is the Lifeguard Feeling?** and **BLM 3.7: How Is the Firefighter Feeling?**

Challenges

Set up some challenges for students. First, discuss how some people will find some of the activities a little bit scary but others won't. Stress that this doesn't mean that one person is braver than the other. It just means that some things scare some people but other things do not. You might be OK with these things but you might get scared if you have to give a talk or when you meet someone new. Then practise as a group the kind of 'tough talk' that will make them feel braver. Set challenges such as:
- walking along balance beams
- doing a handstand
- giving a class talk
- getting to know someone they don't know very well
- spending half a day in another grade
- wearing socks that don't match.

Emergencies

Students can discuss, write about and act out typical emergencies and how to deal with them, for example:
- robbery
- house fire
- being lost in a shop.

Unit 3

Courage

Stress that these are rare events and that being brave mostly means getting help from adults. Then talk about how difficult it can be to stay calm enough to be brave in emergency situations. Fear often makes you feel stuck to the ground and unable to think well. Talk about how people make themselves calmer under these circumstances, for example:
- remind themselves that they have to be brave for someone else
- say, 'I am the only one who can help here'
- remember to call 000 to get help in an emergency ('Be a little hero, dial triple zero')
- say, 'It will be OK if I stay calm'.

→ Follow up with any of these:
- role-plays of different emergencies and the students dialling 000
- making brochures and posters about one of the emergencies.

Consolidation: Courage

Activity

Snakes and ladders
Students can colour in **BLM 3.8: Bravery Snakes and Ladders**, then play the game.

Games

Bingo strips
Use some of these words to play 'Bingo strips' (see **Handbook**, page 89).

afraid	dentist	scared
brave	doctor	skill
cry	fear	talk
dangerous	foolish	tough
difficult	nervous	worried

Other games
The following games reinforce the key concepts in this unit:
- 'Cross-offs' e-game (see **Handbook**, page 89). The secret message is 'Don't let fear beat you'.
- 'Secret word' e-game (see **Handbook**, page 92). The secret word is 'Brave'.

Resources

A complete list of resources (including references for books, poems, films, websites and web links for songs) is available on Pearson Places.

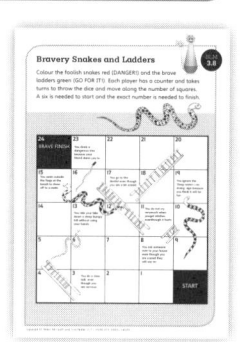

Unit 4

Looking on the bright side

Key points

It's good to look on the bright side of things.
This means being positive and expecting that things will work out well or get better. It also means that you think good things can happen so you try harder and don't give up easily.

It's good to be a positive tracker and look for the good things.
A positive tracker is someone who always tries to look for the good things in themselves, in others and in what happens in their life. Positive trackers have happier lives and happier feelings. They are more fun to be with and people like them more and want to be their friend.

Look for the small good bits in the bad things that happen.
Sometimes things happen that you don't like but you can usually find something good in the situation if you try. Sometimes the good thing is that it could have been worse. Sometimes the good thing is the lesson you learned. Sometimes a small good thing happened anyway even if the rest was not so good.

Bad times don't last. Things soon get better.
When a bad thing happens in your life, it isn't for ever. When you have bad feelings, they don't last very long. Bad things and bad feelings always go away again although it might take a bit of time for this to happen. They will go away faster if you talk about them to someone who cares about you.

It's important to stay hopeful when you have unhappy times.
You will get over unhappy times in your life more easily if you stay hopeful and look on the bright side. Believe that good things will happen and things will get better. If you stay hopeful you don't give up.

Be thankful and appreciative.
Being thankful for the nice things people do for you and the good things that happen in your life helps you feel happy. Letting people know that you are thankful or grateful for how they have supported and cared about you also makes them feel happy too.

Good memories of things help us to bounce back.
When you are feeling sad because you have lost someone or something you love, it helps to remember some of the good times you shared with them to help you feel a bit better.

Just because one unhappy thing has happened in your life doesn't mean that everything else is spoiled too. Lots of other things are still good.
When one thing in your life goes wrong and you feel unhappy or worried, try to remember all the things that are still good in your life. It is just one thing that is going wrong for a while, not everything.

Unit 4

Looking on the bright side

Circle Time: Looking on the bright side of things 72
Picture books 72
  Two Frogs in Trouble
  Tell Me Something Happy Before I Go to Sleep
  The Feel Good Book
Songs 72
  'What a Wonderful World'
  'On the Sunny Side of the Street'
  'Here Comes the Sun'
  'Oh What a Beautiful Morning!'
  'Keep Your Sunnyside Up'
  'Zip-a dee-doo-dah'
  'When You're Smiling'
Activities 73
  Smiley ball questions
  Our 'bright side' tree
  We love our class because …
  Positive portfolios
  Hearts and flowers (or maybe footballs)
  Good news board

Classroom organisation: On-the-spot positive tracking 74
Giving positive feedback

Circle Time: Positive tracking 74
Picture books 75
  Could Be Worse
  Platypus and the Lucky Day
  The Good Mood Hunt
  Cat
  All Pigs Are Beautiful
  Alexander and the Terrible, Horrible, No Good, Very Bad Day
  Edwardo the Horriblest Boy in the Whole Wide World
  That's Good! That's Bad: On Santa's Journey
  The Tricky Truck Track
Song 76
  'Let It Snow'
Activities 76
  Making a snow jar
  Think–ink–pair–share
  Round table
  Story characters
  Making rose-coloured glasses
  Family positives
Picture books 77
  Fish Is Fish
  Sam's Sunday Dad
  Alexander Who's Not (Do You Hear Me? I Mean It!) Going to Move!
Activities 78
  Things always get better: rain and better weather
  Rain rhythm sticks
  It's only one brick in the wall

Circle Time: Expressing gratitude and appreciation 79
Activity 80
  The Appreciation Station
Song 80
  'Our Thankful Song'

Circle Time: Bouncing back by thinking about positive memories 80
Picture books 81
  Badger's Parting Gifts
  Remember Me

Circle Time: Being optimistic 81
Picture books 81
  A Birthday for Bear
  Chester and Gil

Circle Time: Rainbows and sunflowers as symbols of hope 82
Song 82
  'I Can Sing a Rainbow'
Activities 82
  Rainbows
  Rainbow jelly
  Rainbow toast
  Rainbow dance streamers
  Rainbow bubbles
  Making rainbows
  Investigating floating rainbows
  Growing sunflowers
Picture books 84
  The Sunflower that Went Flop
  Circles of Hope
Maths activity 84
  The sunflower and me

Circle Time: Spring as a symbol of hope 84

Consolidation: Looking on the bright side 85
Activities 85
  Cut-up sentences
  Back patting
  Reflections
Games 85
  Bingo strips
  Other games

Resources 85

Circle Time: Looking on the bright side of things

Introduce the topic of being positive by reading *Two Frogs in Trouble* (see below). You could retell this fable without the book if necessary.

Ask: What do we mean by 'positive' and 'negative'? Make two word lists, one of positive words (e.g. good, terrific, happy, hopeful) and one of negative words (e.g. bad, wrong, sad, unhopeful). Highlight that being positive means looking for the good things in what happens, in yourself and in other people. It also means looking for at least one small good bit in every bad thing that happens. Being positive also means 'looking on the bright side' and believing that things will work out well or improve. Ask students to offer examples of when they have been positive.

→ Follow up with:
- students acting out the story
- singing 'Mr Frog' as a class
- making a class book (see **Handbook,** page 97) called 'Our bright side book', in the shape of the sun. Students can each write and illustrate one page about what being positive means.

Picture books

Two Frogs in Trouble
This is a Buddhist fable about staying hopeful and never giving up. Two frogs are leaping around one sunny day when they accidentally leap into a bucket of milk. They both madly swim around trying to get out, but with little success. Finally, the less optimistic of the frogs decides that all is lost and gives up and drowns. The other frog stays hopeful and eventually, by continuing to swim around in a frenzied fashion, he accidentally makes the milk turn into butter and this enables him to climb out. The moral of the story is 'Never lose hope and never give up'.

Tell Me Something Happy Before I Go to Sleep
Willa, a little bunny, is afraid to go to sleep because she is sure she will have nightmares. Her older brother, Willoughby, shows her how to think only about all the happy things that will be waiting for her when she wakes up again.
→ Follow up by asking each student to talk, draw or write about what happy and positive things they can think about just before they go to sleep so that they sleep well and wake up in a good mood. Encourage them to consider cute animals they have seen, holidays or visits they have enjoyed, fun times they have had at school or with a friend or a pet.

The Feel Good Book
With child-like smiling stick figures, bold colour and upbeat text, this book tells us the many different things that can make us feel good, e.g. saying 'I love you' in sign language; having a ladybird land on your hand; making a new friend; sharing your treats. The closing message is that it feels good to think about good things.
→ Follow up with pairs of students creating a poster about what makes them feel good.

Songs

Start each day with a positive song to put students in the right frame of mind and reinforce the concept of being positive. Here are some suggestions for songs, but the students will have many other ideas to contribute. Consider putting the song titles in a lucky-dip container and asking one student each day to draw out a song.

Unit 4

Looking on the bright side

'What a Wonderful World'
'On the Sunny Side of the Street'
'Here Comes the Sun'
'Oh What a Beautiful Morning!'

'Keep Your Sunnyside Up'
'Zip-a dee-doo-dah'
'When You're Smiling'

Activities

Smiley ball questions

Use the 'Smiley ball' strategy (see **Handbook**, page 92) to ask the following positive questions.
- Samantha, what is one good thing that has happened to you today?
- Con, what have you got to look forward to tonight?
- Jamal, what is one thing you have done well today?

Stress that the 'good things' can be quite small. After a while students will start the day ready to answer all those positive questions even if they don't get asked that day! They can also suggest other positive questions.

Our 'bright side' tree

Set up a tree branch in a pot of sand in the classroom. Each time someone in the class or another teacher reports hearing a positive comment or seeing a positive action from a class member, write it on a cut-out green cardboard leaf and attach each leaf to the tree.

We love our class because…

Brainstorm all the good things about the class and its members and then make a class poster. Ask: What do students in this class think is the very best thing about our class? Carry out a survey. Give the students a sheet of paper containing statements of the best things about the class that have been taken from the poster. Then the students colour in, cut out and 'post' their selection of the one 'best' thing into a voting container. Graph the results and have students write a conclusion.

Positive portfolios

Every student has a plastic folder (or an online portfolio) in which they keep their two best pieces of work from the past week. This can be done each Friday afternoon. It is important to make sure that the portfolio doesn't go 'stale'. Ask each student why those two selections were their best piece of work. Folders can be taken home and returned, or shown to the principal or other grades. Consider allowing students to include photos of their products and recorded performances.

Hearts and flowers (or maybe footballs)

For each student you will need:
- a small photo of themselves
- red cardboard
- scissors and rulers to share.

Select two students each week as the focus of this strategy. Students draw and cut out red hearts. Each student first makes one very large one, about 20 cm × 20 cm. Then they make as many smaller hearts as there are students in the class minus one (themselves). Their small ones should be about 10 cm × 10 cm and have a hole in the top for ribbon. If you have a large class, this may need to be done over a few sessions. Students write their name on the back of their large heart, and then store all of the small ones in one plastic bag with their name on it till their turn comes around. Each week, the two selected students stick a photo of themselves onto their large heart. They give their small shapes to the teacher. Over the rest of the week, ask each student in the class to tell you one good thing about each of the two students. Write these in the smaller shapes and place

73

them beneath the photo. You will need to do this individually with each student so that they work hard on finding one very specific good thing and so that you can help them get beyond 'He's nice' to a more specific comment. At the end of the week, read them all out and then the shapes can be strung onto string or ribbon to be taken home and hung up. You could also use football or flower shapes or let students choose their own shape.

Good news board

Keep a section of your wall/bulletin board just for good news (e.g. Bianca has a new baby brother!). Record good things that happen to the students as individuals and as a class. Add your own personal good news as well. Consider adding positive items from the media. If feasible, make class cards to respond to some of the good news (e.g. make a giant class 'welcome' card for Bianca's new brother). Each student can make a smaller lift-up flap with a personal message on the inside and their name on the outside and these are all glued inside the giant card (see **Handbook**, page 97). Their name is on the outside: 'Sam says.' Inside is their message: 'I am glad you have a new baby brother.'

Classroom organisation: On-the-spot positive tracking

Whenever possible, use situations that occur in the classroom or playground to keep the students practising positive tracking. For example, when no one remembers to feed the class budgie for a day, say: Well, it wasn't a good thing to happen. Let's see if we can use some positive tracking here. Any ideas? (At least there was some seed in his feeder left over from the day before.) **Have we learnt anything useful here?** (We've learnt that we have to come up with a better way of reminding ourselves to feed him.) Encourage students to do the same by asking about any negative event they encounter: Was there any good side to this that you can see?

Giving positive feedback

Talk about how we all like to hear about the good parts of the things we do and how that helps us to do things even better than we did before. Then, at every opportunity, invite students to offer other students positive feedback using these rules:
- Concentrate on the good things. Say, 'One thing she could have done to make it even better is …' rather than 'One thing she did wrong was …'
- Think of their feelings and say it kindly.
- Make a chart of 20 ways to say 'Well done'.

Circle Time: Positive tracking

Start by reviewing what 'positive' means. Reiterate that being positive can also mean finding a small positive side to a not-so-good situation. Read the book *Could be Worse* (see below). Have each student take a turn to draw a card from a box and briefly complete the positive (or positive reframing) sentence written on the card. For example:
- It's great for me when …
- I am good at …
- I am looking forward to …
- I am getting better at …
- I am happy when …
- My favourite place/book/lesson/family holiday/movie/song/toy/TV show/game is …

Unit 4

Looking on the bright side

- I feel important when…
- I like it when…
- My favourite lesson is…
- My favourite sport is…
- The best thing about the weekend/my house/class/family/pet/grandparent is …

Alternatively, you could use these (and similar) questions with the 'Animal asks' e-tool (see **Handbook**, page 89).

Picture books

Could Be Worse
This is the classic story of a boy whose grandfather always replies that it could have been worse, whenever his grandchildren tell them their tales of woe. Then Grandpa tells them about an amazing dream he has had in which the most outrageous things happened to him and the children respond that it could have been worse! Ask students to suggest ideas for situations when something has gone wrong. (e.g. missing a plane; tripping over; losing their bag; having a flat tyre on their bike; being dumped by a wave; getting lost in a shopping centre)
→ Follow up: Take one of the ideas suggested by the students and draw and write about it on the top half of an A4 page. On the bottom half of the page they glue on a cardboard lift-up flap (see **Handbook**, page 97). On the front of the flap they write 'But it could have been worse!' Underneath the flap they draw/write how it could have been worse. You could also do this activity with an animal character and his/her adventures, e.g. a rabbit, a mouse, a cat or a koala.

Platypus and the Lucky Day
A platypus demonstrates good optimistic thinking as he plays with his kite and his billy cart and uses positive tracking to cope with a 'not-so-good' day that finally turns out well.

The Good Mood Hunt
Hannah wakes up in an infectious happy mood but then remembers something that makes her good mood disappear. She sets out on a good mood hunt to restore her good mood and focuses on the positives around her.

Cat
The author uses very few words and the illustrations encourage students to put the words together to tell the story of a cat's busy and eventful day, where things may go wrong but the outcome is always positive.

All Pigs Are Beautiful
The author loves pigs, whether they are big, small, ginger, black and white or spotty. He encourages the reader to become excited about the positive features of pigs. He highlights their positive traits and points out that they are very like us, they make really good mothers and he explains why they are so fond of mud. The book comes with a CD.
→ Follow up: students take another animal that is not usually thought of as beautiful and identify all the positive things about it, e.g. a camel, a crocodile, a hippopotamus, a fly or a skunk. You could also make links with the book *The Ugliest Dog in the World* (see Unit 2: People bouncing back, page 47).

Alexander and the Terrible, Horrible, No Good, Very Bad Day
Read this book to the students (even if you have already read it as part of Unit 2: People bouncing back). Ask students to categorise all the bad things that happened to Alexander (e.g. he gets gum in his hair, he gets squashed in the car, he's the only one with a cavity in his tooth). Then go through every incident and ask them to think of how Alexander would have acted in each case if he had been a positive tracker, i.e. looked for the good bit in something bad that happened. For example, when he didn't get a toy in his cereal box,

he could have said, 'Maybe I'll get one next time'. When he messed up his father's office, he could have said, 'I'll remember to be more careful next time'.

Edwardo the Horriblest Boy in the Whole Wide World
Edwardo is a normal less-than-perfect boy but when the adults around him start to use 'negative tracking' and telling him how bad he is, he starts to live up to their expectations. When they change direction and use positive tracking by telling him how terrific he is, he starts to live up their positive expectations.

That's Good! That's Bad: On Santa's Journey
Santa sets off to deliver presents to a little boy on Christmas Eve and has a series of positive experiences but also some misadventures, including a snowstorm, an icy roof, a dusty chimney and a cat to trip over.

The Tricky Truck Track
This simple rhyming big book has six stories to reinforce the letter combination 'ck', including one in which the Truck character alternatively has good news and bad news as it goes about its job of transporting.

Song

'Let It Snow'
The class sings the song 'Let It Snow'.

This Christmas song emphasises how there are lots of good things to focus on, even when it is snowing and miserable outside. Link it with seasons, celebrations, change and the Earth's rotation (why Australia doesn't have snow at Christmas).

→ Follow up with a discussion about the 'up side' and 'down side' of each season, with an emphasis on finding the positives. For example:
- I don't like the burning sand on my feet when we go to the beach, but I really do like the cool feel of the water.
- I don't like very cold weather but I really love the open fires we have in winter.
- I don't like very hot days but I do like that we can go swimming (or have an air conditioner/very cool room).

Students can contribute to a large class poster with the 'Up side' and 'Down side' of each season, but make sure there are more positives than negatives. Students can decorate the poster with illustrations and magazine pictures. Consider making a class digital class book (see **Handbook**, page 97).

Activities

Make a snow jar
You will need:
- a clean and dry small jar with a wide mouth and tight fitting lid for each student
- waterproof glue or silicone sealant
- small toys, plastic flowers, seashells, plasticine, little toy people or animals (try to find things that stand up tall)
- water, glitter, glycerine, paper towels.

Ask each student to make a happy scene with their toys/people/animals to glue securely to the inside of the jar lid. Have different heights, e.g. they can make a plasticine hill with things glued on the top of the hill. Make sure the items are glued away from the edges of the lid so they don't get in the way when the lid is screwed back on.

Fill the jar about ¾ full of water, add glycerine to the water until nearly full, then add a heaped teaspoon of glitter. Squirt waterproof glue all around the inside of the rim of the jar lid, screw the lid on the jar tightly, use paper towel to wipe away excess glue, allow time for the glue to set and then shake it up.

This would be a great activity for each student to do with their older buddy.

Think–ink–pair–share
(See **Handbook**, page 92.) Students discuss the best things about school holidays and about coming back to school.

Round table
(See **Handbook**, page 92.)
- Write one thing that is good about our school/playground/neighbourhood.
- Write one thing that is good about our classroom/this country/state/suburb/town.
- Write one thing that is good about having a brother or sister or cousin.

Story characters
Whenever you read a story or poem to the class or show students a film, ask them to be on the lookout for any character who is using positive tracking. They can also do this as a homework exercise when watching TV or reading a book.

Making rose-coloured glasses
You will need:
- cardboard cylinders (halved) or paper plates
- red/pink cellophane
- sticky tape, glue or rubber bands or craft stick or hat elastic.

Students can cover one end of the cylinder half with the cellophane or join two together and make binoculars. Alternatively, they could use a pair of old sunglasses without lenses and add cellophane. Another alternative is to cut out two eyeholes in a paper plate and add a craft stick and cellophane to make opera glasses. You could also make a mask using a small paper plate with two eyeholes, cellophane and hat elastic.

Whenever you are talking about positive tracking or staying hopeful, a student who wants to identify a positive aspect can put on their rose-coloured glasses first. Alternatively, ask all students to use them when they are trying to think of a positive aspect in some situation, such as what is happening in a story.

Family positives
Point out that although we all love our family, they still have their faults because nobody is perfect. Students make an individual flipbook (see **Handbook**, page 98) using the core sentence, 'My family: The best thing about … is …' For example:
- The best thing about my sister is that she lends me toys.
- The best thing about my grandma is that she plays card games with me.

They include different family members on each page.

Picture books

Read stories to make the point that although things might be bad for a while, they always get better. The books below demonstrate that things always get better.

Fish Is Fish
A tadpole and a minnow are underwater friends until the tadpole grows legs and explores the world beyond the pond. When he returns to tell the fish what he has discovered, the fish is eager to explore. He discovers that he can't breathe outside his pond, but also realises that life in a small pond is pretty good.

Sam's Sunday Dad
In this story, Sam's parents are separated and he only sees his father on weekends. He has learned to save up what he wants to tell him during the week, ready for Sunday.

→ Discuss how Sam might have felt when his parents separated but stress how things are better now. Ask: What was still the same even though Sam's parents had separated? This book is also used in Unit 2: People bouncing back.

Alexander Who's Not (Do You Hear Me? I Mean It!) Going to Move!
Alexander's father has a new job in a new state and they have to move. Initially Alexander hates the idea and lets everyone in the family know how he feels, but he eventually finds some positives in the idea and gets used to it to the point where things not only get better but he starts to feel hopeful about the move.

→ Ask: What was still the same even after they moved? This book is also used in Unit 2: People bouncing back.

Follow up with students making their own simple story where things get better after an initial upset.

Activities

Things always get better: rain and better weather
- Students can investigate how rain occurs by using an eye dropper to slowly fill a suspended sea sponge (from the chemist), a piece of sponge rubber or dishwashing sponge. This is a simulated version of how clouds fill with water and then rain when there is too much water for the cloud to hold.
- Sing some rain songs such as 'Rain Rain Go Away' and 'It's Raining, It's Pouring'. Make rain rhythm sticks (see below) for students to shake when they are singing these songs.
- Discuss why some people prefer it not to rain. Then ask how rain is also a very positive thing. Discuss how farmers and people who have gardens might be hopefully looking for signs of rain when there is a drought. Ask:
  – Who would want to live somewhere where there was never any rain or a change in the weather?
  – What would that be like?
  – In what countries does that happen? (e.g. desert areas)
- Talk about how rain or bad weather may last for a while, sometimes it even floods, but the sun always shines again and good weather returns. Students can also keep records of the weather for a week or two to show that bad weather always clears up. Discuss how, for many people, rainy weather is a really good thing because it fills their empty dams or waters their crops and gardens.
- Ask students to talk about times when things began to look better for them and what the sign of things getting better was. (someone starts to be nice to them at a new school; their baby sister starts to feel better and eat more after being sick)

Rain rhythm sticks
You will need:
- cardboard tubes
- masking tape
- dried beans or rice or cereal
- felt pens
- stickers (optional).

Give each student a cardboard tube to decorate with markers and stickers. Close one end off with masking tape. Let the students partially fill the tube with dried beans or rice. Close the other end with masking tape. When students shake the tube, it will sound like raindrops.

Unit 4

Looking on the bright side

It's only one brick in the wall
This activity makes the point that just because one unhappy thing has happened in your life, it doesn't mean that everything else is spoiled too. The rest of your life goes on as before.

Students use matchboxes or other kinds of boxes (e.g. small tissue boxes) of the same size to make a class brick wall. They all contribute one or two bricks by covering them in paper they have painted to look like bricks. Ask the students to talk about all the parts of their lives. Make a list on the board and write each one on a brick so that when you make the brick wall, the students can see the labels. For example:
◎ Family: being with your mum, dad, brother, sister, grandparents, aunt, uncle
◎ House: bedroom, yard
◎ Holidays
◎ Pets
◎ Neighbourhood: friends, neighbours
◎ Leisure activities: sport, bike, TV, reading, playing on the computer
◎ School: friends, schoolwork, teacher
◎ Being well
◎ Enjoying your food.

Then students help to make a brick wall at the front of the class by standing the boxes on top of each other so they look like bricks, but make sure the labels are visible.

Say: Imagine that this brick wall is the life of a child just like you. Now, what if this child's grandma got very sick? Ask a child to come and take out the brick that says 'Grandma', making sure that no other bricks fall down at the same time. Say: This bit of the child's life would not be going as well as they would like. They would be feeling worried and unhappy about this part of their life. But is the rest of their life still OK? Did taking this brick away make all the other bricks crash to the ground?

Repeat the exercise with other people or activities that are written on the boxes (e.g. a friend moves, or your bike is stolen, the computer breaks down and you can't play your games).

Use **BLM 4.1: One Bad Thing Does Not Mean Everything Turns Bad**. Select a situation for students to use it with according to the needs of your class. Here are some ideas for situations that can be the focus of the activity:
◎ Someone's parents separate
◎ Brianna's best friend wants to be someone else's best friend
◎ Dylan's budgie dies
◎ Ricky hurts his leg and can't play any games for a while
◎ Harry is finding it very hard to do maths.

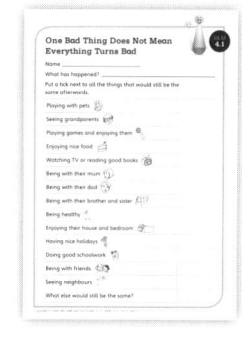

Circle Time: **Expressing gratitude and appreciation**

Expressing appreciation and gratitude towards others is another form of positive tracking. It has been shown in research studies to increase positive mood, self-acceptance, positive relationships and resilient behaviour. Read the book *Have You Filled a Bucket Today? A Guide to Daily Happiness for Kids* (see Unit 1: Core values, page 10) and stress that showing appreciation for the support, kindness, friendship, behaviour and love that we receive from others also helps us to fill our own 'happiness' buckets.

79

Activity

The Appreciation Station

(You could also call it the Thanks Bank or Gratitude Station.) Visit the classroom Appreciation Station each week and ask students to prepare and send emails, cards or letters to express their appreciation and gratitude for what others have done for them or for the love, friendship or support they have shown them. They can use one of the following formats.

- I'm glad you're my… because you/I…
  - I'm glad you're my friend because you have such good ideas for games.
  - I'm glad you're my cousin because I have such fun when I am with you.
- Thank you for being my friend. You/I…
  - Thank you for being my grandma. You are always so kind to me.

Whenever an opportunity arises, send a whole-class message of appreciation, e.g. to a parent helper, to the maintenance staff for repairing a broken chair in the classroom, to another teacher for the extra work they did helping the class prepare a display, to a local business for a donation.

Song

'Our Thankful Song'
(To the tune of 'Yankee Doodle Dandy')

We are thankful for our dad
He tells us lots of stories
He also tells some awful jokes
But Dad is never boring

Chorus

There are lots of special things
We can all be thankful for
Friends and family, food and fun
And many many more

We are thankful for our mum
She joins in with our games
She also makes us do some chores
We love her just the same
Chorus

We are thankful for the beach
In sunshine and in rain
The sand gets in our bathers but
We wash it out again
Chorus

We are thankful for our dog
He takes us for a walk
When he stops at every tree
We feel like such a dork
Chorus

Circle Time: Bouncing back by thinking about positive memories

Read one of the books listed below. Ask: How can thinking a lot about the good things we did with someone or the things they taught us help us to bounce back when we feel sad? Use the 'Think–ink–pair–share' strategy (see **Handbook**, page 92) to ask students this question and also to ask them what good things they have done with an older person or what they have learnt from them. Ask selected students to report when they return to the circle.

Unit 4

Looking on the bright side

→ Follow up with students drawing and writing a sentence (or using Kid Pix) about memories of good times with grandparents or older people they care about.

Picture books

Badger's Parting Gifts
Badger goes down the long tunnel to die and his friends deal with their grief at his loss by recalling the good times they had and the things that he taught them.

Remember Me
Although she may forget many things, Ellie's grandma remembers all the special times the two of them have shared.

Circle Time: Being optimistic

Read *A Birthday for Bear* (see below). Ask: What does 'optimistic' mean? (hopeful; you believe that something good could happen, especially if you have a go and try hard) Then ask students in turn to answer one of the following questions.
- What does it mean to say 'If you believe it is possible then you will try to do it'?
- How do we know that Mouse believed that he could convince Bear to have a party? (he wouldn't give up)
- Why did Mouse want to do that? (Bear was his friend)
- What finally made Bear change his mind?
- Has anyone ever done something special for you on your birthday?
- Have you ever done something special for someone on their birthday?
- Have you ever believed that something was possible so you kept trying to do it? Were you able to make it happen because you believed it was possible?

→ Follow up by reading *Chester and Gil*.

Picture books

A Birthday for Bear
Bear is a bit of a grump and does not like birthdays at all; he would rather spend his birthday alone cleaning his house than celebrate his own birthday. But his ever-cheerful friend Mouse believes that if he tries he can wear Bear down and convince him that a party would be fun. This is a humorous book between the two 'opposite' characters from the book *A Visitor for Bear* (see Unit 6: Relationships, page 130).
→ Follow up with students creating pictures of Bear's house or his party on Kid Pix.

Chester and Gil
Chester and Gil are two goldfish who live in the same bowl. While Gil is happy to do the same old thing every day, Chester embraces life. Chester is a 'glass half full' goldfish, while Gil is the opposite. As it happens, Chester does something special. By using his imagination, he saves an ocean liner full of passengers from crashing into an iceberg, all without leaving his bowl.

Circle Time: Rainbows and sunflowers as symbols of hope

Ask students in advance to use the 'Lightning writing' strategy (see **Handbook,** page 91) to write what they know about rainbows.

In the circle, ask selected students to say one thing they have written about rainbows. Then ask if anyone has seen a rainbow and where. Does anyone know what colours are always in a rainbow and the order they are in? (red, orange, yellow, green, blue, indigo, violet) Then talk about hope and what it is. Ask: Why do people think rainbows are good and make us feel hopeful? (They signal that the rain is probably over and the sun has come out again. They are also beautiful parts of nature that we don't see very often and therefore we are always pleased and surprised when they occur, just as we are when good things happen.)

Song

'I Can Sing a Rainbow'
Have the class sing this rainbow song before they make rainbows (see below).

Activities

Rainbows
The following activities are a mix of Maths, Science and Creative Arts.
- Students count and graph the colours in a box of Smarties that have been spread out as a rainbow.
- Groups of students make collages from materials that are all one colour. Each group uses a different colour of the rainbow.
- Dye macaroni all the colours of the rainbow. Students can string the macaroni to make rainbow necklaces.
- Take the students for a walk to the local park and see how many different things they can find of each colour of the rainbow.
- Using felt pens, students draw different coloured dots onto blotting paper, making sure that they use all the colours of the rainbow. Then they use an eye dropper to drop water onto the blotting paper and watch the colours spread.
- Make many-coloured ice cubes using food colouring. Fill a tall clear container with oil. Put the ice cubes in the water. What happens? Do the colours mix?

Rainbow jelly
This activity will take some time because each layer of colour needs to be set before the next layer can be added. The final effect looks great and it is a good task to teach students that some things take time to complete, and each step has to be done one at a time.
You will need:
- red, orange, yellow, green, blue and purple jelly crystals
- boiling water and jug
- clear plastic cups
- refrigerator.

Make the red jelly according to the instructions on the packet. Pour a small amount in the bottom of each cup (about one-sixth of the cup). When the red jelly has set (a few hours or overnight), repeat using the orange jelly. Then repeat with yellow, green, blue and purple jelly.

Looking on the bright side

Rainbow toast

You will need:
- milk
- food colouring
- cups
- new, clean paintbrushes
- bread
- toaster.

Pour several small cups of milk. Add different food colouring to each cup. Use paintbrushes to paint a rainbow on each piece of bread. Painting means that the bread doesn't get too soggy and the rainbow design can be done with some accuracy. Toast the bread.

Rainbow dance streamers

For each student, you will need:
- red, orange, yellow, green, blue and purple crepe paper streamers (about 1 to 1.5 metres long)
- half a paper plate
- scissors
- stapler.

Students staple the streamers to one side of the plate in the order of the colours of the rainbow.

Rainbow bubbles

You will need:
- detergent
- water
- a little glycerine or cooking oil to make bubbles stronger
- a variety of things to make the bubbles, such as shaped wire, pipe-cleaners, funnels and straws.

Make the bubble mix. Students can experiment with the different bubble makers to see what is best. Making the bubbles in the sun should produce rainbows.

Making rainbows

You will need:
- glass bowl of water
- small mirror
- sunlight.

On a sunny day, place a small mirror in a glass bowl of water so that the mirror rests against the side of the bowl. Set the bowl in direct sunlight to make a rainbow.

Investigating floating rainbows

You will need:
- food colouring
- a large glass jar filled almost to the top with water
- a thin layer of cooking oil floating on the top of the water (the thicker the layer, the longer it takes the colouring to reach the water).

Squeeze a few drops of colouring onto the oil. The bubbles of colouring will slowly ease through the oil, explode into tiny circles and float to the bottom of the jar. Gradually the colours will blend into each other. Food colouring is denser than oil, hence the colouring passes through the oil to mix with the water. Students can predict what will happen before the experiment.

Pairs of students can use Kid Pix, or a similar computer program that allows colour mixing, to make a rainbow.

Growing sunflowers

Sunflowers are another symbol of being positive and hopeful. You can buy some or, preferably, grow some with the class. They are relatively fast growing plants, growing up to three metres at the rate of 30 cm a week. Students will be intrigued to watch such a large flower grow from such a small seed. Sunflowers need a lot of fertiliser and sunlight to grow tall. Spread a few layers of compost on the soil and dig it in well before planting. Make sure they have space to grow.

- Plant the seeds about 30 cm apart at a depth of 5 cm and water thoroughly.
- When the seeds sprout in a week or two, pull out every second seedling so the remaining plants are 60 cm apart to allow room for growth. Water the seedlings often.
- The sunflowers will grow quickly. Students can make a growth chart by measuring the same plant every week and graphing its progress.
- After a flower forms, students can compare their height to that of the sunflower and then paint a life-size picture of the sunflower.

Picture books

The Sunflower that Went Flop

A husband and wife can't work out what to do with their sunflower that keeps going floppy until they realise it needs water.

Circles of Hope

Facile, a young boy in Haiti, wants to follow the local custom and plant a mango tree to celebrate the birth of his new baby sister who is ill in hospital. Each of his attempts fails as the soil washes away. He decides to plant his mango seed in a protective circle of stones and that works. After many months, his mother returns to their mountain village with a now healthy baby and Facile proudly shows her his tree. Other villagers adopt his idea of using protective stone circles to grow new trees.

Maths activity

The sunflower and me

Sunflowers belong to the same family of flowers as daisies. Compare the features of each flower to see the similarities and differences. Compare the sizes of the two flowers with the heights of some of the students. Ask each student to imagine they are a tiny person and all flowers are as tall as the sunflower. Then they can draw a picture in which they are tiny and all the plants and insects are huge, or tell a story on tape.

Circle Time: Spring as a symbol of hope

When spring has just begun, take the students for a walk to find as many signs as they can that spring is here. Back in the circle, ask each student to tell the person next to them one thing they saw. Ask why the season of spring gives people new hope and helps them to look on the bright side. (There is continuity in the fact that things keep growing and renewing, no matter what has happened. Baby animals and new growth suggest new, fresh possibilities.) Link this with seasons, change and life cycles. Conduct a quick class survey on which season makes the students feel most positive, graph the result and ask students to write a sentence about the conclusion.

Consolidation: Looking on the bright side

Activities

Cut-up sentences
(See **Handbook**, page 89) Cut these sentences into individual words and place each cut-up sentence into an envelope. Make enough sets for each pair of students to have one set of six envelopes. Each pair reconstructs the six sentences. You can also use the 'Cut-up sentences' e-activity.
- It is good to play with your friends.
- If you look on the bright side, you will be happier.
- Find the good things in everything you do.
- Look for the good things about everyone you meet.
- Stay hopeful when you are feeling worried.
- Believe you can and then try to do it.

Back patting
Make a 'back patter' by cutting a hand shape into a plastic fly swatter and encourage students to come out and use it when they think they have done something well, however small.

Reflections
Use these questions and statements with the 'Reflections' e-tool (see **Handbook**, page 92).
- What is one thing you are good at?
- What is one good thing about your mum or dad or someone in your family?
- Tell about a time when you hoped something would happen and it did.
- What is one good thing about cold weather?
- What is one good thing about the work we do at school?
- Tell about a time when good luck happened to you or someone you know.
- What is one good thing about our class?
- What is one good thing you have done today?
- What is one good thing you are looking forward to?

Games

Bingo strips
Use some of these words to play 'Bingo strips' (see **Handbook**, page 89).

best	glad	great	lucky	positive	thankful
better	good	happy	memory	rainbow	track
bright	grateful	hope			

Other games
The following games also reinforce the key concepts in this unit.
- 'Cross-offs' e-game (see **Handbook**, page 89). The secret message is 'Always look for the good things'.
- 'Secret word' e-game (see **Handbook**, page 92). The secret word is 'rainbow'.

Resources

A complete list of resources (including references for books, poems, films, websites and web inks for songs) is available on Pearson Places.

Unit 5

Emotions

Key points

Everyone has feelings. They are necessary in your life, even the unpleasant ones.
Feelings are useful, natural and necessary. Pleasant feelings (like feeling pleased, proud and excited) help you to understand the things that make you happy. Happy feelings also help you to cope better when you make a mistake or have a setback. Angry feelings act as alarms to tell you that you might need to protect yourself because you are being treated badly or unfairly. Feeling scared warns you about possible danger and helps you to do something (like tell someone) to make yourself safe. Feeling guilty tells you that you may have done something wrong.

You can change a bad mood into a good mood.
Everyone feels sad, disappointed, angry or worried sometimes. That's normal. But sometimes you can help yourself feel a little better if you do something or think about something that helps you to feel happier.

You can be the boss of your own feelings.
Trying to change your bad mood into a good mood is an example of being the boss of your own feelings. Trying to calm yourself down when you are angry is another example. If you let your unpleasant feelings control you, then they can hurt you and hurt others. If anger is the boss of you, it can cause people to not want to be friends with you. If fear (feeling scared or worried) is the boss of you, you can lose confidence, and not have a go at something. You need to be the boss of your feelings so your unpleasant feelings don't hurt you or make you hurt others.

Find a good and safe way to express your unpleasant feelings that does not hurt anyone.
To be the boss of your angry feelings, you need to be aware that you are feeling angry and then calm yourself down. Then you can speak up for yourself in a calm but strong way. 'No hitting, hurting or name-calling' is the rule. Tell the other person calmly why you feel angry with them. When you are feeling sad or disappointed, it's best if you talk to others about how you are feeling.

Being the boss of your feelings is not the same as trying not to have any feelings!
You need your feelings, even the unpleasant ones. Without pleasant feelings you would never feel happy. Without unpleasant feelings you wouldn't be able to protect yourself, stand up for yourself and what you think is right, or recognise danger.

If you give the right name to your feeling it is easier to be the boss of your feelings.
Sometimes you might make a mistake about the name of the feeling you are having. For example, you might think you are feeling angry when you are really feeling scared or sad. The feelings in your body can be similar. Sometimes you can make a mistake about how strong a feeling is, too. For example, you may think you are really, really angry when you are just cross. Giving the right name to your feelings helps you to better manage your feelings, or be the boss of your feelings.

Talking to yourself in a negative way and exaggerating how bad you are feeling can make you feel more upset.
You can make yourself feel more upset by what you say to yourself. Sometimes it is understandable that you feel angry or sad or have other feelings when things don't go well, but that event or person hasn't made you have that feeling. One of the best ways to be the boss of your feelings is to use more helpful 'self-talk' and thinking.

You need to ask 'did they really mean it?' when you feel hurt and angry.
Sometimes you get upset and angry over something that a person has done, but if they didn't mean to do it and it was an accident, you have to take that into account and understand.

To understand others, you need to work out how they are feeling.
Working out how somebody is feeling (or might feel) is called empathy. Empathy is important for making and keeping friends and for caring about other people.

Unit 5

Emotions

Classroom organisation 89
  'Sing and shout' time 89
    'If You're Happy and You Know It Clap Your Hands'
    'Celebration'

Circle Time: Feelings are necessary, even the unpleasant ones. 89
Picture books 90
  Why Do You Cry?
  What Makes Me Happy?
  I Have Feelings
  Smile-a-Saurus! A Book About Feelings
  Our Feelings from Happy to Sad
  All in a Day
  If You're Happy and You Know It: Jungle Edition
Drama. 91
  Acting with feelings
Activities 91
  Happy/sad feelings
  Circle class story
  Make a feelings board
Picture book 92
  My Many Coloured Days

Circle Time: You can change your bad mood into a good mood 93
Picture books 93
  The Good Mood Hunt
  I Love It When You Smile
  The Bad Mood
  When I'm Feeling Happy
  Feeling Sad
  Our Granny
  Red Sled
Activities 94
  Good mood hunt
  Class book
  Happy cube
Songs 94
  'Shake Your Sillies Out'
  'Put on a Happy Face'
Activity 95
  Pop goes the feeling
Song. 95
  'Pop Goes the Feeling'

Circle Time: Feelings happen inside our body too 95
Activity 96
  One worried wombat
Drama. 96
  Guess the feeling
Games 97
  Fish the feeling out
  Snap and Fish
Activities 97
  Feelings pictures, words and other things

Circle Time: We can have mixed feelings . . 98
Picture book 98
  Ever So Ever So
Drama. 98
  Feelings hats
Activities 98
  A picture dictionary of feelings
  Flipbook or class book
  Feelings dice: throw a feeling
  Round table

Circle Time: How angry do you feel? What do you do? 99
Picture books 100
  Would You Be Angry?
  When I'm Feeling Angry
  When I Feel Angry
  Andrew's Angry Words
Activities 100
  How angry do you feel?
  The hurtful power of angry words

Circle Time: Being the boss of your angry feelings. 101
Picture books 102
  Where the Wild Things Are
  Angry Albert
  Angry Arthur
  Dealing with Anger
  When Sophie Gets Angry—Really Really Angry
Song. 103
  'That Just Makes Things Worse'
Activities 103
  Tashi and Timba Tortoise
  Fridge magnets
Drama. 104
  We don't want to play with you
Song. 104
  'We Don't Want to Play with You'

Circle Time: What to do when someone is angry with you 104

Circle Time: Hands are not for hitting, feet are not for kicking, words are not for hurting. 105
Picture books 105
  Hands Are Not for Hitting
  Feet Are Not for Kicking
  Words Are Not for Hurting
Song. 106
  'Hands Are Not for Hitting'
Activities 106
Discussion 107
  What to do if people are hitting or hurting at home

Circle Time: Did they really mean it? 107

Circle Time: Everyone feels sad sometimes 107
Activity 108
   Good memories
Song. 108
   'My Favourite Things'
Picture books 108
   The Saddest King
   Bear's Last Journey
   Tough Boris
   Toby
   The Tenth Good Thing About Barney
   Old Pig
   Daddy, Will You Miss Me?
   Desser, the Best Ever Cat

Circle Time: Don't be a worry bee. 109
Picture books 109
   Waiting for Mum
   The Worry Monster
   Scaredy Squirrel
   Silly Billy
   Frog Is Frightened
   When I Feel Scared
   Franklin and the Thunderstorm
   Wemberly Worried
   Supposing
Activities 110
   Worry hoops
   I can be a worry bee sometimes

Circle Time: Do you feel jealous? 111
Picture books 111
   Dealing with Jealousy
   Byron and the Chairs
   Two Bad Teddies

Circle Time: How do other people feel? . . 112
Picture books 113
   Just a Little Brown Dog
   Two Tough Teddies
   It's Useful to Have a Duck
   The Truth About Horrie
Activities 114
   How do you know when someone is feeling…?
   Mime a feeling
   Feelings pictures
   Feelings slide show
   Teddy bear
   Animals and empathy
   Babies and empathy

Circle Time: What kind of surprise? 115
Picture books 115
   Boo!
   Snap! Went Chester
   Scary Bear
Activity 116
   Making happy surprises

Consolidation: Emotions. 116
Activities 116
   Cut-up sentences
   Reflections
Games 117
   Memory cards
   Bingo strips
   Other games

Resources. 117

Classroom organisation

'Sing and shout' time

Whenever there is an opportunity, take five minutes to have a 'Sing and shout' session, with students singing songs that could be described as happy, inspiring, celebratory, joyous or just plain loud and fun! A song session with actions is a wonderful way of increasing positive feelings and connecting classmates. Here are some ideas:

'If You're Happy and You Know It Clap Your Hands'.
Other verses can be added:
- If you're sad and you know it say boo-hoo (or tell a friend)
- If you're angry and you know it cross your arms (or take a walk)
- If you're worried and you know it make a frown (or tell a friend)
- If you're scared and you know it hug yourself (or stand up tall)
- If you're proud and you know it give a clap

'Celebration'
This is a wonderful song for everyone to express joy together. Make the point that we are energised and feel happy when we have fun and share together.

Some other songs are:
'Be Kind to Our Web-footed Friends'
'My Grandfather's Clock'
'Happy Days Are Here Again'
'Sing'
'The More We Get Together'
'Teddy Bears' Picnic'
'Ten Little Indian Boys'
'The Grand Old Duke of York'
'Lion Sleeps Tonight'
'We All Sing the Same Song'
'Happy Song'
'Everybody's Song'

Circle Time: Feelings are necessary, even the unpleasant ones

Prior to the lesson, have every student make a paper plate puppet where one side of the paper plate is a happy face and the other is a sad face (see **Handbook**, page 100).
Begin the lesson by reading the following questions (in an appropriate tone of voice) and asking students to show the happy or sad face on their puppet to show how they might feel if they were in each situation. How would you feel if:
- you got soaking wet on the way home from school?
- you were playing your favourite game?
- you were invited to a party?
- someone broke your favourite toy?
- someone pushed you over?
- you broke your favourite pencil case?
- your pet died?
- you got lost at the shopping centre?
- you won a prize for your drawing?
- a friend who had been away for a long time visited you?
- somebody said you were stupid?

Reiterate that most of the time, everyone has pleasant feelings but everyone also has unpleasant feelings sometimes. Ask: What are some other feelings words? Write them on the board. (angry, worried, scared, frightened, proud, excited) What are some other feelings words we could use to describe how we might be feeling for each of the situations above? Read the questions again and ask different students how else they might be feeling. (I felt proud when I won a prize.) Why do we have feelings? (Our feelings are like our antennae—they help us to understand what is happening to us, and what we need to do.)

- *Feeling happy* tells you about the things you love to do.
- *Feeling scared* tells you there might be danger and to find someone to help you (but you need to check your facts because you might be jumping to conclusions).
- *Feeling angry* tells you that you might be being treated badly or unfairly.

Read one of the books listed below. Ask: What feelings did the character(s) in the story have? What was happening inside their body? What did they do (or not do) because of that feeling?

→ Follow up: Use the 'Feelings' e-activity where the whole class sorts feelings into 'pleasant' and 'unpleasant'. Alternatively, you could make feelings cards (disappointed, happy, scared, loving, angry, worried, surprised, excited, jealous, sad, proud, embarrassed) and students can take turns to sort each one into hoops or boxes labelled 'Pleasant feelings' and 'Unpleasant feelings'. After the activity, students can write sentences that start with the following stems:

- I felt proud when I…
- I felt sad when…
- I felt happy when…
- I felt angry when…
- I felt scared when…

Students then can individually, or with a partner, cut out and complete **BLM 5.1: How Feelings Look On Our Faces**. Give every student a copy of **BLM 5.2: Be the Boss of Your Feelings: Poster** and also display it in a prominent position during this unit. You can display the BLM on the interactive whiteboard.

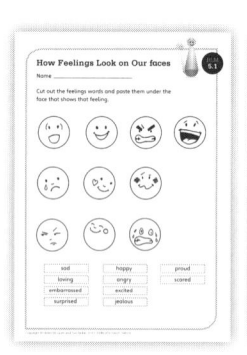

Each day, ask students to choose how they are feeling at that moment and to copy the face on **BLM 5.1** that shows that feeling. Alternatively, they could cut them all out and place the appropriate one on the corner of their desk.

Picture books

Why Do You Cry?
Little Rabbit is about to turn five, and he decides he's all through with crying. He doesn't want cry-babies at his birthday party, so he tells his friends they can come only if they're big, like him, and don't cry any more. When all of his friends admit to crying sometimes, Little Rabbit is shocked. Does everybody cry? They each explain why they cry.

What Makes Me Happy?
This rhyming book explores the kinds of situations that elicit different feelings, e.g. rain makes me sad because no one wants to play.
→ Follow up: Make a wall display of small similar rhymes made by pairs of students.

I Have Feelings
In this simple picture book, each situation is described on one page, with the accompanying feeling on the next page, allowing students to predict the name of the feeling.

Smile-a-Saurus! A Book About Feelings
These dinosaurs love to express their feelings. Fretful-saurus worries. Cry-ceratops weeps. Terror-dactyl is always afraid. Glee-rex smiles all day long. Students can create their own 'emotional dinosaurs'.

Our Feelings from Happy to Sad
This is a non-fiction book about the range of emotions. It is supported by photographs.

All in a Day
The message in this book is that living in the moment and making each day count is what matters. A young farm boy makes the most of the day as he waters his garden, collects the eggs, has a picnic and a nap and stretches out on his back to gaze up at the sky.

If You're Happy and You Know It: Jungle Edition
This is a different version of this classic song in which animals take a different view of what you should do if you're happy, e.g. a puppy thinks you should wave your tail (swirl, twirl), an elephant thinks you should flap your ears (flap, flap) while a crocodile argues that you should snap your teeth (snip, clip).

Drama

Acting with feelings
Write each of the following feelings on a card: happy, sad, angry, excited and scared. Write five 'action' cards, with actions such as:
- Hammer a nail.
- Brush your hair.
- Sit down at the table and start eating.
- Dig the garden.
- Hit a tennis ball several times.
- Eat an apple.
- Take off your shoes and socks.
- Play with Lego.

Students draw one feelings card from a container. They then draw an action card from another container that tells them what action to do with that emotion. For example, 'Brush your hair in an angry way'.

Activities

Happy/sad feelings
Give each pair of students a polystyrene cup. Explain that this will become their special feeling person and ask them to decide on a name for this 'person'. One student in each pair then draws a happy face on one side of the cup and the other student draws a sad face on the other side. Help the students to fill their cups about four-fifths full of potting mix and sprinkle grass seed onto the mix. Show them how to lightly water their plant. Place the plants on a window ledge so they receive indirect sunlight. As the grass grows, each pair can cut their character's grass 'hair' into whatever shape they choose. Every few days, ask two pairs to bring their 'person' into the circle, introduce them and decide whether they are happy or sad today (turning the appropriate face around to face the class). They explain why their character is feeling that way today.

The message to students is that it is normal for people to have many different feelings. Ask:
- What are some things that children your age feel happy about?
- What are some things that children your age feel sad about?

- What are some things that children your age feel excited about?
- What are some things that children your age feel angry about?
- What are some things that children your age feel worried about?
- What are some things that children your age feel proud about?
- What things help children your age to feel safe?

Circle class story

Begin a story with: 'Once upon a time two children about your age went with their family on a picnic. They felt really happy.' Ask pairs of students to discuss why the children were happy, then to share their answers. Repeat the process for other parts of the story: 'When the children arrived at the picnic grounds they felt worried.' (Why?) 'Mum was angry.' (Why?) 'They felt proud.' (Why?)

Make a feelings board

Divide a magnetic whiteboard into four quadrants or use four small quartet whiteboards (available from office suppliers). Draw up the board with headings and 'feelings' words as shown below. Put each student's name on a small magnetic button or use magnetic paper to make small magnetic buttons for each student with a photo of their face. You can use Dr Seuss's *My Many Coloured Days* (see below) to introduce the feelings board. Attach a face drawing to each quadrant to show the main emotion for that quadrant: yellow—excited; black—angry; pink—calm/pleased; purple—sad. Then encourage each student to place their button in the square that shows how they feel today. Students can do this at the beginning of each day and then during the day be encouraged to move their button when their mood/feelings change.

Yellow day	**Black day**
Excited	Angry
Lots of energy (energetic)	Mad
Lots of ideas	Annoyed
Keen to work (enthusiastic)	Cross
Keen to learn	Tense
Bubbly	
Purple day	**Pink day**
Sad	Calm
Feeling alone/left out	Happy
Worried	Glad
Anxious	Peaceful
Scared	Pleased
Tearful	
Unhappy	
Upset	

Picture book

My Many Coloured Days

This simple book introduces the notion of how our feelings can change a lot and how different feelings can be linked to different colours.

Unit 5

Emotions

Circle Time: You can change your bad mood into a good mood

Begin the lesson with everyone standing and singing 'Shake Your Sillies Out' (see over). Then ask the students to sit in the circle and put their hands up if, before the lesson, anyone felt cross, sad, angry or worried. It's OK and natural to have these feelings if our day did not start well. Now, hands up if you feel happier after the song. Why do we now feel happier? (it's fun to sing together; doing fun things together gives us more energy; it helps us to also pay attention to the good things in our life, not just the bad things)

Read *The Good Mood Hunt* or one of the other books listed below. Ask the students to go on a 'good mood hunt' to find something in the classroom that can help them to turn their mood around. For example: things they like doing; things or places that make them feel happy, proud, pleased, excited or relaxed. Ask different students to share what they found and how this thing makes them feel: elicit different positive emotions. Ask: What are other ways you can go on a 'good mood hunt' at home or at school to help change a bad mood or unpleasant feelings into a good mood or happy feelings? (you can find things or people to play with that make you happy; you can find something you like to do that makes you happy, e.g. reading, painting, singing, dancing, talking to someone you like, spending time with your pets', walking in the park; you can find someone to spend time with or be kind to) Ask students to turn to their partner and share one thing that they love to do that helps them feel happy. Ask different students to share; write their ideas on the board to help with a follow-up class flipbook (see **Handbook**, page 98).

Stress that they can also help to make other people feel happy. Ask: What is one thing you could to do to make someone in your family (or a friend) happy?

→ Follow up by singing 'Put on a Happy Face' (see page 95).

Picture books

The Good Mood Hunt
Hannah wakes up happy and then remembers she has nothing for Show and Tell, and her good mood changes to a bad mood. She then goes hunting for things to share for Show and Tell and finds lots of things that help her recover her good mood.
→ Ask questions based on how Hannah's mood changed from a good mood to a bad mood and then back to a good mood. What did she do to change her bad mood to a good mood?

I Love It When You Smile
This is a tale about an extremely cranky kangaroo and his mother's efforts to cheer him up. After some gentle tickling, a game of hide-and-seek and even a fun pile of leaves fail to rouse Little Roo from his down mood, his mum takes him on a ride that just might do the trick.

The Bad Mood
Badger wakes up in a bad mood and he decides that everyone else should feel miserable too. He finds his friends Raccoon, Deer, Fox, Hare and Squirrel and is very rude to them. Badger returns home and does a bit of gardening and soon his bad mood turns into a good mood. He goes off to find his friends but they don't want to spend time with him because he had been so mean. He realises that he has passed on his bad mood to them. He apologises and then plans a party for his friends.
→ Discuss why gardening helps people to feel happy. Ask students to talk about anyone in their family who gets pleasure from gardening. Have they ever helped in the garden? Consider following up with a small garden patch or putting some plants in pots.

When I'm Feeling Happy
The character in this book describes the many things that can help us to feel happy.

Feeling Sad
Duck is feeling sad. The sky is black and her world seems very dark, even though she has her little toy, Dudley, with her. She is overwhelmed with sadness until she makes a plan to bring back the light to her world and sets off with Dudley to find the sun. Frog tells her that the clouds will pass and she must look ahead. She does, and feels happy in her new world, which moves from black and white into full colour.

→ Follow up with an art activity in which students use two halves of a large sheet of paper. They draw one 'sad feelings' side using black, white and grey. On the other side they draw 'good feelings' using bright colours.

Our Granny
The focus of this book is grandmothers and how they are all different (e.g. some babysit, some drive trucks, some travel and some write books) but all are important in the lives of their grandchildren.

→ Talk with students about how spending time with someone you care about and who cares about you, such as a grandparent, can help you to change a bad mood into a good mood. If you can't spend time with them (because they might be as busy as many of the grandmothers in the story!), you can email them or talk to them by phone or via a program such as Skype.

Red Sled
This book has just a few rhyming words (e.g. red sled, sad lad, sad dad) and reminds the reader that having fun can help lift your mood. A young boy and his father are both feeling sad so they put on their outdoor clothing and go outside into the snowy evening with their red sled. They climb a hill and then, laughing, they slide down it together many times. Then they go back inside and have a hot drink, not feeling sad any more. Having fun changed their mood and brought them closer together.

Activities

Good mood hunt
Ask students to bring something from home that helps them feel happy—it might be their favourite book, soft toy or ball, or a photo or drawing of something that makes them happy. Follow up in Circle Time with everyone sharing the 'treasure' that makes them feel happy.

Class book
Make a class book (see **Handbook**, page 97) titled 'Our class good mood hunt'. Each student contributes one page that begins: I can change a bad mood into a good mood by …

Happy cube
Students make a happy cube (see **Handbook**, page 97) On each of the six sides they draw and write about one thing that makes them feel happy.

Songs

'Shake Your Sillies Out'
Other verses could be:
- Jump your jiggles out
- Yawn your sleepies out
- Stretch your stretchies out
- Laugh your troubles out

Unit 5

Emotions

'Put on a Happy Face'

Students can show the happy side of their paper plate puppet (see page 100) or make a happy mask to wear whenever they sing the line 'Put on a happy face' or when singing the entire song. Make the mask from a paper plate and hat elastic. Discuss the usefulness of putting on a happy face so you can feel OK for a while and because things will soon be better. Stress that it is not good to pretend for a long time and not all the time. It is better to talk to someone when you don't feel happy.

Activity

Pop goes the feeling

Blow up three balloons. Draw faces on the balloons with three different expressions: angry, worried and sad. Ask three students to come out the front and give them something to pop a balloon with. When the class sings 'Pop Goes the Feeling' (see below), they pop the balloon that represents the feeling that the class is singing about. You will need to discuss the idea of healing with them at the start. This can be done by making links with changing bad moods into good moods, and finding ways to be the boss of your feelings.

Song

'Pop Goes the Feeling'

(To the tune of 'Pop Goes the Weasel')

> Whenever I am feeling sad
> I help myself with healing,
> I tell someone who cares about me
> Pop! goes the feeling.
>
> Whenever I am feeling cross
> I help myself with healing,
> I tell the person why I'm mad
> Pop! goes the feeling.
>
> Whenever I am feeling scared
> I help myself with healing,
> I think about a happy time
> Pop! goes the feeling.

Circle Time: **Feelings happen inside our body too**

Introduce this Circle Time by passing a smile from student to student—one student turns to the person sitting next to them and smiles, that person then turns to their neighbour and smiles and so on around the circle. Ask students how their body felt when they were smiling and watching everyone else smile. Ask them how the following pleasant feelings feel inside their body: happy, excited, proud, loving. Then explain that unpleasant feelings are felt inside our body too. Pass a frown around the circle. Ask students to think about the last time they felt left out of something and all alone. Then ask them to remember a time when they felt sad because they had lost something or someone important to them. How did their body feel? Ask some students to describe what that felt like. Ask: What might happen inside our heads and bodies if we have uncomfortable and unpleasant feelings and we don't talk to someone about them? Students might offer examples such as: tummy ache, headache, feel scared, heart beats very fast, shake, sweat, weepy eyes, body feels heavy and you have no energy.

Ask: When you have unpleasant and uncomfortable feelings, what are some of the unhelpful ways that you might show them to other people? (yell; cry for a long time; not sleep well; clench your hands; not eat much; look cross or sad all the time; get upset over everything) What are some helpful ways? (talk to someone you trust; keep busy; be kind to someone else; do something else that makes you feel happy)

Activity

One worried wombat

Read the book *One Woolly Wombat* to the class. The book is not essential to the activity but it makes a nice introduction. Read out the 'one worried wombat' version below.

> One worried wombat
> Two excited emus
> Three happy hippos
> Four frightened fish
> Five proud platypuses
> Six sad seals
> Seven surprised snakes
> Eight angry alpacas
> Nine nervous numbats
> Ten contented koalas

- Talk about the feelings that each animal has. Brainstorm with the class what the wombat might be worried about, what the emus might be excited about and so on.
- Make one copy of **BLM 5.3: Animal Pictures** for each student. They colour and cut out each of the ten pictures, then use the pictures to make a class mural using the numbers of each animal as described above. Students could work in groups to draw the habitat of the various animals on the mural.
- Students work in pairs to draw around each other's body shape. Then they can write on the different parts of the body the changes that they experience when they have an unpleasant feeling.

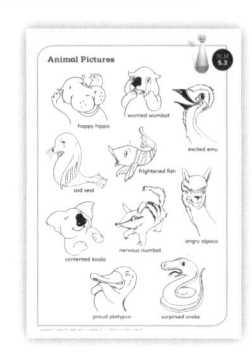

Drama

Guess the feeling

- Use the feelings on **BLM 5.1: How Feelings Look On Our Faces** to make a class set of cards and put them in a container. Then make a set of masks using paper plates for each of the emotions. Copy the characteristics from the feelings faces on the BLM (or photocopy and enlarge them). Students draw out a feelings card and select the correct mask. Use the masks with drama activities.
- Students draw a feeling card from a container and then mime something that might make them have that feeling. They can use their whole body or just their hands. After their mime, ask the class to guess what it was. For unpleasant emotions, ask the performer what they would be saying to themselves (self-talk) at the time. You could use the scenarios on **BLM 5.4: Matching Feelings and Situations**.

Unit 5

Emotions

- Students draw a situation card from a container and mime it. The other class members try to guess the situation and the feeling expressed. Situations could include:
  – having an argument with someone
  – wanting a new basketball like a classmate has
  – not getting what you want for your birthday
  – losing your schoolbag
  – seeing a snake in front of you
  – winning a race
  – getting ready for a party.

Games

Fish the feeling out

Students make fishing rods and feelings bottles. They fish out a bottle, read the feeling inside and make the expression that goes with it or say when they have felt like that. This could also be used with drama or writing activities. You will need:
- eight small, clean plastic soft drink bottles with screw-top lids
- small (about 2 cm) metal key rings (without the tags) to be attached to the outside of the bottles with a thick elastic band. Curtain rings are another option but you may have to cut the elastic band and re-tie it. Insert the elastic band through the key ring. If the bottle tips so that the key ring is under water (it usually doesn't) then add a second key ring to the opposite side to balance it.
- a piece of dowelling or wood with a length of string and a cup hook on the end of it
- container of water for the bottles to float in
- little rolled-up pieces of paper with the names of feelings written on them, tied with an elastic band that can be placed inside the bottles (or write the feeling on a craft stick and place inside the bottle)

Alternatively you could use cut-out fish (with feelings written on them) with paper clips and a rod with a magnet and a container without water.

Snap and Fish

- Make a copy of **BLM 5.4: Matching Feelings and Situations** on thin card for each student. Then they cut out, colour and pool their cards to make pairs to use when playing Snap and Fish.

Activities

Feelings pictures, words and other things

- Students cut out pictures of people from magazines and newspapers. They hold up one of their pictures for the class to see and say what they think that person is feeling and why. The rest of the class gives their ideas. Then the pictures are labelled and displayed or used as a stimulus for writing a story.
- As a class, collect pictures from magazines and newspapers around a specific feeling and make a display.
- Play a selection of music and ask about each piece: What feelings do you have? How do you make that expression/hold your body? Afterwards, say: Let your face and body be… (sad, worried, etc.).
- Students can use Kid Pix or a similar program to construct faces showing different emotions. They can print them and make a collage of the different images.
- Students can draw emotional faces on blown-up balloons and make displays of positive and negative emotions.

Circle Time: We can have mixed feelings

Start this Circle Time with a 'Movers and shakers' activity (see **Handbook**, page 91) using statements such as these:
- Jump on the spot if you have ever felt excited.
- Pretend to cry if you have ever been sad.
- Put your hand on your heart if you feel loved.
- Punch your fists in the air if you have ever felt angry.
- Fold your arms if you have ever felt jealous.
- Shake all over if you have ever been worried.
- Give yourself a pat on the back if you have ever felt proud.

Ask: Is it possible to have two feelings at once? Some feelings are more likely to happen together even if they are not very much like each other. Point out that it is possible to be excited and nervous at the same time (e.g. in a class play or presenting a talk to the class); happy and disappointed (e.g. at present-opening time at Christmas or birthdays); excited and jealous (e.g. when a new baby comes home); angry and sad or worried (e.g. when Mum and Dad have an argument). Discuss times when students remember feeling two feelings about the same event or situation. Make a chart on the board.

→ Follow up with students completing **BLM 5.5: Two Feelings at Once**.

Picture book

Ever So Ever So
The arrival of a baby sister in the family creates many mixed feelings in a young girl, e.g. excitement, rejection and jealousy.

Drama

Feelings hats
Put together a collection of hats. You can get these from the supermarket, a party shop or a second-hand shop (clean them first) or the students can make them. A headband with a label works well, too. Place a clearly visible 'feelings label' (happy, excited, sad, worried, etc.) on each. Two students put on hats and then act out those feelings.

Activities

A picture dictionary of feelings
Students make a class picture dictionary of feelings illustrated with magazine pictures. Give each pair several different letters to work on.

Flipbook or class book
(See **Handbook**, pages 97 and 98.) Students write and draw their own flipbook or contribute a page to a class book using one of these sentences:
- The happiest I have ever felt was when…
- The most angry I have ever felt was when…
- The most surprised I have ever felt was when…
- The most worried I have ever felt was when…
- The most excited I have ever felt was when…
- The most proud I have ever felt when was…

Unit 5

Emotions

Feelings dice: throw a feeling

Make a feelings dice using the cube pattern on page 97 of the **Handbook**. Write one of the sentence stems below on each of the six sides. Students throw the dice and complete the various sentences. The 'Animal asks' e-tool (see **Handbook**, page 89) could also be used with eight of these sentence stems.
- A time when I felt sad was…
- A time when I felt angry was…
- A time when I felt worried was…
- A time when I felt surprised was…
- A time when I felt proud was …
- A time when I felt happy was…
- A time when I felt excited was…
- A time when I felt disappointed was…
- A time when I felt surprised was…
- A time when I felt like I belonged was…

Round table (two activities)

1. (See **Handbook**, page 92.) Give each child in a group of four an A3 piece of paper with one of the questions below written on it. Each student takes a turn to write or draw an example of when a child their age would feel that emotion. They then pass the paper clockwise to the next student. Every student contributes one drawing/ example per sheet.
   - When do children feel sad?
   - When do children feel angry?
   - When do children feel worried?
   - When do children feel excited?

2. Choose four different situations and write each one in the middle of an A3 piece of paper, e.g. two girls laugh at you; a friend comes over to play; you fall over; you win a prize. Each student draws a face that shows how they would feel and pastes it on the poster around the statement. For the situation 'Two girls laugh at you', they could write under their face, for example:
   - Caitlin would feel sad.
   - Zac would feel angry.
   The posters can then be displayed.

   A second poster can be placed underneath. Write a statement such as 'This is what we could do about it if it happened'. Then each student cuts out a strip of paper and writes their name and what they think would be the best way to handle the situation. For example:
   - Caitlin thinks the best thing to do is to just move away from them.
   - Zac thinks the best thing to do is say 'Go away'.

Circle Time: How angry do you feel? What do you do?

Read one of the books listed below. Talk about the situations in the book that the character(s) felt angry about. Discuss how different animals express their anger and ask students to mime each one, e.g. cats hiss, bulls snort and paw the ground, birds flap and squawk. Ask: What does it feel like when you are angry and what do you feel like doing? (saying something mean; throwing something) Stress that it's OK to have that feeling as long as you don't turn the feeling into a hurtful action. Your feelings don't hurt other people or get you into trouble, but your actions do. Also stress that other people and what they do don't *make* you angry. It's how you think and feel about what happens that makes you angry. When you feel the strong, hot feeling of anger you need to do something to cool down that feeling, so you don't hurt someone and get into trouble. In other words, you have to try to be the boss of your feelings and find some safe ways to show that you are angry. Ask: How will other students behave towards you if they think you will not be able to be the boss of your angry feelings? (they will not want to play with you or be your friend; you will get into trouble; you will get a bad reputation) Ask: How will you feel if you are not the boss of your angry feelings? (you will not feel proud of yourself; you will not feel so confident)

Picture books

Would You Be Angry?
Many of the situations presented are the normal ones that children experience, such as when a friend accidentally breaks your toy. Others are humorously whimsical, such as when a baby elephant steps on your foot. Some of the situations make interesting discussions, e.g. when the grown-ups take too long to finish their coffee and you are dying to go to the beach.
→ Follow up by making a class version of the book, with students contributing typical scenarios as well as silly ones.

When I'm Feeling Angry
This book gives the message that it is OK to feel angry sometimes, as long as you don't hurt anyone.

When I Feel Angry
This book contains some interesting metaphors for anger (e.g. volcano, bull in a china shop, water boiling over in a pot).
→ Follow up by having students draw the different metaphors.

Andrew's Angry Words
Andrew gets into an angry mood when his older sister accidentally trips over him. He swears angrily at her and the angry words 'escape' (with Andrew following them on their travels), touching many people's lives. The angry words eventually travel to another country and touch a woman selling fruit in a market. She collects them, throws them into the sea and gives Andrew some nice, kind words to replace them with. Link Andrew's irrational anger towards his sister to his not asking 'Did she really mean it?'
→ Follow up with the activity 'The hurtful power of angry words' (see over) or use the activity to introduce the book.

Activities

How angry do you feel?
Make a big 'anger warning device' (like a fire-risk warning device) from cardboard. Cut out a spinner and attach it at the centre of the base with a split pin. Ask individual students to come to the front and indicate how angry they would feel in the situations you describe (see below). Hopefully, different students will give different answers to the same situation. Point that out and then talk about how angry they feel influences how they act (walk away, shrug their shoulders, hit back, etc.).
- When someone makes fun of you.
- When you have to stop playing and clean up your toys.
- When it rains and stops you going on a picnic or to the beach.
- When you try really hard but you still can't make your drawing look good.
- When you accidentally spill something and get into trouble.
- When other kids won't let you play in their game.

Unit 5

Emotions

- When you aren't allowed to play on the computer.
- When someone tries to mess up your game.
- When another kid takes what you are playing with without asking first.
- When someone pushes you.
- When someone calls you a name you don't like.
- When someone knocks you over in a game, even though they didn't mean to.
- When someone teases you and calls you names.
- When someone comes up behind you and makes you jump.
- When you make a mistake in front of the class.
- When your favourite toy is broken.

Link the fire-risk warning device to fire safety. Ask students if they have ever seen one of these and talk about why they are helpful.

The hurtful power of angry words
You will need:
- a bag—write on the outside 'Some angry words'
- between six and eight small blank cards
- some talcum powder with a strong smell

Explain that students are going to see how angry words go from one person to another and change things for everyone involved. Ask them to think of some angry words or phrases. (I hate you. I don't like you; go away! I'm not going to play with you any more.) Write each one on a separate card, place it in the bag and then sprinkle them heavily with the talcum powder.

Take out one of the cards and read it. Say: What do you notice? Yes, the air smells different because of the angry words that I have. I am the only one who has the angry words but you can see that things have changed in the room for all of us because of them. Then pass the bag and ask each student to take out one card, read it out (or pass it you to you to read out), put it back in the bag and pass it to the next student. When the bag of cards returns to you, ask them to smell their hands. Point out that even after they no longer have the angry words, there is still something left behind that has affected them. Ask: How is this like angry words that we sometimes say to someone else? Something still remains and it can take a little while to go away. Saying sorry, trying to fix things and being the boss of your angry feelings can help you and the other person feel better and make the 'left-over' smell go away more quickly.

Circle Time: **Being the boss of your angry feelings**

Begin by playing 'Feelings circle charades'. Prepare a set of 'feelings words' flash cards and place them in an envelope. The students pass a ball to each other in a clockwise direction while music plays. When it stops, the student who is holding the ball draws out a flash card and acts it out while the rest of the class guesses what the feeling is. Ask: What kinds of situations might children your age feel angry about? (Try to avoid the term 'makes me angry'. Instead say, 'Well, we can understand that you felt angry when that happened, but it didn't *make* you angry.) Then ask: What does it mean to be the boss your feelings? (you are in control; you can stay calm; you think before you act)

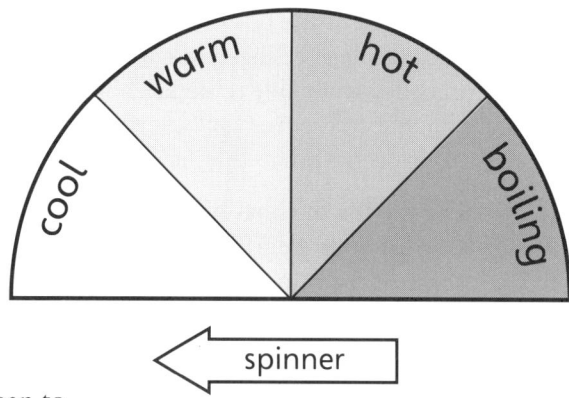

101

Read one of the books listed below. Ask: What was the character feeling? Were they the boss of their feelings? Ask if anyone can tell the class about a time when they felt angry but they were able to be the boss of their feelings. Ask them to talk about what they thought to themselves (I can stay calm) or what they did (went away for a while and sat on the swing to calm down) that helped them to be the boss of their anger.

Use the 'Be the boss of your feelings' e-activity and **BLM 5.6: Be the Boss of your Angry Feelings**. Stress that sometimes you can't change some of the things that you feel angry about, e.g. when your friend moves away to another school, when your favourite toy gets broken or when it rains and you were planning to go somewhere special. The best thing to do if you can't change it is to say to yourself, 'Well, it's not the end of the world and I can't do anything about it anyway'. It also helps to remind yourself that sometimes you are angry because you are also sad. You can talk to someone about sad feelings.

→ Follow up by asking the students to make a mobile using **BLM 5.7: Good and Bad Ways to Be the Boss of Your Angry Feelings**. Students then make and illustrate a digital class poster, an individual flipbook, a class book or lift-up flaps (see **Handbook**, pages 97 to 98) using the sentence: 'A good way to cool down when you feel angry is…' or 'A good way to be the boss of your angry feelings is…'

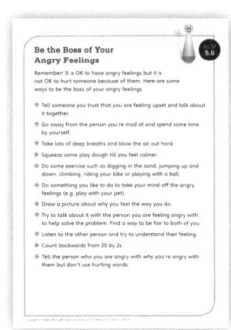

Picture books

Where the Wild Things Are
Read the story, then re-read it and at each point ask: How was Max feeling? Why did he feel like that? What was he saying to himself that would make him feel like that? What did Max do to help him be the boss of his angry feelings? (He imagined a faraway place where angry creatures lived.) How would you have felt if you were Max? What could Max have done if his feelings had been the boss of him? Has anyone ever had a similar experience? Students can make a class book (see **Handbook**, page 97) called 'When we felt like being wild things!' Consider showing the DVD of *Where the Wild Things Are*.

Angry Albert
Albert constantly throws temper tantrums and everyone avoids him until he learns not to. This is written in a tongue-in-cheek style but it helps to reinforce the idea that people who are not the boss of their anger lose friends or do not make them.
→ Follow up by having students make a class book (see **Handbook**, page 97) for the library using the sentence: 'If you let anger be the boss of you then…'

Angry Arthur
All the stages of a full-blown tantrum are captured in this picture book. Arthur is peaceful, then defiant, then he gets angry and the results are spectacular. His room falls apart, then his house and the whole town; the world splits, and there is finally a 'universequake'. And then Arthur can't remember what he was angry about!

Dealing with Anger
In this book, two or three simple scenarios are described in which the children in the photographs experience being angry.
→ Follow up by taking photographs for a book or display in which students make angry faces. Write captions underneath describing what happened. Avoid the use of the term

'makes/made X angry'. Instead use the expression 'X feels angry when'. Then ask them to write a sentence about how they dealt with their anger: 'X was the boss of his/her angry feelings because he/she …'

When Sophie Gets Angry—Really Really Angry

When Sophie's sister takes away a toy that Sophie was playing with, Sophie gets so angry that she runs out of the house and keeps running until she falls exhausted to the ground and bursts into tears. Eventually she goes for a walk, climbs a tree and is soothed and calmed by the sights and sounds of nature.

→ Use this as a lead-in to a discussion about how nature can help us to soothe strong feelings such as anger (and sadness). Students can discuss and then draw their favourite outdoor place that helps them to calm down and feel better. The use of colour in this book is very interesting and students could work with a partner and use the same colour approach to digitally illustrate a three-frame story of an angry outburst. When Sophie is angry, she is illustrated in red, but as she calms down the colour changes to yellow. Remind students that they shouldn't go for a walk away from their own home without permission.

Song

'That Just Makes Things Worse'
(To the tune of 'Polly Wolly Doodle')

    I don't hit when I feel mad
    That just makes things worse
    I don't call names or try to hurt
    That just makes things worse
    Tell them why
    Tell them why
    I tell them why I'm mad
    I find a way to still be friends
    Then I don't feel bad

Activities

Tashi and Timba Tortoise

Tashi and Timba Tortoise are young tortoises who live with their grandparents. Grandpa and Grandma Tortoise teach them that the purpose of having a shell is so that they can 'pull their heads in' when they feel upset and think about the best way to be the boss of their angry feelings. Students can act out the tortoise characters having their conversation.

→ Read out some of the anger-provoking scenarios described in 'How angry do you feel?' (page 100). Ask the students to make their own 'shell' by folding their arms on the desk and putting their head down between their arms so that they can have time to think, like Tashi and Timba. Students can write stories about the two characters and use them for drama activities, using **BLM 5.8: Tortoise Puppets**. They cut out the front and back of the tortoise and use a glue stick to paste around the edge of the front and back, leaving the neck and between the legs without paste. They paste craft sticks to the necks of the tortoises so they can be slipped into the body. Then they can move the stick up and down to pull the tortoise's head in as they tell or respond to storytelling.

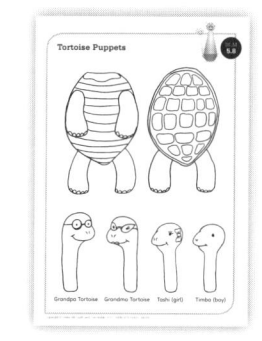

Fridge magnets

Students make a fridge magnet (see **Handbook**, page 99) showing the statement 'Be the boss of your feelings'.

Drama

We don't want to play with you

Students make balloon puppets (see **Handbook**, page 100). Then they act out this play using the puppets and sing the song (below) as part of their play. The puppets de-personalise the unpleasant message. Use the 'Freeze frame' and 'Good fairy/bad fairy' strategies (see **Handbook**, pages 89 and 90). The characters in the play are:

- a puppet called Aggro who is not the boss of his/her feelings and hits, yells and insults when angry
- three other puppets who get sick of being hurt by this puppet.

The story can be based on any of the scenarios listed in the 'How angry do you feel?' activity (see page 100). Aggro might lose his/her temper when:

- someone accidentally bumps him/her
- he/she loses in a card game such as Snap
- someone says he/she can't have one of their chips
- he/she thinks it is his/her turn to have the ball.

Aggro then starts to realise what is happening because of the way in which the other puppets respond to him (the 'Before' song below), so he starts to find better ways to be the boss of his angry feelings and the children change their response to him ('After' song below).

Song

'We Don't Want to Play with You'

(To the tune of 'Popeye the Sailor Man')

'Before' song

We don't want to play with you
We don't want to play with you
When you get mad
You make us feel bad
We don't want to play with you

'After' song

We're happy to play with you
We're happy to play with you
You may feel mad
But we don't feel bad
We're happy to play with you

Circle Time: What to do when someone is angry with you

Pretend to be angry with the class. Tell them off a little for some minor infringement. Ask: What feeling did I have? How did you know I was feeling angry? Then debrief and explain that you were not really as angry as you seemed, but you wanted them to think about how they know when someone is angry with them. Ask: What things do people say or do that tell you they are feeling angry? (frown a bit more than usual; use a slightly louder voice; don't smile much; have angry narrow eyes and stare more)

Talk about good ways to respond to another person's anger. For example:
◎ apologise if you really have done something to upset them
◎ stay calm so they will get calmer too
◎ don't yell back or try to hurt them or call them nasty names
◎ say, 'Is there a problem?'
◎ go away until they calm down a bit more.

→ Follow up with drama or puppet activities in which one person is angry and the other deals well with the anger.

Circle Time: Hands are not for hitting, feet are not for kicking, words are not for hurting

Start with students using the 'Think–ink–pair–share' strategy (see **Handbook,** page 92) to talk about how they felt when someone hurt them by hitting, pushing, punching and so on (no names). Ask selected students to report what was said. Explain that when someone hurts your body or says hurtful and mean words to you, they also hurt your feelings. Talk about why people sometimes hit/kick/push or use hurtful words when they feel angry.
For example:
◎ They are feeling left out.
◎ They are worried about something (e.g. that boy always laughs at me and I feel silly).
◎ They don't know what else to do to show they are angry and we need to help them to learn better ways to be the boss of their angry feelings.

Ask: What could you do if someone hurts you? (you do not have to hurt back, you can walk away; you can find something else to do; you can find an older person who can help; you can remind the person who hurt you that hands are not for hurting)

Picture books

Hands Are Not for Hitting
Read the book *Hands Are Not for Hitting* (note: this not a storybook). Discuss what hands are for, e.g. saying hello and goodbye (waving, shaking hands and blowing kisses), writing, counting, drawing and painting.

Feet Are Not for Kicking
The message in this book is that feet are for fun, not for hurting others. It is a similar book to *Hands Are Not for Hitting* (see above). It also contains some useful activities.

Words Are Not for Hurting
The message in this book is that words are for helping and connecting, not for hurting others. It is a similar book to *Hands Are Not for Hitting* (see above). It also contains some useful activities.

You can also discuss 'Computers and phones are not for hurting' and discuss sending nasty emails or text messages (if age-appropriate for your students).

Song

'Hands Are Not for Hitting'

Students can learn this song and do the actions as they sing.
(To the tune of 'Sing a Song of Sixpence')

Hands are not for hitting	Hands are not for hitting
This is what they're for	This is what they're for
Shaking hands with classmates	Playing with your pet
Who walk in through the door	Sweeping the floor
Saying bye to Grandma	Throwing a ball
Cleaning your teeth	Opening a box
Lifting up the beach rocks	Tying up your laces
To see what's underneath	Putting on your socks
Hands are not for hitting	Hands are not for hitting
This is what they're for	This is what they're for
Using lots of crayons	Putting on your seatbelt
To write and to draw	Using a saw
Patting your teddy bear	Blowing lots of kisses
Putting clothes away	Eating up your meal
Hammering a nail in	Putting on a bandaid
Or modelling some clay	Removing orange peel

Activities

- Students act out all the things that hands *are* for and others try to guess what the behaviour is.
- Make a wall collage of hands with the heading 'Hands are not for hitting!' Students trace around their own hands, colour them and cut them out. On the hands they write some of things that hands *are* for.
- Make a mobile of hands. Students trace around their hand twice, then write an example of what hands can be used for on each side. Staple or glue the paper hands together and stuff them with cotton balls or crushed-up newspaper. You could also use cheap white cotton cleaning gloves and stuff them with newspaper, cotton fill or cut-up plastic bags.
- Make a class book of what hands *are* for.
- Teach the students some sign language.
- Teach the students a series of friendly gestures they can make with their hands, e.g. the OK sign (thumb and forefinger in a circle), a salute, high fives, low fives, a spaghetti shake (limp and wobbly up and down), little finger shake.
- Students can use their hands in a 'feely box' and try to guess what they are feeling (e.g. different fruit and vegetables, play dough, pencils, felt pens, erasers, rulers, small toys).
- Students work in pairs to complete tasks that need two hands, with one student using only their left hand and the other using only their right. Tasks could include: tie a bow, build with Lego, draw shapes, hold and read a book and turn the pages together.
- Students put both hands behind their back and see what happens when they run or hop (they will lose their balance), talk or try to eat.

Unit 5

Emotions

> **Discussion**

What to do if people are hitting or hurting at home
Talk to students about what a child could do if they were at home and the adults or older children hit or hurt others. Don't ask them to share experiences, just talk about what you could do. For example:
- Plan a safe place in the house where they could go to next time.
- Go to their safe place and draw, read, play a game or play music.
- If they don't feel safe, call Kids Helpline.
- Talk about it with a teacher or other grown-up they trust.

Circle Time: Did they really mean it?

Before you start the circle activity, arrange in advance for one student to accidentally knock over something of yours (such as a pile of books) as they arrive in the circle and then say 'sorry' in a genuine way. Ask the students: Do you think they meant to upset me when they did that? If you tripped over someone's feet, how would you expect them to behave if they had not meant to trip you? (They would apologise in a real way.) If someone said something that hurt your feelings and you told them so, what would you expect them to say if they hadn't meant to hurt your feelings? (I'm sorry.) Ask selected students: What signs tell you that someone who has just hurt you or hurt your feelings actually meant to upset you, rather than did so accidentally? For example:
- They say everything in a nasty voice.
- They say or do mean things more than just once.
- They have a nasty pretend smile, which is called a smirk.
- They look pleased or laugh when they have upset you.

→ Follow up with a drama activity in which one puppet deliberately does something mean to another, such as knocking something out of their hands, taking their toy or scribbling on their work. Ask the students watching what they noticed about what the puppet did when it was deliberately trying to make someone upset. Use the 'Freeze frame' strategy (see **Handbook**, page 89). Some ideas are:
- A child kicks someone's ball too far away and it is deliberate/accidental.
- A child bumps someone's desk as they pass between school desks and it is deliberate/accidental.
- A child tears someone's drawing and it is deliberate/accidental.
- A child steps on someone's foot and it is deliberate/accidental.
- A child tells someone else a private fact about someone and it is a mean act/just thoughtless.

Circle Time: Everyone feels sad sometimes

Start by playing 'Pass the feeling'. Give the first student a card with a feeling written on it. They then make an expression to match the feeling and pass it to the next student in the circle and so on. Do this several times with different cards. Finish with 'feeling sad about'. Then ask a student to name some times or things that they have felt sad about. Read one of the books listed below. Ask: Does everyone feel sad sometimes? (Yes.) What is the same about all the things that we feel sad about? (most sad situations are about loss, i.e. no longer having something we really liked or wanted, or losing someone or a pet we really loved) **Sometimes** sadness can be about feeling the sad feelings of someone else and empathising or feeling upset that someone or something we love is being hurt or is distressed. Ask: Will you keep feeling sad forever? (No, over time you will start to feel happier.) **What can you do to help you get through a sad time?** (you can talk to someone about how you are feeling; you can go on a good mood hunt and find things to do that will make you feel better)

Activity

Good memories

Memories of good things can last forever. They can help to cancel out or soften the memories of sad or unpleasant events. Just thinking of them can bring happiness to your heart and a smile to your face. Each student can make and keep adding to a 'Happy scrapbook' in which they write and draw about happy memories or add copies of photographs, or things they found at the beach and so on. Give them an opportunity to decorate it in their own way. Students can be encouraged to read their 'Happy scrapbook' if they are feeling sad. The class can sing the song below as part of this activity.

Song

'My Favourite Things' PP

Picture books

The Saddest King
The Saddest King is the story of a land of very happy people. By order of the King, everyone has to be happy all the time. So when a young boy flouts the law by crying, he is sent to see the King at once. He is able to convince the King that there's nothing wrong with feeling sad sometimes and that emotions are nothing to be scared of.

Bear's Last Journey
This book tells the story of how Fox and the other forest animals deal with the loss of their friend Bear and seek answers to questions about grief and loss.

Tough Boris
This is the story of a mean pirate whose pet parrot dies. Despite what you would expect from the way he lives his life, he grieves openly for his lost pet.

Toby
When a family's beloved dog has to be put down, a young girl finds it difficult to deal with her feelings of sadness and covers them up.

The Tenth Good Thing About Barney
Again, the death of a dog is the main storyline but this one stresses the importance of celebrating all the good things about something important that you have lost to help deal with sadness. Stress that sadness can take a while to disappear but it always goes away and lovely memories are left in its place.

Old Pig
Old Pig and her grand-daughter have lived together for a long time. Old Pig begins to make plans for her death. She puts all her affairs in order and takes one last long walk—looking, listening, smelling and tasting.
→ Ask students how the characters deal with their sad feelings and what they offer to help us to understand how to deal with feeling sad. Discuss their experiences of losing a pet or someone who was important to them. Ask: What was one wonderful thing about them that you can tell us about?

Daddy, Will You Miss Me?
A young boy is very sad and lonely when his father has to go to Africa to work for four weeks, but he copes well by making a special box of things to show his father when he returns.
→ Follow up by having students draw what they would put in their box to show someone who hadn't seen them for a while.

Desser, the Best Ever Cat
The young narrator links events in her own life with stories about the beloved family cat Desser, which has recently died. The story balances humour and sadness and stresses the importance of re-living happy memories and also moving on.

Circle Time: Don't be a worry bee

Start by reading one of the books listed below. Then talk to the students about what 'worry' means. Worry is fear about what *might* happen. It usually doesn't happen. Ask: Can you think of any other words that mean 'worried'? (anxious, nervous, scared) Tell students that a worry is usually something that starts with 'What if…'. The best thing to do when you are worried is to talk to someone you trust and do a reality check. This means checking whether the thing you are worried about is likely to happen or not. A reality check can also help you to find ways to feel less worried.

Picture books

Waiting for Mum
Mum is late collecting her daughter after school but the young girl manages to find ways to handle her anxious thoughts.

The Worry Monster
Sally Blueshoes tells a lie and blames her dog for eating the missing cake and the dog is banished outdoors. Sally's conscience starts to trouble her and she is followed around by an ever-growing monster (i.e. her conscience) until she tells her mother the truth.
→ Make links with Unit 1: Core values (honesty).

Scaredy Squirrel
Scaredy Squirrel is scared of absolutely everything. His emergency kit contains all sorts of things he thinks will be useful—a parachute, antibacterial soap and sardines.
   Eventually he realises that always assuming that the worst stops him from enjoying life. Other titles in this series include *Scaredy Squirrel Makes a Friend* and *Scaredy Squirrel at the Beach*.

Silly Billy
Billy worries about all kinds of things such as hats, shoes and clouds. Grandma gives him some worry dolls. He then tells his worries to the worry dolls and he stops worrying.
→ This is a good book to talk about how a lot of our worries are impossible and won't ever happen. The students could all make a worry doll.

Frog Is Frightened
Frog hears strange noises while lying in bed and becomes so scared that he runs through the woods to Duck's house. Duck invites Frog to stay but they both become frightened and run to Pig's house. Pig is cross at being woken up, but he lets them stay. All three lie awake listening to the noises in the woods. Next morning their friend, Hare, finds their empty houses and, very frightened, he runs to find them. When he hears their story, he tells them that everyone is frightened sometimes.

When I Feel Scared

This book focuses on how to cope and feel better when feeling scared.

Franklin and the Thunderstorm

Franklin, a turtle, is terrified of thunderstorms but his friends find them exciting. One day, as a storm approaches, he becomes more and more anxious until a sudden flash of lightning sends him into his shell. He refuses to come out until his friends Fox, Hawk and Beaver make him laugh with their exaggerated tales about how cloud giants cause storms by playing sky drums, bowling in the sky and turning their lights on and off. When Beaver finally explains to Franklin the science of what really causes lightning and thunder, Franklin begins to feel less anxious. The storm subsides and a rainbow appears.

→ Discuss the importance of getting information and checking facts to minimise worry.

Wemberly Worried

Wemberly is a little mouse who worries about everything. When she gets to school on the first day she finds a friend who is just as worried as she is and she feels better.

→ Follow up by having the students draw and classify the worries in the book. Ask students if they can remember some of the silly worries they had when they were little. Refer back to the poems on fear in Unit 3: Courage (see pages 54 and 62).

Supposing

A little monster catastrophises and supposes the worst. His mother responds with positive alternatives and reassurances.

→ Follow up by having students write one of their own 'supposing' questions and then write a positive version as in the book.

Activities

Worry hoops

Write the following questions on cards:
- What if a pig flies into our classroom?
- What if all my shoes get up and walk away?
- What if it starts raining in my bedroom?
- What if Mum and Dad move away while I'm sleeping?
- What if a big bird flies in my bedroom and carries me away?
- What if Mum or Dad loses their job?
- What if I eat too much and I burst?
- What if I get bad comments on my school report?
- What if people are talking about me at school?
- What if my parents can't pay the water bill?
- What if my best friend moves away?
- What if I catch the flu?
- What if a war happens and there are bombs?
- What if I fall over and scratch my knee?
- What if my sister doesn't do well in her exams?

Label four hoops as follows:
- Impossible: could never happen
- Very unlikely: could happen but probably won't
- Likely: could happen but not very awful or important
- Other people's worries

Unit 5

Emotions

Read each question in turn and ask different students to put the card in the appropriate hoop. Then ask the students to:
- Write out one of the 'impossible what ifs' and add 'but this is impossible'.
- Write out one of the 'very unlikely what ifs' and add 'but this is very unlikely to happen'.
- Draw out one of the 'likely what ifs' and add 'but that wouldn't be the end of the world'.

I can be a worry bee sometimes

For each student you will need:
- the template on **BLM 5.9: I Can Be a Worry Bee Sometimes**, enlarged and photocopied onto card
- brown and yellow pencils or felt pens
- black pen
- two black pipe-cleaners
- scissors and glue to share.

Students cut out the bee and colour it brown with yellow stripes. They add pipe-cleaner antennae and curl them up. On each yellow stripe they write (in black) a worry they sometimes have and what they can do about it. For example:
- Think about whether it is likely or unlikely to happen.
- Talk to someone else and get a reality check to see if it is likely to happen.
- Keep busy and don't keep thinking about it all the time.
- Write it down and then think of all the things I could do to help myself.

Circle Time: Do you feel jealous?

Begin by having everyone standing in the circle. Bounce a small rubber ball to a student and before you bounce it say: 'Hi Hayley, catch the ball.' Hayley then has five seconds to name a feeling. Then she bounces the ball to somebody else and they have to name a different feeling within five seconds. The same feeling cannot be said twice in a row. After everyone has had a turn, ask them to list all the feelings used in the game. Then read one of the books listed below. Talk about how the character felt jealous. Ask: When do we sometimes feel jealous? (when we feel someone else is getting more of something than we are and that it isn't fair, such as attention, more friends; when we feel that someone has something that we would really like to have, such as an item of clothing or a toy; when we feel that someone has achieved something that we would like to achieve, such as a prize or award or high mark) **Tell each student to turn to a partner and say one time when they felt a bit jealous or envious. Then ask some students to share.**

Ask: What are some good ways to feel less jealous? (focus on the good things about us and what we have; try to work harder to get the things we envy; tell ourselves that it is a good thing to be pleased for someone else when they have something nice; try to find good ways to engage the people whose attention we want)

Picture books

Dealing with Jealousy
A few simple scenarios are presented in photographic form, e.g. a child wishing she had won a prize like her friend and a sister resenting the fuss being made over her sick brother. The text explains what jealousy is, explains that everyone feels jealous sometimes and suggests some ways to deal with it.

111

Byron and the Chairs

Byron has a new baby brother called Max and he feels very jealous of all the attention the new baby is getting. His mother gives his favourite yellow 'baby' chair to Max because Byron is now too big for it. She replaces it with a new blue chair for Byron that is more appropriate for his age and size, but he isn't happy about it. Byron learns how to cope with these changes by turning his jealous feelings into a little monster that has to be managed.

→ Follow up by having students draw a green-eyed jealousy monster.

Two Bad Teddies

Gruffy Ted and Tilly Ted are Mollie-Sue's two much-loved teddies and they do everything with her. One day, a present arrives from Grandma. It's a new toy, Bendy Bill, and Mollie-Sue is very taken with him and gives him all her attention. Feeling pangs of jealousy, the two teddies plan to get rid of Bendy Bill but things don't go quite as planned. Eventually they realise that Bendy Bill does have some good points and there is enough room in the house for them all.

→ Follow up by having students write about when they have felt jealous and how they became the boss of those feelings. You could also use the 'Good fairy/bad fairy' strategy (see **Handbook**, page 90) and set up a drama around people feeling jealous. The bad fairy encourages them to be nasty, to damage the thing they envy, to say bad things about or hurt the person they are jealous of or to throw a tantrum to get attention. The good fairy encourages them to focus on the good things and qualities they have.

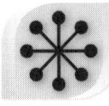

Circle Time: How do other people feel?

Prior to the lesson, buy a pair of extra large old shoes from a charity shop or ask parents for a donation. Make sure they are a pair that can easily slip on and off. Clean them up, especially on the inside, and paint them bright red with different coloured spots. Students should be given clean socks before they put them on. Use these as 'empathy shoes'.

Begin the circle by greeting each student, varying your voice in each greeting to reflect a different emotion (happy, sad, loud/angry, loud/confident, soft/shy, spooky/scary, worried/nervous). Ask each student to greet you with the same kind of voice. After you have used the same tone for three or four students and they have replied in the same voice, ask the class: How were we feeling? Then repeat with another mood. Ask selected students: How can we understand how someone else might be feeling? (look at their face; listen to their voice; ask them; remember how we felt when that happened to us)

When we try to understand how someone else is feeling, we try to guess what it's like to be in their shoes. Introduce the empathy shoes.

Invite students to think about what it would be like to be in someone else's shoes in a particular situation (see below). Focus on the feelings they would have and how you would see those feelings in what they said, did or how they looked (their facial expression). Ask different students to come out to the front and stand in the shoes. Before you discuss each situation, ask students if they have had any similar experience or feelings that help them to understand how the person was feeling. Situations could include:

- someone who performed at school assembly
- someone who won a prize
- a mum or dad who spent a lot of time cooking dinner and no one said they liked it
- someone travelling on a plane for the first time
- a person whose pet is run over
- someone who volunteered to take a friend's dog for a walk and lost it

Unit 5

Emotions

- a student who forgets their costume for a dress-up day
- someone who is pushed over
- a student who arrives at a new school
- a student who has no one to play with at recess and lunchtime
- someone who was teased and called mean names
- someone who has a new baby brother or sister.

→ Follow up with the activities below and/or by reading one of the books with a focus on how the characters are feeling. Use some of these prompts:
- What feelings is this character having? How do you know? What can you see on their face and in the way they behave?
- What can you learn about their feelings from what they are doing?
- Have you ever had any similar experience or feelings that help you to understand how they might be feeling?

Consider using 'Restorative conversations' (see **Handbook**, page 69, and Pearson Places for more information) in situations where one student has been distressed by another, to model seeing the other person's point of view and listening to their feelings.

Picture books

Just a Little Brown Dog
Sally Morgan, a descendant of the Palku people, is the author of this book about a little brown puppy, the last of his litter, who is fearful of being rejected and hopeful that he will find a home. Aboriginal illustrator Bronwyn Bancroft's illustrations add depth to the story.
→ Discuss how the illustrations and the text let us know how the little dog is feeling. Ask if anyone has felt like the little dog feels.

Two Tough Teddies
Two unkempt teddy bears, Tilly and Gruffy, are abandoned in a box of unwanted toys. They decide to try to find another owner to love them. They practise being loud, bold and brave but only manage to frighten away some cats. Finally a little girl discovers them and takes them home to scrub up and love.

It's Useful to Have a Duck
This accordion-style, double-sided board book tells the same simple story from two different perspectives. The first perspective is that of little boy who finds a rubber duck and uses him as a plaything, e.g. as a hat, to dry his ears, as a straw and as a plug for the bath. The second perspective is that of the toy duck, who turns the boy into a plaything, e.g. sitting on the boy's head allows him to get a better view and he uses the boy's ear to wax his bill. Don't be put off by the fact that it's presented as a board book.
→ Follow up by having pairs of students make a similar story with two characters, each seeing things differently, e.g. two characters in a fairy tale such as Hansel/Gretel and the Wicked Witch.

The Truth About Horrie
Horrie is a wombat who has been raised by humans. Horrie is devastated to learn that he is not really human but adopted. The story deals sensitively with the issue of adoption as a sub-theme. Link with people caring for animals in Unit 1: Core values (page 13).
→ Follow up with inquiry-based about learning wombats (see **Handbook**, page 90).

Activities

How do you know when someone is feeling…?
Students discuss and make posters about how you can recognise when someone else is feeling a particular way. Stress facial expression, posture, tone of voice, how the eyes look, what is said and what is done. For example, how do you know when:
- your parent or grandparent is feeling sad? What expression do they have on their face? What do they do? What do they say? How can you help them and show them that you care when they feel like this? Remind students not to say anything that will hurt their family's feelings.
- a friend is sad? What do they do? What do they say?

→ Follow up with the students completing **BLM 5.10: Creating Feelings in Others**.

Mime a feeling
Students draw a feelings card from a box and mime it while other students try to guess what it is.

Feelings pictures
Give students magazines and advertising brochures and ask them to work with a partner to find and cut out a picture of someone who is showing how they are feeling and then paste it onto a large piece of card. Ask them to look for simple feelings such as happy, sad, angry, scared or proud. As they work, move around the class asking them to name the feeling of the person in the selected picture and their reasons for deciding on that feeling. (they are smiling; their eyes look angry) Alternatively, they could photograph their pictures and upload them onto the interactive whiteboard. Each pair then shows and explains their picture to the class, describing what they can see in the person's face or posture that tells them how they are feeling.

Feelings slide show
Students take photographs of each other expressing different emotions. They upload them onto the computer, add a label to name the feeling and create a slide show.

Teddy bear
You will need a soft teddy bear or toy, not necessarily a new one, plus heart-shaped self-adhesive stickers. Alternatively, you could use Velcro dots with some small red cardboard hearts made by the students (you will need to have corresponding Velcro dots on the teddy). Keep them in a container. Each time a student feels that someone has understood their feelings or listened to them talk about their feelings, they tell you about it and then add a heart to the teddy bear. You could also sing 'The Teddy Bear's Picnic' and have a special afternoon tea with small teddy bear biscuits.

Animals and empathy
Observation and care of animals can be the starting point for empathy. Ask students to watch their pets (or the class pet) or ask parents to consider bringing in a pet to share an observation experience with the students. Ask students to observe the animal and comment on what feelings the animal seems to express and how and when they express them. Distressed? Wants something? How do the animal's feelings make the students feel? (if a dog is excited it might make them feel excited too and want to play with the dog; if it seems scared it might make them feel worried too and try to soothe the animal) Students can work with a partner to make a simple digital book (see **Handbook**, page 97) of their observations. They could also make a class book or an individual flipbook (see **Handbook**, page 98) using the sentence: When my… feels… he/she…

Babies and empathy

Observing babies and young children is another way to teach empathy. You could use an observation approach as described above if you have a parent who would be willing to bring in their baby or young child. You could ask students who have a baby or young child in their home to watch, observe and report. Ask them when they know when their baby brother or sister is happy, sad, distressed, hungry, tired and so on. What are some of the things that lead to babies feeling happy, sad, distressed and so on? What can they do to help their baby feel happy, and not sad or distressed?

Circle Time: What kind of surprise?

Take in a nice surprise for the students to start the session, e.g. some small treats, a visiting kitten or baby rabbit, a special book, a video clip or a special song. Then read one of the books listed below. Talk about what a surprise is and how some surprises are pleasant and some are unpleasant. Ask students for examples of when they have felt surprised. Write them on the board. Then write them on pieces of paper and place them into a container. Students can take turns drawing an example out of the container and categorising it as 'unpleasant' or 'pleasant'. Talk to students about nasty practical jokes and tricks and how people do not like the unpleasant surprise that accompanies them. Stress that we need empathy if we are planning a surprise for someone so that we can try to imagine how the other person will feel about it.

→ Follow up with illustrated sentence writing, for example: 'Surprises we like' and 'Surprises we don't like'.

Picture books

Boo!
Preston Pig, the 'Masked Avenger', loves to jump out at night and give people an unpleasant surprise when he yells 'Boo!' His father gives him some of his own medicine but it doesn't completely cure him of his ways. Ask: Why did people not like Preston's surprises? How did they feel when he surprised them? What kind of feelings might they have towards him? How could that affect their relationship with him?

Snap! Went Chester
Chester the crocodile is bored until he discovers that it's great fun to loudly snap his jaws at all the creatures around the waterhole. He enjoys their frightened reactions until eventually a pelican turns on him and snaps back and he realises how bad it feels to be frightened like that.

Scary Bear
When Bear wakes early from his long winter sleep, he decides to find his friends and surprise them. They are certainly surprised, but not in a pleasant way. The other animals are frightened by the arrival of a huge scary bear who doesn't look like their little bear cub friend who went into hibernation. Chaos ensues as Bear scares each new friend without meaning to and becomes increasingly confused by their reactions. At last he realises how they feel and why, and that helps him to solve the problem.

→ Follow up by having pairs of students write the bear's diary entry for that night. Students could also undertake inquiry-based learning about bears and hibernation (see **Handbook**, page 90).

Activity

Making happy surprises

Encourage students to make some happy surprises for others. Ask: How will it be a surprise? Stress that it is a surprise if the person wasn't expecting anything at all, but also a surprise if they were not expecting what you gave them. Stress the importance of trying to imagine how the person might feel about their surprise. They could make:

- birthday cards (using a computer drawing program) for people who didn't expect to get a birthday card from them
- happy cards to cheer someone up or just say hello
- happy rocks for the same purpose (students collect smooth stones from the beach and paint happy scenes on them; one or two coats of varnish afterwards make the pictures last longer)
- surprise boxes with a special message inside (make them from matchboxes or other small boxes)
- a nice surprise for someone in their family (e.g. breakfast in bed for Mum or Dad, setting the table for dinner).

Consolidation: Emotions

Activities

Cut-up sentences

(See **Handbook**, page 89.) Cut these sentences into individual words and place each cut-up sentence into an envelope. Make enough sets for each pair of students to have one set of six envelopes. Each pair reconstructs the six sentences.

- I can be the boss of my feelings.
- We can change a bad mood into a good mood.
- Everyone has good and bad feelings.
- We can be kind to babies and pets.
- We can be kind when a friend feels sad.
- Good thinking helps us feel better.

You can also use the 'Cut-up sentences' e-activity with these sentences.

Reflections

Use the 'Smiley ball' strategy (see **Handbook**, page 92), 'Reflections' e-tool (see **Handbook**, page 92) or the 'Animal asks' e-tool (see **Handbook**, page 89) with statements such as these:

- Tell about one time you were the boss of your angry feelings.
- What is one good way to be the boss of your angry feelings?
- What is one way you can change a bad mood into a good mood?
- Tell about something at school that makes you happy.
- Tell about something at home that makes you happy.
- What is one way you can help someone who is feeling sad?
- What is one way you can help someone who is feeling left out?
- What is something you can do when you feel nervous or worried?

Unit 5

Emotions

Games

Memory cards

Play the 'Memory cards' e-game with the class using words related to feelings. Students can also play the games on the computer individually or with a partner (see **Handbook**, page 91).

Bingo strips

Play 'Bingo strips' (see **Handbook**, page 89).

angry	lonely
bored	nervous
cross	pleased
disappointed	proud
excited	sad
frightened	scared
happy	unhappy
jealous	worried

Other games

The following games also reinforce the key concepts in this unit.
- 'Cross-offs' e-game (see **Handbook**, page 89). The secret message is 'Be the boss of your feelings'.
- 'Secret word' e-game (see **Handbook**, page 92). The secret word is 'Feelings'.

Resources

A complete list of resources (including references for books, poems, films, websites and weblinks for songs) is available on Pearson Places.

Unit 6

Relationships

Key points

Getting along well with others and making friends will make you feel happier.
If you have good friendships and can get along well with others, you will be happier. It's fun to do things with friends and friends are good to talk to when you are worried or upset.

No one has friends all the time. Everyone feels lonely sometimes.
Many people have times in their life when they feel like they don't have a friend, but this is usually only for a short time. If you try to get to know people and get on well with other people, you will make some friends.

Sometimes friendships change and are no longer as strong as they were.
People change as they grow and friendships don't always last. Sometimes your friends move on to other friendships and don't spend as much time with you any more. Sometimes you are the one who moves on and lets the friendship go. This is normal and it happens to everyone at some points in their life. It doesn't mean anything bad about you.

It takes hard work to learn how to get along with other people and be a good friend.
We aren't born knowing how to be a friend and get along with others. We all have to learn how to do it just like we have to learn to read and do maths. Then we have to practise what we have learned. To get along well with someone else you have to stop and think about their feelings, not just your own. You also have to think about what is fair for them as well as fair for you.

Social skills are things that you can do to get along well and make friends.
People will want to keep playing with you if you play fairly and you are a good winner and loser. They will like you more if you share and take turns, if you are kind, if you are thoughtful, if you smile a lot and talk to them, and if you tell them a little bit about yourself.

If you want to HAVE a good friend, then you have to BE a good friend.
You are more likely to find someone who wants to be your special friend if you act like a good friend towards them. A good friend is loyal, kind and thoughtful, stands up for their friend, spends time with them, tells their friend about their feelings, listens to their friend's problems and keeps their friend's secrets. A good friend looks for the good things their friend does.

It's OK to have more than one friend.
Many people have more than one friend at a time. However, sometimes you may not have a friend for a while or you may only have one friend. It's good to try to make friends with several people because there usually are a lot of nice people to be friends with and, if one of your friends is away, the rest of you can play together.

It's OK to have an argument as long as you don't hurt the other person.
Disagreement (also called conflict) is what happens when people don't agree, when they want different things or when they think someone has been unfair. You have to speak up when you think that things are not fair or when you don't agree about something but you need to do so in a way that doesn't hurt someone else and remember to try to see things from their point of view as well. It is important to find a way to disagree that lets you find a solution to the problem and still be friends.

You can't sort things out until you are the boss of your angry feelings.
The main reason why people try to hurt other people when they disagree is because they get angry and then they can't remember the good things to do to sort out the disagreement. You have to try hard to be the boss of your angry feelings if you want to sort out arguments in a way that lets you still be friends. See Unit 5: Emotions for activities on anger management.

Unit 6

Relationships

Circle Time: Feeling shy and lonely......121
Picture books 121
  The Very Lonely Firefly
  The Lonely Little Bear
  The Shy Little Girl
  So Shy
  Will I Have a Friend?
  I'll Be Your Friend Smudge

Circle Time: Getting to know others.....122
Picture books 122
  Crusher Is Coming!
  Big Al
Activity 123
  Someone in my class I don't know very well
Drama................................123
  Getting to know someone

Circle Time: What do children like about other children?......................123
Picture books 124
  The Rainbow Fish
  The Biggest Boast
  I'm Terrific
  Franklin Is Bossy
  A Weekend with Wendell
  Friends
  Kickball Rules
Activity 125
  Friendship mobile

Circle Time: It's important to listen well when people talk to you 125
Game 125
  Chinese whispers
Activities............................125
  Picture listening
  'Good listening ears' morning talk
  Class books: About me
Game 126
  Who am I?
Activity 126
  Common bonds

Circle Time: Being noticed.............127

Circle Time: Including others..........127
Activity 127
  Take a bow! Social feedback sessions

Circle Time: Friendship 129
Activities............................129
  Smiley ball: Making friends
  Matchbox jigsaw
Song................................129
  'Consider Yourself'

Circle Time: Making new friends........130
Picture books 130
  Franklin's New Friend
  Do You Know Millie?
  A Visitor for Bear
  Bear's New Friend
  Clancy and Millie and the Very Fine House
  Jessica's Box
  Stinky! or 'How the Beautiful Smelly Warthog Found a Friend'
  Quincy and Oscar
Activity 131
  New friends poster and tree

Circle Time: Being a good friend........131
Picture books 131
  My Friend John
  Frog and Toad Are Friends
  Is That What Friends Do?
  I Very Really Miss You
  Emily and Alfie
Song................................132
  'You've Got a Friend in Me'
Activity 132
  Friendship collage

Circle Time: Friends can be different 133
Picture books 133
  Bear and Chook
  Cat and Fish
  Chester's Way
  Henry and Amy
  A Rainbow of Friends
Activity 134
  Rainbow friendship hands wreath

Circle Time: Friendship and loyalty......134
Song................................134
  'Together, Wherever We Go'
Picture books 134
  Alice and Anatole
  Giddy the Great
  Wombat Stew
  The Ugliest Dog in the World

Circle Time: How to be a thoughtful friend..............................135
Picture book 135
  Wombat Divine
Activities............................136
  The Tigger Movie
  Friendship lift-up flaps
  Making a friendship circle

119

Circle Time: Being separated from a friend **136**
Picture books 137
   Amy and Louis
   We Are Best Friends
   Best Friends Together Again
   Alexander Who's Not (Do You Hear Me? I Mean It!)
     Going to Move
Activity 138
   Class wall chart or poster

Circle Time: Good and bad ways to disagree **138**
Picture books 138
   Elephant and Crocodile
   The Rainbow Fish and the Blue Whale
   Pumpkin Soup
   Chill
Activity 139
   The problem-solving mat

Circle Time: Apologising and being friends again. **139**
Drama 139
   Saying sorry
   Fights and arguments
Activity 140
   Practising negotiation and fair deals

Consolidation: Relationships **140**
Activities 140
   Cut-up sentences
   Friendship tree
   Friendship mobile
   Photos
   Design a friendship card
   Discussion: How to treat a friend who visits
   Are you a good friend?
   Reflections
Games 141
   Bingo strips
   Other games

Resources. **142**

Unit 6

Relationships

Circle Time: Feeling shy and lonely

Read one of the books listed below to introduce the topic of shyness and loneliness. Ask: What is shyness? (When you feel shy, you are scared that the other person will not talk to you or like you. You feel a bit scared about what to say or do.) How does it feel to be shy? How do you know when someone else is feeling shy? Students turn to a partner and tell about one time when they felt shy. Select some students to tell either what they or their partner said. Explain that shyness can look like being unfriendly (even though it isn't) and we should always consider the possibility that someone who seems unfriendly is just shy. Stress that even if you feel shy, it is good to be brave and try to talk to other people to get to know them and to make friends. Remind them that smiling, talking, listening and sharing are the main ways in which people make friends and that most people are kind and responsive and will want to talk to you if you try to be friendly. Discuss loneliness in the same way.

→ Follow up by having pairs of students talk about good things to do if you feel shy or lonely and want to get to know other people.

Picture books

The Very Lonely Firefly
A lonely firefly, while looking for a friend, mistakenly tries to interact with headlights, lanterns and fireworks. Eventually he finds another firefly. The last page contains a battery that makes the page of fireflies light up.

The Lonely Little Bear
A lonely little toy polar bear cannot find a home and ends up being placed at the top of the highest shelf in the toy shop. There are other toys in the same predicament but they eventually find new owners. Even when he is bought, the child returns him to the toy shop because she really wanted a racing car. Finally he is bought for Eleanor, who adores him, and he no longer feels lonely or rejected.
→ Ask: What can we learn from this story about feeling lonely and coping with feeling rejected? Stress that everyone feels lonely and rejected sometimes and that's normal. Not everyone we meet will like us just as we don't like everyone we meet. The solution to feeling lonely (and perhaps rejected) is to keep busy with things we enjoy doing and get to know other people by smiling, saying hello, telling them a bit about yourself, listening to what they say and showing interest and doing things together that you both like.

The Shy Little Girl
Anne never raises her hand to answer a question in class because she is too shy. She doesn't like her freckles and her soft voice. She never invites anyone home and spends most of recess time by herself looking for flowers. In the beginning of the story, Anne's isolation is shown by her being depicted in colour while the rest of the children are in black and white. A new girl called Claudia arrives at school and befriends Anne. She shares Anne's love of nature and brings out the best in her. Soon Anne is acting more confidently, speaking more clearly and loudly, and being more involved in classroom activities.
→ Ask:
◉ How did making friends with Claudia help Anne to be less shy?
◉ If Claudia hadn't arrived, what could Anne have done to be less shy?

So Shy
Jake is shy and lonely and hasn't been able to make friends. His only playmate is his shadow. When Jake comes across a girl who is crying because her cat is stuck in a tree, he forgets his own shyness and helps her to rescue it. This is the start of his first friendship.

Will I Have a Friend?

Jim is worried on his first day at school that he might not have a friend. For much of the day he is lonely and by himself, but then he meets someone who feels the same way and it's the start of a friendship.

→ Ask the students how Jim's friendship started (because the two boys began to talk and listen to each other, shared their feelings and enjoyed playing with similar things). Ask: What else could Jim have done to make a new friend?

I'll Be Your Friend Smudge

Smudge is a little mouse and she is having her first birthday in her new house in a new neighbourhood. Smudge feels sad and lonely because she doesn't know anyone in her new neighbourhood and has no one to invite to her birthday party. Hare comes across Smudge and notices that she is crying. He befriends her and introduces her to others. Her new playmates gather for her birthday tea.

→ Discuss how you could help someone get to know other people by introducing them to people you know. Students could act out some of the suggested ideas and practise the social skill of introducing people to each other.

Circle Time: Getting to know others

Before reading one of the stories below, ask the school librarian to help you find a really good (but short) story book to read to the students that has a boring or tatty cover (or put a brown paper cover on the one you choose to read). Show this to them and then read it. Talk about the expression 'You can't judge a book by its cover'. Ask what it means. Ask students for examples of times when they have thought someone was mean or unfriendly or not nice, but then they found out that they weren't like that at all, and that they were just shy or someone had said unkind things about them. Ask students to volunteer information about themselves that they think others might not know (e.g. born in another country/state/town; their pet's name; their favourite colour/toy/ice-cream flavour/book/movie) to demonstrate that it can take a while to get to know someone and find out what kind of person they really are.

→ Follow up by having students make an individual flipbook (see **Handbook**, page 98) titled 'I bet you didn't know that I ...'.

Picture books

Crusher Is Coming!

'Crusher' has a reputation at school as an aggressive and nasty bigger boy. When he comes to stay for a few hours at Peter's house, Peter realises that he has believed all the stories about Crusher and that in fact Crusher is actually kind and gentle and not at all as he expected.

→ Ask: What message does the name 'Crusher' give us? How do we expect someone with that name to act and behave? Does Crusher live up to our expectations? What do the pictures tell us?

Big Al

This is the story of a very ugly and mean-looking fish who finds it hard to make a friend because he looks so big and mean. Eventually he is accepted for who he is and the other sea animals realise they have misjudged him.

Unit 6

Relationships

Activity

Someone in my class I don't know very well

Draw a picture of balloons with strings, one for each student in the class. Write a student's name in each and make a copy for each child. Ask students to colour in the name balloon of anyone in the class they don't know very well. With some students who don't read well, you will need to do this individually and then put a small colour slash in the balloons they select so they can finish off colouring. Alternatively, you could use a camera or scanner to make a sheet with photos in each balloon and ask students to cut out the ones they don't know very well and glue them on a sheet of paper. An older student or buddy may like to take on this task. Use this information to pair students who don't know each other well for activities or to organise them to play together with Lego, a card game, etc. Encourage them to find out two interesting things about their new partner that they can tell the class. You could also ask students to complete **BLM 6.1: About Me**, and swap with their new partner to encourage them to talk with each other. You could also use some of the cooperative activities in Unit 1: Core values.

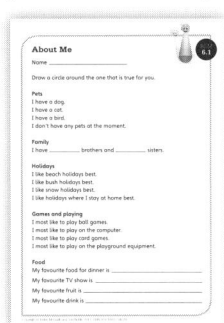

Drama

Getting to know someone

Set up some drama activities (with students acting or as a puppet play) based on getting to know someone:

- in the playground at the park (stress safety here)
- who has moved in next door to you
- who is new to your class
- who is at a family party that you go to.

After each enactment, ask the class: What did they do well? (Elicit several answers.) What is one thing they could have done to make this even better? (Elicit only one or two answers.) A good opening line is 'Hello. My name is (Tyson). I like ice-cream. Do you?'

Circle Time: What do children like about other children?

Start by asking the students to use the 'Lightning writing' strategy (see **Handbook**, page 91) on the topic of what they know about children who are good to play with. Ask students to talk about the people they like to play with and say why. Place the emphasis on what they do rather than who they are so that students feel encouraged to use more successful behaviours, such as:

- being kind and generous
- cooperating
- sharing and taking turns
- playing fairly, and being a good winner and loser
- being a good listener
- sharing information about themselves
- having good ideas for games or activities.

→ Follow up by asking selected students to mime a good way to be liked or a bad way to be liked. Use the 'Who is good to play with?' e-activity with the whole class or with students working in pairs on the computer.

Picture books

The Rainbow Fish
Introduce the topic of getting along well with other students by reading this book (original version only) to the class. This is a simple book that makes the point that if you share with others and show some generosity people will like you more. The rainbow fish has lovely shiny scales but nobody is keen to be his friend until he realises that he needs to share his lovely scales, not just boast about having them.
→ Follow up by having students make a rainbow fish from a paper plate covered with pieces of pink, blue and silver foil, with a mouth and a tail.

The Biggest Boast
Ben and Sally are lonely at school and become friends but Ben finds Sally boasts an awful lot, especially about her father who Sally claims to be everything from a rock star to an astronaut. When her fabrications become apparent, Ben and Sally are able to sort it out and stay friends.
→ Follow up by discussing what 'boasting' is and asking why children don't like to hear other children boasting. Ask selected students to act out either 'boasting' or 'just giving information about yourself' and see if the other students can work out which one it is. Let each student draw a card from a container that tells them which one to act out.

I'm Terrific
Jason Bear awards himself gold stars for being so helpful, hardworking, organised and thoughtful. He tells everyone how terrific he is, and alienates all his potential friends until he works out how not to boast.

Franklin Is Bossy
Franklin, a young turtle, is alienating all his friends because he is being selfish and bossy. He won't listen to their ideas or take turns and he always wants things to be his way when they are deciding what to do or play. After spending some time alone, he realises he needs to change his behaviour.

A Weekend with Wendell
Wendell is spending the weekend at Sophie's house but Wendell always makes sure that things go the way he wants them to and Sophie feels unfairly treated and ignored. Wendell also likes teasing and playing tricks on Sophie, who dislikes being annoyed in this way. Eventually, Sophie has had enough and finds that being assertive can save a friendship.
→ Discuss what 'assertive' means (standing up for yourself without being nasty or hurting the other person) and why it is important to be assertive if things really aren't fair or you are being mistreated.

Friends
A rabbit named Oscar moves to a new neighborhood but finds it difficult to make friends because he only wants to do what he likes (mostly swimming) and gets grumpy about doing the things the others want to do. He stays lonely for a few days and then realises that there has to be some compromise and consideration for what others want to do.

Kickball Rules
Barney isn't much fun to play with because he always wants to be the boss of the game and keeps changing the rules without anyone else having a say in the decision. Eventually, the other children get sick of it and decide that they won't play kickball with him. He starts to realise that if he doesn't change his way of doing things, then he won't have anyone to play with.

Unit 6

Relationships

Activity

Friendship mobile

Students can make a mobile (see **Handbook,** page 99) with pictures on cards to illustrate the kind and caring things that children can do for each other and the behaviours that help them to make fiends and get along well with others. Images can be found in magazines or on the Internet.

Circle Time: It's important to listen well when people talk to you

Start with a brief drama activity for a pair of students. Have a private chat beforehand with the 'second' student in this activity so they know what to do. Ask one student to talk about their pet or holiday, while the second one makes sure that they do not look at them while they are speaking. Then ask the student who spoke how it felt when the other person didn't look at them or pay attention. Repeat the activity several times with different pairs to make the point. These re-enactments will be different to the first one as students will be aware that one person is being ignored. Discuss how we show interest in another person (e.g. by making eye contact when they speak, listening and asking good questions based on what they said).

Game

Chinese whispers

Play 'Chinese whispers' to demonstrate how easy it is to *not* listen properly. Use sentences such as:
- If you go to the beach, remember not to leave your rubbish there and to take your towel home.
- If you don't shut the door properly, the cat might get out and run away again like he did last time.
- Vegetables, fruit and fish are good for you and you should eat them often.
- If you want to get on well with others, remember to be kind and share.

Keep records (that the students can see or be told about) of how similar/different each sentence sounded when it got to the last person in the circle. Then play the 'Whisper game' (see **Handbook,** page 92).

Activities

Picture listening

Cut out a selection of general magazine pictures or pictures based on your current theme. Try to include pictures with people in them. Place each picture in an envelope so that you have two envelopes for each pair of students. The students can help with this preparation. Prepare a series of questions (see below) that can be asked about the pictures and write them on cards. Go through the questions as a class to ensure that the students understand them. Add a picture prompt to each card if needed. Place one question in each envelope with each picture. Examples:
- What colours are in the picture?
- What are the people in the picture like?
- What can you see in this picture?

125

- Do you like this picture? Why?
- What does this picture remind you of/make you think about?

In pairs, one student takes out the picture from the envelope and shows it to the other. The other reads out the question and then answers it. Then the first student briefly sums up what was said. (*You said that you like this picture because it makes you feel happy.*) Remind them that the summing up doesn't have to include everything they said, just the most important part of it. They swap roles with the second envelope. On a signal they can place the pictures and the questions back in the envelopes and pass them on to another pair.

'Good listening ears' morning talk

Make three sets of big ears out of cardboard and attach each set to a headband. Alternatively, buy large ears from a novelty/bargain shop. When you have morning talk, choose three students to be the 'best listener' and to wear the 'Good listening ears'. Their job is to give a quick summary of what the person said. Remind them to leave out detail and just say the most important bits. Alternatively, place all students' names in a container (they could make their own name cards) and after each person has spoken, draw a name and ask that person to give a brief summary while wearing the 'Good listening ears'. Make sure that the students know in advance that this will happen.

Class books: About me

Ask: Why is it important to remember what someone has told you about themselves? Discuss why we like it when someone remembers our name and details about us. Emphasise that remembering things about people helps them to see that we are interested in them and like them. Students complete **BLM 6.1: About Me** with information about themselves (if you haven't used this BLM before). Then make a class book (see **Handbook**, page 97) of everyone's completed sheets and leave time for students to read and look at it. Then match students according to similar answers for a five-minute 'chat session'.

Game

Who am I?

Each student can use their completed **BLM 6.1: About me** and other information to make a 'Who am I?' sheet with four or five personal facts on it. Mix them up, hand them out and then have students try to work out who the person is. For example:

- I am a girl.
- I have a pet goldfish.
- I like to play skipping.
- I have two younger sisters.

This can be done at the front of the class or in pairs.

Activity

Common bonds

Have students write 'Me too' on a paper plate and attach a craft stick as a handle. Discuss why people are more likely to become friends and get along well if they both like some similar things and have some of the same kinds of experiences in their life. Ask individual students about their likes, interests and families, and ask students to raise their paper plate if they like the same thing, e.g. 'Raise your paper plate if you like to play checkers like Milly does'. This could also be used as a Circle Time activity.

Unit 6

Relationships

Circle Time: **Being noticed**

Ask three or four of the more socially confident students to 'perform' in some way (e.g. tell a riddle, sing a song, say a nursery rhyme, do a very high jump). Talk about how they all enjoyed doing it in front of the class. Ask: Why do we like other people to notice us and pay attention to us? Does everyone like this? (No, some children do not. They feel a bit shyer about being noticed in a group, but they are not necessarily shy with a friend.) Students then turn to the person next to them and talk about some good ways to try to get other students to notice you and get to know you. Select some students (or ask what their partner said) to share with the class. Then ask for some of the bad ways that students try to be noticed.

→ Follow up by having pairs each contribute one good or bad way of being noticed to a class poster. Then use the 'Good and bad ways' e-activity as a whole class or with pairs on a computer.

Circle Time: **Including others**

There are links to this topic in Unit 1: Core values (see page 1).

Ask students to write or draw about a time when someone let them into a game. Discuss what they have written. Ask: Why is it good to let someone who is by themselves join in your games? How does it feel when you are included? Not included? How does it feel when you have made someone happy by including them? How do you know when someone would like to be included in what you are doing? Ask individual students: What are some ways to let someone else join in your game or activity? Give them specific examples of games, e.g. Tiggy, skipping, Lego, a card game.

→ Follow up by having students act out inviting someone in to a specific game or activity (or have them write and draw about some good ways to do this).

Consider having a Friendship Committee (lasting for a week at a time), in which three or four students look for other students in the class who are by themselves at lunchtime. Then they can ask them if they would like to play and either invite them to join the 'committee' in a game/activity or take other action to facilitate their inclusion in other people's games or activities. It is helpful to brainstorm (as a class) some lunchtime games and activities that they could organise for this purpose. Over the year, try to have different combinations of three or four students work in this committee for a week at a time.

Activity

Take a bow! Social feedback sessions
This strategy is designed to improve students' behaviour in getting along with others through positive peer feedback. Have two sessions of 20 to 30 minutes each week (preferably just before lunch or recess) in which students work cooperatively in pairs or in small groups of three. This might be an educational game or any activity where they work with a 'learning partner'. Using **BLM 6.2: Take a Bow! Cards,** make enough Applause cards for about half of the students in the class and enough Performance cards for the rest. All cards should be the same colour and students shouldn't be able to see through them.

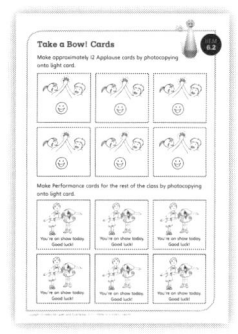

Briefing session

Before you first use this strategy, explain that each week there will be one or two 'Take a bow!' sessions when the class will practise the skills of getting along well with others. During this activity, one student in each pair will give positive feedback to the other student whenever they see or hear them using good 'getting along' behaviours. Ask the students if they can remember and describe some examples of behaviours that help people to get along well with others. Encourage them to focus on social skills such as: sharing resources, sharing the work, cooperating with others, taking turns with equipment, taking turns to talk, playing fairly, being a good winner or loser, listening to others and showing interest, being thoughtful, sorting things out in a friendly way if disagreement occurs, etc.

Put students into pairs. Ask each student to write down a different number between 1 and 10. Then the teacher does the same. The student in each pair whose number is closest to the teacher's number gets a Performance card and is the 'Performer' for that activity. If the two numbers are equally close to the teacher's number, the one closest to 1 is the Performer. Having a Performance card means that they must try very hard to use good 'getting along' behaviours. The other student in each pair is given an Applause card. This means they watch for whenever their partner uses good 'getting along' behaviours and give them positive feedback in one of the following ways:

◎ A smiley gesture: The student looks at the other student, smiles and makes a semi-circle (facing up) smile with their thumb and index finger from one hand. Then they also make a positive verbal comment about what the student did well.

◎ A two-finger clap: The student looks at the other student, smiles, gives a two-finger clap using their index fingers and makes a positive verbal comment about what the student did well.

◎ A very gentle high or low five: They say 'High/Low five' to signal the other student to get ready and then gently clap one of their hands against one of the other student's outstretched hands while making a positive verbal comment about what the student did well.

Positive comments might be:

◎ A 'thank you' comment, e.g. 'Thank you for (sharing/helping me/listening well, playing fairly, etc.).'

◎ A 'well done' comment, e.g. 'You shared the felt pens very well'; 'You cooperated well'; 'You listened well to what other people were saying.'

◎ An 'I noticed' comment, e.g. 'I noticed that you cooperated a lot when we were playing the game. That was great.'

◎ An 'I liked' comment, e.g. 'I liked the way you listened so well when I was explaining my idea to you.'

You may find it helpful to have a short 'briefing' time with just the observing group and give each one a copy of **BLM 6.3: Good Ways to Get Along with Others** as a prompt.

While the session is taking place, wander around the room and make some notes on how effectively and regularly the students with Applause cards are giving feedback and give them positive feedback on this in a short 'debriefing' at the end of the activity. Consider providing occasional whole-class rewards (e.g. free time or a special game) for any observed improvement in the effective use of some (or all) of the 'getting along' behaviours by the class.

You can also use this activity in a whole-class setting where everyone is working or playing independently or in groups of various sizes or in different parts of the room. Give Applause cards to ten students and, if possible, identify them in some way (e.g. by asking them to wear a coloured sash) so that the students with the Applause cards don't give feedback to other students with Applause cards.

Unit 6

Relationships

Circle Time: **Friendship**

Introduce the topic of friendship by using the 'Smiley ball' activity below. Alternatively, use a 'Round table' activity (see **Handbook**, page 92). In a group of three, the students pass around the sheets and write:
- one good thing to say or do to be a good friend to someone
- one thing that children do with their friends
- a word that describes how you feel when you are with your friends.

Use their sheets to launch the Circle Time discussion. Ask: Why do we like to have friends? Where do we meet the people who become our friends? Ask selected students to talk about their very first friend and where they met them. Do they still spend time with that person?

→ Follow up by having students write about how and where they met one of their friends. Students can sing 'Consider Yourself' (see below) as a class, then discuss what the song means about friendship.

Activities

Smiley ball: Making friends
(See **Handbook**, page 92.) Use the smiley ball to elicit responses to these questions:
- What is a friend?
- Why do we like having friends?
- How do you meet people who become your friends?
- What are some good ways to get to know another child you meet with your parents at the playground or at the beach?
- What are some good ways to get to know another student who is new to the class?

→ Follow up by having students make a class book (see **Handbook**, page 97) using the sentence: 'One good way to get to know someone you don't know very well is…' Here are some suggestions:
- smile
- say hello and tell them what your name is, then ask what their name is
- say, 'I have a dog. Her name is Mimi. Do you have a dog?' (or something similar)
- tell them something interesting about your pet or your house or your toys or your holiday and ask them about theirs
- talk about something you think is good fun to do
- start to do whatever they are doing
- ask them a question about their pets, their holidays or their toys.

Matchbox jigsaw
Students can make a matchbox jigsaw using a scanned photograph of themselves and a friend. Each jigsaw needs nine matchboxes. Each picture is cut into nine equal rectangles to match each matchbox. Paste onto the matchboxes.

Song

'Consider Yourself'

129

Circle Time: Making new friends

Choose one or more of the books below to read to the class. Ask students to talk to the person next to them about some good ways to make new friends. Ask each pair to say one of their ideas and make a board chart. Discuss times when students have found it hard to make friends. (when going to a new school; starting in a club or team; moving to a new neighbourhood) Discuss: How would you try to make new friends if you had to move to a new school in a new area? Some good suggestions might be:

- join a club (e.g. an athletics club or Cubs)
- join a sports team
- look for someone friendly and ask them to help you get to know people
- introduce yourself to someone and ask them about themselves. Don't forget to smile and look interested.

Picture books

Franklin's New Friend
Franklin, a little turtle, gets some new neighbours—the Moose family—and they are BIG! Franklin's teacher, Mr Owl, asks him to be Moose's buddy at school and help him to get to know the school and the other students. Initially Franklin is scared of Moose because he is so much bigger than Franklin, but he soon realises that despite their differences, Moose is now a new friend.

Do You Know Millie?
Sarah and her family are moving to the city and she has to leave her friends behind. To cheer her up, a neighbour tells her that Millie lives in the big city and will be her friend. When she and her family arrive in the city, Sarah asks the furniture removalist, the pilot of the plane, the taxi driver, the hotel porter, the postman, the cashier who works in the supermarket, the hairdresser, the policeman, a whole team of footballers and a team of workmen if they know Millie and where she lives. Their amusing responses will make students chuckle (as will the sly detail in some of the illustrations). Sarah finally finds Millie in a serendipitous way.

A Visitor for Bear
Bear is grumpy, fastidious and self-contained and he seems very happy living by himself. He even has a sign posted on his door that says 'No visitors'. A mouse who knocks on Bear's door looking for friendship is told to go away, but he doesn't give up that easily. Eventually, Bear realises it's actually very pleasant having someone else around to share jokes and stories with.

Bear's New Friend
The bear in this story is the character from *Bear Snores On*. One summer morning as Bear is heading off to play, he hears someone in the trees but can't work out who it is. He uses a process of elimination to work out that it isn't any of his current friends and finally a new friend (Owl) reveals himself. The clue is in the repetition by the animals of the word 'Who?'

Clancy and Millie and the Very Fine House
Clancy is unhappy about moving from his old house even if the rest of his family thinks the new house is better. He finds it large and lonely and he feels very sad. While he is playing among the packing boxes he meets Millie, the little girl next door, and together they invent a game using the boxes to build a 'safe' house like the one that the three little pigs built. Finding a new friend helps him to cope with the changes.

Jessica's Box
Jessica is excited about her first day at school and is particularly keen to make new friends. To make it easier to make new friends she takes a box in which she has packed her favourite teddy bear, hoping that other students will be interested and want to be her friend. But this doesn't work as she had planned and the other students laugh at her. She persists in her efforts, putting something new in the box each time but without success. Finally, she gets into the box herself and that attracts the curiosity of a classmate. The basic message is 'Be yourself'.

Stinky! or 'How the Beautiful Smelly Warthog Found a Friend'
This story is about how it feels to be left out and the difficulty of making new friends. Stinky is a beautiful baby warthog who just wants to play. But he's very smelly, and every time he tries to make friends, the nasty flies that surround him create havoc. Finally Stinky makes a friend—a bird who not only doesn't mind the flies but actually enjoys eating them.

Quincy and Oscar
The themes of this story are belonging and making friends. Oscar and his dog Quincy do everything and go everywhere together. When Oscar and his family move to a new neighbourhood they feel isolated. Oscar feels alone when he goes to his new school each day while Quincy feels all alone when he is at home all day. One day, Oscar takes Quincy to school and finds that classmates want to share experiences with them. Eventually people in the neighbourhood start to join in too.

→ Follow up with a discussion about how pets can help you to make new friends.

Activity

New friends poster and tree
Pairs of students could make a poster or digital poster about what someone could do to make new friends if they moved to a new school. You could also follow up with students making a 'New friends tree'. You will need:
- cardboard
- green paint
- construction paper
- crayons/felt pens.

Cut a tree shape out of cardboard and paint it green. Give students construction paper and have them each design one big leaf. They can draw themselves on one side and write one thing they would try when they wanted to make a new friend on the other. Attach the leaves to the tree.

Circle Time: Being a good friend

Over a few days before the Circle Time session, read some of the books listed below. During Circle Time, discuss what makes a good friend. Ask each student to say one thing that they would like a friend to say or do. Stress that nobody can ever be a perfect friend, so even a very good friend might sometimes disappoint you.

Picture books

My Friend John
The narrator describes his relationship with his friend, John. The boys know each other's secrets, strengths and limitations. One is good at maths but the other is good at spelling.

They have great fun and undertake projects together such as bringing home a dead tree branch and using it to make a pulley system to lift food and furniture (and even the dog) up into their tree. The story is full of acceptance, closeness and unconditional caring.

Frog and Toad Are Friends
This book contains five little stories about Frog and Toad who are friends with very different personalities. Frog is usually quite cheerful, while Toad is a bit more pessimistic. They help and support each other. Toad thinks of a story to cheer Frog up when he feels ill; Frog helps Toad look for a lost button; Toad understands and protects Frog from an embarrassing moment; Frog writes a letter to Toad who is sad because no one has ever sent him a letter.

Is That What Friends Do?
Monkey and Elephant are both by themselves; Monkey offers to be Elephant's friend because he has had lots of experience with friends and Elephant has never had a friend before. Monkey takes the lead and soon is encouraging Elephant to do all the things that he, Monkey, likes doing best such as swinging through trees, with Elephant repeatedly asking 'Is this what friends do?' Elephant isn't having much fun and doesn't have the skills to do these things so he decides to go back to being alone and friendless. Monkey admits that although he has had 'many friends' none of them stayed for very long and he suggests that they try again, which they do because 'That's what friends do'.

I Very Really Miss You
Sam's big brother Ben is going away on a school trip and Sam is glad because it means he can play with all the toys, have the whole bedroom to himself and be free of his big brother's teasing. But Sam starts to miss his big brother. He writes Ben a postcard to say he really misses him and he is surprised to learn that Ben misses him too.
→ Discuss whether your brother or sister can also be your friend.

Emily and Alfie
Emily and Alfie are two penguin friends who venture into an ice cave that their parents have warned them to never explore. They find themselves in a predicament that they need to deal with together.

Song

'You've Got a Friend in Me'
This song is from *Toy Story*.

Activity

Friendship collage
With a partner, students cut out magazine pictures of people being friends and doing things with each other and make a 'Friendship' wall collage. Alternatively, they could find images and words related to friendship on the Internet and make a digital collage, or print them out. As a class they can follow up by singing the song above. Follow up with students playing **BLM 6.4: Friendship Game**.

Unit 6

Relationships

Circle Time: Friends can be different

Students could complete **BLM 6.5: How My Friend and I Are Alike and Different** before this discussion, with a focus on a current or former friend from school or elsewhere. Cousins can also be friends for the purpose of this activity. Read one of the books listed below and then ask each student to give an example from their BLM of one way in which they are different to a friend.

Picture books

Bear and Chook
Two unlikely animals, a polar bear and his mate Chook, are the best of friends. They have very different perspectives on what is important in life. Bear wants to try out a range of adventurous careers when he grows up, and Chook patiently tolerates the madcap schemes, narrowly avoiding injury in the process.

Cat and Fish
Cat lives on the land and Fish lives in the water but they still form a friendship. They try to share in each other's way of life but Fish misses the sea and Cat misses her home. They finally understand each other's different needs and find a solution that will enable them to stay friends. They compromise by living together where the sea and land meet. This is a good example of a negotiated situation where both get part of what they want but not all of it. The book's black and white pen-and-ink illustrations and motifs are similar to the illustrations of M.C. Escher, the batik designs of Southeast Asia and 19th-century engravings in children's picture books.

Chester's Way
Chester and Wilson (animal characters) are best friends and both are creatures of habit who like to do things in very precise ways and stick to their routines. When Lilly moves into the neighbourhood she overwhelms them with her exuberance and chaos. Chester and Wilson avoid her and reject her offers of friendship until they are harassed by some older children and Lilly comes to their rescue. They start to accept her and become friends, discovering that they all have a lot in common.

Henry and Amy
This story is about two friends who are very different from each other. Henry is clumsy and chaotic and finds many things hard to learn but has wonderfully creative ideas. Amy is neat and organised and finds schoolwork easy but is not very creative. Together they make an amazing tree house with wonderful decorations. They are good friends despite being very different.
→ Follow up with an art activity in which students choose one item in Henry and Amy's tree house to make. Find a tree branch for them to hang their items on (or make one from papier mâché).

Discuss how friends are usually similar in some ways but different in other ways too, and that it is important to let your friends feel free to be themselves and not have to pretend to be someone else. Discuss what 'free to be yourself' means.

A Rainbow of Friends
This book highlights the importance of acceptance and celebrates friendships between all kinds of people who are different to each other in terms of viewpoints, interests, dress, strengths and weaknesses. Follow up with the activity below.

Activity

Rainbow friendship hands wreath
What you need:
- different coloured construction paper (one for each student)
- glue
- stickers, felt pens, glitter
- two or three paper plates (one per group), each with the centre cut out

Divide class into two or three groups. Give each student in the group a different coloured sheet of construction paper. Each student traces their hand on the paper and then cuts out their hand print. They decorate their hand print with felt pens, stickers, glitter, etc. Then each group makes a rainbow friendship wreath by gluing or stapling their hand prints around the paper plate. This is a great way of showing that you can put the works of different people together to make something fabulous.

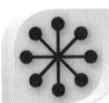

Circle Time: Friendship and loyalty

Introduce the topic of loyalty by reading one of the books listed below. Then ask: What do we mean by 'being loyal'? Ask for examples and encourage students to talk about how members of their family are loyal to each other. Loyalty usually means:
- considering the other person to be special and important to you
- seeing them as more important than the other people in your life (with the exception of family) and putting them ahead of others
- protecting them when you can
- standing up for them in an argument or if someone is being mean to them
- not saying bad things about them behind their back
- helping them when they need it
- keeping their secrets
- remaining their friend even if they are not able to be with you or see you very much
- trying to understand their problems and see their point of view
- saying good things about them to other people.

→ Follow up by having students write sentences about one way they have been loyal to a friend and/or singing the song below.

Song

'Together, Wherever We Go' **PP**

Picture books

Alice and Anatole
This is a story about a shy, lonely girl called Alice and her friendship with an anteater called Anatole. Alice doesn't really know how to make friends at school and is delighted when she discovers that taking the mischievous Anatole to school draws other students to her. She is having so much fun with her new friends that she begins to neglect Anatole, who is rather put out and begins to behave petulantly. After Anatole helps Alice sort out a difficult situation with her shoes, she realises that she has been neglecting a very loyal friend and changes her ways.

→ Follow up with a discussion about whether you can have more than one friend. The message is that it is good to have a number of friends if possible, because if one is away there are others to play or be with.

Giddy the Great
Giddy the Great wants to be the greatest car-racing hill climber in the world. One day he has to make a choice between winning the Giant Pinnacle hill-climbing race and saving his friendship with Edmund the Sheep. Friendship wins out.

Wombat Stew
Platypus, Emu, Lizard, Echidna and Koala help their friend Wombat outsmart the wily dingo who has caught him and wants to eat him.
→ Ask: How did the animals show that they cared about what happened to Wombat?

The Ugliest Dog in the World
This book is about the love of a girl for her very ugly dog. No one else can see much to appreciate in the dog, but she loves him anyway. This book is also used in Unit 2: People bouncing back (see page 47).

Circle Time: How to be a thoughtful friend

Start by reading the book *Wombat Divine* (see below). Discuss: What do we mean when we say that someone is being thoughtful? Thoughtfulness usually means trying to find a good way to make the other person feel special and cared about. Ask students for examples of when people have been thoughtful towards them. Talk about ways that their family members are thoughtful towards people they care about (e.g. parents, siblings, grandparents, neighbours). Then brainstorm all the ways to be thoughtful towards a friend, for example:
- remembering when it is their birthday
- helping them with schoolwork they don't understand
- helping them carry heavy things
- including them in what you are doing
- telling them about what they have missed if they are away from school
- lending them something if they have forgotten their own
- letting them play with something of yours
- listening to them and caring if they have a problem.

→ Make a class book (see **Handbook**, page 97) using the sentence: 'One good way to be thoughtful to a friend is …' Older students can make a poster with a partner.

Picture book

Wombat Divine
The animals are planning their nativity play. Wombat is very excited at the idea of playing a part, but they can't work out what role he can play. He's too big to be Mary and too short to be a king. His friends finally work out how to make the best of his strengths in the play and everyone is delighted. This book is also used in Unit 1: Core values (page 20).

Activities

The Tigger Movie

This Disney movie is based around the theme of friendship. Tigger is sad that he has no family, so his friends, somewhat misguidedly, put on Tigger masks and pretend to be members of his family. Students make tiger masks from the template on **BLM 2.4: Tiger Mask** and act out the story.

Friendship lift-up flaps

Students make lift-up flaps or circles (see **Handbook**, page 97). On the top they write 'One way to be a thoughtful friend is…', with the sentence completed underneath, e.g. 'to share your toys'. Alternatively, they could write 'Is this a good way to be a good friend?' on the top, e.g. 'playing together'. Then write 'Yes' underneath. Another example could be 'hitting someone', with 'No' written underneath. This activity could also be done using a computer.

Making a friendship circle

On a piece of A4 paper, draw a circle with a diameter of approximately 20 cm. Inside this circle draw another one of approximately 7 cm diameter. This becomes a friendship circle. Photocopy or print (on to light card) one copy for each student. They cut around the outside of the large circle and the inside of the small circle so they have a ring. They add words and drawings in the friendship circle. The friendship circles (or rings) are then suspended by a piece of string or stapled to the bulletin board. Here are some ideas for students to use.

- Stand up for friends and be on their side.
- Talk to friends about your feelings.
- Keep friends' secrets.
- Be thoughtful and kind.
- Spend time with friends.
- Look for the good things friends do.
- Help them.

Circle Time: Being separated from a friend

Start with students standing in a circle and use a 'Movers and shakers' activity (see **Handbook**, page 91) using statements about being separated from a friend, for example:

- Show with your face and body how you would feel if you had to move to a new school and be separated from a friend.
- Nod your head if you think that a friendship can continue even if your friend goes to live somewhere else or goes to a new school.
- Shake your head if you think that a friendship will stop if your friend goes to live somewhere else or goes to a new school.
- Flap your arms (like a plane flying) if you have a friend who lives in another country or another state.

When they sit down, students can tell the person next to them how they would think and feel if their friend moved away to another suburb and/or another school. Share some responses. Discuss how the most common reaction is feeling scared, lonely and sometimes angry. Usually the fear is that:

- your friend will make new friends and forget about you
- you will no longer be special to anyone
- you won't find any other friends where you live or at your school
- you will never see your friend again.

Read one or more of the books listed below. In the follow-up discussion, stress that:
- even if your friend has moved, it doesn't mean that everything in your life has been spoiled
- there are lots of other people who will like you and care about you when they get to know you
- these unpleasant feelings will go away again and things will get better
- look the bright side and think:
  - I will see them again
  - I can stay in touch with them
  - I will also find other friends where I live or go to school.

Students can then work with a partner to think of two ways in which the characters in the story could stay in touch with their friend who moved away, for example:
- visiting
- ringing, writing or emailing
- sharing photographs, images and souvenirs from where they have been and what they have done
- using a wiki to organise an activity together
- having a 'Me too day' where they arrange to do the same thing at the same time on the same day
- posting DVDs containing home movies.

Picture books

Amy and Louis
Amy and Louis are next-door neighbours and friends, but Amy's family moves across the world and Louis is anxious that she may not want to be his friend any more.

We Are Best Friends
When his best friend Peter moves away, Robert feels sad and lonely because he no longer has a friend to play with. They stay in touch through letters but they both miss each other. Then Robert forms a new friendship with Will, who is also feeling lonely. The book reinforces the idea that you can have a friendship with more than one person and that even when friends have to separate geographically, they can still be friends.

Best Friends Together Again
This is a sequel to *We Are Best Friends* (above), in which Robert's best friend Peter moved away with his family and both of them felt sad to be apart. In this story Peter comes back for a visit with Robert, who is both very excited and also a bit nervous that Peter might not be the same any more. When Peter arrives they both realise that, although some things are a bit different, the friendship is still strong. As soon as they start playing and having fun together, the differences disappear. When it is time for Peter to return home, they are both excitedly looking forward to their next reunion. The book highlights how friendships don't have to end when people move away.

Alexander Who's Not (Do You Hear Me? I Mean It!) Going to Move
Alexander's family announces that they are moving to a new state. Initially he wails and laments about all the losses attached to moving, but finally starts to see the exciting possibilities. This book is also used in Unit 2: People bouncing back and Unit 4: Looking on the bright side.

Activity

Class wall chart or poster

Make a class wall chart of all the things you can do to stay in touch with a friend who moves. Each student can contribute a small lift-up flap (see **Handbook**, page 97) to paste on the chart. On the front they can write 'A good way to stay in touch with a friend'. Alternatively, make a class poster or a class or individual flipbook (see **Handbook**, page 98) with the sentence: 'If my friend and I couldn't be together, we could…'

Circle Time: Good and bad ways to disagree

Make a copy of **BLM 6.6: Good and Bad Ways to Disagree** for each student. Read one of the books listed below to the class.

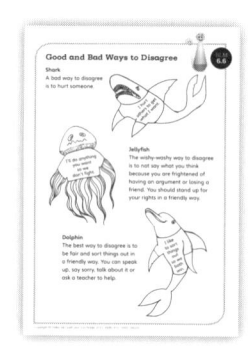

Ask students to make an expression on their face to show how they feel when they have a disagreement with a classmate or friend. Discuss how having a disagreement with someone initially makes most people feel sad, angry and worried. Then ask them to offer other words that mean 'disagreement'. (fight, conflict, argument, problem, dispute) Stress that having a disagreement occasionally is not terrible, it is normal. Even friends have to sort things out and find ways to solve a problem between them and be fair. Disagreements don't necessarily mean the end of friendships. It can actually be helpful to have a disagreement because things can get sorted out. You also learn to trust each other because it shows that the relationship is important to you. Highlight that disagreements occur because people do not agree about what should happen, what did happen or what is fair. Ask: What sorts of things do children argue and disagree about? Make a list on the board. Ask selected students to tell about some of the things they have seen others fight and argue about. Then discuss **BLM 6.6** and apply the three ways to the book(s) you have read, i.e. they can act like a jellyfish (no backbone and so doesn't stand up for itself), a shark (hurts the other person) or a dolphin (speaks up in a friendly voice, says sorry or tries to sort things out peacefully).

Picture books

Elephant and Crocodile
Elephant is angry about the amount of noise that Crocodile makes practising his violin so he takes up the trumpet in competition. Things get worse and worse until eventually tempers flare and Elephant knocks down the wall between their houses. They finally find a peaceful solution to their conflict.

The Rainbow Fish and the Blue Whale
Blue Whale wants to be friends but Rainbow Fish and his friends misunderstand and reject him. In anger, Blue Whale deliberately annoys them. Finally, Rainbow Fish sorts out the conflict with Blue Whale and peace and friendship are the order of the day.

Pumpkin Soup
Every night, Cat, Squirrel and Duck make pumpkin soup together, with each one having their own job to do. One night, Duck decides that this is unfair and that he should have a turn at stirring. This results in major conflict and Duck leaves. They finally realise that they need to sort things out and they reach a compromise.
→ Follow up by making pumpkin soup.

Unit 6

Relationships

Chill
In this story of friendship and making up, Dolly and Jack argue over the pictures that they have painted of each other, with each feeling offended about how they have been portrayed. They calm down and find a way to sort it out

Activity

The problem-solving mat
Make a problem-solving mat (use a large mat or piece of carpet) and display **BLM 6.6: Good and Bad Ways to Disagree**. When two students have a fight over something, you can ask them to both go to the problem-solving mat to deal with it. Have prompts, such as those below, written on a sheet so that they can prepare for a discussion either in a written form or oral form.
- I want…
- I feel…
- My reasons for this are…
- I think you feel…
- I think you want…
- Two things we could do to solve our problem are…
- The first one we could try i…

Circle Time: Apologising and being friends again

Discuss when saying 'sorry' would be helpful in a fight and why. Ask students to talk about times when people have said sorry to them or they have said sorry to others. What was the result? How did it make them feel? Then use large speech bubbles to make a display of different ways to say 'I'm sorry'. For example:
- I didn't mean to upset you.
- I made a bit of a mistake.
- I wish I hadn't said that.
- I didn't really mean what I said.
- Let's be friends again.

Drama

Saying sorry
Read out the following scenarios and ask different students how they would say they were sorry. They could act them out.
- You don't wait for your friend who has to clean up the mess they made when they were cutting out. Afterwards, your friend is unhappy that you didn't wait for them. How do you say you are sorry?
- You take a classmate's best felt pens without asking. How do you say you are sorry?
- You take a classmate's pencil and you accidentally break it. How do you say you are sorry?
- You laugh at a classmate when they make a mistake in reading. How do you say you are sorry?
- You forget to say happy birthday to your friend when you first see them at school on their birthday. Your friend reminds you that it is their birthday. How do you say you are sorry?
- You told the person on the computer that it was your turn and they let you take over. Then you find out it was not your turn. How do you say you are sorry?

Fights and arguments

Use **BLM 6.6: Good and Bad Ways to Disagree** to make jellyfish, shark and dolphin puppets. Students can act out one of the conflict scenarios below and the puppet can whisper good or bad advice in the student's ear. Discuss how the playlets will go before they start. Use 'Freeze frame and rewind' (see **Handbook**, page 89).

- One person pushes in at the tap to wash their hands.
- One person says 'You're stupid'.
- One person will not let another use the scissors at the table because they are using them.
- One person says 'That's my book' and the other says 'It's not'.
- One person is helping the teacher pack up some chairs and another student, who is also supposed to be helping, is doing hardly any work.
- One person is playing alone, kicking a ball, and Jack goes past and kicks it a long way away.
- One person is trying to finish their story on the computer. Kirsty comes over and says she has to use the computer for ten minutes to finish off her story.
- A person's friend told their secret about their parent losing his job.

Activity

Practising negotiation and fair deals

Use games and activities to give students practice in negotiating and both getting a fair deal. The best kinds are those where a decision has to be made. For example:

- Deciding on a Lego structure to build together or a drawing to complete together. They must tell the teacher what they have decided to build before they start.
- Choosing a book together to be read to the class. Give each pair four books to choose from.
- Deciding on a song to sing just before recess or at the end of the day.

Unit 1: Core values (pages 16 to 19) has more cooperative tasks that require negotiation.

Consolidation: Relationships

Activities

Cut-up sentences

(See **Handbook**, page 89.) Cut these sentences into individual words and place each cut-up sentence into an envelope. Make enough sets for each pair of students to have one set of five envelopes. Each pair reconstructs the five sentences.

- It is good to stand up for a friend.
- It is good to be kind to a friend.
- It is good to not tell a friend's secret.
- Friends make you feel special.
- Everyone feels lonely sometimes.

You can also use the 'Cut-up sentences' e-activity with these sentences.

Friendship tree

Place a small tree branch in a pot of sand. Students can cut out boy and girl coloured paper dolls to make a collection for later class use. Whenever a student talks about an act of friendship, they write it on the doll and hang it from the tree.

Unit 6

Relationships

Friendship mobile

Students can make a mobile (see **Handbook,** page 99) with pictures on cards to illustrate the kind and caring things that friends do for each other. Images can be found in magazines or on the Internet.

Photos

Take photographs of students being friends and make a display or a class book (see **Handbook,** page 97).

Design a friendship card

Students can use the computer and a drawing program such as Kid Pix to design and make a friendship card to give to a friend.

Discussion: How to treat a friend who visits

(This could also be an additional Circle Time.) Discuss good ways to treat a friend when they come to your house to play. For example:

- show them what games and toys you have
- ask them what they would like to do and then do what they choose, not just what you like
- show them where the toilet and bathroom are.

Then students can make a smiley-face-shaped and decorated booklet around the theme of 'How to treat a friend who visits you'.

Are you a good friend?

Students can complete **BLM 6.7: Are You a Good Friend?**

Reflections

Use the 'Smiley ball' strategy (see **Handbook,** page 92) 'Reflections' e-tool (see **Handbook,** page 92) or the 'Animal asks' e-tool (see **Handbook,** page 89) with questions such as these:

- What does a good friend do?
- Have you ever been scared of talking to someone in case they didn't like you? What happened?
- Have you ever felt shy? What did you do about it?
- Why is it important to try to sort things out when you disagree with someone?
- What sort of behaviour makes you *not* want to play with someone?
- Why is it important to listen well and show interest?
- What is one way to get to know another child you meet for the first time?

Games

Bingo strips

Use some of these words to play 'Bingo strips' (see **Handbook,** page 89).

anger	hello	shy
argue	kind	smile
disagree	listen	talk
fight	lonely	thoughtful
friend	loyal	
good	new	

141

Other games
The following games also reinforce the key concepts in this unit:
- 'Memory cards' e-game (see **Handbook**, page 91)
- 'Cross-offs' e-game (see **Handbook**, page 89). The secret message is 'You can disagree and still be friends'.
- 'Secret word' e-game (see **Handbook**, page 92). The secret word is 'Friend'.

Resources

A complete list of resources (including references for books, poems, films, websites and weblinks for songs) is available on Pearson Places.

Unit 7

Humour

Key points

Humour is healthy!
When we laugh a lot we stay healthy. Laughter helps our body to fight disease and illness. Humour is like exercise for our mind and our emotions.

Humour can make you feel better.
Having a laugh can make you feel a little bit better when you are feeling unhappy, sad or worried.

You can use humour to help someone else feel a little bit better.
You can cheer someone up when they have a problem, or they are feeling sad or worried, by being funny in a nice way. Stop doing it if the other person says they don't like it.

Humour can help people to be friends.
Friends can have a laugh together and be funny together as a way of saying they like each other.

Laughing should not be used to pretend that you don't feel sad or worried.
Even though laughter can help you feel better when you have a problem, you still need to try to solve the problem, or deal with the unhappy feeling. Laughter doesn't make problems go away. It just helps you to cope with them a little better.

It isn't good to be the class clown.
Trying to be funny to make other students laugh at you is not a good way to behave in class when there is work to be done. It can get you into trouble and stop you from learning well. If you want to try to make other kids laugh, do so at lunchtime or recess. Do it in a good way that doesn't get you into trouble or hurt others.

It is OK to find the funny side to your own problems or bad luck.
It is OK to see the funny side of your own bad luck and bad times. Finding the funny side helps you to not take things too seriously and it can help you to feel more hopeful.

Humour can be hurtful.
It is mean and unkind to laugh at someone else's problems or bad luck. It is also mean to laugh at or make fun of the way another person looks, thinks, speaks or acts. Unkindness can become a habit if you don't stop it quickly.

Note: Check that students' comments, throw-away lines, jokes and riddles are not sexist, racist or offensive to any other group. Monitor classroom humour for put-downs. Students often reply, 'But we were just having a joke'. One good response is 'If you're having a joke, does everyone think it's funny?'

Classroom organisation **145**
   Giggle Gym. 145
   I need an extra laugh today. 145

Circle Time: Humour is healthy! **145**
   Picture books 146
      Suddenly!
      Peace at Last
      The Trouble with Gran
      Nighty Night
      A Nice Walk in the Jungle
      Who's Laughing?
      Why Do I Have to Eat Off the Floor?
      Fearless
      Don't Let the Pigeon Drive the Bus
      A Pig Called Pete
      The Wheels of the Bus
      Jasper McFlea Will Not Eat His Tea
      Bear Snores On
      Bear Wants More

Circle Time: That's nonsense! **148**
   Picture books 148
      The Boy Who Lost His Belly Button
      Parts
      More Parts
      The Wrong Book
      Not Last Night but the Night Before
   Poems and nonsense rhymes 148
      'Upside-down Town'
      'The Owl and the Pussy Cat Went to Sea'
      'Disobedience'
   Activities 149
      Train chants
      Drawing funny trees
   Game 149
      Confusions!
   Poem 150
      'Silly Billies'
   Game 150
      Swimming chickens
   Picture books 151
      Would You Rather?
      If
   Activities 151
      Bundling
      Rating funny stories or poems
      Riddle voting

Circle Time: What makes you laugh? **152**
   Games 152
      Cooperative riddles and answers
      Big lift-up flap riddles

   Activities 152
      Making alien balloon puppets
      Making riddle jars
      Making funny biscuit faces
      Sequencing a funny story

Circle Time: Clowns and the circus. **153**
   Activities 153
      Charlie the clown
      Making funny things
      Funny face flipbooks
      Funny new faces
      Family interview
   Games 154
      Funny face or funny walk competitions
      Stoneface
      Funny memory cards
      Chinese whispers
   Drama. 155
      Mimes

Circle Time: Humour can be hurtful **155**
   Songs. 155
      'The Laughter Song'
      'The Humour Song'
      'Laugh, laugh, laugh'
   Other funny songs, action songs or dances
   and poems 157
      Funny songs
      Funny action songs or dances
      Funny poems
   Funny games and activities. 158
      Mrs Mumbly Bumbly
      Hot potato
      Pass the chicken
      Preposition game (funny version)
      Movers and shakers
      Zoo game
      Speed passing
      Cotton ball relay race
      All up, all catch
      Look, no hands!

Consolidation: Humour **160**
   Activities 160
      Cut-up sentences
      Reflections
   Games 160
      Bingo strips
      Other games

Resources. **160**

Unit 7

Humour

Classroom organisation

Giggle Gym

If possible, have a short (five to fifteen minutes) Giggle Gym session once a day. It could be linked with literacy, language, music, dance, maths or any relevant learning area. Introduce the laughter break by reviewing with students why it is good to have some laughter in your day. (to help you feel relaxed; to help you cope; to give you hope; to keep you healthy; to make you feel less anxious; to build friendships) Choose a humorous or silly dance, game, song, poem, story or book from the suggestions in this unit or from your own collection. You could also have a riddle telling session. Consider making an index file with every humorous poem, book, song, activity, etc. numbered and asking students to draw one number out for each Giggle Gym session. Remove the numbers when they have been drawn out. Replace all numbers every six weeks to make sure of a good mix. You could also offer students the chance to vote on what will be in Giggle Gym next week. You can combine this with behaviour management or practising social skills. Provide points (or point cards) for specified behaviours. Students who earn three points during the previous week can vote on what will be in the Giggle Gym sessions for the next week.

I need an extra laugh today

Explain to students that if they are having a hard day or feeling upset or worried, they can ask for an extra laughter exercise. If this is asked for, provide a very brief extra five-minute activity if you can fit it in. Silly songs and poems are probably the quickest things. If more than one student asks on a given day (and this is unusual), use the same extra session for all of them. This is another way of encouraging students to talk to someone if they are feeling down.

Circle Time: **Humour is healthy!**

Start by reading a short funny story book from those listed on the next pages or from your own collection. Follow this by asking each student to say any word that they think of about humour or being funny. (joke, laugh, giggle, etc.) Write each word on the board. Then ask students to help you to categorise the words: Which words are a kind of laugh? Which ones are things that people laugh at? Then ask: Who likes funny stories? Who likes funny TV shows? Who likes cartoons? What is humour? Why do we like to laugh? Can anyone tell us why laughing is good for us? (laughing and seeing the funny side helps us cope and feel stronger; it helps us to feel more hopeful when we are sad or worried, i.e. it helps us to think that things will get better soon; it helps us to relax our bodies, feel less worried and stay healthy because our bodies fight illness and disease better if we laugh; it helps us to have good friendships when we laugh together) Ask: Can anyone tell us about a time when something sad or worrying happened in their lives or in their family but people were able to find one small thing about it to laugh about?

→ Follow up by having students write and draw (e.g. sentences, a poster, a flipbook or digital class book—see **Handbook**, page 97) about why it is good to laugh.

Picture books

Suddenly!
The plot of this silly little book involves a wolf trying to sneak up and eat the main character, who is unaware that he is being followed. Each time the wolf lunges at him, the main character unwittingly manages to escape by sheer good luck.
→ Follow up with students acting out the scenes.

Peace at Last
Father Bear suffers badly from insomnia one night, and when he finally falls asleep as dawn breaks, the alarm goes off and the children run in and jump all over him.

The Trouble with Gran
The trouble with Gran is that she is really an alien from outer space and occasionally reveals her true self.

Nighty Night
This is a simple story with little plot in which some piglets are going to bed. They give lots of different reasons for not going to sleep and at the end they need to go 'wee'!

A Nice Walk in the Jungle
Miss Jellaby's class is eaten by a boa constrictor on an excursion but she manages to get them back.
→ Follow up by having students draw a boa constrictor using Kid Pix. Then have the class sing 'I'm Being Swallowed by a Boa Constrictor'.

Who's Laughing?
Hippo is trying to get some sleep but every time he starts to drift off, someone starts laughing. On each page, Hippo asks 'Who's laughing?' and on the opposite page a partially hidden animal (e.g. a donkey, a lion) laughs their unique laugh. With his friend, a little blue bird, Hippo sets off to find the answer and discovers that it is Hippo himself who's laughing because Monkey is tickling everyone with a feather.
→ Follow up with a digital class book (see **Handbook**, page 97) about animals that laugh.

Why Do I Have to Eat Off the Floor?
This humorous tale is based around the kinds of questions and answers that a child would typically ask a parent. The twist is that the questions are being asked not by a child, but by Murphy, a pet dog. The girl answers her pet's questions patiently but finally needs to remind him that he is in fact a dog, not a human.

Fearless
Fearless is a scary-looking bulldog but he's really quite friendly. When he bares his teeth to smile at people they think he is about to bite them, which makes Fearless feel confused and disappointed. When a burglar breaks into the family house, Fearless ends up catching him by trying to befriend him. The humorous illustrations are very appealing.

Don't Let the Pigeon Drive the Bus
There is a pigeon on the school bus with an overwhelming desire to drive the bus. The bus driver has to leave for a while, and tells the reader not to let the pigeon drive the bus. The bird then begins his campaign to drive by pleading sweetly with the reader and the kids on the bus to let him be the driver. Everyone replies 'No' to his repeated requests so he starts to bargain, and then moves to petulant whining. Finally, he throws a full-on tantrum. The driver returns and the pigeon leaves in a huff but then starts to transfer his interest to driving to a beautiful tractor trailer parked nearby. The students will really enjoy the repetitive refrain.

→ Follow up with a discussion about young children and their temper tantrums, and responsibility. Ask:
◎ Did you ever act like this when you were younger?
◎ Have you ever seen a preschooler behave like this?
◎ Did the children/reader act responsibly when they wouldn't let the pigeon drive the bus?

Ask the students to act out the story.

The pigeon has its own website for children (see the Resources list on Pearson Places).

A Pig Called Pete

Pete the Pig is a very different type of pig. For a start, he isn't pink (he's purple), he isn't smelly (he washes twice a day) and he doesn't like to play in the mud. And this pig can fly. He travels all over the world 'just for fun' and, for example, to dance the Can Can in Paris, climb the Great Pyramid of Giza and eat cucumber sandwiches in London with the Queen.

→ Follow up by having students draw and write or make digital stories (see **Handbook**, page 97) about additional places and experiences for Pete.

The Wheels of the Bus

This book is based on the classic children's song. A collection of cartoon-like Australian animals (kangaroos, emus, frill-necked lizard and koala) take a trip around Australia in a red-and-white bus, visiting Coober Pedy, Tasmania, Bondi, Philip Island, the Daintree, the Great Barrier Reef, the Pilbara, the Blue Mountains, Darwin and the Opera House. The book includes a map of Australia showing the places that the bus will go to. There is also a tiny green gecko on each page that the reader will have lots of fun trying to find.

→ Follow up with the song as well as activities based around the website that gives information about all the places that are visited in the story.

Jasper McFlea Will Not Eat His Tea

Jasper McFlea is a very fussy eater who will simply not eat his tea unless it is pasta, no matter how hard everyone tries to make him do so. He is very different to his twin sister, Ginger McFlea, who eats almost everything. Jasper is finally convinced about the need to eat properly when his sister implies that his cricketing career might suffer. From then on, he starts to eat healthier foods and his cricket improves.

→ Follow up with links to healthy eating.

Bear Snores On

A small mouse creeps into the den of a hibernating bear cub to escape the cold outside. Soon many small forest animals (e.g. badger, wren, hare and mole) join him and they have a fun time brewing tea, popping corn and making a lot of noise. The bear snores on until he is woken when some pepper from their stew causes him to sneeze. The bear is quite cross, not because his den has been invaded but because he feels left out. That is soon fixed and they all party on.

→ Follow up with inquiry-based learning (see **Handbook**, page 90) about animals that hibernate.

Bear Wants More

This is the follow-up book to *Bear Snores On*. Spring has arrived and after all that hibernation, Bear's feeling very hungry. His new animal friends take him to places where he can get some food, but he always wants more. When they all return to his den, Bear finds that he has eaten so much that he gets stuck in his own doorway. His friends find a way to help him get out and he lies down for a snooze. But now his friends want more!

Circle Time: That's nonsense!

Students become more interested in nonsense words and rhymes as they develop their use of language. They can only appreciate nonsense rhymes that 'misuse' language when they understand that the language or meaning being presented to them is not correct. Then they find it funny. Read *The Boy Who Lost His Belly Button* (see below) and/or one or more of the nonsense poems below. Ask: What do you think the word 'nonsense' means? (it describes something that makes 'no sense') Explain that nonsense songs, stories or poems are so silly or so exaggerated that no one could possibly believe they are true. They are also meant to make us laugh.

Picture books

The Boy Who Lost His Belly Button
A small boy wakes up and discovers that his belly button has gone missing. He heads off to the jungle to try to find it and questions each animal that he meets about the lost belly button. He finds that each animal has one of its own and doesn't know where the boy's belly button could be. He works out that the crocodile is the belly button thief, although the croc claims that he was only intending to give the belly button a wash. The boy then manages to get it back.

Parts
This is a humorous rhyming story about a little boy who thinks he's falling apart. His hair has started to fall out, his skin has started to peel, he has a loose tooth and he's feeling very worried! His parents manage to convince him that it is all normal.

More Parts
This is a humorous rhyming story about a little boy who takes various 'body' expressions quite literally (e.g. give me your hand, hold your tongue, scream your lungs out) and becomes very worried.

The Wrong Book
While Nicholas Ickle is trying to tell a story, he is constantly interrupted by characters from other stories: a pirate, a queen, some monsters. To get an opportunity to tell his story, Nicholas has to convince the other characters that they are all in the wrong book!

Not Last Night but the Night Before
One night a small boy discovers that a collection of fairytale and nursery rhyme characters, including Miss Muffet and the three little pigs, have arrived at his home to wish him a happy birthday. They all begin to sing a very different version of 'Happy birthday'.

Poems and nonsense rhymes

'Upside-down Town'
'The Owl and the Pussy Cat Went to Sea'
'Disobedience'

Unit 7

Humour

Students can learn to say one or more of the following five rhymes and then illustrate them. Ask them to check with their parents about any that they might know.

I went to the pictures tomorrow
I took a front seat at the back
I fell from the floor to the ceiling
And broke a front bone in my back.

One two three
Mother caught a flea
She put it in a teapot
And made a cup of tea.

Little peanut on the train line
Little heart all aflutter,
Along came the next train
Toot, Toot! Peanut butter!

Dictation, dictation, dictation
Three sausages went to the station
One got lost, one got squashed,
And one had a big operation.

(You might like to give students an opportunity to do some simple dictation around the topic of 'funny' or 'silly'.)

Mrs White
Had a fright
In the middle of the night
She saw a ghost
Eating toast
Climbing up a lamp post.

Activities

Train chants
Train chants are nonsensical and fun. They encourage children to enjoy language.
This one is a chant about the menu in the dining car of a train:
- start with 'bacon and eggs' chanted four times to the rhythm of train wheels
- then 'fish and chips' four times at a slightly faster rate
- then, getting faster, 'apple and custard' four times
- then, getting even faster still, chant 'cheese and biscuits' three times, building up to 'sooooooooooooooup' (like a train whistle).

Drawing funny trees
Ask students to think about what grows on trees. Then ask: What could grow on trees that would make us laugh if we saw them? (umbrellas) Then the students can draw their funny tree.

Game

Confusions!
Students sit in a circle with two players in the middle. The aim is to confuse the other person with a silly combination of statement and movement so that they make a mistake. The first person says 'This is my nose' and then they touch their ear. The second person has to copy this exactly. If they get it right, they perform their own confusion such as 'This is my toe' while touching their eyebrow to see if the other person can follow it. Change pairs often.

Poem

'Silly Billies'

There was a girl named Polly Pink
She washed her budgie in the sink.

There was a boy named Benjy Black
His pet cat said 'quack, quack, quack'.

There was a girl named Ruby Red
She wore her shoes upon her head.

There was a boy named Billy Blue
He grew wings and away he flew.

There was a girl named Britney Brown
She walked to school upside down.

There was a boy named Will White
He slept all day and played all night.

There was a girl named Yasmine Yellow
She grew flowers in her pillow.

There was a boy named Gary Green
He swept his garden to keep it clean.

There was a girl named Milly Mauve
She made her bed upon the stove.

There was a boy named Grantley Grey
He fell over and yelled 'Hooray'!

Toni Noble and Helen McGrath,
in the style of *ABC Blue Book*

Ask students why each verse is nonsensical.
→ Follow up by having students colour in **BLM 7.1: Silly Billies** and then making up and illustrating a similar 'Silly' two-line rhyme with a partner.

Game

Swimming chickens

This is a nonsensical version of 'Simon says'. Play it in a large space. Call out a combination of animals and actions (e.g. barking dogs). If the combination is correct, students do it. If the combination is wrong (e.g. swimming chickens) they do nothing. Students are 'out' if they perform the wrong combination. Here are some ideas:

- swimming dolphins
- flying frogs
- waddling cats
- flying elephants
- swimming chickens
- slithering lions
- jumping giraffes
- bouncing kangaroos
- skipping fish.

Unit 7

Humour

Picture books

Would You Rather?

This book presents students with ridiculous options such as: Would rather be chased by a crab, a lion or wolves? Be covered in jam or soaked with water?' Discuss each option and ask students which one they would 'rather' and why.

→ Follow up by having students make their own illustrated sentences or flipbooks (see **Handbook**, page 98), using the same format but only two options. You could also conduct a class survey on some of the options in the book or one of those below and make a class pictograph.

- Would you rather go to school at midnight or at noon?
- Would you rather shrink to be as small as an ant or grow to be as large as an elephant (just for the day)?
- Would you rather stay for a week in an igloo or a tree house in the jungle?
- Would you rather eat only chocolate for a day or only chips?
- Would you rather have a dinosaur as a pet or an elephant?

If

Each two-page spread in this book presents illustrations of strange 'What if…' possibilities, e.g. if zebras had stars and stripes; if the moon was square; if worms had wheels; if frogs ate rainbows; if mice were hair; if toes were teeth; if cats could fly. At the end, the reader is invited to come up with some more.

→ Students can work with a partner to identify some more and use them to create a class book or class digital book (see **Handbook**, page 97).

Activities

Bundling

Students write down three things that make them laugh. As a class, put different categories together (e.g. jokes, cartoons, TV shows) and make a class poster or pictograph of 'What our class likes to laugh at'.

Rating funny stories or poems

Read a funny story or poem and then ask students to indicate how funny they found it. They can choose from:

- very funny
- a bit funny
- not funny.

They write their vote on a piece of paper and place it in a voting box. While the teacher tallies the responses, the students can use 'Think–ink–pair–share' strategy (see **Handbook**, page 92) and explain why they rated the story/poem in that way. Make a pictograph of the results and ask students to write a sentence about the conclusion. Alternatively, you could use the 'Paper plate quiz' strategy (see **Handbook**, page 91).

Riddle voting

Type riddles in large print on three separate and different coloured cards. Near the riddles, place small pieces of paper with a circle on them, a voting box (try a swing-top table bin) and three felt pens that correspond to the card colours. Over one day, ask each student to choose which of the three riddles they think is the funniest. They vote by taking a piece of paper, writing their name on it and colouring the circle on the paper in the colour of the card they chose as having the funniest riddle.

→ Follow up by making a class graph and having students write conclusions.

151

Circle Time: What makes you laugh?

Use the 'Think–ink–pair–share' strategy (see **Handbook**, page 92) and ask students to talk about a book or TV show that has made them laugh. Select some students to tell what their partner said. Ask: Why do different people find different things funny? Why did students have different ideas as to which of the riddles was the funniest in our survey? Stress that it is OK to be different (refer back to Unit 1: Core values) and that humour is a very individual thing, but should never be hurtful.

→ Follow up by having each student make a flipbook (see **Handbook**, page 98) with the sentence 'I like to laugh at …'

Games

Cooperative riddles and answers
Make up pairs of cards, one with a riddle and the other with the answer. Using many different coloured cards will make the activity visually attractive. Make enough pairs so that everyone in the class can have one card (i.e. if there are 26 players you will need 13 sets of cards). Everyone draws a card. Then they walk around the room trying to find the person with the matching riddle or answer card. They may not talk to any other player except to say what is on their card. If they find a 'match' they quickly sit down and watch the others. When everyone has found their partner they take turns at reading their riddle and answer.

Big lift-up flap riddles
Students can make their own riddle-and-answer pairs as big lift-up flaps (see **Handbook**, page 97). The riddles can be researched online, in joke books or after interviewing parents and other family members.

Activities

Making alien balloon puppets
For the class you will need:
◉ large and small party balloons
◉ felt pens and scissors to share
◉ thick coloured cardboard
◉ bits and pieces such as coloured construction paper, adhesive spots, feathers, craft sticks, foil, pipe-cleaners, paper clips, corks, ping-pong balls, circle and star stickers, felt pieces, wool, bottle tops, buttons, beads, nuts and bolts.

Before students start to make their creatures, prompt with questions such as:
◉ How many eyes does your alien have?
◉ Does it have hair? What can you make hair from?
◉ What special features does it have?
◉ Does it eat with its nose or eyes or mouth?
◉ Does it have arms and legs?
◉ Does it have horns or antennae?
◉ Are its eyes, nose and mouth in the same place as they are on your face?
◉ What planet does your creature come from? What is its name? Who is in its family? What does it eat? What friends does it have? What happens when it comes to Earth?

Make the alien into a puppet by tying elastic or rubber bands to the balloon neck and tying to a stick. Students take turns to tell a story using their balloon alien puppet. Play and sing the song 'Purple People Eater'. Students can make their puppet move in funny ways or walk and dance.

Making riddle jars

For each student you will need:
- small clean jars with lids (e.g. baby food jars)
- construction paper
- glue and scissors to share
- decorating materials (e.g. magazine pictures or own drawings)
- felt pens and pencils
- riddles.

1. Trace around the top of the jar twice on the construction paper.
2. Cut out both circles. Trim one circle so that it fits snugly inside the lid.
3. On the bigger circle, print the riddle question. Print the answer on the smaller circle.
4. Glue the question circle to the top of the lid and the answer circle to the inside of the lid. Let it dry.
5. Cut out a picture or paint to decorate the inside of the jar and put the lid on

Making funny biscuit faces

You will need:
- plain biscuits
- icing sugar, food colouring and water (to make icing)
- knives to spread the icing
- things to make faces with (e.g. Smarties, snakes, banana lollies, sultanas).

Students make icing and ice the biscuits, then decorate them with funny faces.

Sequencing a funny story

Students can make their own set of three funny story pictures for other students to place in the correct order.

Circle Time: **Clowns and the circus**

Start by showing pictures of clowns. Ask: Has anyone seen a clown perform? What do you remember about how they were dressed and what they did? What do clowns look like? How do they dress? What sort of faces do they have? What do clowns do to be funny and why do we laugh at them? Discuss with students how clown make-up is usually sad and funny at the same time. Make the link between clowns as sad people and clowns as people who cheer themselves and others up when they are sad or worried. Laughter can make us feel a bit better and a bit more hopeful if we have a problem.

→ Follow up with one of the clown activities below. Students could also make simple clown clothes by using a box attached to braces made from elastic, an oversized bow tie and a hat with a flower on a stem.

Activities

Charlie the clown

Students work with a partner to make a clown picture using simple drawing software such as Kid Pix.

Making funny things

Students can make:
- A clown frieze using A3 coloured paper. Students cut the paper in half lengthways then fold it into four, backwards and forwards like a concertina. They draw a clown shape

on the top fold, making sure that its hands and feet go to the edge of the fold. They cut around the clown then open the paper out to make a chain of clowns. Decorate the clowns with paper hats, eyes, bow ties, buttons, etc.
- A clown mobile by drawing clown pictures, each with different make-up or with funny expressions from pictures cut from magazines.
- A collage of people laughing and smiling or things that they find funny.
- A funny house using cardboard boxes and cylinders of different sizes.
- Funny creatures using play dough.

Funny face flipbooks
Take close-up photos of the faces of all the students in the class. Print and cut the photographs in half with nose and eyes in the top section, mouth and chin in the bottom section. Students write their first name on the top half and their second name on the bottom half. Make it into a flipbook (see **Handbook**, page 98). Students will have great fun mixing each other up.

Funny new faces
You will need:
- old magazines
- light cardboard
- craft sticks or hat elastic
- glue, scissors and masking tape to share.
1. Students cut out eyes, noses and mouths from the magazines to make masks (or they can use the whole face). Small holes should be cut out for the eyes.
2. Glue the pictures onto card. Carefully trim around the picture.
3. Attach hat elastic so it can be worn or tape a craft stick onto the bottom so it can be held up to cover the face.

Family interview
Students interview a family member about a time when they felt very sad or worried but having a bit of a laugh or finding a funny side to the situation helped them to feel a bit better. They share what they found in class and write some sentences about what was said. Summarise findings in a class poster.

Games

Funny face or funny walk competitions
Have a class competition to see who can make the most people laugh with the funny face they pull. Then discuss why the best three were so funny. Repeat with funny walks.

Stoneface
Play 'Stoneface'. Students play in two teams of five or six. One team at a time attempts to make all the people in the opposite team laugh within three minutes. Teams sit on the floor facing each other. The first team starts. They cannot say any words. They can make funny noises (quiet ones that aren't rude!), funny faces or funny movements (but they must stay seated on the floor).

Funny memory cards
Students work in pairs and use **BLM 7.1: Silly Billies** to make cards to play their own Silly Billies memory game.

Chinese whispers
Pass on a funny riddle reworked as a sentence, such as:
- The man threw his clock out of the window because he wanted to see time fly.
- If a sheep married a kangaroo their baby would be a woolly jumper.

- A fairy that won't have a bath is called Stinkerbell.
- The chewing gum said to the shoe, 'I think I'm stuck on you'.
- You can't play basketball with pigs because they hog the ball.

Drama

Mimes

Students mime funny actions for the rest of the class to try to guess. Here are some suggestions:
- washing an elephant
- getting stuck in a too-tight jumper
- losing one shoe
- getting chewing gum on one's shoe.

Circle Time: Humour can be hurtful

Start with a puppet play in which two puppets make fun of another puppet and laugh at him/her (see **Handbook**, pages 99 to 101, for puppet ideas). Ask: How could being funny hurt someone's feelings? What sorts of funny but nasty things do some people do that hurt other people's feelings? (mimic; laugh if they make a mistake; call other people funny but nasty names; say funny things about their real name; say funny things about their family) **Make a chart on the board as you go.** Ask: What does it feel like to have someone make fun of you? Does the person making fun mean to hurt the other's feelings? (sometimes they are deliberately being mean, but sometimes they just don't stop and think about the effect of what they are doing) Why would someone *want* to be mean to another child? (to show off; to make people not like the person they are making fun of because they are jealous) What could we do to make sure we don't make fun of others? (think about how it would feel if someone said the same thing to us)

→ Follow up with one of these:
- A 'Smiley ball' activity (see **Handbook**, page 92): roll the ball to different students and ask them one way we can have fun with someone that does not hurt their feelings (tell a joke or riddle; share a game; look at a funny book or movie together; sing a silly song).
- An activity in which students write 'commitment' sentences along the lines of 'Making fun of someone else hurts their feelings. I would not like someone to laugh at me. I will try not to laugh at other people in a hurtful way'.

Songs

'The Laughter Song'

(To the tune of 'The Wheels of the Bus Go Round and Round')

The donkey told a joke and everybody laughed

Even the zebra and the tall giraffe

Then he sailed away on a wooden raft

Hee haw, Hee haw, hee Haw.

The horse told a riddle and we giggled a lot

We told each other and danced on the spot

Then the horse ran away with a gallop and a trot

Ha ha, Ha ha, Ha ha.

The monkey pulled a face and we chuckled all day
We jumped up and down and had a play
Then the monkey climbed a tree and swung away
Hee hee, Hee hee, Hee hee.
The lion was doing a funny dance
His partner was a tiger with funny pants
Then they left without a glance
Ho ho, Ho ho, Ho ho.
They everyone returned and we all had a laugh
The monkey and the tiger and the tall giraffe
The lion and the donkey and the zebra too
And this is how we laughed:
Hee haw, Hee haw, Hee haw, Hee haw
Ha ha, Ha ha, Ha ha, Ha ha
Hee hee, Hee hee, Hee hee, Hee hee
Ho ho, Ho ho, Ho ho.

'The Humour Song'
(To the tune of 'A Sailor Went to Sea Sea Sea')

When I'm feeling sad sad sad
Or when I'm feeling mad mad mad
I try to see the funny side
So I don't feel so bad bad bad.
'Cos It's Really Healthy'

'Laugh, laugh, laugh'
(To the tune of 'Jump Jump Jump if You Feel You Want To')
Students can add actions and voice changes.

Laugh laugh laugh 'cos it's really healthy
Laugh laugh laugh 'cos it's good for you
Laugh laugh laugh when things aren't working
Laugh laugh laugh when you're feeling blue.
Laugh laugh laugh with all your friends
Laugh laugh laugh and stand up tall
Laugh laugh laugh make it very loud
Laugh laugh laugh make it very small
Laugh laugh laugh make it very fast
Laugh laugh laugh make it very slow
Laugh laugh laugh in a very high voice
Laugh laugh laugh down very low
Laugh laugh laugh like a kookaburra
Laugh laugh laugh like Santa Claus
Laugh laugh laugh like a silly donkey
Laugh laugh laugh like a happy horse.

Unit 7

Humour

Other funny songs, action songs or dances and poems

Funny songs
'Frog Went A-Courtin'
'Ants Go Marching'
'Do You Wear Your Hat on Your Feet?'
'Do Your Ears Hang Low?'
'Five Little Monkeys (jumping on the bed)'
'How Much Is That Doggie in the Window?'
'I Know a Song That Gets on Everybody's Nerves'
'I Wish I Was a Little Bar of Soap'
'I'm Being Swallowed by a Boa Constrictor"
'Little Sir Echo'
'Little White Duck'
'Michael Finnegan'
'Mr Frog'
'On Top of Spaghetti'
'Rubber Ducky'
'Rumbly in My Tummy' (a Winnie the Pooh song about hunger)
'Spider and the Fly'
'Supercalifragilisticexpialidocious'
'Ten Green Bottles'
'The Bear Went Over the Mountain'
'The Green Grass Grew All Round'
'There Was an Old Lady Who Swallowed a Fly'
'There Were Five in the Bed'
'Three Little Fishies'
'Yes, We Have No Bananas'

Funny action songs or dances
'Animal Fair'
'Back of a Crocodile'
'Hand on My Head'
'Head and Shoulders, Knees and Toes'
'Hokey Pokey'
'I'm a Gummy Bear'
'She Sailed Away on a Lovely Summer's Day on the Back of a Crocodile'
'The Chicken Dance'
'They're Digging a Hole in the Road'

Funny poems
'Baby Bumblebee'
'Be Glad Your Nose is on Your Face' (Jack Prelutsky)
'Five Grey Elephants Balancing'
'Mother Doesn't Want a Dog' (Judith Viorst)
'My Baby Brother' (Jack Prelutsky)
'Ning Nang Nong' (Spike Milligan)
'Nobody Loves Me, Everybody Hates Me'
'Open Shut Them'
'Upside-down Town' (Jack Prelutsky)
'Upsy Down Town'

Funny games and activities

Mrs Mumbly Bumbly

Students ask/say these 'questions and answers' around the circle without showing their teeth when they speak. 'Have you seen Mrs Mumbly Bumbly?' The reply is 'No, I haven't seen her, but I'll ask my neighbour'. Then they turn to the next person, repeat the question and play continues.

Hot potato

Use the 'Timer' e-tool and set it each time to one minute.

Make a list on the board of all the words the students can think of that are associated with humour, being funny, laughing or smiling. (chuckle, grin, smile, chortle, cackle, guffaw, snicker, beam, shriek, smirk, roar, break up, crack up, be in stitches, giggle, laugh, tee-hee, fun, comic, comedian, funny, silly, nonsense, ridiculous, hilarious, humour, humorous, joke, joking, jolly, relax, tickle, riddle, cartoon, clown, healthy, kookaburra, hyena) Prepare a card on which you have written 'Say a word about being funny'. The game is played with students sitting in a circle but working with a partner. The aim of the game is to avoid being the pair who is saying their word about being funny when the timer goes off. Give each pair a few minutes to revise and practise saying the list of words on the board before the words are covered up or removed. The first pair is given the card, says one of the words about being funny (e.g. *joke*) and then passes the card to the pair on their left. No pair can repeat a word that has already been given within the same round. A round finishes when the timer goes off. The pair who is holding the card when the timer goes off sits out of the game. Keep playing until there is one winning pair. Alternatively, give each pair two chances before they are 'out' and play the game for a set time rather than until every pair is eliminated.

Pass the chicken

Use the same initial preparation procedure as in 'Hot potato', i.e. make a list of 'humour' words on the board. Then give the class a few minutes to revise and practise saying the words before the words are covered up or removed.

You will need a rubber chicken or similar humorous object. To begin the game, all students sit in a circle. Select one person to be 'It'. That person holds the rubber chicken. The teacher says to 'It', 'Pass the chicken and then say three words about being funny'. As soon as the teacher says, 'Pass the chicken', the student who is 'It' passes the chicken to the right and tries to quickly say three words before the chicken is passed around the circle and comes back to them. The aim is to stop being 'It' by being quick enough to say the three words before the chicken returns to you. If they do this, then the person who happens to be holding the chicken when 'It' completes the task becomes the new 'It'.

Preposition game (funny version)

You will need two silly objects, e.g. a toy crocodile and a 'slimy' toy spider. Make slips of paper to pull out of a container and write one of the following phrases on each slip:

- The person before the crocodile
- The person with the crocodile
- The person after the crocodile
- The person before the spider
- The person with the spider
- The person after the spider

Students stand or sit in a circle. Give the crocodile to one person and the spider to someone across from them. Play music while they pass the objects around the circle. When the music stops, pull out a slip of paper and ask one student to read it. The student who is in the position described on the paper sits out of the game, e.g. they might be the person before the spider. This activity could also be used with five or six shapes being passed around to reinforce the names of shapes (but then it won't be as funny).

Unit 7

Humour

Movers and shakers

(See **Handbook,** page 91.) Use funny movements and expressions (perhaps after asking the students for some ideas) with statements such as:
- Clap your hands silently while nodding your head if you like … (name of a cartoon).
- Make a silly face if you have ever seen a clown.
- Wobble like a jelly if you have ever told a joke that made someone laugh.
- Be as floppy as a jellyfish with no bones if you know a really funny riddle.
- Suck in your cheeks and roll your eyes if an animal has ever done something that made you laugh.
- Poke out your tongue if you have ever played a funny game.

Zoo game

Give each student the name of an animal that makes a distinctive noise, e.g. lion, cow, cat, dog, snake, bird. Walk around the room with two other students (but not walking together) and greet each student by their real name (Hello Ben). They must only answer you with their animal noise (Moo!).

Speed passing

Sit with the students in a circle. Hold up a flash card with an animal word written on it (e.g. giraffe) and say what it is. Pass it on to the student beside you, who loudly repeats it and passes it on to the next student. Start slowly but encourage the students to go faster and faster and the game gets sillier and sillier. Consider using a stopwatch to see how fast they can pass the card (and say the word) around the circle back to you.

Cotton ball relay race

This game is played in two teams. You will need one large spoon for each team, lots of cotton balls and four containers. Establish a starting and turning line. Give students some time to practise. Put two containers full of cotton balls at the starting line—one for each team. Put an empty container for each team at the turning line. In turn, each player uses a spoon to scoop one cotton ball from their team's container and then (using only one hand) runs to the turning line and drops it into the other container. If they drop it along the way they can't stop and pick it up. But they can go back to their team's container and get another cotton ball. After they have successfully dropped one cotton ball into the container, they race back and pass the spoon to the next member of their team. The race continues until one team wins. For more giggles, ask students to use their non-preferred hand.

All up, all catch

Everyone has a tennis ball and, on a signal from the teacher, they throw it high up in the air. Each student then has to catch somebody else's ball, not their own. How many balls are missed? Can the class do better next time?

Look, no hands!

Use the 'Timer' e-tool. Organise students into groups of six to eight. One group plays at a time (sitting or standing in a circle) while the others watch. The aim is to pass a blown-up balloon as quickly as possible around the circle without using your hands.

159

Consolidation: Humour

Activities

Cut-up sentences

(See **Handbook**, page 89.) Cut these sentences into individual words and place each cut-up sentence into an envelope. Make enough sets for each pair of students to have one set of six envelopes. Each pair reconstructs the six sentences.
- Laughing helps us to be more healthy.
- Laughing can make us feel better if we are sad.
- You can cheer someone up by making them laugh.
- Laughing can help us to be friends.
- Having fun together makes us feel great.
- It is mean to make fun of other people.

You can also use the 'Cut-up sentences' e-activity with these sentences.

Reflections

Use the 'Smiley ball' strategy (see **Handbook**, page 92), 'Reflections' e-tool (see **Handbook**, page 92) or the 'Animal asks' e-tool (see **Handbook**, page 89) with questions such as these:
- Who is your favourite cartoon character?
- Have you ever seen a clown in a show or on TV? Tell us about it.
- Have you ever seen your pet or an animal do something that made you laugh?
- Who is a funny person in your family and how do they make you laugh?
- What is your favourite riddle or joke? Tell it to us.
- What is a funny thing that has happened in your family? (Remember not to hurt your family's feelings by what you tell us.)
- What is a funny commercial that you like? Why do you think it's funny?
- What is something that made you laugh a lot?

Games

Bingo strips

Use some of these words to play 'Bingo strips' (see **Handbook**, page 89).

cartoon	giggle	laugh
chuckle	grin	riddle
clown	joke	silly
fun	joking	smile
funny	jolly	tickle

Other games
- 'Cross-offs' e-game (see **Handbook**, page 89). The secret message is 'It is good to laugh with friends and classmates'.
- 'Secret word' e-game (see **Handbook**, page 92). The secret word is 'Funny'.

Resources

A complete list of resources (including references for books, poems, films, websites and weblinks for songs) is available on Pearson Places.

Unit 8

No bullying

Key points

It is important to know what bullying is and what it is not.
It is mean and unkind to bully someone. Bullying is when someone keeps picking on someone else in an unkind way over days, or weeks or longer. A student who is bullying will often say, write, text or do mean things that hurt the other student's body, their things or their feelings. Sometimes they keep trying to stop them from joining in and being liked or write mean things when they are online. It's NOT bullying if students just have an argument or if someone says or does just one nasty thing to someone else.

Bullying is never OK.
It is never OK for anyone in our class or school to bully someone else. Bullying is very serious misbehaviour and you will get into trouble if you bully others. Our school and teachers take it seriously and will quickly act to stop it. If you bully someone, then your parents may be asked to come to the school and talk to the teacher (and perhaps the principal).

Bullying is everyone's problem. Bullying spoils things for all of us.
If someone in our school is being bullied, it spoils things for all of us. It makes us all feel worried and unsafe. None of us can feel safe and happy if bullying is happening to someone we know. So we all have to make sure that nobody gets bullied. If bullying does happen to someone, then we all have to work together to stop it and to help the person who is being bullied.

Put-downs are not OK.
A put-down is a deliberately mean comment or gesture that tries to make someone look bad or silly. Put-downs are not allowed in our class or in our school.

Think for yourself. Don't just copy others.
Think for yourself and don't just copy others if they are being mean to someone else. If you bully someone too, then you have made a bad decision and you can't blame other people for your bad choices. Even if you take part in the smallest way, you will get into trouble. It is not OK to say 'someone else started it' or 'someone else made me do it' or 'everyone else was doing it too'. Think for yourself and decide not to take part in mean behaviour or bullying.

Students who often bully others need our help too.
Sometimes students don't realise that the mean things they keep doing to someone are really bullying. We all need to help other people to understand that they are bullying when they act in a mean and unkind way towards one person again and again. Bullying hurts us all and it is not OK. We must all help our classmates and other students in our school not to bully so that they don't grow up to be criminals or people who hurt and bully their wives, husbands, partners or children.

If someone gets bullied it is not their fault.
Nobody deserves to be bullied. The student who is doing the bullying is the one doing the wrong thing. It is not the fault of the student who is being bullied. They might be different in some way, but it is OK to be different. We don't all have to be the same. They might sometimes annoy you or disappoint you, but you can tell them this without bullying them or making it a big deal. Everyone can be annoying or can disappoint you at times.

Bullying is not OK after you stop being friends with someone.
Friends don't always stay friends. Sometimes we don't see as much of a friend and we make new friends. If someone stops being your friend it is not OK to bully them because you (or they) feel sad about the loss of the friendship. Don't keep thinking about it. Make new friends.

If someone starts to bully you, stand tall, stare into their eyes and tell them to stop doing it.
When someone is trying to hurt or upset you, try to stand tall, look firmly into their eyes and tell them to stop because you don't like it. If you can't stop them from doing it, ask a teacher to help you solve the problem. Teachers care about you and want to stop any bullying that occurs as soon as it starts. They cannot help you unless they know what is happening.

Asking for help is not the same as dobbing.
When you have firmly told someone to stop bullying you but they still won't stop, then you must talk to a teacher about what is happening so they can help you solve the problem. This is not the same as dobbing. When you ask a teacher for help you are asking for help to fix a problem, not just trying to get someone into trouble.

Do the right and kind thing and let a teacher know if someone else is being bullied.
If you know that another student is being bullied, then the right and kind thing to do is to talk to a teacher so that the teacher can stop it from happening. This is not the same as dobbing. When you dob, you just try to get someone into trouble. When you let a teacher know what is going on, you are trying to help someone else who is in trouble. You have to be brave to do this for someone else, but it is the right and kind thing to do and helps our school to be a caring and safe school.

You can be a friend to someone who is being bullied.
Students who are being bullied feel better if you show them that you think it is not fair. You can show them you care that they feel sad and worried about being bullied. You can encourage them to go somewhere that is safe with you or to join your game. You can let a teacher know about the bullying so that they can solve the problem. You can also try to be brave and say or do something that lets the student who is bullying know that you think what they are doing is wrong and mean. It takes courage and kindness to do this for someone.

Unit 8

No bullying

Circle Time: Protecting animals 164

Circle Time: What is bullying? 164
Picture books 165
   Big Bully Hippo
   Oliver Button Is a Sissy
   Hooway for Wodney Wat
   No More Teasing
   Ant and the Big Bad Bully Goat
   Chrysanthemum
Film. 166
   A Bug's Life

Circle Time: How it feels to be bullied ... 166

Circle Time: Put-downs can lead to bullying or be a part of bullying 167
Picture books 167
   I'm Number One!
   Stand Tall, Molly Lou Melon
   Pig Enough
Drama. 168
   Put-downs
Activities 168
   Put-down rubbish bin
   'No put-down zone' rewards
Game 169
   Greedy pig

Circle Time: Bullying spoils things for everyone 169

Circle Time: Think for yourself (Part 1) ... 170

Circle Time: Think for yourself (Part 2) ... 170
Activities 171
   Making sheep
   Making a poster
Song. 171
   'We're Two Little Sheep'

Circle Time: What you can do if you are bullied. 172
Drama. 173
   Act confidently and speak up
Picture books 173
   Lucy and the Bully
   King of the Playground
   Willy the Wimp
Activities 174
   Being prickly
   Make a book
   Animal warnings
   The frill-necked lizard

Circle Time: Cyberbullying. 175

Circle Time: How to help someone who is being bullied or cyberbullied. 176
Activity 177
   Is this dobbing?

Consolidation: No bullying 177
Drama. 177
   Bullying scenarios
Activities 178
   End-of-the-day personal reflections
   Cut-up sentences
   Missing words
   Reflections
Games 179
   Bingo strips
   Other games

Resources. 179

Circle Time: **Protecting animals**

Ask if anyone knows what kind of work the RSPCA (Royal Society for the Prevention of Cruelty to Animals) does. Then ask if anyone has seen or heard about someone mistreating an animal. Ask: How would you feel if you saw an animal being mistreated and what could you do about it? Make the link between bullying and animal mistreatment. This helps the students understand that we need to care about and help other people if they are mistreated (i.e. bullied), just like we stand up for animals that are being mistreated. Explain that 'mistreat' means to hurt or to deliberately be horrible to someone or to an animal. Describe a scene in which two children are throwing sticks at a dog. Ask students what they could do if they saw this happening. Then ask: Why is it harder to speak out or do something when a person is being hurt or mistreated than when an animal is being mistreated? Stress that it is not a good idea to put yourself in danger by directly confronting someone or trying to physically stop someone who is mistreating an animal or a person. Sometimes you can make a difference by saying something like 'I/we don't like what you are doing. You're bullying. Please stop it. It's cruel', but usually it is best to tell an adult who can help.

→ Follow up with inquiry-based learning (see **Handbook**, page 90) about the RSPCA and/or the RSPCC (Royal Society for the Prevention of Cruelty to Children) and/or the Rights of the Child.

Circle Time: **What is bullying?**

Start by reading one of the books listed below or show the film *A Bug's Life* in three segments, asking students to summarise what has happened so far at the end of each segment and then again before the next segment. Ask them what was happening in the story that we would call bullying. Stress that bullying is repeated unkindness towards the same person (not just a single or occasional unkind act, not just nastiness towards a number of people and not an argument between two children). Ask students if they have ever seen a student being deliberately mean more than once to the same person. Stress the 'no names' rule in the circle, but let them know they can talk to you in private if they want to. Students can turn to the person next to them and tell each other about a time when they have seen someone being mean to another person (again, no names). Ask selected students to tell what their partner said. Draw out the different ways in which students might bully someone else. They may be trying to hurt their body, their things or their feelings, or stop them from joining in or being liked. Put up a chart on the board and classify their answers into the categories below. Ask them to draw one of the examples.

- Hurting someone's body (e.g. hitting, pushing, kicking)
- Hurting someone's things (e.g. drawing on their work or deleting it, kicking their school bag)
- Saying nasty things or using nasty teasing (e.g. calling someone nasty names, telling lies about them, saying mean things such as 'nobody likes you' in person, to others in writing or by email or text message)
- Playing nasty tricks (e.g. hiding someone's things or running away from them)
- Forcing (e.g. making someone hand over their food or their toys)
- Blocking (e.g. stopping someone from playing or doing what they want to do)
- Trying to stop them from joining in or being liked (e.g. telling others not to play with them or refusing to let them join in a game)

→ Follow up by having students make an illustrated classroom chart by pasting their drawings into the labelled categories.

Unit 8

No bullying

Emphasise that doing any of these things even once is still mean, unkind and wrong, but it is not bullying, Bullying is when one person is being picked on and treated this way a lot. Use the bullying scenarios on page 177. Discuss why some students choose to bully others. Then make a list of reasons on the board. For example:
- They might be trying to make others think that they are tough and important.
- They might want to seem popular or be the boss and tell people what to do, and say who can and cannot play.
- They might not think about other people's feelings enough and don't understand how much their actions hurt.
- They might feel angry with someone who used to be their friend and want to make them feel bad.
- They might feel jealous of someone else and want others not to like them.
- They don't understand that what they are doing is wrong and think it is OK to hurt someone else to get what they want.

Make the point that these are not good reasons. There are other ways to be well liked and popular or deal with a friendship break-up. There are other ways to impress other students. They should try to understand other people's feelings. Talk about some of the other ways they could be popular or give others a good impression of themselves. Then talk about the behaviours we would like to see people use to impress others and make friends. (being cooperative; being kind; helping others)

→ Follow up by having students make digital posters with a partner that stress that bullying is mean and unkind and that it is not OK to bully.

Picture books

Big Bully Hippo
Hippo plays mean jokes on some of the other animals in the jungle and his behaviour borders on bullying. He deliberately pops Baby Monkey's balloon, drinks Lion's drink and splashes the ducks. When he tries to kick the meerkats' ball away, he gets more than he bargained for. The other animals help him despite his behaviour.
→ Ask: If Hippo deliberately did something nasty to Monkey again the next day, what would we call that? (bullying) Stress that Hippo's behaviour was leading him to become a bully and he was lucky that he was able to learn to stop his behaviour.

Oliver Button Is a Sissy
This is the story of a boy who is different, in that he doesn't like sports like the other boys do and prefers to read, draw, dress up, sing and dance. Although he is hurt by their repeated teasing and nastiness, he stands up to those who bully him by staying true to himself and eventually he earns their respect.

Hooway for Wodney Wat
Rodney Rat gets a hard time from his classmates because he can't pronounce the letter 'r' properly. They intentionally ask him questions to embarrass him, such as another name for 'bunny' (he, of course, replies 'wabbit'). Rodney feels so embarrassed that he eats lunch alone and buries his head in his jacket. A very big and nasty new classmate called Camilla arrives at the school. She pushes the others around and everyone is afraid of her. Rodney is chosen to lead a game of 'Simon says' and he gives Camilla a taste of her own medicine by giving instructions that confuse her because she doesn't realise that Rodney can't pronounce 'r'. Camilla is the one who looks foolish as she tries to follow the instructions literally.

No More Teasing
Mimi is a monkey. Her older cousin Momo is bigger than Mimi and constantly teases her. He is always telling her that the 'Grizzly Grilla' will get her. Mimi talks to her

grandmother about the teasing and together they hatch a plan to teach Momo a lesson. Grandma dresses up like Grizzly Grilla and Mimi yells out to Momo that 'Grizzly Grilla' is coming. He, of course, knowing that he has made this creature up, laughs at her. But when he sees Grandma in her Grizzly Grilla outfit, he runs away in terror with Mimi calling out to him to stop teasing. He finally starts to understand what he has done.

Ant and the Big Bad Bully Goat
Badger is happy living in his neat and tidy burrow, until Big Bad Bully Goat decides to takes over Badger's house. Badger needs help to get rid of him and have his house back, but Bully Goat has such a scary reputation that even Badger's biggest and toughest friends are too scared to help him. Help finally arrives from an unexpected source—an ant with a nasty bite. This story is based on a traditional Iberian tale.

Chrysanthemum
Chrysanthemum is a confident young mouse who has always really liked her unusual name. But when she starts school, several of the other girls keep teasing her about it. She starts to hate her name and going to school, and loses her confidence. She becomes more confident again when her teacher, who is helping her to solve the problem, reveals that she is also named after a flower—the delphinium. After this revelation, Chrysanthemum regains her confidence.

→ Follow up with one or more of these activities.
- Make a class graph of the number of letters in each student's name. What is each name worth if each letter is worth $1 (a) up to $26 (z)? Do more students have fewer than five letters in their names?
- Find the little words in the big word 'chrysanthemum'.
- Have students plant a chrysanthemum with a partner and then observe, measure and describe its growth in a digital report for the school library.
- Have students ask their parents about their own name: What does it mean? Why was that name chosen? Do they have a nickname and, if so, how did they get it? Are there are any well-known people with the same name?
- Line up from the shortest to longest name or according to the number of syllables.

Film

A Bug's Life
This is a good film to introduce the idea of bullying. The grasshoppers push the ants around, and finally the ants outsmart them. The ant who leads them in their rebellion is hardly a typical hero, as he is kind-hearted and well-intentioned but clumsy. Talk to the students about what happened in the film and how it relates to bullying at school.

Circle Time: How it feels to be bullied

Read one of the books listed above. Research has highlighted that many students either bully or don't stand up for a student being mistreated because they fail to understand how that child is feeling. Ask: How did the character in the story feel when they were being bullied? How would you feel if someone bullied you? (Choose one example of what might be said or done in a bullying situation—see the bullying scenarios on page 177). Discuss with the students how someone who is being bullied might feel. They can use balloon puppets or paper plate puppets (see **Handbook**, page 100) to act out a bullying scene. Use the 'Freeze frame' technique (see **Handbook**, page 89) to stop the action where you can ask the question 'How might X be feeling right now?' Highlight feelings such as:

- sadness
- helplessness (not knowing what to do)
- fear
- anger
- worry (that they are not liked or that it will happen again soon).

Ask students to close their eyes and imagine one of those unkind things being done to them. How would they feel? They can work with a partner to trace around their bodies onto butcher's paper and then write in some of the feelings they would have and where they might feel it (e.g. heart, head, eyes, hands). Then they can write sentences: 'I would hate to be bullied because I would feel...'

→ Follow up by making an X-chart and ask students to identify what bullying looks, sounds, feels and thinks like. In the 'Thinks like' section, write 'It's OK to make somebody else feel bad to get what I want' and 'It's OK to bully someone'.

Circle Time: Put-downs can lead to bullying or be a part of bullying

Read one of the books listed below. Ask: What are put-downs? How does it feel when someone says a put-down to you? Are all put-downs things that someone says to you? What are some put-downs that are not said? (gestures; nasty looks; giggling at someone's mistakes) Why do some students use put-downs? Ask: What do we mean by 'hinting'? Talk about the ways some people will 'hint' bad things about you to other people by what they do with their body and expressions, e.g. making a rude sign about you, using a nasty smile or laugh to hint that you are stupid, mimicking you and so on. Students who use this kind of behaviour have chosen to be mean and nasty to someone but they don't want to get into trouble so they try to pretend they are not doing it when they really are. Ask: What is the difference between put-downs and having a joke (which is what some students claim to be doing when in fact they are making a put-down or bullying)? If it really is a joke and is fun, then both people should find it funny, not just the person doing it.

Picture books

I'm Number One!
A-one is a little wind-up toy soldier who tells all the other toys that he is in charge. He bullies Maddy, Sally and Sid. When he orders them to turn his key and wind him up, they do what he tells them. When he tells them they're no good and hopeless, they feel bad. But eventually his ranting and raving starts to sound ridiculous even to him and he starts to laugh at himself and see the silliness of what he is doing. They all realise that A-one really needs the others because without them he can't go anywhere!

→ Follow up with a display of wind-up toys that students bring from home.

Stand Tall, Molly Lou Melon
Molly Lou Melon is being subjected to nasty put-down remarks at her new school. Her grandmother has always reassured her with encouraging words. With her grandmother in mind, Molly Lou is able to confidently confront the classmate who has been bullying her. She also manages to impress her classmates with her talents (e.g. making a giant snowflake) and gain acceptance.

Pig Enough
Willy is a guinea pig but he thinks he is enough of a pig to join the Pig Scouts despite the snickering of the 'real' pigs. Peyton, a nasty pig scout, is the ringleader and starts a teasing chant. As it turns out, Peyton is teamed up with Willy for a hiking activity and thanks to Willy they get out of a sticky situation. Discuss how bullying can happen when people aren't prepared to accept differences in others and the importance of believing in yourself even when others are putting you down.
→ Follow up with a discussion about guinea pigs as pets.

Drama

Put-downs
Using puppet drama (see **Handbook**, pages 99 to 101, for ideas for puppets), ask students to act out the following situations where put-downs are used towards others.
- One student says 'That's dumb' when another brings a special book or toy and shows it round.
- One student says to a group 'I can skip now, look' and another says 'Who can't do *that*!'
- One student says 'We're going out for dinner tonight' and another replies 'We don't care what you're going to do'.
- One student says 'I like to read fairy stories' and another replies 'That's what babies do'.
- One student in class answers the teacher's question about a maths problem and another says 'Who doesn't know *that*!'
- A teacher asks a student a question (e.g. 'How do you spell …') and the child gives the wrong answer and three other students laugh.

Remember to safely debrief the role-play (see **Handbook**, page 88). In a follow-up discussion ask students what they noticed about how the put-down was done, such as:
- a nasty voice
- being laughed at in a nasty way
- nasty words
- the person using the put-down wants everyone else to think the other person is no good (e.g. they look at other people when they are doing it to tell them this message)
- a nasty pretend smile (called a smirk).

→ Follow up by making a Y-chart on the board showing what a put-down looks, feels and sounds like.

Activities

Put-down rubbish bin
- Bring a small pedal rubbish bin into class. Show how it works. Discuss the kinds of mean things that people sometimes say or do towards others either through words or by hinting through body language such as smirks and laughs. Talk about how it feels when someone does that to you.
- Write some examples on the board and discuss with the students how it would feel if someone said or hinted mean things about them. Emphasise that just because someone says a mean thing about a person doesn't make it true.
- Then ask students to draw or write down all the mean things people have said to them or when people have laughed at them in a mean way. Have a ceremonial dumping of the put-downs into the bin. They belong in the rubbish bin because that is what they are—rubbish.

Unit 8

No bullying

'No put-down zone' rewards

Discuss and display the 'No put-down zone' poster and give students **BLM 8.1: No Put-Down Zone** to colour. Then set up games and discussions where you reinforce not using put-downs and accepting classmates' right to be themselves and their right to be different without fear of being mistreated. The most likely situations occur when students are discussing their different views or playing competitive games. Stress the following before each game or discussion.

- You may think that someone else isn't playing/thinking the way you would, but everyone can do it their own way and have their own opinion. Your way is only one way, not necessarily the best or the only way.
- Put-downs are not OK. Don't say or make them (remind them of what not to do by referring back to the put-down Y chart).

Use one or both of these strategies:

- When a designated time period has elapsed with no put-downs occurring, give the class a quick five-minute game or five minutes of 'chat time'. This is best just before recess, lunch or going-home time. Make it clear that they have earned the special time because of their kind and accepting behaviour and the fact that there have been no put-downs.
- Draw ten circles on the board and write 'one minute' in each circle. Each time you see or hear a put-down in the class, or one is reported to you by the yard duty teacher, cross off one circle. At the end of the day, give the class the amount of time left as 'special earned time'.

Game

Greedy pig

This game reinforces 'no put-downs'. Students play in pairs. One pair competes against another pair. Each student takes a turn at throwing a dice and adding each number they throw to get their total score for that round. This total score is added to their partner's score. They keep throwing the dice until they decide to stop or until they throw a six. If they throw a six, all of their numbers for that round are discarded. The strategy in the game involves deciding to stop after a reasonable number of throws because, statistically, the six is going to turn up eventually, even though the likelihood is the same (a one in six chance) each time the dice is thrown. They have five rounds. The aim is to be the team with the highest pair score. Emphasise that if your partner decides to keep going and then throws a six so that their score is wasted, you must not do or say anything that is a put-down. Use the 'No put-downs' rewards system outlined above.

Circle Time: Bullying spoils things for everyone

Use the 'Think–ink–pair–share' strategy (see **Handbook**, page 92) and ask students to discuss: How does bullying spoil things for all of us? How would you feel if someone in our class was bullied and you knew about it? Debrief with selected pairs. Then discuss the many ways in which bullying spoils things for all of us:

- everyone feels unhappy
- everyone feels worried that they might be bullied too
- it upsets us to see someone else being hurt and to not know what to do about it
- it makes people think that our class isn't very kind.

169

→ Follow up by having students work in pairs to make a simple digital story (see **Handbook**, page 97) around the theme of 'Bullying spoils things for all of us' or 'Bullying is everyone's problem'.

Circle Time: **Think for yourself (Part 1)**

Talk about how some students start to bully someone because others are already bullying that person. Some other students don't actually bully but they help others to bully by watching, by laughing at what they say or do or by doing little things to help them (e.g. passing on someone's pencil case when it is passed to them as part of a nasty trick). Sometimes they do this because they think it's fun, they don't realise how hurtful it is, they think it will make others like them, or they are scared of the person who started it. Ask: How do students help others bully and why? Why do students copy others who are already bullying someone? Select students who wish to comment to say their ideas and make a summary on the board using two charts, one labelled 'What do they do?' and the other labelled 'Why do they do it?'. Lead into a discussion about how other students might sometimes try to get you to think like they do and do what they do, even though you don't want to. Students take it in turns (applying the 'no names' rule) to say one of the following:

- one thing that kids sometimes try to get other kids to think or do that is unkind, mean **or wrong** (don't play with that kid; say mean things about the kid; break a class or school rule; say you don't like that person)
- one reason why it can sometimes be hard to ignore someone who wants you to be **mean or bully someone with them** (they may not like me or play with me if I don't do what they say; they might try to make other people not like me too if I don't; they may say nasty things about me too; I may have no one to play with)

Stress that it takes courage to think for yourself and not just let other people tell you what to do or think.

→ Follow up by having each student make a poster that says 'I will try to think for myself and not let others tell me what to do or think'.

Circle Time: **Think for yourself (Part 2)**

Talk about sheep. Quickly collect classroom statistics (or use 'Movers and shakers', see **Handbook**, page 91, or 'Paper plate quiz and people pie', see **Handbook**, page 91) around questions such as:

- Who has been to a farm and seen a sheep?
- Who has touched or patted a sheep and felt its wool?
- Who has a woollen jumper?
- Who has a lamb's wool item in their home?

Discuss the one major problem that sheep have (i.e. the blind, unthinking, following behaviour that is typical of sheep). If one sheep does something stupid, such as running across a busy road, all the other sheep do the same thing. Sheep do not think for themselves. Link the idea of students acting like sheep when they copy bullying or any other wrong behaviour. Talk about how sometimes people behave in a particular way just because others do, just like sheep. Discuss the importance of thinking for yourself and making up your own mind instead of blindly following what everyone else is doing. Ask for examples of the kinds of wrong behaviours that students might copy.

Activities

Making sheep

Make a set of six different animal cards (pictures or words). Photocopy the set of cards four times so you can have six groups of four in a class of 24 students. Put all 24 cards in an ice-cream container. Ask each student to take one. Then ask them to move around the room making the noise of their animal until they find the other three people who are making the noise of the same animal. Then they sit down in the group of four. Repeat three times and then, as a class, sing 'Baa Baa Black Sheep'. Students can then make sheep. Here are several different ideas on how they can do this.

- For very young students, use a 'cloud' sheep shape. They can paste cotton wool or lambs' wool offcuts on their shape and add toothpick legs. They can make a class collage of sheep on green hills. Underneath they can write 'I'm not a sheep because I don't copy others'.
- Make sheep finger puppets or sheep hand strappers (see **Handbook,** page 100), then students can use their fingers in the holes as legs. Cover with cotton balls or lamb's wool offcuts.
- Join two of the twelve segments from an egg carton as a body, and another segment from the egg carton as a face. Cover in lamb's wool offcuts or cotton wool. Add toothpicks for legs, either taped on or inserted into the egg carton segments. Add two ears made from pink paper.
- Make papier-mâché sheep out of two balls of paper covered with PVC glue and strips of white paper. Egg carton legs can be added with masking tape. The sheep can stand in front of a sheet of paper that says 'We're not sheep because we think for ourselves'.
- Make the body from a cardboard tube. Cover it with cotton balls or a sheet of cotton wool. Make a head from the top of a toothpaste tube. Use toothpicks for legs and cover with cotton wool rolled flat to fit. Make the tail from a pipe-cleaner or roll a cotton ball into a sausage shape. Add two ears made from pink paper. Students can write in them 'I'm not a sheep because…'

Making a poster

Students can make posters or digital posters that say 'Don't be a sheep. Think for yourself'. Alternatively, they can cut out sheep patterns and write a message on each one. For example:

- Sheep don't think for themselves.
- Sheep just copy others.
- Don't be a sheep.
- Think for yourself.
- I will think for myself.
- Don't copy other people when they do a mean/wrong thing.
- Don't be a bully just because someone else is.

Song

Sing the following song with the class all wearing their sheep hand strapper puppets (see 'Making sheep' above). You could also have two students at a time singing it in sheep costumes. Sheep costumes can be made using a white skivvy and white tights. Or you can use a lamb's wool cot cover (or similar) worn over the student's back and tied around the waist so it doesn't slip off. Make a headband out of cardboard with cotton wool or lamb's wool offcuts glued to it and two pink ears attached.

'We're Two Little Sheep'

(To the tune of 'We're Poor Little Lambs Who Have Lost Our Way')

We're two little sheep, Barbie and Stu

Baa baa baa

We just copy what others do

Baa baa baa

We're two little sheep, Bobby and Sue

Baa baa baa

If someone else bullies, we bully too

Baa baa baa

We're two little sheep, Tommy and Lou

Baa baa baa

Whatever you do we'll follow you

Baa baa baa

We're two little sheep, Billy and Boo

Baa baa baa

Whatever you do, we'll do it too

Baa baa baa

We're two little sheep, Milly and Drew

Baa baa baa

If you break a rule, we'll do it too

Baa baa baa

We're two little sheep, Barry and Prue

Baa baa baa

If you are mean, then we're mean too

Baa baa baa

Circle Time: What you can do if you are bullied

Read one or more of the books listed below. Ask: What did the character who was being bullied do?

Ask each student to say one thing that would be good for someone to do if they were being bullied. It is important to stress again and again that the wrongdoer is the student who does the bullying or uses the put-downs and that if someone gets bullied it is *not* their fault. There are things you can do that might make it stop it quickly and if they don't work, you need to talk to a teacher and ask them to help you to stop the bullying. Highlight the following points, particularly in face-to-face situations.

- If you smile a lot, stand tall, look and act confidently and have your own ideas rather than just agreeing all the time, you are less likely to be bullied.
- If someone starts to pick on you, the first thing you can try is to ignore them.
- If that doesn't work, the next thing you can try is to walk away from them and go somewhere close to a teacher.
- If that doesn't work or you can't move away or there is no teacher close by, the next thing to do is to ask them to stop it and say you don't like what they are doing.

Unit 8

No bullying

- If that doesn't work then stare into their eyes (and don't look away) and tell them loudly to stop what they are doing or saying to you, for example:
  - Enough! Stop! I don't like it.
  - Go away!
  - Stop bothering me!
  - Don't do/say that any more!
- If that doesn't work, talk to a teacher and ask for help to solve the problem. They care about you and will help you.

Introduce students to **BLM 8.2: What to Do If You Are Bullied**. This is a memory jogger to help them remember what to do if someone starts to pick on them or if they are being bullied face-to-face.[1] They use their left hand. Note: The right hand is used as a memory jogger for what to do to help if someone else is being bullied (see page 177).

- Finger 1 (thumb): Ignore them.
- Finger 2: Move away.
- Finger 3: Ask them to stop in a polite voice.
- Finger 4: Stare at them and tell them loudly and strongly to stop. Don't smile.
- Finger 5: Ask a teacher for support in solving the problem.

Talk about how you start with finger 1; if that doesn't work, go to finger 2; if that doesn't work go to finger 3 and so on. Students can cut out the hand on the BLM and colour each finger in a different colour, or trace around their own and write in the messages. The hands can be displayed around the school and the students' traced hands can be displayed in their classroom.

The messages on both hands should be learned to mastery so that students can easily recall them. Ask them to practise reciting the steps with a partner as they touch each finger one at a time.

Drama

Act confidently and speak up

- Challenge all students to smile at least five extra times a day. You can set up an activity in which one student counts how often another smiles in a school day. They will do this activity with enthusiasm if they have a counting device.
- Have a 'staring out' competition. Call it the 'Stare dare'. Use a stopwatch to time how long each student can maintain a stare without smiling or looking away.
- Have 'strong voice' drama activity or reader's theatre where all the actors have to use really strong voices. Tell them to imagine that there is a strong wind and people will not be able to hear them unless they speak strongly. This does not mean yelling but speaking in a confident, strong voice.
- Play some of the games in Unit 7: Humour, where attempts are made to make them laugh or to break their composure. This helps them to learn to maintain an assertive stare or glare and stay in control if they are being bullied.

Picture books

Lucy and the Bully

In class, everyone asks Lucy (a little lamb) to draw for them because she is so good at it. Tommy, a little bull, starts to wait for Lucy after school and break or tear what she has

---

[1] This strategy is adapted from an idea developed by Gill Brown and Liz Harrop from the Doveton Heights and Wallarano Social Adjustment Centre in Victoria.

made or drawn at school. Her mother realises what is happening and asks the teacher to deal with it. Tommy's mother comes up and the family has a 'chat' with the teacher about what has been happening. Tommy stops giving Lucy a hard time and, over time, Lucy is able to reach out to him. It is a gentle story with a realistic outcome. Lucy and Tommy don't become great friends, they just heal the rift.

→ Stress that Tommy hadn't learned to be kind and that Lucy told her mother and then they talked to the teacher, who helped Lucy to solve the problem and helped Tommy learn to be kind.

King of the Playground
Sammy declares himself the 'King' of the playground and keeps blocking Kevin's attempts to play on the equipment and making threats about what he will do to him. Kevin's father suggests some helpful thinking (e.g. checking your facts and thinking through consequences) and some non-aggressive ways to overcome Sammy's bullying behaviour. Kevin finds the courage to confidently confront Sammy and respond verbally (but not aggressively) to his threats. Eventually, the situation improves and Kevin is able to play alongside Sammy in a reasonably friendly way.

Willy the Wimp
Willy the chimp feels unable to defend his girlfriend Milly when she is given a hard time by thugs. So he undertakes a bodybuilding course and develops muscles. This makes him feel more confident and when it happens again he is able to stand taller and frighten them off. The main point of the story is that Willy never really gets nasty, mean or tough, he just bluffs when he warns them off. The last scene shows that Willy is still the same person, as he walks into a lamp post and immediately apologises to it.

→ Stress that most people have to learn to bluff and pretend they are tougher than they are when they are being mistreated, but they don't change who they really are. Make the link between how Willy bluffed the bullies and how animals bluff predators. Ask them if they remember some of the ways that animals 'bluff' and outsmart the predator (act as if they are tougher and less scared than they really are).

Activities

Being prickly
Grow a cactus in the classroom or take the students to visit a cacti garden. Emphasise that the cactus protects itself by having some prickles to defend it against people or animals who want to hurt it. Take students for a walk in the school grounds, the local botanical gardens or a nearby park and see which other plants have some prickles to stop people and animals from getting too close and hurting them (e.g. roses, bougainvillea). Compare the prickles of plants with being 'prickly' and speaking up loudly and saying 'Stop it'.

Make a book
Students can make flipbooks or class books (see **Handbook**, pages 97 and 98) using these sentence stems:
- If you are being bullied, you can …
- To be kind to someone who is being bullied, you can …

Animal warnings
Conduct inquiry-based learning (see **Handbook**, page 90) about what animals (including insects) do to warn people and other animals to leave them alone when they feel unsafe. Don't focus on how they can sometimes attack, just on their warnings. Make the link between animals warning people to go away and stop annoying them and students warning someone who is picking on them to go away and leave them alone. The most common strategies animals use are:

Unit 8

No bullying

- making a loud noise to sound confident
- bluffing, i.e. looking and sounding confident even when they aren't (as children can do when they stand tall, stare firmly and speak up loudly).

For example:
- An echidna raises its spines to make itself look bigger and more confident.
- A skunk emits a strong smell.
- A dog barks, growls and bares its teeth.

The frill-necked lizard

Discuss this Australian lizard with the students. It has to protect itself against animals that try to hurt it, but its only real defence lies in bluffing, i.e. looking bigger and more scary than it really is and making a loud noise. This is what it does:
- It puffs out its cheeks and then opens its mouth and hisses. This action makes the frill around its neck stand up so that the lizard looks larger and more dangerous.
- It stands up on its two back legs to look taller.
- If this doesn't work, it escapes by running as fast as it can on its two back legs to the nearest tree and climbs it.

Point out to students that we sometimes have to bluff too and try to look confident when we say 'Leave me alone'. We have to stand tall, make firm eye contact and not smile. If this doesn't work, we have to move away and then, if they follow us, we have to let a teacher know what is happening.

Follow up with students singing and dancing to 'Do the Frill-necked Lizard'.

Circle Time: Cyberbullying

Start with a mobile phone and a computer in or near the circle. Select some of these questions to get the discussion going, according to the age of your students. You could use the 'Animal asks' e-tool (see **Handbook**, page 89) with eight of them.

Emailing
- Who has sent/received an email to a friend or family member? What are the good things about being able to send or receive an email?
- What are some good manners that we should use when emailing? (don't use capitals because they mean that you are feeling angry and shouting)
- What should we avoid doing when we use email because we might harm someone else? (Don't say mean things in your email—imagine how the person who gets it might feel. You wouldn't want someone to do that to you.)
- How can we protect ourselves from other people using email in way that might harm us? (Don't give your email address or password to anyone you don't know well or are not sure you can trust. There is a risk that they might use your email address to be mean to you or use your address and password to pretend to be you and send nasty messages to someone else to cause trouble for you. Don't send a reply to anyone who emails you if you don't know them. If you know them but their emailing you makes you feel 'unsafe', don't send any message back and then talk to a parent/carer about it.)

Mobile phones
- What is texting? Who has texted someone? How can it be helpful to be able to text someone? What does it cost to text someone? What is predictive text?
- What should we avoid doing when we text because we might harm someone else? (Don't say mean things in your text message. Imagine how the person who gets it might feel. You wouldn't want someone to do that to you. Don't use anyone else's mobile phone for any reason without their permission. Don't take anyone's photo with your mobile phone without that person's permission.)

175

◎ How can we protect ourselves from other people using a mobile phone in a way that might harm us? (Don't give your mobile phone number to anyone you don't know well or are not sure you can trust. There is a risk that they might use it to be mean to you. Take care of your mobile phone. Don't leave it lying around because there is a risk that someone else might pretend to be you and use your phone and send nasty text messages to another person to cause trouble for you.)

Online games
◎ What is an online role-playing game? (e.g. Club Penguin) Who has played one? What are the good things about them?
◎ How can we make sure we don't harm anyone in an online role-playing game? (Don't say nasty things about them or to them. Don't single someone out for attack during the game.)

Social networking sites for children
◎ What is a website that someone your age might use to talk to other people? (e.g. SuperclubsPlus) Who is a member of one? What are the good things about them?
◎ How can we make sure we don't harm anyone on a social networking site? (Don't say nasty things to or about somebody. Don't pretend to be someone else.)
◎ How can we make sure that we stay safe on a social networking site? (Don't give other people our access codes in case they use them to pretend to be us.)

Then ask: What should we do if someone harms us using email or a mobile phone or in a role-playing game or on a social networking site? Focus on:
◎ Show a teacher or parent or talk to them about what has happened.
◎ Keep the evidence if there is any, e.g. by saving, downloading, cutting and pasting or using Screen Capture to take a photo of a page.

→ Follow up by having pairs of students make a short slide show about one of these safety/bullying issues (i.e. using email, using a mobile phone, playing online role-playing games or using a social networking site).

Circle Time: How to help someone who is being bullied or cyberbullied

Ask students how they could help someone who was being bullied. For example:
◎ They can refuse to join in with the bullying or help with it.
◎ They can let the student being bullied know that they understand how sad and worried they must feel and that it isn't fair.
◎ They can act disgusted when someone is bullying and being mean so that they know they are doing the wrong thing.
◎ They can tell the child who is bullying what they are doing ('You are bullying') and to stop doing it because it's mean and cruel.
◎ They can show disgust towards unkind or bullying behaviour when they see it. Use role-plays to identify ways to do this safely, e.g. shaking their head and staring at the person doing it; saying 'We don't do that in our class/school' or 'What you are doing/saying to X makes us all feel bad'.
◎ They can help the person being bullied to move somewhere else and do something else.
◎ They can tell a teacher what is happening and ask them to help solve the problem.

Ask the students if they can think of any reasons why children might not let the teacher know if they knew someone else was being bullied. Write them on the board. Then go through each one, and ask every third student, 'Why is this not a good reason?' For example:

Unit 8

No bullying

Reason	Counter argument
It is dobbing.	This is not dobbing. Dobbing is when you want to get someone into trouble. Letting the teacher know what is happening is acting in a kind and responsible way, not trying to get someone into trouble.
The others will hurt or reject me.	The teacher will keep it a secret. The students who are bullying will not know about it.
It's not my problem.	It's everyone's problem. It might be you next time.

Introduce the students to **BLM 8.3: What to Do to Help Someone Being Bullied**. They use the right hand and they can remember to use their *right* hand because it is the *right* thing to do.[2]

- Finger 1: Show the person who is being bullied that you understand how they feel and that it isn't fair.
- Finger 2: Show your disgust to the person who is bullying.
- Finger 3: Tell the person bullying to stop it.
- Finger 4: Encourage the person being bullied to move away and then find ways to include them.
- Finger 5 (thumb): Tell a teacher what is happening so that they can help solve the problem.

Activity

Is this dobbing?

Use the 'Dobbing or asking for help?' e-activity with the whole class. Students sort actions that involve talking to the teacher into:
- dobbing and just trying to get someone into trouble
- asking for help because they are being bullied.

Consolidation: No bullying

Drama

Bullying scenarios

It can be distressing and counter-productive to have students act the role of being a bully. You run the risk of teaching what you want to eliminate. Use balloon puppets or paper plate puppets (see **Handbook**, page 100) to act out the bullying scenarios listed below and some good ways of responding to them. Talk about good ways to handle the situations first to give the puppeteers some ideas of what to do. Use the 'Freeze frame and rewind' strategy (see **Handbook**, page 89) with the performances. Here are some possible scenarios:
- Ben often tries to upset Adam. He does lots of mean things to him such as taking his sun hat and throwing it in the dirt and then stepping on it. He also follows him around and says, 'You're yucky and we don't like you'. Adam doesn't like what Ben does and he gets very upset with Ben.
- Kylie doesn't like school because Kym is always trying to make her feel bad. Kym says to the other girls on the table, 'Don't let Kylie have any of the good felt pens'.
- Klara and Suzi follow Jessica around during lunchtime and keep saying to her, 'No one likes you'.

[2]This strategy is adapted from an idea developed by Gill Brown and Liz Harrop from the Doveton Heights and Wallarano Social Adjustment Centre in Victoria.

- Carl hates it when two girls in his class, Erica and Katie, use the 'germ lock' sign when he comes near them (they are hinting that he has germs).
- Drago likes to push Liam's lunch on the ground and step on it, pretending that he has knocked it over accidentally.
- Jenni gets lots of other students in the class to hide Daria's pencil case (and other things belonging to her) during the day. She enjoys seeing Daria crying and upset because she can't find her things.
- Harry often goes over to Darren at lunchtime and says, 'Give me some of your chips or I'll bash you'.
- Jake and Tyson enjoy saying 'You can't be in our game, ha ha', but they only say it to Kenji and they say it whenever they can.
- Several kids say 'You are smelly' every day to Jaya.
- Whenever Anoushka tries to go to her school bag in the corridor, Aaron and Henry deliberately bump or block her.
- Several boys and girls walk behind Martina and copy whatever she does. They try to get lots of other students to do it too.
- Two girls splash water at Indrani whenever she goes near the tap or the drinking fountains.
- Koula and her friend Kimi send nasty emails to Graden telling him that nobody likes him or wants to play with him.

Activities

End-of-the-day personal reflections

At the end of each day, ask the students to put their heads down on the desk and close their eyes. Then ask them to think about the day at school as if they were running a movie of the day in their head while you ask them some questions (see below). This can also be done as a written exercise or you can ask parents to use the reflection questions at home with their children before bedtime.

- Do you remember anyone in this class feeling very sad today? Could you have helped them to feel happier? What could you have said or done?
- Do you remember anyone in this class being hurt by someone else today? Could you have done something about that and helped them? What could you have said or done?
- Do you remember anyone in this class having their feelings hurt today? Could you have helped them to feel happier? What could you have said or done?
- Can you think of anything hurtful that someone did that you should have told a teacher about?
- Think about any of your own small acts of unkindness. Did they hurt anyone? How can you try not to do those kinds of things again?
- Did you stand up for anyone who was being mistreated today?
- Were you strong enough to refuse to help someone bully today?

Cut-up sentences

(See **Handbook**, page 89.) Cut these sentences into individual words and place each cut-up sentence into an envelope. Make enough sets for each pair of students to have one set of six envelopes. Each pair reconstructs the six sentences.
- Be a friend to someone who is being bullied.
- Bullying is never OK in our school.
- Talk to a teacher if you are being bullied.
- Speak up loudly and say 'Stop it now!'
- Help someone if they are being bullied.
- Put-downs are not OK in our classroom.

You can also use the 'Cut-up sentences' e-activity with these sentences.

Unit 8

No bullying

Missing words

Students can complete the 'Missing words' e-activity.

Reflections

Use the 'Smiley ball' strategy (see **Handbook**, page 92), 'Animal asks' e-took (see **Handbook**, page 89) or 'Reflections' e-tool (see **Handbook**, page 92) questions such as these:

- What is one thing you could do if you saw some children throwing stones at a dog?
- Why does bullying spoil things for all of us, even if we aren't being bullied ourselves?
- Why is it hard to stand up for someone else when they are being badly treated?
- How will we feel if we don't help people who are being badly treated?
- How could you help someone who is being bullied?
- What is one thing you could do if someone was bullying you?

Games

Bingo strips

Use some of these words to play 'Bingo strips' (see **Handbook**, page 89).

bullying	mean	teacher
email	nasty	tease
help	safe	text
kind	stop	unkind
loudly	talk	unsafe

Other games

- 'Cross-offs' e-game (see **Handbook**, page 89). The secret message is 'Let a teacher know if someone is being bullied'.
- 'Secret word' e-game (see **Handbook**, page 92). The secret word is 'Bullying'.

Resources

A complete list of resources (including references for books, poems, films, websites and weblinks for songs) is available on Pearson Places.

Unit 9

STAR! (Success)

Key points

You feel successful and happy when you achieve your goal.
It's important to have goals because when you achieve a goal you feel happier and more successful. The STAR statements help you to remember the important messages about achieving your goals.

Stick with it and don't give up.
Think about yourself: What are you good at? How do you know?
Always make a plan.
Remember to try hard, work hard and have a go.

Stick with it and don't give up.
When something proves hard to do, keep on trying. Stick to your plan and don't give up. If things get in the way, find another way to solve the problem or try something new.

Mistakes help you to learn.
Everybody makes mistakes and fails at some things when they are trying to achieve their goals. All mistakes are useful because you can learn from them, even if you don't feel too happy when you make them.

Think about yourself: What are you good at? How do you know?
It's helpful to think about what you are good at, how you know, what you have learned, what mistakes you have made and need to fix, what kind of person you are, and how you can improve.

There are two kinds of strengths.
Your strengths can be personal strengths, such as being kind or brave, and ability strengths, such as being good at something.

Look for evidence of what you are good at.
No one is good at everything. You need to know what you are best at. These things are called your strengths. Look for evidence before you decide if you have strength in some area.

As you get older, you get better at things.
When you were a small child, there were lots of things that you couldn't do that you can do now because you have tried hard and learned things. As you get older, you will learn to do many new things that you can't do now.

Always make a plan.
Goals are the things you want to achieve and be successful at. To achieve your goals, you need to make a plan before you start. A plan helps you decide the best way to do things.

Remember to try hard and work hard.
Trying hard and working hard make it more likely that you will succeed at what you are trying to do.

Have a go and believe in yourself.
Even if something is hard to do, take a risk and try to do it—'have a go'. You can't be successful if you don't try. You also can't be successful all the time. Taking a risk is when you might fail at what you try to do but you try anyway. It means believing in yourself and having a go at something that is hard for you to do. Believing in yourself doesn't mean you can do anything you'd like to. It means you need to believe in your ability to try hard and work hard to achieve something that is OK for someone your age.

Solve problems.
If you have a problem, then don't give up. Stick with it, and look for a different way to solve the problem if the first way didn't work.

Try to be the boss of yourself.
If you want to succeed at things, you must try hard to be the boss of your own behaviour. This means doing things for yourself, being organised, remembering the things you have to do, being able to find the things you need and not being late for things.

Use your strengths to help others.
When you use your strengths to help others or our school, other people feel happy and so do you.

Unit 9

STAR! (Success)

Circle Time: You feel successful and happy when you achieve a goal **183**
Activities 183
  Make a starfish or STARfish fridge magnet
  Starfish sponge painting

Circle Time: Stick with it and don't give up **184**
Picture books 184
  Try Again Sally Jane
  The Three Little Pigs
  Bobbie Dazzler
  Possum Tale
  Little Bat
  The Hare and the Tortoise
Activities 185
  Inquiry-based learning about starfish
  Draw a sea picture
Drama. 185
  Mime
Game 185
  Fish gobbler

Circle Time: Think about yourself. How are you clever? How do you know? **186**
Picture books 186
  Yes We Can!
  Ella Sets the Stage
  Cleversticks
  Wombat Divine
Activities 187
  Make a flipbook
  Multiple intelligences (MI) class graph
  People scavenger hunt
  Four corners
  How we are clever (or smart): class lift-up flaps

Circle Time: What kind of person are you? How do you know?. **188**
Picture book 188
  Wilfrid Gordon McDonald Partridge
Activity 188
  Strengths cards

Circle Time: Liking yourself **189**
Picture books 189
  The Great Big Animal Ask
  I Like Myself
  Just the Way You Are
  I Want Your Moo
  Samantha Seagull's Sandals
  Alexander and the Wind-up Mouse

Circle Time: As I grow, I get better at things **190**
Picture book 190
  Clem Always Could

Circle Time: Believe in yourself and have a go **190**
Picture books 191
  Small Florence: Piggy Pop Star
  Sink or Swim
  Giraffes Can't Dance
  I'm Special, I'm Me
  The Little Engine That Could
Song. 192
  'The Little Red Engine'

Circle Time: Always make a plan when you want to make something happen . . **192**
Picture books 193
  Alex's Bed
  Try Again Sally Jane
  Little Bat
  Possum Tale
Activities 193
  Setting goals
  Classroom STAR celebrations
  Step-by-step calendars
  Class goals
  Success chains
  Class vouchers
Games 195
  Speedy Gonzales
  Alphabet relay
  Clap race
Activities 195
  Challenge box
  Personal bests
  Stargirl and Starboy

Circle Time: Remember to try hard and work hard **196**
Picture books 197
  The Little Red Hen
  The Very Busy Spider
  The Ants and the Grasshopper
Songs. 197
  'Ants Go Marching'
  'Heigh Ho'

Circle Time: Solving problems. **197**
Picture books 198
  The Great Goat Chase
  Our Daft Dog Danny
  Swimmy
  Big Bad Wolf Is Good
  Too Many Pears
  Where Do You Hide Two Elephants?

181

Circle Time: Be the boss of yourself: be organised. **199**

Picture books 199
- *Max Cleans Up*
- *Franklin Is Messy*
- *Hurry Up Franklin*
- *Jillian Jiggs*
- *Hurry Up Oscar*

Song. 200
- 'Get Up! Get Up!'

Activity 200
- Rise and shine!

Circle Time: Using our strengths to help others **200**

Consolidation: STAR! (Success) **201**

Activities 201
- Class projects
- Star biscuits
- Reflections

Games 202
- Bingo strips
- Memory games
- Other games

Resources. **202**

Unit 9

STAR! (Success)

Circle Time: You feel successful and happy when you achieve a goal

Tell the students about a time when you set a goal and stuck with it and didn't give up, even though it was sometimes hard and lots of other things got in the way. Emphasise how happy you felt when you succeeded. Link this to some of the goals the class has worked on, where everyone tried hard and how happy you all felt when you achieved your goal. What did you do to achieve your goal? Did you stick to it and not give up? Did you think about what you are good at? Did you make a plan? Did you work hard? Then teach the STAR! acronym using the 'STAR!' e-tool and **BLM 9.1: STAR! Poster**. Discuss what each line means.

→ Follow up by playing 'STAR box' as a whole-class activity, with one group of six at a time, or have teams compete against each other. You will need:
◎ one ball (one per team if you are using teams)
◎ a set of four boxes; write one letter of STAR on each box.

Students take turns throwing a ball into one of the boxes. When their ball lands in the box, they say what the letter on the box stands for.

Find ways to give the students daily practice in learning the acronym until they have learned it to mastery and can recite it spontaneously.

Activities

Make a starfish or STARfish fridge magnet
You will need:
◎ one round clear plastic take-away food container per student
◎ tissue paper
◎ white round stickers (for eyes) or googly eyes
◎ felt pens, sticky tape and scissors to share.

1. Cut the side of the plastic container from the base. Cut around the inner circle of the base. Cut five triangles from the side piece of the container.
2. Tape the five triangles around the base of the container to make the starfish.
3. Wrap two layers of tissue paper around the starfish and tape down on the back.
4. Stick extra bits of scrunched-up tissue paper on the top of the star for a bumpy look.
5. Draw pupils on two round stickers for eyes and stick on (or use googly eyes).
6. Punch a hole in one point of the star and thread enough string through so the starfish can be hung, with all the others, across the classroom.

To make a STARfish fridge magnet, tape a small magnet on each starfish. Students could tape the words of the acronym on their starfish and take it home.

Starfish sponge painting
Make a star template for students to use to draw a starfish shape on a kitchen sponge and cut it out. They can then experiment with how the sponge soaks up water. The starfish sponge shapes can also be used to make sponge paintings. Have containers of different coloured watery paint with one starfish shape for each container. Hold each shape with a coloured peg, each peg matching the colour of the paint (e.g. blue paint = blue peg).

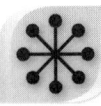

Circle Time: Stick with it and don't give up

Read one of the books listed below. Use the 'Think–ink–pair–share' strategy (see **Handbook**, page 92) and ask students to talk with their partner about something the character did that was hard for them but they kept trying and did not give up. With a new partner, students then share one thing they did that was hard for them to learn but they stuck to it and didn't give up until they were successful (e.g. learning to ride a bike, swim, read, do sums, tie shoelaces, write their name). Ask one student from each pair to tell about one of the things they talked about. Link each example to STAR messages. Highlight their feelings of satisfaction and happiness when they achieved their goal.

Picture books

Try Again Sally Jane
Sally Jane is learning to roller skate. She ends up in the pond and is ready to give up. She meets a frog, a butterfly, a flamingo, a chameleon and a snake, and each one talks about the things they have learned that were difficult for them to do. They each ask Sally Jane whether that was easy to do. The book communicates the message that 'if at first you don't succeed, you try and try again'.

The Three Little Pigs
Students can act out the story and then write about how the three little pigs didn't give up, solved their problem and defeated the wolf. This story could also be used with the Circle Time discussion 'Remember to try hard and work hard' (see page 196).
→ Follow up by singing 'Who's Afraid of the Big Bad Wolf?'

Bobbie Dazzler
Bobbie the Red Wallaby can jump, bounce, skip, hop on her left and then her right leg, walk on her heels, and even walk on her toes. She can keep her balance while walking across a fallen log. She can twirl, stand on her head, do hand springs, and do somersaults forwards and backwards. But she can't do the splits. She is determined not to give up. Her friends watch and encourage her to persist. At last Bobbie does the splits, but then she can't get back up again!

Possum Tale
A ring-tailed possum seeks a house to live in and persists in trying every option he can think of to achieve his goal (even highly inappropriate ones such as in a chimney).
→ Follow up by asking students about their family's experiences with possums who like to live in or near houses.

Little Bat
This is a simple, colourful book with minimal text, which features a range of Australian animals and birds, such as a kingfisher, a possum, a parrot, an owl, a butterfly, a sunbird, a quoll and a python. A baby bat is nervously trying to fly for the first time and the other animals offer positive and encouraging remarks. The story stresses persistence and self-belief.
→ Follow up by having students make a story map and/or undertake inquiry-based learning (see **Handbook**, page 90) about some of the beautiful animals that appear in the book.

The Hare and the Tortoise
Read the story and then talk about the importance of persistence, not giving up, and believing in your own ability to succeed. Link it to STAR! Students can draw a tortoise, make a tortoise finger puppet (see **Handbook**, page 100) or make one out of play dough.

Unit 9

STAR! (Success)

→ Follow up with any of these activities.
- Students make a poster of what they have learned that was hard for them and where they had to keep trying and not give up. They can write the statement 'I tried and tried again' or the statement from *Try Again Sally Jane*, 'Was that easy to do?'
- Give each student a copy of a cube pattern (see **Handbook**, page 97) to make a 'Me' cube with each side of the cube showing a picture of something they have learned that was difficult at first.
- As a class, sing the 'Never Never Never Give Up' song (from the TV series *Thomas the Tank Engine*). Some of the verses are good but others are a bit difficult to sing. The chorus is excellent and could be sung by itself.

Activities

Inquiry-based learning about starfish
Conduct inquiry-based learning (see **Handbook**, page 90) about starfish. Starfish have five tentacles that stick to things because they have hundreds of suckers underneath. Link this 'sticking' capacity to the need for students to stick to things they try to do and not give up.

Draw a sea picture
Students can draw a picture using the following oral instructions read out one at a time by the teacher or another student:
- There is a starfish sticking to a rock.
- The waves are washing over it.
- Three fish are swimming near the rock.
- An octopus with eight tentacles is next to the fish.
- Four seagulls are flying overhead.
- There are two clouds and an aeroplane in the sky.

Drama

Mime
As a whole class or in groups of six, students can create a mime set at a beach (e.g. starfish, waves, fish and children swimming) about not giving up.

Game

Fish gobbler
This game can also be used as part of Giggle Gym (see Unit 7: Humour, page 145). You will need a large area for this game. The purpose of the game is to follow the fish gobbler's instructions. Appoint someone to be the fish gobbler. Make one end of the room or playground the beach and the other end the ship. When the fish gobbler says:
- 'Ship': all students run to one end of the space.
- 'Beach': all students run to the other end of the space.
- 'Fishnet': all students join hands and make waves.
- 'Starfish': all students lie down or stand against the wall and pretend their arms and legs are tentacles that stick to the ground/wall.
- 'School': all students move together slowly around the space in a large, close mass.
- 'Sardines': all students squash together with their hands by their sides.

The fish gobbler can then combine two instructions such as:
- 'Go to the beach and be starfish.'
- 'Move to the ship as a school.'

Circle Time: Think about yourself. How are you clever? How do you know?

Prior to the lesson, send home **BLM 9.2: Multiple Intelligences: Parent Letter and Survey**. Then use the information from the survey for this lesson. From the parent feedback, make a list of one strength for each student in the class.

Start Circle Time by naming one of your own strengths (using the multiple intelligences framework) and give two pieces of evidence for that strength (e.g. I'm good at painting and I've had my paintings in a gallery exhibition. I won an art prize at school). Then read one of the books listed below. Talk about strengths. Explain that strengths are things that you are good at. When you are using one of your strengths you enjoy doing the activity and you get a 'brain buzz'. Talk about how the characters in the story all had different strengths. Ask students if they can remember what each character's strength was. Stress that every student in the class has 'ability' strengths too, but not all the same ones.

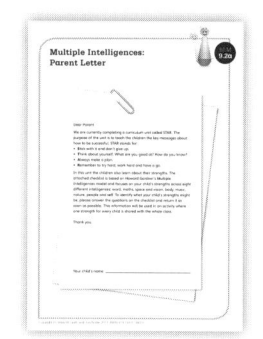

→ Follow up with 'Movers and shakers' (see **Handbook**, page 91) based on the multiple intelligences. Here are some suggestions:
- Do a star jump if can ride a bike well.
- Draw a big circle in the air if you are good at drawing.
- Pretend to read a book if you are good at reading.
- Make a big plus sign in the air if you are good at maths.
- Shake hands with someone if you are good at including others.
- Make a fist if you are good at being the boss of yourself.
- Pretend to dig the ground if you help someone do the gardening and like watching things grow.
- Turn around on the spot if you are good at dancing.
- Pretend to paint a picture if you are good at painting.
- Mime counting 1 2 3 4 5 with your fingers if you are good at counting.
- Pretend to sing (silently!) if you are good at remembering tunes and singing songs.
- Play an air guitar if you know how to play a musical instrument.
- Pretend to shake hands with someone if making friends is easy for you.
- Pretend to pat a dog if you know a lot about how to look after an animal.
- Make a big letter S in the air if you are a good speller.

Then use the 'Smiley ball' strategy (see **Handbook**, page 92) and ask each student to say one of their strengths and give an example (if they can) of one thing they do that shows that they have that strength. If students have forgotten, use parents' responses to the survey to remind them. Highlight that we all have different strengths and there are many different ways that we are clever.

Picture books

Yes We Can!
Four animal friends start making fun of each other because of things they can't easily do (e.g. Quacker Duck can swim well but can't jump over a big log, while Little Roo can easily jump over the log but can't swim). They all end up feeling angry and grumpy with each other but eventually realise that they each have their own strengths and nobody is good at everything.

Unit 9

STAR! (Success)

Ella Sets the Stage
Ella the little elephant lives on Elephant Island and her school is holding a talent show. Everybody seems to find a special talent except Ella. She tries drumming, juggling and singing but she can't do any of them well and she begins to feel down-hearted. However, when the talent show committee asks for assistance, she helps classmates with their acts, makes the program, makes awards and helps deal with the inevitable last-minute problems and a potential disaster during the show. She finally recognises that her talent is organisation and supporting others.

Cleversticks
Ling Sung is feeling sad because all the other students in his class can do things he can't do, but he is the only person in the class who can use chopsticks.

Wombat Divine
The animals (all Australian) are planning their nativity play. Wombat is very excited at the idea of playing a part, but they can't work out what role he can play. He's too big to be Mary and too short to be a king. His friends finally work out how to make the best of his strengths in the play and everyone is delighted. Talk about how everyone has different strengths and how everyone has something they are good at. This book is also used in Unit 1: Core values (page 20).

Activities

Make a flipbook
(See **Handbook**, page 98.) Begin with the sentence stem 'I can' on the top half and one drawing of what they can do on the bottom half. Students can also complete **BLM 9.3: Me Maths**.

Multiple intelligences (MI) class graph
Ask students to complete **BLM 9.4: Multiple Intelligences Checklist**. Explain that the sheet tells about eight different ways in which children can be clever. Then they choose one of their very best strengths and complete the sentences. Collect statistics on students' strengths using information from this checklist. Make multiple copies of the pictures of the eight intelligences and get each student to find the picture of their best strength, colour it in and then paste it on a pictograph titled 'How are we clever in different ways?' Use the data from the pictograph to write sentences in response to that question.

People scavenger hunt
Use BLM **9.5: People Scavenger Hunt**. Students take turns to ask a classmate to say one thing they are clever at. They write the student's name next to the correct 'smart' image on the BLM (or the other student can write their own name on their classmate's sheet). They need to find a different person for each intelligence.

Four corners
(See **Handbook**, page 89.) Make A3 pictures of each of the eight intelligences from **BLM 9.4**. Display two pictures in each corner of the room. Ask the students to go to the corner that shows one of their strengths. When they get there, they find a partner and share their top strength and one thing they can do well to show that strength.

187

How we are clever (or smart): class lift-up flaps
Get each student to make a lift-up flap (see **Handbook,** page 97) for a class display. On the outside, write: Guess what X is good at? Then on the inside, include a drawing and description of what the student can do well.

Circle Time: What kind of person are you? How do you know?

Prior to the lesson, send home **BLM 9.6: My Child's Personal Strengths: Parent Letter and Survey.** Ask parents to discuss what they tick with their child. Then collect them from the students and use the information, plus your own knowledge, to make a summary of each student's perceived strengths to use as the basis of this lesson.

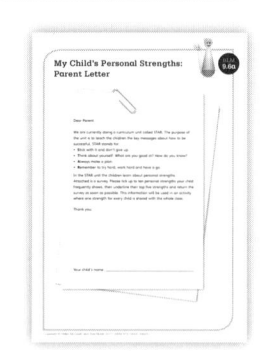

Begin Circle Time by reading *Wilfrid Gordon McDonald Partridge* (see below). Explain that we not only have 'clever' or 'smart' strengths but personal strengths such as being brave, being kind, trying hard and so on. Then ask: What kind of person was the boy in the story trying to be? How do we know? What is the evidence? Share one of your personal strengths and talk about how it is a personal strength about the kind of person you are trying to be. Explain how you know that this is a personal strength for you, i.e. give some evidence. Then roll the smiley ball to each child and ask them to name one of the top five strengths that their parent indicated for them and give one way they have shown that strength. Prompt students who may have forgotten by using your summary.

Picture book

Wilfrid Gordon McDonald Partridge
Wilfrid is a small boy who lives next door to an aged care facility. He discovers that his favourite person in the home has lost her memory. He sets out to help her find it and discovers the benefits of memory joggers, or concrete aids to memory. This book is also used in Unit 1: Core values (see page 11).
→ Follow up by using 'Strengths cards' (see below).

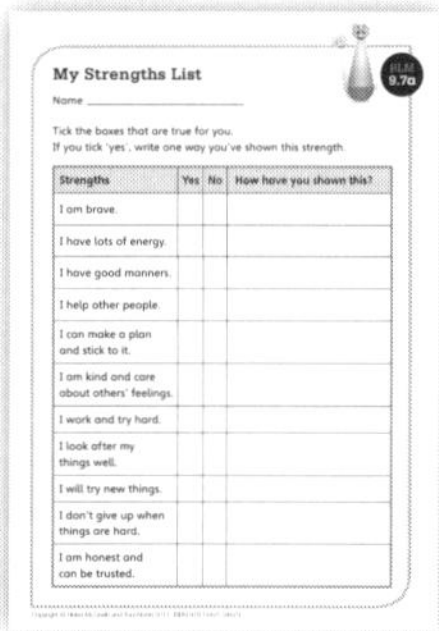

Activity

Strengths cards
Make 'Strengths cards' using the list on **BLM 9.7: My strengths list.** Make ten cards, writing one strength on each card (e.g. I am brave. I am honest and can be trusted.). Mix up the cards and ask ten students in turn to take one that they think is true about them. Then encourage them to share one way they have demonstrated that strength. When they have finished they return the cards and the next ten take a card and share. Repeat the activity with different cards over time. Keep a record of which ones have been used by which students.

Variation: Ask each student in turn to take a card and place it in front of a person they think has that strength. Repeat with different cards over time.

Ask students to write down the statement from one card each week and then look for evidence over a week to see if they think it is true of them or not. They can write it up as follows:

Do I have good manners?
Yes, this is true because…
No, this is not true yet because…

BLM 9.7: My Strengths List will also act as a prompt to remind the student of their strengths. Sending the list home to parents will encourage parents (and grandparents, brothers and sisters, etc.) to provide some evidence of the strengths that the child chooses. This stresses the importance of connecting beliefs about what you are good at with facts. Older students can write their own examples.

Circle Time: **Liking yourself**

Read one of the books listed below. Then ask the students to loudly chant 'I like myself, I'm glad I'm me. There's no one else I'd rather be'. Ask several students to explain what those words mean and why it is important to like yourself and think you are OK and not wish you were someone else.

→ Follow up by having students write and draw two reasons why they like themselves and think they are OK. Highlight the importance of continuing to work on building your strengths so that you eventually become the kind of person you are trying to be.

Picture books

The Great Big Animal Ask
This is a reworking of the Noah's Ark story in which animals, concerned that they will not be good enough to go onto the ark, ask Noah questions.

I Like Myself
This book uses chants to encourage students to value their own characteristics and strengths. Students can repeat them in appropriate contexts.

Just the Way You Are
This is a comical story about acceptance of one's self and friendship. The animals are having a party and they all want to look special. This circular story ends with the animals realising and valuing their individual qualities.

I Want Your Moo
Toodles the turkey hates her feathers, her skinny legs and her 'gobble gobble' sound and wants a better sound such as a 'moo'. Toodles is sad and unhappy about not having a 'moo' until one day her loud 'gobble gobble' saves her friend. Then she starts to accept herself and value her strengths.

Samantha Seagull's Sandals
Samantha, a young seagull, wants to be different. She doesn't want to be like all the other seagulls. She decides that a new pair of silver shoes is what she needs to make her stand out from the other seagulls. But her plan backfires and she ends up embarrassed. Only her friend Simon stands by her.

Alexander and the Wind-up Mouse

Alexander is a little mouse who learns the importance of appreciating who you are and not wanting to be someone else. People scream and throw things at him whenever they see him in the house where he lives. One day, he sneaks into Annie's room and discovers a mechanical toy mouse, Willy, who tells Alexander how good it is to be a pampered favourite toy. Alexander and Willy become friends and Alexander decides that he would rather be a wind-up mouse like his friend than be himself. He hears of a magical purple lizard that can change one animal into another animal and he determines to ask him to change him into a wind-up mouse. But when Annie's birthday arrives, Willy and some of the other toys in her room are replaced by new toys. Alexander finds the purple pebble that is required by the purple lizard to transform one animal into another but he decides to use it to turn Willy into a real mouse instead of a wind-up toy mouse.

Circle Time: As I grow, I get better at things

Prior to the lesson, ask students to bring in two photos of themselves—a current one and one when they were younger (about three to four years old). Make a labelled display. Make sure they have completed **BLM 9.3: Me Maths** before the lesson.

Begin Circle Time by asking each student to share one thing that they can do now that they couldn't do when they were little, or some of the ways in which they have changed. Read the book *Clem Always Could* (see below). Ask students to name some of the things they have had to learn. Then use **BLM 9.8: I'm Growing**. Read through the worksheet and revise the concepts of same and different. Students then decide whether they are the same in each category as when they were younger or whether they are different.

→ Follow up by having each student draw two pictures on a page. On one half of the page, they draw something they can now do that they could not do when they were three or four years old. On the other half of the page, they draw something they would like to be able to do in two years' time that they cannot easily do now.

Picture book

Clem Always Could

Clem is a enthusiastic young boy who is proud of his achievements. But then Clem finds something he can't do—swim—and he's sure he'll never be able to do it. His mother can't coax him into the swimming pool for his first lesson and they spend the lesson watching the other children. Although Clem is convinced that he was always able to drink from a cup and clean his teeth, his mother explains that he actually had to learn to do those things and there are lots more things to come. Back at the pool the next week, Clem tries to avoid getting into the pool but then his friend arrives and invites him in.

Circle Time: Believe in yourself and have a go

Begin the lesson with a story of a time when you wanted to achieve or learn something that you had never done before. You wondered if you would be able to do it, then you

Unit 9

STAR! (Success)

thought about what you can do and thought it was worth 'having a go'. For example, you wanted to learn to ski but you had never been skiing before, you knew you were fit and good at other sports and were pretty brave so you believed in yourself and had a go. You were sensible in the risk you took because you had lessons to teach you how to ski. All through life we have the opportunity to learn new things. If we don't have a go, we don't learn and we don't grow. But we have to believe in ourselves to have a go at new things. We will make mistakes and that's OK because we are learning something new. Read one of the books listed below. Then ask the students what the character in the book wanted to learn. Did they have a go? Did they believe in themselves? Then do a 'Think–ink–pair–share' (see **Handbook**, page 92) where students share with a partner a time when they believed in themselves and had a go.

→ Follow up by having students finish this sentence: 'I believe in myself so I will have a go at learning (or doing)…'

Picture books

Small Florence: Piggy Pop Star
This is a funny and inspiring tale about believing in yourself and has similarities to the story of Cinderella (but without the Prince!). Florence, a young pig, has big dreams of becoming a pop star but her two older sisters laugh at her when she tries to sing and, because she's so worried about their taunts, she can manage no more than a weird little squeak. But she still believes that she can sing well and practises in secret. Her sisters get the chance to sing in a TV competition but on the day, they lose their nerve and Florence has to sing instead. She wins the competition and becomes famous singing 'songs about love, life and vegetarianism'.

Sink or Swim
It's a hot day and Ralph the cow, after watching a family of ducks enjoying themselves in the water, decides he would like to learn to swim. When he asks the ducks to teach him, they are overcome with laughter and tell him that cows can't swim. But Ralph is persistent. He believes in himself and is prepared to do whatever it takes to learn to swim. He gets the right equipment (a swimsuit, goggles, nose plugs, flippers and a surf board) and follows the skills training provided by the ducks. By the end of the story, he can not only float and swim, but also surf. This is also a good book to use in Giggle Gym.

Giraffes Can't Dance
In this rhyming poem, Gerald the giraffe desperately wants to be able to dance along with all the animals at the annual Jungle Dance, but the other jungle animals make fun of him because he is different. He can't dance like they can because his legs are too skinny and his neck is too long. Then Gerald hears a new and different song being played and, without thinking, he starts to dance exuberantly, stunning the other animals. Hearing the right music helped Gerald to believe in himself and gave him the confidence to think that he could dance, so he had a go and he was able to dance his own special dance.

I'm Special, I'm Me
Milo enjoys playing imaginative games with his friends but they never let him be what he wants to be. He wants to be a pirate captain, but the other kids tell him he's too short. He wants to be the lion in their jungle game but they tell him he isn't strong enough so he has to be the monkey. Each day, he goes home feeling sad, but when he tells his mum about the character he played she reframes his experience, telling him about all the positive things his character could do. At the start of the story he asks other kids what he could be, then he moves to saying what he would like to be (but still doesn't get anywhere), and by the end of the story he is telling them what he's going to be. This highlights how Milo

starts to believe in himself, becomes more confident and then has a go at trying to get the part in the game that he wants.

The Little Engine That Could
This classic story promotes the power of believing in yourself and having a go. A little blue (girl) engine is carrying loads of toys for all of the boys and girls on the other side of the mountain but is confronted with a seemingly impassable mountain to get up and over. Neither the Shiny New Engine nor the Big Strong Engine (who are very arrogant and unhelpful) will help pull the load. She overcomes the odds and pulls the train to the other side using the classic motivating chant of 'I think I can, I think I can'.

See the Resource list on Pearson Places for information about where to find the online version of this story.
→ Follow up by singing the 'The Little Red Engine' (see below).

Song

'The Little Red Engine'
(This has a similar tune to 'Down by the Station, Early in the Morning')

The little red engine was taking the passengers
And the children's toys to another town
Suddenly he came to a great big mountain
He had to go up and he had to go down
(*Slowly*)
I think I can, I think I can, I think that I can do this
I must keep puffing and never stop
So he puffed and he puffed and he tooted and he tooted
And finally he got to the very top
I knew I could, I knew I could, I never should have doubted
I worked so hard and I really tried
I carried the passengers and the heavy parcels
Over the mountain to the other side.

There are details of another song version of this story on Pearson Places.
◎ Students can make a train by joining together and moving around the room while the song is being sung.
◎ One student can act as the conductor to make sure the second verse is sung more slowly.
◎ Students can each make one carriage for the train out of boxes such as fruit juice boxes. They write their name on the side of their carriage. They can write on a card one thing they wanted to learn and have learnt, and put the card in their carriage.
◎ Students can use open boxes as carriages and make tiny parcels to go in them.

Circle Time: Always make a plan when you want to make something happen

Read one of the books listed below. Discuss what the characters did in the book to set goals and make a plan. Ask: What is a goal? (something you want to do or make happen) **Why is it good to have goals?** (they help you to make your life the way you want it to be; they help you to feel good about what you can do; achieving your goal helps you to feel happier) **Go through the** story again and ask students to identify all the things the characters do to achieve their goal. Use the 'STAR!' e-tool and ask students to identify where in the book each of the ideas in the STAR! acronym can be seen (i.e. thinking carefully about what you want to do, making a plan, not giving up, taking the risk of perhaps not being able to do it, and learning from mistakes). Ask students to volunteer to say one goal they have achieved in the past. Give them some ideas, e.g. learning to ride a bike, saving money for a present, making something specific with Lego, doing a good drawing for a project, making a parent breakfast on their birthday, tidying their room.

→ Follow up by having each student say one thing they would like to do to re-organise their bedroom. Then ask them to draw or write down their plan. Remind them each day of their plan and then follow up in Circle Time in a few days.

Picture books

Alex's Bed
This is a story of how Alex and his parents make a goal to improve Alex's bedroom.

Try Again Sally Jane
See page 184.

Little Bat
See page 184.

Possum Tale
See page 184.

Activities

Setting goals
Help each student to set goals in a number of areas of their personal and school life. The goal must be something that is very concrete and possible for them to achieve in a relatively short time. For example:
- remember to bring and wear their sun hat each day for a week
- eat a piece of fruit each day at school
- learn to spell five new words
- read two books in a week
- be extra kind to their brother or sister for a week.

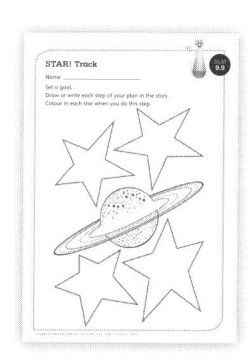

Give each student a copy of **BLM 9.9: STAR! Track** and get them to draw/write each step of their plan. For example, if they have chosen 'eat a piece of fruit each day', they might write the following steps in three of the stars:
- Decide on the five pieces of fruit.
- Help mum or dad to buy them.
- Remember to put one piece in my lunchbox each day.

Allocate several times during the week when they can colour in any of the steps in their plan that they have taken so far.

Classroom STAR celebrations
When a student has successfully set a goal, made a plan and achieved the goal, share their success with the whole class. Make a wand with a star on the top. When student achieves their goal, they can be touched by the star wand. You could also have a cloak covered in stars that the student can wear for the singing of the following song. Use the tune of 'Twinkle, Twinkle Little Star' and ask the whole class to sing it. Incorporate the student's name into the song.

Bella, Bella classroom star
Now we know just who you are
You're a girl (boy) who made a plan
Did not give up, and now you can
Tell the world 'I can go far!
Because I am a classroom star!'

- Cut out a large star for each student. They draw themselves in the middle of the star or use a photo. On the back of the star, the student (or the teacher) writes what their goal was and when they achieved it.
- You can also use STAR mobiles or display **BLM 9.9: STAR! Track**.
- Students can use a computer publishing program to make banners, cards, certificates or badges of the STAR acronym.
- Use a star shape as a lift-up flap (see **Handbook**, page 97). On the top star, students write their name and the sentence 'Guess what Sarah can do now?' On the star underneath, they write what they can do now that they couldn't do before ('She can say her four times tables').

Step-by-step calendars

In discussions, help students realise that there are steps along the way in a plan. If you choose not to use **BLM 9.9: STAR! Track**, you could make a step-by-step calendar. Have students plan and write down three or four steps to achieve a goal and then make a small three- or four-door Advent-style calendar with each step behind a door (e.g. reading one page of a book, then two pages of the book, then three pages, then finishing the whole book). The door is opened when that step is achieved. Using a similar calendar with whole-class goals (e.g. to throw all rubbish in the bin for the week—see more below) also shows students how to monitor progress in achieving a goal.

Class goals

One of the best ways to teach goal setting is to set a whole-class goal. Refer to the STAR acronym along the way so that students can see the step-by-step process of planning, sticking to it (persistence), thinking about themselves and using their strengths and trying and working hard.

You could:

- reorganise the classroom
- make a class garden
- set up a web page or organise email pals with another school
- organise a class picnic
- have a class nature hunt followed by a nature collage activity. Students work with a partner in the yard or in a nearby park to find interesting things from nature (that are readily available on the ground and don't have to be picked) to contribute to a class nature collage on a large sheet of cardboard. Before they start, briefly discuss how to 'stay safe' while they are looking, e.g. be careful when turning over a rock. When you return to the classroom, ask each pair to show and explain what they have and suggest where it could go on the collage.

Success chains

Use paper chains similar to Christmas decorations. The chains are made up of strips of coloured paper about 4 cm wide and 20 cm long. Students write their name and a personal goal on the paper ('My name is' and 'My goal is'). When they have achieved the goal, they can write 'I did it' on their strip of paper. They make the strip into a circle and glue the ends, then add it to the class chain to be displayed. Alternatively, students can make their own personal chains to hang on the back of their chair or elsewhere in the room.

STAR! (Success)

Class vouchers

Consider giving students a voucher to acknowledge the successful completion of a goal. Vouchers can be rewards such as extra computer time, using special felt pens, being an official 'helper', choosing a class game, a visit to the library with a buddy, playing a game on the computer, an extra Giggle Gym, visiting another classroom, ten minutes of playing a board game with a friend, jigsaw rental (to take home), pop-up book rental, a ten-minute card game with a friend, use of teacher's ruler, etc. Make the vouchers on different coloured card and negotiate a time when the students can swap the voucher for the reward.

Games

Speedy Gonzales

Students play games in pairs. Their goal is to improve their performance and hence their scores or times over four rounds. Use a timer for each game. Some ideas for different games are:
- Sort letter cards into alphabetical order.
- Sort playing cards from Ace (one) to King.
- Sort the same set of 20 picture cards into four piles. Five pictures start with the letter F, five with the letter B, five with the letter J and five with the letter M.
- List as many words as possible starting with B (or Th, Sh, etc.) in four minutes. The key letter combination can be selected by drawing one card from a pile.

Alphabet relay

Each team of four students has a pile of 26 alphabet cards in a container some distance in front of them. Each player runs up, finds and collects the next letter in the alphabet (e.g. A for the first player, B for the second player, etc.). They place their card in a row in front of their team and then tag the next runner. The aim is to improve the team's time each time they play. This could also be used with numbers.

Clap race

Sit in a circle. Start a clap that passes from person to person around the circle (domino style). Practise to see how fast it can travel (use a stopwatch to time it). Set a class goal to improve the class's time each time you do this. Look for evidence of the degree to which students are focusing and trying hard to try and achieve the class goal.

Activities

Challenge box

You will need:
- a box with a lid
- blank cards on which you write challenges that the students can undertake to practise goal-setting.

Ask the students for suggestions for challenges. Make up the challenge cards and put them in a large closed box. Once a week, each student reaches into the box with their eyes shut and pulls out a card. They take the card away and copy the task down and then return the card to the box so all cards are available all the time. The students can then choose whether or not to take up the challenge. When they complete three challenges (i.e. achieve their goal) they can be a 'classroom star' (see page 193).

Some ideas for challenge cards:
- Sing a song of your choice to the class for one minute.
- Tell a riddle or joke.
- Mime an animal and ask the class to guess what it is.
- Dance for one minute.

- Skip for one minute.
- Go and play with two kids from another class that you don't know very well.
- Ask someone to your house to play who hasn't been there before.
- Learn five hard spelling words and then spell them out loud without looking.
- Practise hopping until you can hop 20 times in a row.
- Teach the teacher how to do something that they don't know how to do.

Personal bests

Students can work in pairs and staple sheets of paper together to make a 'Personal bests' diary' or keep a record on the computer in their 'Personal bests' file. They keep records of their personal bests in areas that can be measured, such as how many, how long, etc. They update their records as they set and achieve improvement goals.
For example:
- How many times they and a partner can hit a table tennis ball before one person misses.
- How long they can keep a balloon up in the air without it falling to the ground or bursting.
- Their combined scores on quizzes based on spelling, words, etc.
- How many books they have read in a week, etc.

Stargirl and Starboy

Students colour in the Stargirl and Starboy cartoon characters on **BLM 9.10: Stargirl and Starboy**. These characters can be made into stick puppets using craft sticks and used in drama with stories based on when either Stargirl or Starboy wanted to achieve a goal. Here are some scenarios but the students will suggest others:
- They wanted to save some money to buy their grandmother a present for her birthday.
- They needed to learn how to play the recorder.
- They wanted to get better at shooting basketball goals.
- They wanted to make a friend at the new school they went to.
- They wanted to be better at their times tables.
- They wanted to help their next-door neighbour who had been ill.
- They wanted to raise money for the victims of an earthquake in another country.

In the discussion, encourage students to think and talk about how Stargirl and Starboy thought about their strengths, made a plan, worked hard on their plan over a long time and learned from their mistakes along the way. Discuss who might have helped them to achieve their plan (you may need to make other puppets such as Mum, Dad, teacher, Grandma, big sister). Discuss how they knew when they were finally successful (evidence) and how they felt when they had achieved their goal (proud, happy, pleased, etc).

Circle Time: Remember to try hard and work hard

This main point of this lesson is that effort and having a go are more important than how good you are at something (although obviously that helps a lot too!).

Tell the students about a time in your life when you worked very hard to achieve a goal and because you worked so hard you felt very pleased with yourself when you succeeded. Ask: Do you think I would be pleased with myself if I hadn't worked hard? If the task was really easy? (No, you feel more pleased, happy, satisfied and proud when you have achieved something that is difficult to do.) Do you always succeed when you try hard? (No, but you mostly do and if you don't succeed at least you can be happy that you tried and did the best you could.)

Then read one of the stories listed below. Ask the students what helped the character(s) to achieve their goal. In your summary of their responses, make links to actions such as: they tried hard, they worked hard, they stuck to it and didn't give up, they made a plan, etc. Ask: What if the character(s) had not worked hard? (They would not have achieved their goal.) Link back to the STAR! acronym by using the 'STAR!' e-tool or **BLM 9.1: STAR! Poster**.

→ Follow up by having each student finish the sentence: 'I worked really hard when I … and I felt happy'. Then give all students paper and felt pens to write and draw this and make the pages into a class book (see **Handbook**, page 97). Play the 'STAR box' game (see page 183) as a competitive game with students in teams of six. Students can also sing one of the songs listed below.

Picture books

The Little Red Hen
This story stresses the importance of hard work.
→ Follow up by having students act out the story or make a story map. Also make the link with the core value of 'cooperation'.

The Very Busy Spider
This is the story of a spider busily spinning her web and refusing to be distracted. She works all day and doesn't give up.
→ Follow up by singing 'Incy Wincy Spider'. Talk about how Incy Wincy did not give up when he was washed down. He tried again and climbed up the spout again. Make Incy Wincy spider out of an egg carton and pipe-cleaners. There are more activities about spiders in Unit 7: Humour and in the Elasticity unit.

The Ants and the Grasshopper
All summer long the ants worked hard building their nests and storing food for winter while the grasshopper spent summer playing and singing songs. When winter came, the grasshopper had no food, no home and was starving.
→ Follow up by having students make a bulletin board display featuring cut-out ants going along a trail carrying food and one lazy grasshopper. Sing some related songs such as those listed below.

Songs

'Ants Go Marching'
'Heigh Ho Heigh Ho (it's off to work we go)'

Circle Time: Solving problems

Ask the class to help you to solve some problems. Put a maths problem on the board, think aloud as you are solving the problem and ask for their help. Ask them if they can remember any problem that happened in the classroom that was well solved (e.g. not being able to find something, spilling something, having a bird fly inside, having too much rubbish on the floor). Stress that these were all problems that needed to be solved. Ask: Does everyone have problems? (Yes.) What are some of the things we can do to solve problems? (don't give up; think of lots of different ways to solve the problem; ask people for help) Read one of the books listed below. Ask what the character(s) did to solve the problem.

→ Follow up by having students work with a partner to think of as many ways as they can to solve one of the following imaginary problems.
- A new student joins our class halfway through the year.
- We don't have enough felt pens/computers for everyone to use whenever they want to.
- Nobody can find what they need in our classroom because it is so messy.
- We all need to have more exercise.

Picture books

The Great Goat Chase
When Mr Farmer's three greedy goats get into his turnip field, everyone tries to get them out so that they don't eat all of his turnips. Mr Farmer tries first, then the dog, horse, cow and pig. A tiny bee offers to help solve the problem in an unusual way but the other animals just laugh and ignore him. Ultimately it is the bee who solves the problem by threatening to bite the three goats on the bottom if they don't leave the turnip field.

Our Daft Dog Danny
The two children in this story love to visit their Uncle Peter and his dog Millie at the beach, especially in winter. One day, they take their dog Danny with them and chaos erupts because Danny spends all of his time at the beach trying to bite Millie's tail instead of chasing the ball they throw. Uncle Peter tries to solve the problem by putting chilli powder on Millie's tail to deter Danny from biting it. But when Danny tries to bite her tail again he is in such distress from the chilli powder that the children become very upset. They then come up with a better solution to the problem. They teach Danny a new game that involves a ball and a long rope that he can chase and chew on as much as he likes instead of chewing on Millie's tail.

Swimmy
A small black fish teaches a school of red fish to frighten their enemies by swimming close together so that they look like one large fish.

Big Bad Wolf Is Good
Big Bad Wolf is very lonely and he begins to realise that if he changes into a Big Good Wolf he might be able to make some friends. But it isn't easy to make a change, especially when you have been so bad. Big Bad Wolf finally manages to perform a noble deed (he searches for, finds and returns a lost duckling to its mother) that helps others to see him differently.
→ Follow up by having students act out the story.

Too Many Pears
Pamela the cow loves to eat pears and will stop at nothing to get at them. But her obsession deprives everyone else in the household of the joy of eating pears. A successful plan is hatched to turn her off pears by allowing her to eat as many as she wants until she never wants to see another pear.

Where Do You Hide Two Elephants?
Resourcefulness is the focus of this simple rhyming story of a young boy who is asked by two escaped circus elephants to help them to hide from those who seek to recapture them. He finds some very imaginative hiding places for them.

Unit 9

STAR! (Success)

Circle Time: Be the boss of yourself: be organised

Tell the students all the things you did to get organised for the lesson (e.g. keep an eye on the time, find and read a book, organise resources and space, work out the order of the lesson, have the computer ready for the 'STAR!' e-tool). Tell them how you managed to find everything you needed (e.g. you had them in a labelled box, you put them in the same drawer as last time, you made a list). Ask: What would happen if I wasn't organised? (the lesson would not work well; students wouldn't know what to do; there would be no resources) Explain that you would have liked to be doing other things, but you had to be the 'boss of yourself' and make yourself do what was needed because 'sometimes you have to do what you *have* to do not just what you *want* to do'.

Read one of the books listed below. Ask: Was the character in the story the boss of themselves? Were they organised or disorganised? What happened when they weren't organised? Stress that there are three things to remember to be the 'boss of yourself' and be organised:

- Organise your time, i.e. watch the time so that you are not late, don't waste time and don't take too much time to so something.
- Organise your things, i.e. sort (e.g. into a drawer or container) and label them so that you are able to easily find them when you need them.
- Have good ways to remember what you have to do, e.g. make a list, use a calendar or diary.

Ask: What do your parents do to make sure you get up and get to school on time? What do they do to make sure the family can remember what they have to do? How do you and your parents make sure everyone can find the things they need at home? (Are drawers labelled? Are things put away in the same place? Do they have their names on things like their school bag and clothes?)

Then ask half the students to walk around the classroom and find the items that help them to remember things (e.g. alphabet friezes, times tables, posters of rules). Ask the other half of the students to walk around the classroom and find the things that have been done to make it easy for the teacher and students to find things. Then have a circle discussion where different students share what they noticed about:

- how to remember things such as tables, spelling and rules
- how to find things.

Picture books

Max Cleans Up

Max's room is a disaster and has lots of messy 'boy junk'. His sister supervises him cleaning up his room but most of what she tells him to throw out (old Easter eggs, his ant farm, etc.) ends up hidden in his pockets.

→ Follow up with:
- Make a puppet play (see **Handbook**, pages 99 to 101, for puppet ideas) about why it's good to have a tidy room.
- Conduct inquiry-based learning (see **Handbook**, page 90) about ants and ant farms. Students could draw an ant farm with ants in the tunnels.
- Students can identify where each of the following materials were used in the book's illustrations: ink, watercolours, rubber stamps, string, cotton, cloth, silver foil, a glue gun, feathers, fabric paint and bubbles.

199

Franklin Is Messy
When the mess in his room becomes overwhelming and results in him breaking one of his favourite toys, Franklin, a little turtle, is helped by his parents to work out a way to make his room neater and better organised.

Hurry Up Franklin
Franklin is slow, even for a turtle! Everyone is always telling him to hurry up. He intends to be on time, but gets distracted by all the things there are to see and do. He is determined to be on time for a birthday party and manages to avoid the tempting distractions on the way and arrive on time.

Jillian Jiggs
Jillian Jiggs promises to clean up her room but just can't seem to get round to doing it, until eventually she annoys everyone around her and has to get on with it. Use the book as a discussion starter and talk about how she could have been the 'boss of herself' and got it done.

Hurry Up Oscar
This simple text describes a totally chaotic and disorganised Oscar getting ready for school. It could be used as a fun introduction to how being organised and having a place for everything makes your life (and Mum's) easier. This book also can be a lead-in to 'Rise and shine!' (see below).
→ Follow up by having students ask their parents about things they do to help them to organise their time (e.g. use watches, clocks and alarms) and remember things, such as what to buy at the shops, things to do and appointments. Make a class chart the next day.

Song
'Get Up! Get Up!'

Activity

Rise and shine!
For each student you will need:
- one enlarged copy of **BLM 9.11: Getting Ready in the Morning**
- backing card for each BLM
- paste to share.

One aspect of being disorganised that causes distress in many families is getting children up and ready for school. This activity demonstrates the process of time management. Students cut out the pictures at the top of the BLM, then paste the grid onto backing card. Then they sequence the pictures in order of what they do in the morning to get ready for school, then paste them in sequence along the top of the grid. Students can take the chart home and when they complete each step they can stick a star on the chart or colour in the star that is there. Encourage a parent/guardian or older sibling to supervise and initial each star when the step is successfully completed. The grid allows students to record their progress for three weeks. At the end of each week, the students can bring their chart to share their progress with the rest of the class.

Circle Time: Using our strengths to help others

This Circle Time session can be linked to the book *Have You Filled a Bucket Today?* and activities in Unit 1: Core values (page 10). The focus here is on helping students start to

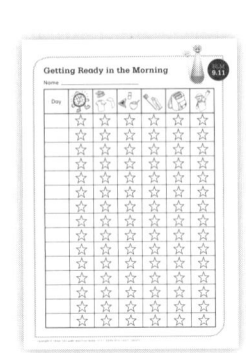

Unit 9

STAR! (Success)

develop a sense of meaning and purpose by using their strengths to help others or to make a contribution to their school or community.

Ask each student to remind the class about one of their 'ability' strengths or their 'personal' strengths. Then ask volunteer students to tell about a time when they did something for someone else that made the other person happy but also made them feel happy. When we do something for the wellbeing of other people, it makes us feel happy too and increases our own wellbeing. Ask students to think about and discuss with a partner ways in which each of them could help others in our classroom. For example, Tess is good at drawing dogs: she could teach others how to draw a dog. Jack is good at shooting basketballs: he could teach people how to do this. Ella is good at reading: she could listen to people read and help them with hard words. Zack knows how to insert pictures in a Microsoft® PowerPoint®; presentation and he could help others to do this.

→ Follow up by making an online 'Classroom directory of children's skills' that can be organised either alphabetically by name ('These are things that Adam can help others with') or by skill.

Consolidation: STAR! (Success)

Activities

Class projects
Organise a series of whole-class projects where everyone works together on a project that benefits others and contributes according to their multiple intelligences and personal strengths. These projects will also help to consolidate the STAR messages. Some suggestions:
- Plan and make a class vegetable garden and invite other classes to visit it as a stimulus for their writing or drawing activities. Students can use a digital camera to record and display what each person contributes along the way.
- Collect and donate used toys and board games to a charity such as The Smith Family.
- Organise an event to celebrate a special day such as Harmony Day (usually March 21) or Playday (usually August 4 or 5). Playday celebrates the rights of children to play as enshrined in the United Nations Convention on the Rights of the Child. Invite another class to join in with the celebration (e.g. younger students or those in the same year level but a different class) or invite parents and/or grandparents, residents of local retirement villages or school neighbours.
- Make STAR biscuits (see below) or do something else to sell to raise money for a charity.

Star biscuits
You will need:
- 250 g butter
- 1 cup caster sugar
- 2 eggs
- vanilla essence (optional)
- 1 cup self-raising flour
- 1 cup plain flour
- greased tray
- star-shaped biscuit cutter.

1. Cream butter and sugar, add eggs (and vanilla) and mix thoroughly.
2. Add sifted flours and mix to a smooth dough.
3. Knead dough on a floured surface.
4. Roll out to about 4–5 mm thick.
5. Cut out biscuits with a star-shaped biscuit cutter.
6. Bake on a greased tray in moderate oven (180°C) for 15–20 mins.

Reflections

Use the 'Smiley ball' strategy (see **Handbook**, page 92) or 'Reflections' e-tool (see **Handbook**, page 92) with questions such as these:
- What is one of your ability strengths?
- What is one of your personal strengths?
- What is something you can do now that you couldn't do when you were three years old?
- What is something you have learned that was hard for you?
- When did you stick to learning something and not give up?
- What is something new that you would like to learn?
- When did you make a mistake? What did you learn?
- What is one way you have helped others?

Games

Bingo strips

Use some of these words to play 'Bingo strips' (see **Handbook**, page 89):

alarm	goal	remember
believe	hard	stick
boss	help	smart
clever	improve	solve
diary	list	strength
difficult	mistake	try
effort	organise	watch
finish	plan	work
go	problem	yourself

Memory games

You can use the 'Memory cards' e-game (see **Handbook**, page 91) or play a game such as: I went shopping and bought… (or 'The class went on a picnic and we took…')

Other games

The following games reinforce the key concepts in this unit:
- 'Cross-offs' e-game (see **Handbook**, page 89). The secret message is 'Stick with it and don't give up'.
- 'Secret word' e-game (see **Handbook**, page 92). The secret word is 'Planning'.

Resources

A complete list of resources (including references for books, poems, films, websites and weblinks for songs) is available on Pearson Places.

Bounce Back!

A Wellbeing and Resilience Program
2nd edition

Years **K–2**
Handbook

Helen McGrath and Toni Noble

Contents

Preface iv
What's in this Handbook? v
What's on Pearson Places? vi

Chapter 1 Introduction 1
    What is the Bounce Back! program? 2
    The core features of Bounce Back! 3
    The background of the program 4
    What outcomes can you expect from Bounce Back? 5
    The Bounce Back! curriculum 5
    The classroom units 6
    Additional features of Bounce Back! 14
    In summary 17
    References 18

Chapter 2 Wellbeing and resilience 21
    What responsibility do schools have in enhancing student wellbeing? ... 21
    What is student wellbeing? 22
    What is resilience? 22
    Resilience is more than dealing with adversity 23
    The emergence of the constructs of wellbeing and resilience 23
    The protective processes and resources that promote student wellbeing and resilience 23
    Environments that promote student wellbeing and resilience 26
    Personal skills and attitudes for wellbeing and academic success 30
    In summary 32
    References 33

Chapter 3 Personal coping skills for wellbeing and resilience 35
    Everyday and major stressors 35
    Optimistic thinking 35
    Self-efficacy 40
    Hope and goal setting 40
    Luck 41
    Help-seeking and self-disclosure 41
    Helpful and rational thinking 42
    Normalising 42
    Using humour 43
    Social and emotional skills 45
    Self-knowledge 46
    Experiencing 'psychological flow' by using one's strengths 48
    A sense of meaning and purpose 49
    Being resourceful and adaptable 50
    In summary 50
    References 51

Chapter 4 Teaching the BOUNCE BACK! acronym 53
    Guidelines for teaching the acronym 53
    The key principles in BOUNCE! and BOUNCE BACK! 54
    Different ways to use the BOUNCE BACK! acronym 56
    Using the BOUNCE BACK! critical question prompts 56
    How the BOUNCE BACK! acronym addresses specific emotional and behavioural patterns 57
    Myths and realities about resilience 57

    Indicators for referring a student for professional help 60
    References 61

Chapter 5   School environments for student wellbeing and resilience **62**
    1. Enhancing school, peer and class connectedness 62
    2. Teacher optimism about student academic achievement 63
    3. Provision of opportunities for meaningful participation and taking initiative 65
    4. Positive teacher-student relationships 66
    5. Establishing peer support structures 67
    6. Positive behaviour management approaches 69
    7. Developing safe and supportive school communities 69
    8. Focusing on teacher wellbeing 70
    References 71

Chapter 6   Implementation and maintenance of Bounce Back! **74**
    Effective leadership 74
    Development of a positive school culture 75
    Effective implementation 78
    FAQs about implementing Bounce Back! 79
    Case studies of three schools implementing Bounce Back! in slightly different ways 80
    Planning for sustainability 81
    Seeking system support 82
    In summary 83
    References 83

Chapter 7   Teaching strategies in Bounce Back! **84**
    Section A: Using Circle Time and creating psychological safety in class discussions. 84
    Section B: Core K–2 teaching strategies and games. 89
    Section C: Organising students into pairs and groups 93
    References 93

Chapter 8   Years K–2 resources **94**
    Section A: Books, films and songs 94
    Section B: Classroom resources 94
    Section C: An example of a Years K–2 scope and sequence chart 102

Preface

We share a long held passion for helping teachers to enhance the wellbeing and resilience of students and young people so that they can meet life's challenges and have more satisfying lives. We wrote and developed the first edition of *Bounce Back!* (2003) to provide teachers and psychologists with an evidence-informed and classroom-friendly program that could also be used in community settings. We drew on our experience as teachers, practising psychologists, researchers and teacher educators to ensure that the program was based on both sound psychological theory and evidence-informed approaches to engaging students and effective teaching. In 2003, *Bounce Back!* was awarded the Robin Winkler Community Psychology Award by the Australian Psychological Society in recognition of its applied research base and its focus on prevention. We have been delighted by the widespread implementation of *Bounce Back!* both nationally in Australia, and internationally in countries such as the United Kingdom and South Africa.

Our roles as teacher educators and researchers have also enabled us to link the program to contemporary national and international educational issues and policies. Since we wrote the first edition, there has been an increasing understanding in psychology and education of the ways in which student wellbeing and resilience affects student engagement, learning outcomes and academic success. The focus is also embedded in the new discipline of Positive Psychology/Positive Education, and in the understanding of the importance of social–emotional learning to student engagement and success.

This revision of *Bounce Back!* is based on new research and feedback from hundreds of schools and teachers using online surveys, focus groups and personal contact with individual schools and psychologists with whom we have worked on implementation of the program. This revision also draws extensively on the outcomes from our own work as key researchers in a number of large state and Commonwealth research projects that have included investigations into effective practices for reducing bullying in schools, research into effective approaches for increasing student engagement and attendance, a scoping study on student wellbeing and the 2010 revision of the Australian National Safe Schools Framework.

We are confident that the key psychological and teaching principles that underpin the program are still relevant, rigorous and supported by research. This revised edition focuses even more strongly on the key psychological messages in the first edition. It also includes the following additions and changes:

- a new flipbook format that has been designed to make it easier, when planning for the implementation of the activities, to quickly reference the theory, research, resources and teaching strategies that underpin them
- an increased focus on translating the theory and research from the new discipline of Positive Psychology/Positive Education into classroom activities
- a number of additional cooperative learning strategies, new educational games and activities, especially activities with a focus on promoting higher order thinking, social skills and perspective taking
- more than 300 picture books and junior novels
- new links to relevant websites and online video music clips
- the 'Elasticity' unit, assessment tools, blackline masters and resource lists are now available online to provide more flexibility
- information for parents is also available online
- an extensive collection of online interactive whiteboard (IWB) games and activities to support every unit.

We are confident that you (and the young people with whom you work) will enjoy and benefit from this revision of *Bounce Back!*

Helen McGrath and Toni Noble

What's in this Handbook?

This Teacher's Handbook is divided into the following sections.

Chapter 1: Introduction
Chapter 1 provides an overview of the evidence that informs the *Bounce Back!* wellbeing and resilience program and a summary of the nine units of work that appear in the three Classroom Resource books. One is designed for Lower Primary (Years K–2), one for Middle Primary (Years 3 & 4) and one for Upper Primary–Junior Secondary (Years 5–8).

Chapter 2: Wellbeing and resilience
Chapter 2 looks at the constructs of wellbeing and resilience in greater detail and links to current national educational policies. It provides a chart of the environmental protective factors and the personal skills that have been identified by research as significant resources in helping young people grow stronger.

Chapter 3: Personal coping skills for wellbeing and resilience
Chapter 3 details the personal coping skills taught in *Bounce Back!* and outlines their theoretical rationale. Myths and realities relating to the concept of resilience are also discussed.

Chapter 4: Teaching the BOUNCE BACK! acronym
Chapter 4 explains the ten coping statements that make up the acronym BOUNCE BACK and six coping statements that make up the K–2 version BOUNCE. The two acronyms form the core of the program and have been designed to help students learn and use effective coping skills.

Chapter 5: School environments for student wellbeing and resilience
Chapter 5 discusses strategies for creating strong levels of school connectedness, peer connectedness and teacher connectedness: three significant environmental factors that contribute to resilient behaviour in students. From an educator's point of view, these are the most accessible of all the protective environmental factors that foster resilience in young people.

Chapter 6: Implementation and maintenance of Bounce Back!
Chapter 6 draws on the school leadership research literature to identify key factors that facilitate success in leading the implementation and maintenance of a school-wide wellbeing and resilience program such as *Bounce Back!* The key factors are effective leadership, the development of a positive school culture, effective implementation and planning for sustainability, and seeking system support.

Chapter 7: Years K–2 teaching strategies in Bounce Back!
Chapter 7 includes a description of all the teaching strategies used in the K–2 curriculum units. It begins with guidelines for running Circle Time and creating psychological safety during Circle Time discussions. Step-by-step guidelines for the teaching strategies follow, and finally ideas for randomly grouping students.

Chapter 8: Years K–2 resources
Chapter 8 provides ideas on how to find books, films, songs, video clips and websites used in the program, plus step-by-step instructions on how students can make the resources referred to in the nine units. There is also a sample scope and sequence chart to show how a school can coordinate the teaching of the *Bounce Back!* curriculum units.

What's on Pearson Places?

Supplementary materials for *Bounce Back!* are available on www.pearsonplaces.com.au/bounceback.aspx, your online destination for:

- Comprehensive and up-to-date lists of resources used in each of the nine curriculum units: books, songs, films, websites and video clips
- Blackline masters
- Digital or e-games, activities and teacher tools for the IWB and classroom computers
- The 'Elasticity' unit: this is an additional unit, focusing mostly on Maths and Science, that links human resilience to the scientific concept of elasticity
- Tools for measuring student wellbeing and resilience
- Information for families to help them build student wellbeing and resilience.

These are indicated by the following symbol:

Chapter 1

Introduction

Life is an exciting and often unpredictable journey with joys, satisfactions and highlights, but also some difficulties, challenges and disappointments along the way. In meeting life's challenges, we grow stronger and gain personal coping skills and a sense of who we are. We become more resilient. When we talk about human resilience we mean the capacity of a person to address challenges and cope with adversity and hardship, and then return to a state of wellbeing.

Young people have always needed coping skills to deal with challenges, but there is an ever-increasing body of evidence from different disciplines that suggests that the world of today's young people is different from that of previous generations in the following significant ways.

- Young people today are more likely to encounter a greater range of difficult and more complex circumstances, negative events and down times than previous generations. The challenges include: higher levels of family break-up, greater incidence of blended families, pressure to complete higher levels of education, issues related to cybersafety, and easier access to drugs.
- At the same time, young people may be less equipped than previous generations to cope well with these challenges. The parents of previous generations of children who lived through difficult times such as economic recessions and world wars taught them skills and attitudes that helped them to become independent and resilient, and their families were usually part of close-knit and supportive communities. Inter-generational studies suggest that today's parents are more likely to over-protect their children and are less likely to receive community support.
- In response to stress, children and young people today are more likely to become anxious and/or depressed and turn to maladaptive strategies such as overusing drugs and alcohol, and behaving in anti-social or risky ways, and suicidal thinking. For example, statistics released by the Australian Institute of Health and Welfare show that between 1996 and 2006, hospitalisation of young people as a result of intentional self-harm increased by 43% (and continues to increase) and teenagers aged 15–19 years have the highest hospitalisation rates for acute intoxication from alcohol among all age groups[1].
- Studies suggest that an increasing number of young people suffer from anxiety, depression and disorders related to substance abuse[2]. Being depressed makes it even more difficult for some young people to cope with normal but negative life events. Depression itself can also become one of the hardships that a young person has to face.
- The World Health Organization predicts that depression will be the world's leading cause of disability by 2020 and is also expected to be the second most important determinant of the burden of human disease in the world by 2020[3].

That's the bad news. The good news is that research has identified many of the significant coping skills and protective life circumstances that help young people to become more resilient. The teaching of life skills that enhance wellbeing and resilience has become a powerful tool in our ongoing battle to prevent youth depression, suicide, self-harm, violence and substance abuse. Teaching resilience and enhancing student wellbeing can enable students to respond positively and adaptively to their current life issues. It can also inoculate them against the possibility of not coping when faced with future difficulties, just as vaccinations can protect them against the adverse effects of future diseases.

Social and emotional learning is the process through which young people acquire the knowledge, attitudes and skills to:

◎ recognise and manage their emotions
◎ set and achieve positive goals
◎ demonstrate caring and concern for others
◎ establish and maintain positive relationships
◎ manage difficult situations and times resiliently
◎ make responsible decisions
◎ handle interpersonal situations effectively[4].

Social and emotional learning programs such as *Bounce Back!* are among the most successful interventions ever offered to school-aged young people[5]. Research suggests that they can be effective in school settings and for students with and without behavioural and emotional problems.

What is the Bounce Back! program?

Bounce Back! is a preventative whole-school social and emotional learning program. It has been developed to support schools and teachers in their efforts to promote positive mental health and wellbeing in their students and, in particular, to enable them to act resiliently when faced with challenges and adversity. The program predominantly focuses on classroom strategies and activities that teach students those positive social and emotional skills that might best be described as 'life skills'. *Bounce Back!* also focuses on ways to develop the types of learning environments and teacher–student relationships that foster resilience and wellbeing.

Bounce Back! is informed by the research evidence on the factors that contribute to effective prevention programs and/or social-emotional learning (SEL) programs. The evidence strongly suggests that the presence of the following features increases the effectiveness of prevention programs designed to foster positive mental health and wellbeing in students.

◎ *The program is a whole-school program.* This means that the program is not just an 'add-on', but is embedded in the curriculum and general life of the classroom and the school[6,7] and involves partnerships with families and the community[8,9]. When a program is embedded, the skills, concepts and understandings in it are linked to other curriculum areas and applied in a variety of classroom and playground contexts. The values, skills and concepts are also supported by teaching practices, interactions and other school activities and experiences, and teachers try to act in accordance with what they are teaching.

◎ *The program is delivered by teachers and integrated with academic learning.* Academic improvement is more likely when teachers (rather than external consultants or professionals) implement a SEL program[4,10].

◎ *The program is universal.* This means it is delivered to all students and not just those who are identified as 'at risk' for mental health difficulties[4,11,12].

◎ *The program is long-term and multi-year.* Multi-year programs are more likely to produce enduring benefits and are more sustainable, especially when taught across ages[7,9,11,13].

◎ *The program uses a multi-strategic approach.* This involves the inclusion of a collection of coordinated 'active ingredients', rather than a single focus[11,14,15]. Effective programs

contain at least five different aspects of social and emotional learning[16] and focus on both promoting positive behaviour and reducing anti-social behaviour[17].
- *The program is initially delivered to students early in their schooling.* Most reviews of preventative research stress that programs that start when students are very young are more likely to be effective[9,18,19]. Reivich[20] has identified that students develop the habit of thinking optimistically or pessimistically by the end of primary school.
- *The program includes a significant component of skills derived from cognitive behaviour (CBT) approaches*[3,6,21]. This point is further elaborated below.

The core features of Bounce Back!

1. *Bounce Back! contains all the evidence-informed features that have been identified as leading to higher levels of effectiveness in improving student wellbeing and resilience.*
   - *Bounce Back!* is a long-term, multi-year, whole-school program and not just an 'add-on'. It is intended that students are introduced to *Bounce Back!* in their first year of schooling and the program is continued every year thereafter.
   - *Bounce Back!* is a universal program taught to all students, not just selected students. However, concepts and skills from the program can be further consolidated in individual or small-group sessions.
   - *Bounce Back!* is taught by the teacher who has the closest relationship with a particular class of students. In primary schools, that is usually the classroom teacher. In secondary schools, the Health or English teacher can deliver the program, as can teachers who have responsibility for Personal Development or Pastoral Care. Many aspects of the program can also be picked up by teachers in other subject areas. For example, the 'Courage' unit (see **Classroom Resources**) can be integrated with aspects of English, History, Health, Religious Education and Social Studies.
   - *Bounce Back!* uses a multi-strategic approach, contains more than five different aspects of social and emotional learning, and focuses on both the promotion of positive behaviour and the reduction of anti-social behaviour.
   - The content of *Bounce Back!* is predominantly drawn from cognitive behaviour approaches.
   - Wherever possible, the social and emotional knowledge, skills and concepts in *Bounce Back!* are integrated with academic content.
2. *The content of Bounce Back! is based on evidence-informed psychological principles.*
   The content of the program is based significantly on the core psychological principles of cognitive behaviour therapy (CBT). There is more research support for the efficacy of CBT in changing feelings and behaviour than there is for any other type of therapy.[3] CBT, which was orginally developed by Aaron Beck[22], is based on the understanding that how you think affects how you feel, which in turn influences how you behave. Therefore, by adopting more positive and rational thinking you can help yourself to change your behaviour. Two specific and more sophisticated applications/refinements of the basic model of CBT have particularly influenced the content of *Bounce Back!*. These are Albert Ellis's Rational Emotive Behaviour Therapy[23] and Martin Seligman's Learned Optimism[24]. Recognition for the psychological rigour of the program is evidenced by its being awarded the Robin Winkler Award in 2003 for Excellence in Community Psychology (Applied Research) by the Australian Psychological Society.
3. *The overall approach in Bounce Back! reflects the Positive Psychology model.*
   Positive Psychology is a model that has shifted the primary focus of psychological and educational intervention away from a focus on deficits, problems and treatment and towards a focus on prevention. This includes: support for engagement and positive emotions, the development of a sense of meaning and purpose in life, the identification and building of individual strengths, and the intentional development of social and emotional skills that contribute to positive relationships, resilience and overall wellbeing. Positive Psychology, although a relatively new model, is also significantly supported by research[25].

4. *Bounce Back! uses teaching approaches that are evidence-informed and/or theoretically sound.*

The most frequently used teaching strategies in the program are based on cooperative learning, for which there is extensive evidence support (e.g.[26-30]). Other teaching strategies in the program include the use of educational games (e.g.[26,31]), Circle Time discussions[32], and high-quality literature (e.g. picture books, poetry and junior novels) as an entry point for discussions on wellbeing topics such as relationships, values, courage and resilience.

5. *The content in Bounce Back! can be integrated with other curriculum areas.*

The content has been developed in a way that enables it to be integrated with many other curriculum areas, such as English, Social Sciences, Science, Mathematics, Religious Education and the Visual and Performing Arts. Integrating social and emotional learning with academic content has been shown to increase program effectiveness[10].

The background of the program

An abbreviated version of the *Bounce Back!* program was trialled in a joint research project between the Drug Education section of the Department of Education in Victoria and the Faculty of Education at Deakin University[33]. Eight teachers were involved in trialling the program in their Year 5 or Year 6 classrooms over 14 weeks. These teachers taught in diverse school communities that included schools from different socio-economic areas, secular and private schools, and rural, inner-city and suburban schools.

All the teachers in the study reported that the *Bounce Back!* program was user-friendly and easy to implement. At the end of 14 weeks of teaching the program, seven of the eight teachers reported greater confidence in teaching the coping skills that underpin the program. They also reported marked improvements and greater confidence in their ability to counsel and support their students. They perceived that their use of the program facilitated better communication with their students, which helped in the students' management of personal issues as well as schoolwork issues. All teachers reported that teaching the program improved their own personal and professional resilience and their capacity to cope with difficult times.

The research also demonstrated that the students in the eight classes were able to learn, understand and recall the BOUNCE BACK! acronym with an average 80% success rate after 14 weeks of the program. At the end of the program, students showed an increase in resilient thinking, especially optimistic and helpful thinking, when asked to solve problems in hypothetical difficult situations. In focus group interviews, many students reported using the coping skills in their own lives, including difficult family situations. Some students mentioned they had taught some of the *Bounce Back!* coping skills to members of their family. During the 14 weeks of the program, teachers also observed some students spontaneously using the *Bounce Back!* statements in real-life stressful situations and in supporting their classmates and friends.

The program was further developed in consultation with several of the trial schools as well as a range of additional primary schools. The teachers and students in these schools provided important feedback on the implementation of *Bounce Back!* curriculum activities.

KidsMatter

KidsMatter is an Australian Primary Schools Mental Health Initiative, which is supported by a partnership between the Commonwealth Department of Health and Ageing, Beyond Blue: The National Depression Initiative, The Australian Psychological Society, Principals Australia and Australian Rotary Health. It aims to improve the mental health and wellbeing of primary school students, reduce mental health problems among students and achieve greater support for students experiencing mental health problems. In 2007 and 2008, grants were provided to 100 primary schools for this purpose. *Bounce Back!* was selected by 64% of the schools that chose to implement a specific social and emotional learning program. The findings of the evaluation of the effectiveness of the KidsMatter initiative indicated that there were significant and positive changes in schools, teachers, parents/caregivers and students over the two-year trial. In particular, there were statistically and practically significant improvements in students' measured mental health in terms of both reduced mental health difficulties and increased mental health strengths. The impact of KidsMatter was especially apparent for students who were rated as having higher levels of mental health difficulties at the start of the trial[34].

International examples

Bounce Back! has also been implemented in many schools outside Australia, including in South Africa and Scotland. A two-year evaluation of the implementation of *Bounce Back!* in primary schools in the Perth-Kinross area in Scotland found similar benefits for both students and teachers to those obtained in the original *Bounce Back!* trial research study conducted in Victoria[35]. Students reported that they had really enjoyed the *Bounce Back!* activities and particularly liked the variety of activities and opportunities for active and cooperative learning in the program.

What outcomes can you expect from Bounce Back?

The research on which the program is based, the Kidsmatter research and research outcomes identified by CASEL[36,37] indicate that the following outcomes are likely to be achieved for many students after consistent and effective implementation of *Bounce Back!* across the school and over time:

- improvement in students' social and emotional skills and pro-social behaviour
- improvements in mental health for all students but especially for those who could be considered 'at risk'; a reduction in emotional distress (i.e anxiety and depression)
- a more positive, supportive and pro-social school culture that contributes to the reduction of school bullying
- higher levels of students' connectedness to school
- greater likelihood of students offering peer support to friends and classmates
- improvements in students' academic learning outcomes
- higher levels of teacher resilience and wellbeing
- more effective teacher support and counselling for students.

The Bounce Back! curriculum

There are three levels in this program:
1. **Years K–2**, which is suitable for students in the first three years of primary schooling, i.e. students aged approximately five to seven years.
2. **Years 3 & 4**, which is suitable for students in the third and fourth years of primary schooling, i.e. students aged approximately eight to ten years.
3. **Years 5–8**, which is suitable for students in the fifth and sixth years of primary schooling and the first two years of junior secondary, i.e students aged approximately 11 to 14 years.

There are three *Bounce Back!* books, as well as online resources. On one side of each book is the **Handbook**, which outlines the theory, rationale and research that underpins *Bounce Back!* and describes in detail the key teaching strategies and resources for its delivery. On the flipside is **Classroom Resources**, which contains all classroom activities pertaining to the level.

The books are also supported by online resources that include:
- the 'Elasticity' unit
- blackline masters for student activities
- information for families on the resilience and wellbeing messages
- tools for measuring student wellbeing and resilience
- detailed lists of all the books, songs, films and videos referred to
- interactive games and activities
- digital teacher tools.

These are available on www.pearsonplaces.com.au/bounceback.aspx and are indicated by the following symbol:

The classroom units

Each **Classroom Resources** book contains nine units of work at the appropriate year levels and curriculum outcomes. These are:
1. Core values
2. People bouncing back
3. Courage
4. Looking on the bright side
5. Emotions
6. Relationships
7. Humour
8. No bullying
9. Success (STAR! in the Years K–2 book, CHAMP! in the Years 3 & 4 book and WINNERS! in the Years 5–8 book).

An additional unit called 'Elasticity' can be found online on Pearson Places. This is mostly a Maths and Science unit that links human resilience to the scientific concept of elasticity.

Unit 1: Core values

> No act of kindness, no matter how small, is ever wasted. (Aesop)
>
> Watch your thoughts, for they become words. Watch your words, for they become actions. Watch your actions, for they become habits. Watch your habits, for they become character. Watch your character, for it becomes your destiny. (Aristotle)

The 'Core values' unit provides concrete and practical activities to help students understand the importance of eight core pro-social values and how these values determine how they behave and relate with others. The discussions and activities in this unit focus on teaching students how to behave in ways that reflect the following values:
- Honesty
- Fairness (including social justice)
- Responsibility
- Support (being kind, showing care and compassion)
- Cooperation
- Acceptance of differences (accepting, respecting, living with and finding the positive side of differences in others)
- Respect (for the rights and feelings of others; self-respect, e.g cybersafe behaviour and protective behaviours)
- Friendliness and inclusion (being friendly and socially responsible, including others in games, activities and conversations).

Values are the relatively stable, pervasive and enduring beliefs that each person holds about what is right and wrong and most important in life. They are the principles or standards that guide our behaviour and choices. Our values form our 'moral map', which we consult every time we have to make a value-based decision or we face a moral dilemma. They also form the basis of how we see ourselves as individuals, how we see others and how we interpret the world in general.

A caring and supportive school and classroom environment with a focus on pro-social values and behaviours makes it less likely that students will behave in anti-social ways[38]. Lovat and Toomey[39], who reviewed the Australian Government's Good Practices Schools Project, concluded that teaching values is at the heart of quality teaching and significantly influences the development of positive relationships in schools.

Pro-social values emphasise the importance of harmony, i.e. getting along well, collaborating, treating other people fairly and kindly, and sorting out social problems in a manner that maintains friendliness and peace. The core pro-social values of honesty, fairness, responsibility, support (also called 'care' or 'compassion'), cooperation, acceptance of differences, respect and friendliness/inclusion are universal values that are linked to the development of wellbeing and resilience. Empathy for others underpins all these values.

When students behave consistently with these pro-social values, it increases the likelihood that students will be more accepted and supported by others. These values also help young people to be connected to their family, peers and teachers. In a large-scale study of 9000 young people[40], a belief in core values was identified as one of three most prevalent protective factors for young people in Australia today. Belonging and feeling supported are critical protective processes in helping students to cope when they experience difficulties, frustrations and hard times. Acting on strong pro-social values can increase one's sense of being a decent, successful and worthwhile person, and at the same time provide some support for peers who might need it.

The teaching of pro-social values is a starting point for helping students to develop pro-social behaviour. The values of compassion and respect become stepping stones to a disposition towards responding with empathy which, in turn, is an essential aspect of treating others with understanding and kindness rather than behaving aggressively or engaging in bullying behaviour. When students adopt the value of cooperation, they are more open to learning and practising the social and emotional skills that enable teamwork and effective management of conflict. Acceptance of the values of fairness and honesty directs students to learn and use social skills such as playing fairly rather than cheating and being a good winner and loser.

Living one's life according to pro-social values also contributes to students' sense of meaning or purpose and has a strong positive impact on their wellbeing and mental health. This process is illustrated by a longitudinal study that followed high school students into late adulthood, a time interval of more than 50 years[41]. The students were first interviewed in the 1930s and then again every ten years until the late 1990s. The results of the study indicated that those adolescents who had tried to live according to their values became both psychologically and physically healthier adults.

Unit 2: People bouncing back

> Our greatest glory is not in 'never falling', but in rising every time we fall. (Confucius)

This unit introduces human resilience, or the capacity of people to bounce back after experiencing difficulties, challenges or hard times. In the Years K–2 book, students are introduced to the acronym of BOUNCE! In the Years 3 & 4 and Years 5–8 books, they are introduced to the acronym of BOUNCE BACK! The acronyms are formed by the key principles underpinning the coping statements.

Bad times don't last. Things always get better. Stay optimistic.
Other people can help if you talk to them. Get a reality check.
Unhelpful thinking makes you feel more upset. Think again.
Nobody is perfect—not you and not others.
Concentrate on the positives (no matter how small) and use laughter.
Everybody experiences sadness, hurt, failure, rejection and setbacks sometimes, not just you. They are a normal part of life. Try not to personalise them.

Blame fairly. How much of what happened was due to you, to others and to bad luck or circumstances?
Accept what can't be changed (but try to change what you can change first).
Catastrophising exaggerates your worries. Don't believe the worst possible picture.
Keep things in perspective. It's only part of your life.

The acronyms help students to learn the statements. There is also a focus on the ways in which nature bounces back (e.g. bush regeneration, skin repair, the immune system) and how people can 'bounce back' after hardship.

Teaching students coping skills makes it more likely that they will be able to respond effectively and adaptively to challenges and times of adversity, manage emotional distress and have optimal levels of wellbeing. Coping skills provide them with cognition, behaviours and attitudes for making their lives in the classroom and playground less distressing, happier and more productive.

Unit 3: Courage

> We become brave by doing brave acts. (Aristotle)
> Courage is resilience to fear, mastery of fear, not absence of fear. (Mark Twain)

The focus of this unit is on:
- understanding that if there is no fear, there is no courage
- understanding the differences between everyday courage, heroism (acting bravely to help someone else), thrill-seeking, professional risk-taking and foolhardiness
- recognising that everyday courage can be either physical (e.g. learning to snorkel), psychological (e.g. sorting out a disagreement with a friend) or moral (e.g. supporting someone who is being treated unfairly despite the risk of losing friends or being criticised)
- understanding that fear is relative—what makes one person scared or nervous may not make another person scared or nervous
- developing the skills and perceptions that lead to being more courageous in many areas of one's life (e.g. public speaking).

Courage is defined as the capacity to face threatening or difficult situations that cause strong emotions such as anxiety or fear, without giving in to those feelings. Courage is needed to persist and deal with hardships or setbacks or tackle a difficult and threatening task. It is a 'voluntary' action and there is risk attached that may lead to undesirable consequences. Courage is not the absence of fear or distress but the capacity to act despite the fear. The courageous person faces the fearful situation and tries to resolve it, despite the discomfort produced by their fearful thoughts, feelings and/or physical reactions.

Rachman[42], an early researcher in courage, investigated the courage of army bomb disposal experts. He identified that the main factor that helped them be courageous was their confidence in their training. This suggests that teachers can help students develop courage to tackle something that is difficult or anxiety-provoking for them (e.g giving a class talk) if they are taught the relevant skills.

Courage is an important life skill that can help young people be more resilient when faced with adversity. Aristotle believed that a person develops courage by doing courageous acts. Teachers can play an important role in 'encouraging' students to be courageous by facilitating them to self-reflect on their courageous behaviour. This type of self-reflection helps a student to develop a courageous mindset to encourage their future acts of courage[43].

Unit 4: Looking on the bright side

> It is better to light a candle than to curse the darkness. (Chinese proverb)

The focus of this unit is on skills and strategies associated with optimistic thinking and positivity. These include:
- positive tracking, i.e. the skill of focusing on the positive aspects of a negative situation, however small they may be
- positive conversion of negative events and mistakes into opportunities and learning experiences
- developing an optimistic explanatory style when faced with setbacks or difficulties, perceiving that setbacks and difficult times:
  - are only temporary ('things will get better')
  - happen to other people too ('not just me')
  - are limited to the immediate incident(s) ('just this')

- skills for challenging a pessimistic explanatory style when faced with a setback or failure. A pessimistic explanatory style is perceiving that a setback is permanent ('it always happens this way'), personal ('it only happens to me; it's my fault, I'm useless') and pervasive ('it affects everything I do')
- focusing on gratitude by being thankful for the good things that happen and taking time to express thanks and show appreciation towards others
- thinking and feeling positive about the past (being grateful), the present (taking time out to think about and feel good about the good things that happen) and the future (being optimistic and expecting good things to happen)
- finding hope in difficult times
- being open-minded and flexible when solving problems and having confidence in one's own ability to solve problems and take positive actions.

The activities in this unit also help to build class optimism. Optimism has been described by Peterson[44] as the 'Velcro' construct of resilience, to which everything else sticks. A student who thinks optimistically tends to look on the bright side of situations and hope for the best, even when things are not looking good. Being optimistic can empower students and help them to get on top of challenges and manage life's difficulties. Conversely, pessimism is expecting failure, anticipating bad outcomes, or a tendency to take a gloomy view of things.

Optimism can play a vital role in helping students and young people adapt to new situations or cope with setbacks. There are two forms of optimism: expectancy and explanatory style. Both are included in the 'Looking on the bright side' unit. From the expectancy perspective, optimism is having a disposition or tendency to expect things to work out, to be forward looking and proactive and to have the confidence to persevere when faced with adversity[45]. From the explanatory-style perspective, an optimistic or pessimistic style refers to the way you explain the cause of events to yourself when they happen[24]. Optimism is also a contributing factor to getting along well with others and having good physical health. In contrast, pessimism, especially a pessimistic explanatory style[3,21], is linked to a sense of hopelessness and despair and, sometimes, depression.

Unit 5: Emotions

Joy is not in things, it is in us. (Richard Wagner)

The focus of this unit is on teaching students to:
- understand that very few events are good or bad in themselves and that how you think about something strongly influences how you feel about it
- recognise, enjoy and recall their own positive emotions such as happiness, pride, contentment, surprise and excitement and the events that promote these positive feelings; teaching them to amplify and enhance those feelings by sharing them with others
- recognise and manage their negative emotions such as anger, sadness, worry, disappointment and embarrassment and understanding that they have choices about how they manage these emotions and the actions they take
- recognise the feelings and intentions of others
- respond with empathy to the feelings of others
- use positive self-talk and low-key emotional language.

In the past, psychologists have focused more on how to manage negative emotions and attitudes (e.g. depression, anxiety and anger) than on how to amplify positive emotions. However, more recent research has shown the benefits of positive emotions. Positive emotions can increase 'behavioural flexibility' and build cognitive and emotional resources. Positive emotions can enhance people's capacity for optimistic thinking, problem solving and decision making and lead to more flexible, innovative and creative solutions[46,47]. Experiencing positive emotions such as joyfulness, pride and excitement helps to broaden students' capacity to learn, connects them to others and builds on the classroom and school's capacity to thrive[48].

Research has demonstrated that positive emotions also have the ability to 'undo' the effects of stress more quickly and encourage both emotional and physical resilience[49].

Positive emotions are promoted in the classroom in **Bounce Back!** For example:
- feelings of belonging are promoted through relational strategies such as Circle Time and cooperative learning
- feelings of excitement and enjoyment in learning are generated through educational games, including interactive whiteboard games
- feelings of optimism about academic success are promoted through learning skills for setting realistic goals, framing success in terms of student effort and persistence, encouraging positive thinking and challenging unhelpful thinking
- feelings of satisfaction and pride are promoted by students identifying and recognising different strengths and valuing and celebrating different learning products.

Correctly recognising and naming their emotions helps students to understand and manage their lives and their relationships more effectively and less stressfully. This unit incorporates activities that help young people to understand how their thoughts affect their feelings and their behaviour. An important message is that their perception or interpretation of an event helps to determine how they feel, not just the event per se. If they are over-aroused and interpret an event in a negative, hopeless or threatening light, then they are more likely to experience strong negative emotions. Strong negative emotions may make it more difficult for them to be resilient and bounce back. If they are able to stay calm and find a helpful way to interpret a situation, then they are more able to cope and to problem-solve.

Poor management of strong emotions such as anxiety, anger, fear and sadness narrows a person's range of thoughts and limits action choices. People who allow their negative emotions to overwhelm them are more likely to act impulsively and be more vulnerable to substance abuse and other acts of self-harm. Learning how to express emotions in a positive and assertive way helps people to feel more in control when things are difficult for them. The unit also encourages young people to reflect on what makes them happy, proud and satisfied, a theme that is picked up again in the STAR! (Success) unit.

Unit 6: Relationships

> Alone we can do so little. Together we can do so much. (Helen Keller)
> In order to have friends, you must first be one. (Elbert Hubbard)

The focus of this unit is skills and attitudes that help students to:
- develop skills for making and keeping friends
- develop skills for getting along well with others
- develop skills for managing disagreements
- self-reflect about their own current levels of skills in these areas.

Having a friend is a very important source of wellbeing for students, as it is for all of us. Although all students would like to be well accepted by their peers or be popular, their relationships with their friends are more important. Having a friend gives a student a sense of self-worth; someone who can provide loyalty, support and companionship; someone to bounce ideas off; someone to help with problem solving; and provide an opportunity to receive and give affection. Having a friend also enables a student to practise essential social skills such as conflict resolution, empathic thinking and negotiation. Social skills are described as 'academic enablers' because they not only help students to develop positive relationships with their peers and teachers, but they also facilitate student learning and academic performance[50].

Although many social skills are practised in students' everyday classroom and playground interactions, their use in the context of deeper and more intimate relationships with friends enables students to prepare for the more significant relationships they will have later in their lives. Long-term romantic partnerships are the goal of most people in adult life. Married people report being more resilient, happier and more satisfied with life[51,52]. The social skills that contribute to satisfying friendships and peer relationships are almost identical to the social skills that contribute to satisfying romantic relationships. Among married people, those whose spouse is:

- agreeable (cooperative, positive and able to handle conflict well)
- conscientious (responsible, hard working and able to achieve goals)
- emotionally stable (able to manage their emotions) and
- open to experience (flexible and risk-taking)

tend to be more emotionally and sexually satisfied with their relationships than do those who do not have spouses with these qualities[53].

The long-term research of John Gottman[54,55] has shown that the most satisfying and sustainable romantic relationships are those where both partners have the skills to handle conflict well and focus more on the positives than the negatives in their relationship. He also identified that one of the main reasons many couples find it so hard to deal with conflict effectively is their inability to manage the 'flood' of anxious and angry emotions that overwhelm them during conflict situations. Relationship skills are not the only factors that contribute to a satisfying and sustainable relationship, but such skills do make a significant difference to the quality of the relationship. More details can be found in McGrath and Edwards[56]. The social skills we can teach students at school will contribute to their later success in adult relationships.

In summary, if we teach relationship skills to students:

- In the short term, they are more likely to feel satisfied with school, have higher levels of wellbeing and be more resilient because they will have social support, a sense of social value and people with whom to cross-check their perceptions about life.
- In the longer term, they will be more likely to:
  - attract supportive partners
  - have successful adult friendships that provide support in adverse circumstances
  - have sustainable romantic relationships that will be protective for themselves as well as for their own children
  - be able to model effective relationship skills for their own children.

Unit 7: Humour

> A person without a sense of humour is like a wagon without springs. It's jolted by every pebble on the road. (Henry Ward Beecher)

The focus of this unit is on:
- activities that develop an understanding of the processes and styles of humour
- activities that highlight how humour can be used to help with coping in hard times as well as with supporting others
- activities to help students to differentiate between humour that helps and humour that harms, stereotypes, trivialises or denies
- opportunities for students to participate with classmates in humorous activities through 'Giggle Gym' sessions. These are brief daily humorous activities that can be used as a stress break in class.

Humour is one of the processes of optimism that significantly contributes to personal resilience. We are able to feel more hopeful and light-hearted when we can see a funny side of a difficult situation. Humour helps us to gain a sense of perspective on our problems because it can throw a little light in an otherwise black situation. It reminds us that life goes on. It helps us to cope with what we can't change. Humour can provide an opportunity to reduce the tension created by strong and uncomfortable emotions such as sorrow, fear and anger. When we laugh we experience pleasure and a greater openness to discussion and interaction. Research consistently demonstrates that laughing results in beneficial physiological changes in our bodies that improve our health and help us to fight illness[57,58]. This understanding underpins the therapeutic use of humour in medical contexts.

Shared laughter is also a unique human bond that helps us to connect with others. Having fun with peers and incorporating humour into classroom activities helps students to feel more connected with each other and with their teacher and to stay engaged and on task. Laughter and humour hold students' attention and create positive emotions, thereby helping students to retain the information they are learning. Cognitively, humour usually involves the perception of incongruity or paradox in a playful context. However, humour can also be demeaning and hurtful when it reinforces sexual or cultural stereotypes, or is at the expense of another person through the use of cynical or sarcastic comments.

Unit 8: No bullying

> The world is a dangerous place to live, not because of the people who are evil, but because of the people who don't do anything about it. (Albert Einstein)

The focus of this unit is on:
- understanding terms such as bullying, cyberbullying and cyberharassment and helping students discriminate between bullying behaviour and other kinds of anti-social behaviour
- understanding the difference between asking for support, acting responsibly to support someone else and 'dobbing'
- skills for acting confidently and assertively; this should not lead students to believe that if they are bullied it is their fault
- skills and attitudes that help students to respond adaptively to being bullied or put down, for example:
  - accepting that if you have 'self-respect' then you 'self-protect'
  - asking for support
  - verbal and non-verbal assertiveness
- skills for understanding and managing negative peer pressure
- skills for discouraging bullying and offering bystander support.

Bullying continues to be a problem in our schools and a new form, cyberbullying, appears to be increasing. One in four students reports being bullied in a school term and one in ten reports being cyberbullied. Increasingly, students are both bullied and cyberbullied[59,60]. Cyberbullying is more likely to occur outside school hours and off the school site, but the effects are felt in school hours because of the breakdown of relationships when school resumes.

Unit 9: STAR! (Success)

> An aim in life is the only fortune worth finding. (Robert Louis Stevenson)

The focus of the unit is on activities that:
- teach students how to identify their own relative strengths and limitations; strengths can be ability-based (e.g. across the eight intelligences identified by Howard Gardner in his Multiple Intelligences Model[61] or character-based (e.g. being kind, friendly, a good organiser, etc.)
- help students to understand that strengths can be developed and limitations also need to be improved through effort
- teach students to use this self-knowledge of their strengths to help them be successful across many areas of their life, with a particular emphasis on collecting evidence for these conclusions about oneself, not just hoping or making unwarranted, unrealistic and deflated or inflated assumptions
- teach students that success is mostly a result of effort and persistence (but ability contributes too)
- develop skills of self-discipline and self-management (e.g. willpower, effort, time management and organisational skills)

- teach the skills and processes of achieving goals (e.g. setting goals, identifying different pathways to goal achievement, making a plan with small steps, taking sensible risks, persisting in the face of obstacles, problem solving and being resourceful when things are challenging or when something goes wrong)
- challenge students to use their initiative and be resourceful, and hence understand the real-life 'rocky up-and-down' process of goal achievement
- help students to understand the concept of 'psychological flow'[62], a positive outcome that occurs when they are using their strengths and are immersed in an activity that offers them a challenge and fully absorbs their attention in a positive way
- encourage meaningful participation and a sense of meaning and purpose through engagement in school and community-based projects in the service of others. This can involve, for example, an older student working with younger students to teach wellbeing themes; school-based projects such as anti-bullying campaigns; and community projects such as reciprocal learning projects in a nearby retirement village, where students teach Internet skills and residents teach card games.

This unit is based on a core acronym at each of the three different levels:

- STAR! in Years K–2
- CHAMP! in Years 3 & 4
- WINNERS! in Years 5–8.

Each acronym reinforces age-appropriate key messages for success.

Being successful includes knowing your strengths and limitations and using that self-knowledge to set goals, monitor progress and achieve in different areas deemed important by oneself and others. Achieving one's goals is linked to being hopeful or optimistic that you can be successful. With hope, you are more likely to be a successful problem solver and find different pathways to achieve one's goals[63]. A 'success mindset' involves believing that effort rather than ability is the most important ingredient in being successful and leads to persevering and working hard, rather than giving up easily when faced with setbacks and obstacles[64]. A strengths-based approach is strongly advocated by the new disciplines of Positive Psychology and Positive Education[65]. Meaningful participation in school and community-based activities helps students to gain a sense of meaning and purpose—a critical component of student wellbeing. The kinds of activities that are most likely to create a sense of 'purpose' for students are those that are worthwhile, and the activities that affect other people, not just themselves, are most likely to create a sense of 'meaning'.

Additional online unit: Elasticity

This unit introduces the scientific concept of physical resilience or 'bouncing back'. When something is resilient, it is elastic and capable of returning to its original shape after being stretched, squashed or bent. The 'Elasticity' unit can serve as an introduction to the 'People bouncing back' unit. The focus of the 'Elasticity' unit is on:

- investigating and experimenting with elastic forces (e.g. rubber bands, bouncing balls) and stretching (e.g. elasticised fabrics, skin)
- springs (how they work and their uses)
- linking scientific resilience to human resilience.

This unit can be found on www.pearsonplaces.com.au/bounceback.aspx.

Additional features of Bounce Back!

'Key points' to teach students are identified at the start of each unit.

The key points at the beginning of each unit in the three **Classroom Resources** books provide a succinct summary of the most important unit concepts for students to understand. Many different activities and engaging teaching strategies in each unit offer students opportunities to demonstrate and apply their understanding of these key concepts.

Key concepts and messages are repeated.

The nine curriculum topics are introduced in the Years K–2 book and then repeated in the Years 3 & 4 and Years 5–8 books. This means that the key wellbeing and resilience concepts, skills and understandings in the nine units are repeated with age-appropriate curriculum, so that students develop a deep understanding of these concepts and therefore can apply them in their lives.

Links are made with common curriculum topics.

Where possible, links have been made between aspects of social and emotional learning and common topics that are often covered in years K–8. For example, concepts such as courage, persistence and dealing with setbacks can be addressed through age-appropriate literature and also through the topics of explorers, inventors, those who have stood against injustice such as Mahatma Ghandi and Nelson Mandela, and researchers who have made great breakthroughs in science and medicine.

All three levels can be adapted for older or younger classes.

If you require more ideas on how to teach a particular key point or concept, activities can be found in the two other **Classroom Resources** books. Many activities in the three books can be readily adapted to make them appropriate for younger or older students.

There is a strong focus on high-quality literature.

Stories are powerful ways to introduce and reinforce important aspects of social and emotional learning and can serve as a stimulus for a range of engaging teaching and learning activities. Each unit of work in *Bounce Back!* incorporates a large selection of literature. An age-appropriate critical literacy approach is adopted through discussion questions and activities. General 'literacy' and 'visual literacy' question prompts are provided in Chapter 8: Years K–2 resources (see, page 94), and can be selectively used to help students to understand and think critically about the texts. There are also *Bounce Back!* 'literacy' prompts that specifically focus students' attention on social and emotional aspects of the texts (e.g. Who was the most optimistic character? Where was courage shown in this scene?). Many of the picture books offer sound psychological insights and social criticisms, and provide different layers of meaning through visual and verbal images that appeal to young and old. Detailed resource lists of all literature referred to are available online at www.pearsonplaces.com.au/bounceback.aspx so that they can be regularly updated. There is also information on how to find out whether books are still in print.

Strengths-based storytelling is encouraged.

The books and novels that are recommended in *Bounce Back!* provide stimuli for further storytelling by teachers, retelling by students and students' own storytelling. Students can orally tell stories about times when they bounced back, showed courage or kindness, or they can use drama or digital technology to tell their story.

There is a focus on outcomes for literacy and multi-literacies.

All units of work actively engage students in traditional literacy outcomes such as talking, listening, reading and writing. All students require literacy skills and those who are low on resilience often have poor literacy skills[66]. The global move towards digital technology now means that classrooms are moving to learning environments characterised by multi-literacies. Therefore the texts that students read or write now often rely on processing several modes of

Chapter 1
Introduction

text simultaneously in order to communicate and interpret meaning. 'Multi-literacies' means the simultaneous reading, processing and/or producing of various modes of print, images, movement, graphics, animation, sound and music.

A focus on multi-literacies is illustrated in many of the *Bounce Back!* units in which students are asked to create and produce a digital story, book trailer or podcast. These activities require traditional print literacies (to record information and ideas), visual literacies (for overall layout and design, to understand meanings conveyed by visual imagery and to manipulate different images for best effect), aural and musical literacies (to integrate voiceover and music) and numeracies (to calculate design dimensions).

Digital technology is incorporated wherever possible.

There are many suggestions in each unit as to how students might use digital technology such as Microsoft® Office PowerPoint® displays, podcasts, blogs, digital still and video cameras for photographic displays, digital storytelling and book trailers, short movies, animation, visual records of their learning products, topic-related Internet research, hunting for songs on different Internet sites, creating their own music with musical software, and using software such as Microsoft® Office Publisher™ or Kid Pix.

There are many interactive whiteboard activities.

The revised *Bounce Back!* incorporates a variety of new IWB activities that actively engage the whole class in learning and reinforce key *Bounce Back!* concepts for each of the nine main units. Activities include e-quizzes, multiple-choice activities, sorting tasks, sequencing activities, word games and more. These can also be completed individually on classroom computers or in pairs and small groups.

The IWB screen can also be used to display or present teacher material or student products on *Bounce Back!* themes, e.g. PowerPoints®, digital storytelling or book trailers, student-made videos of puppet plays, role-plays and animated stories. Specific pages of texts or illustrations can be enlarged and displayed for more detailed analysis. It can also be used for videos of songs or websites on *Bounce Back!* themes and to display to blackline masters.

There are opportunities for older students to work with younger students.

There are many activities that involve older students working directly or indirectly with students in the first four years of their schooling. These activities are usually based on educational games, literacy activities or a specific children's picture book. For example, older students are encouraged to write and illustrate the text for picture storybooks on wellbeing themes. As they prepare to work with the younger children, the older students gain a deeper understanding of wellbeing concepts so they can effectively teach and work with the younger children. Older students who need a boost in self-confidence particularly benefit from opportunities to work with younger children. They are able to feel more knowledgeable. This helps them to develop confidence in their skills and abilities as well as to learn skills in relating positively to others. They also gain a sense of meaning and purpose through helping someone else. This cross-age contact can be based around:

◎ direct classroom visits to teach to the class, run a game, make a craft activity or work with a buddy
◎ preparation of lessons, materials or products for younger students to use
◎ using digital technology to develop a product to teach wellbeing concepts to younger students, such as moviemaking, podcasts, book trailers and PowerPoints®/slide shows that may include sound, video, images, digital storytelling, animation and so on.

There is a strong emphasis on cooperative learning in all units.

Working cooperatively helps to create a sense of belonging in the classroom. Cooperative learning has been shown to be effective in engaging students and developing a sense of 'psychological flow' as well as superior academic outcomes across all key learning areas[67]. Students learn more about social skills such as taking turns, negotiating, reaching consensus and developing positive respectful relationships when cooperative learning is used well.

Cooperative learning also enhances literacy outcomes as students are actively engaged in social dialogue that encourages deeper understanding and promotes different perspectives and a range of acceptable responses. For these reasons, the use of cooperative learning is incorporated throughout all the *Bounce Back!* curriculum units. Chapter 7: Teaching strategies in Bounce Back! (see page 84) details many cooperative learning structures, with guidelines on how to adapt them to make them age-appropriate.

Circle Time introduces each Bounce Back! lesson.

Like cooperative learning, Circle Time builds classroom community, positive relationships and teaches social-emotional learning[68, 69]. Circle Time is used in all units to introduce key concepts and facilitate whole-class and small-group discussions and activities and games to teach those concepts. Each Circle Time is followed up with individual or small-group activities that provide opportunities for to students apply the concepts in a meaningful way. Classroom Discussion Time can replace Circle Time in the upper units.

There are multiple entry points into the program, based on Howard Gardner's model of multiple intelligences.

Activities engaging each of the eight intelligences, identified in Howard Gardner's model of multiple intelligences, are incorporated in the program. What attracts one student's interest and allows them to demonstrate what they are good at may not do the same for another student. Diversity in teaching and learning strategies creates a greater likelihood that all students will become engaged and succeed in learning, rather than a 'one size fits all' approach. Multiple entry points enable students to experience success and to develop an understanding of their relative strengths and weaknesses across the multiple intelligences.

Many of the activities provide opportunities to develop students' higher order thinking skills.

Giving students a challenging task that is designed to foster higher order thinking skills doesn't mean they will actually use such skills. A student is more likely to persist at a task that is intellectually challenging if they find the task intrinsically interesting. *Bounce Back!* includes many topics that are relevant to the world of young people today. This revised edition includes many new higher order thinking strategies that encourage students to consider different perspectives and different values on important social justice and life issues, and come to a group consensus. Many of the activities are open-ended and encourage students to develop skills in solving problems, making decisions and thinking critically and creatively. These higher order thinking skills are crucial in coping with the complexity of life in the 21st century.

Songs and music are used to consolidate some of the main understandings of the program.

Throughout history, music has been used to help maintain people's spirits during difficult times. For example, Australian convicts sang songs such as 'Botany Bay' to raise their spirits. Similarly, gospel singing in North America emanated from the times of slavery. Singing together builds a sense of community and cooperation and the lyrics of songs can convey important messages of hope and strength. Many of the key social and emotional learning concepts and the key wellbeing and resilience messages in the K–4 programs have been incorporated into newly composed songs that are based on well-known tunes.

Each unit also refers to well-known tunes with wellbeing themes, and links to age-appropriate video clips of the songs can be found on www.pearsonplaces.com.au/bounceback.aspx. These links will be continually updated as they change. Regularly singing the songs creates opportunities for students to revisit the key wellbeing messages many times. This repetition makes it more likely that students will then transfer this learning to their real-life experiences and problems. In the Years 5–8 book, students are also encouraged to go 'song hunting' and bring to school songs that they believe are consistent with a particular message related to wellbeing and resilience.

Visual and performing arts are a core part of most units.

Most units of work in the program include opportunities for students to demonstrate their understandings of wellbeing concepts through drawing, painting, constructing, modelling, singing or drama. The activities are developmentally appropriate and meet various outcomes for the visual and performing arts syllabus at different levels.

Students are continually encouraged to self-reflect.

Throughout the program, students are asked to reflect on their own strengths and weaknesses, and the effect of their behaviour on themselves and others. They are also asked to reflect on what they can do to improve their learning, their behaviour and their own wellbeing. These skills of self-reflection (linked to their self-knowledge and self-management) have been identified by Howard Gardner[70] as probably the most important skills for surviving in the 21st century.

There are many educational games.

The revised **Bounce Back!** includes many new games. Games are effective in improving student engagement and learning outcomes as well as creating classroom energy and a sense of fun[71]. Calling schoolwork a game rather than work has been found to sustain students' attention longer and have them more prepared to 'have a go' at an intellectually challenging game[64]. All the games require students to play in teams, either in pairs or a small group, to contribute to a collaborative classroom. Partners/teams can help and teach each other and make the learning (and losing) less threatening and celebrating successes more fun. Playing cooperatively also provides opportunities for practising organisational skills (such as recording data and time management), language skills, hypothesis testing and strategic problem solving.

There are consolidation activities at the end of each unit.

All units incorporate consolidation activities such as games, group tasks, word puzzles and activities. Blackline masters of student activities and IWB activities that are designed to consolidate core concepts and skills are also available on www.pearsonplaces.com.au/bounceback.aspx.

In summary

This chapter reviewed the evidence base that underpins **Bounce Back!** The review explained the psychological principles that underpin the program, plus the teaching strategies employed in the program that will actively engage all learners and improve learning outcomes. This chapter also outlined the special features of **Bounce Back!** that ensure it not only effectively teaches life skills that affect student learning in the short term and their overall happiness and wellbeing in the long term, but also is enjoyed by both students and teachers.

References

1. *Making progress: the health, development and wellbeing of Australia's children and young people*, 2008, Australian Institute of Health and Welfare.
2. *The economic impact of youth mental illness and the cost effectiveness of early intervention*, 2009, Access Economics, Centre of Excellence, Orygen Youth Health Research Centre, funded by the Australian Government, Parkville, Victoria.
3. Andrews, G., M. Szabó & J. Burns 2001, *Avertable Risk Factors for Depression*, beyondblue, the Australian National Depression Initiative.
4. Collaborative for Academic, Social and Emotional Learning, 2007 [cited 18/1/10], available from www.casel.org
5. Payton, J., et al. 2008, 'The positive impact of social and emotional learning for kindergarten to eighth-grade students: Findings from three scientific reviews', retrieved 11/2/10 from www.casel.org/downloads/PackardTR.pdf, Collaborative for Academic, Social and Emotional Learning, Chicago.
6. Scheckner, S., et al. 2002, 'School violence in children and adolescents: A meta-analysis of the effectiveness of current interventions', *Journal of School Violence*, vol. 1, no. 2, pp. 5–32.
7. Wells, J., Barlow, J. & Stewart-Brown S. 2003, 'A systematic review of the universal approaches to mental health promotion in schools', *Health Education*, vol. 103, no. 4, pp. 197–220.
8. Dryfoos, J.G. 1990, *Adolescents at Risk. Prevalence and Prevention*, Oxford University Press, New York.
9. Greenberg, M., et al. 2003, 'Enhancing school-based prevention and youth development through coordinated social, emotional, and academic learning', *American Psychologist*, vol. 58, pp. 466–474.
10. Weissberg, R.P. & O'Brien, M.U. 2004, 'What works in school-based social and emotional learning programs for positive youth development', *The Annals of the American Academy of Political and Social Science*, vol. 591, pp. 86–97.
11. Greenberg, M.T., Domitrovich, C. & Bumbarger, B. 2001, 'Preventing mental disorders in school-age children: a review of the effectiveness of prevention programs', Center for Mental Health Services (CMHS), Substance Abuse Mental Health Services Administration, US Department of Health and Human Services.
12. 'Effective school health promotion: Towards health promoting schools', 1996, The National Health and Medical Research Council's Health Advancement Committee.
13. CPPRG, 1999, 'Initial impact of the fast track prevention trial for conduct problems: 11 classroom effects', *Journal of Consulting and Clinical Psychology*, vol. 67, pp. 648–657.
14. Kellerman, A.L., et al., 1998, 'Preventing youth violence: what works?', *Annual Review of Public Health*, vol. 19, pp. 271–292.
15. Resnick, M.D., et al. 1997, 'Protecting adolescents from harm–Findings from the national longitudinal study on adolescent health', *Journal of the American Medical Association*, vol. 278, no. 10, pp. 823–832.
16. Catalano, R.F., et al. June 2003, 'The importance of bonding to school for healthy development: Findings from the Social Development Research Group', in *Wingspread Conference on School Connectedness*, Racine, Wisconsin.
17. Catalano, R.F., et al. 1998, 'Effectiveness of prevention interventions with youth at high-risk of drug abuse', in Bukoski, W.J. & Evans, R.I. (eds.), *Cost-benefit/Cost-effectiveness Research of Drug Abuse Prevention: Implications for Programming and Policy*, NIDA Research Monograph no.176, pp. 83-110.
18. O'Shaughnessy, T.E., et al. 2002, 'Students with or at risk for emotional-behavioral difficulties', in *Interventions for children with or at risk for emotional and behavioral disorders*, Lane K.L., Gresham F.M. & O'Shaughnessy T.E. (eds), Allyn & Bacon, Boston.
19. Severson, H.H. & Walker, H.M. 2002, 'Proactive approaches for identifying children at risk for sociobehavioral problems', in *Interventions for children with or at risk for emotional and behavioral disorders*, Lane K.L., Gresham F.M. & O'Shaughnessy T.E. (eds), Allyn & Bacon, Boston.
20. Reivich, K. 2005, 'Optimism lecture' in *Authentic Happiness Coaching*, University of Pennsylvania.
21. Andrews, G., Szabo. M., & Burns, J. 2002, 'Preventing major depression in young people', *British Journal of Psychiatry*, no. 181, pp. 460–462.
22. Beck, A.T. 1979, *Cognitive Therapy and the Emotional Disorders*, Penguin Books, New York.
23. Ellis, A. & Harper, R. 2008, *A New Guide to Rational Living (3rd edn)*, Wilshire Book Company.
24. Seligman, M.E.P. 1995, *The Optimistic Child*, Random House, Sydney.
25. Seligman, M.E.P. 2007, 'Coaching and positive psychology', *Australian Psychologist*, vol. 42, no. 4, pp. 266–267.
26. Hattie, J. 2009, *Visible Learning: A Synthesis of Over 800 Meta-analyses Relating to Achievement*, Routledge, London.
27. Johnson, D.W., Johnson, R.T. & Stanne, M.B. 2001, 'Cooperative learning methods: A meta-analysis', www.co-operation.org/pages/cl-methods.html, accessed 10/12/07.

28. Marzano, R.J., Pickering, D.J. & Pollock, J.E. 2001, *Classroom Instruction that Works: Research-based Strategies for Increasing Student Achievement*, Association for Supervision and Curriculum Development, Alexandria, Virginia.
29. Munro, S., et al. 2006, 'Cooperative learning helps create the essential skill of working (and compromising) within a group', *Edutopia*, vol. 2, no. 6, pp. 53–58.
30. Roseth, C.J., Johnson, D.W. & Johnson, R.T. 2008, 'Promoting early adolescents' achievement and peer relationships: The effects of cooperative, competitive and individualistic goal structures', *Psychological Bulletin*, vol. 134, no. 2, pp. 223–246.
31. Dempsey, J.V., Rasmussen, K. & Lucassen, B. 1994, 'Instructional gaming: Implications for instructional technology', in *Annual Meeting of Association for Educational Communications and Technology*, Nashville.
32. McCarthy, F.E. 2009, *Circle Time Solutions: Creating Caring School Communites*, Report for the NSW Department of Education and Training.
33. McGrath, H. & Anders E. 2000, 'The Bounce Back! Program', *Turning the Tide in Schools Drug Education Project*, Victorian Department of Education.
34. Dix, K.L., et al. 2009, 'KidsMatter Evaluation Executive Summary', beyondblue, downloaded 7/1/10 from www.kidsmatter.edu.au/wp/wp-content/uploads/2009/10/kidsmatter-executive-summary
35. Axford, S., Blyth, K. & Schepens, R. 2010, 'A Study of the Impact of the Bounce Back Programme on Resilience, Wellbeing and Connectedness of Children and Teachers in Sixteen Primary Schools in Perth and Kinross, Scotland, Midpoint Report', Perth and Kinross Council, Scotland.
36. Collaborative for Academic, Social and Emotional Learning, 2009, *Social and Emotional Learning and Bullying Prevention*, www.casel.org/downloads/2009_bullyingbrief.pdf
37. Collaborative for Academic, Social and Emotional Learning, n.d., *Social and Emotional Learning (SEL) and Student Benefits: Implications for the Safe Schools/Healthy Students Core Elements*, www.casel.org/downloads/EDC_CASELSELResearchBrief.pdf
38. Wentzel, K.R. 2003, 'Motivating students to behave in socially competent ways', *Theory into Practice*, vol. 42, no. 4, pp. 319–326.
39. Lovat, T. & Toomey, R. 2007, *Values Education and Quality Teaching: The Double Helix Effect*, David Barlow, Sydney.
40. Bond, L., et al. 2000, *Improving the Lives of Young Victorians in Our Community – A Survey of Risk and Protective Factors*, Centre for Adolescent Health (available from www.dhs.vic.gov.au/commcare), Melbourne.
41. Wink, P., et al. 2007, 'Religiousness, spiritual seeking, and personality. Findings from a longitudinal study', *Journal of Personality*, vol. 75, no. 5, p. 1051.
42. Rachman, S.J. 1990, *Fear and Courage (2nd edn)*, W.H. Freeman and Company, New York.
43. Hannah, S.T., Sweeney, P.J. & Lester, P.B. 2007, 'Toward a courageous mindset: The subjective act and experience of courage', *The Journal of Positive Psychology*, vol. 2, no. 2, pp. 129–135.
44. Peterson, C. 2000, 'The future of optimism', *American Psychologist*, vol. 55, no. 1, pp. 44–55.
45. Carver, C.S. & Scheier, M.E. 1999, 'Optimism', in *Coping. The Psychology of What Works*, Snyder, C.R. (ed), Oxford University Press, New York, pp. 182–204.
46. Isen, A.M. 2001, 'An influence of positive affect on decision making in complex situations: Theoretical issues with practical implications', *Journal of Consumer Psychology*, vol. 11, no. 2, pp. 75–85.
47. Isen, A.M. 2003, 'Positive affect, systematic cognitive processing, and behavior: Toward integration of affect, cognition, and motivation', in *Multi-level Issues in Organizational Behavior and Strategy*, Dansereau, F. & Yammarino, F.J. (eds), JAI/Elsevier Science, Oxford, United Kingdom, pp. 52–62.
48. Fredrickson, B. & Joiner, T. 2002, 'Positive emotions trigger upward spirals toward emotional well-being', *Psychological Science*, vol. 13, pp. 172–175.
49. Fredrickson, B. & Tugade, M. 2004, 'Resilient individuals use positive emotions to bounce back from negative emotional experiences', *Journal of Personality and Social Psychology*, vol. 86, no. 2, pp. 320–333.
50. Wentzel, K.R. & Watkins D.E. 2002, 'Peer relationships and collaborative learning as contexts for academic enablers', *School Psychology Review*, vol. 31, no. 3, pp. 366–377.
51. Lyubomirsky, S., King, L. & Diener, E. 2005, 'The benefits of frequent positive affect: Does happiness lead to success?', *Psychological Bulletin*, vol. 131, no. 6, pp. 803–855.
52. Myers, D.G. 2000, 'The funds, friends and faith of happy people', *American Psychologist*, vol. 55, no. 1, pp. 56–67.
53. Buss, D.M. 2000, 'The evolution of happiness', *American Psychologist*, vol. 55, no. 1, pp. 15–23.
54. Gottman, J. 1995, *Why Marriages Succeed or Fail*, Simon & Schuster, New York.
55. Gottman, J. & Silver, N. 2004, *The Seven Principles for Making Marriage Work*, Crown Publishers, New York.
56. McGrath, H. & Edwards, H. 2010, *Difficult Personalities*, Penguin, Melbourne.

57. Lefcourt, H.M. 2001, *Humor: The Psychology of Living Buoyantly*, Plenum Publishers, New York.
58. Martin, R.A. 2001, 'Humor, laughter and physical health: Methodological issues and research findings', *Psychological Bulletin*, vol. 127, pp. 504–519.
59. Cross, D., et al. 2009, 'Australian Covert Bullying Prevalence Study (ACBPS)', Child Health Promotion Research Centre, Edith Cowan University, Perth, retrieved 2/3/10 from: www.deewr.gov.au/Schooling/NationalSafeSchools/Pages/research.aspx
60. Smith, P.K., et al. 2008, 'Cyberbullying: Its nature and impact in secondary school pupils', *Journal of Child Psychology and Psychiatry*, vol. 49, no. 4, pp. 376–385.
61. McGrath, H. & Noble, T. 2005, *Eight ways at once. Book One: Multiple Intelligences + Bloom's Revised Taxonomy = 200 differentiated classroom strategies*, Pearson Education, Sydney.
62. Shernoff, D.J. & Csikszentmihalyi, M.P. 2009, 'Flow in schools: Cultivating engaged learners and optimal learning environments', in *Promoting Wellness in Children and Youth: Handbook of Positive Psychology in the Schools*, Gilman, R., Huebner, E.S. & Furlong, M. (eds), Lawrence Erlbaum, Mahwah, New Jersey, pp. 131–146.
63. Lopez, S.J., et al. 2009, 'Measuring and promoting hope in schoolchildren', in *Promoting Wellness in Children and Youth: Handbook of Positive Psychology in the Schools*, Gilman, R., Huebner, E.S. & Furlong, M. (eds), Lawrence Erlbaum, Mahwah, New Jersey.
64. Dweck, C.S. 2006, *Mindset. The New Psychology of Success*, Random House, New York.
65. Seligman, M. 2009, 'Positive psychology and positive education workshop notes', in Mind & its Potential Conference, Sydney.
66. Howard, S. & Johnson, B. 2000, 'Young adolescents displaying resilient and non-resilient behaviour: Insights from a qualitative study–Can schools make a difference?', in AARE Conference, University of Sydney.
67. Johnson, D.W., Johnson, R.T. & Stane, M.B. 2000, 'Cooperative Learning Methods: A Meta-Analysis', www.clcrc.com/pages/cl-methods.html
68. McCarthy, F. E. 2009, 'Circle Time Solutions. Creating Caring School Communities', Report for the NSW Department of Education and Training.
69. Roffey, S. 2006, *Circle Time for Emotional Literacy*, Sage Publications, London.
70. Noble, T. & Grant, M. 1997, 'An interview with Howard Gardner', *EQ Australia*, vol. 5, no. 1, pp. 24–26.
71. Marzano, R.J. 2007, *The Art & Science of Teaching: A Comprehensive Framework for Effective Instruction,* Association for Supervision and Curriculum Development, Alexandria, Virginia.

Chapter 2

Wellbeing and resilience

Student wellbeing is linked to student learning. Students with optimal levels of wellbeing and resilience are more likely to have higher academic achievement and complete their schooling, have better mental and physical health, be more resistant to stress and to engage in a more socially responsible lifestyle[1,2]. Such students are more likely to be connected to school, their teachers and their peers; to be actively engaged in learning; to be motivated to participate in class activities and school life; and to exhibit positive behaviour at school. Their high attendance means they are likely to complete school and perform better academically than those whose attendance is poor. There is a two-way relationship between many student wellbeing factors and student academic engagement. For example, school connectedness contributes to student academic outcomes, but student academic outcomes also contribute to school connectedness.

The flipside is that students with low levels of wellbeing and resilience are more likely to drop out of school and therefore can expect to earn approximately $500 000 less in their working life than someone who completes school[3]. The social impact of low academic outcomes not only means higher risk of unemployment and poverty, but also lower levels of participation in the community. The psychological costs are in terms of their mental health and wellbeing in the both short and long term.

Students with optimal levels of wellbeing at school are more likely to become happy and more satisfied adults. A comprehensive meta-analysis of studies into wellbeing outlines the multiple benefits[4]. Adults with higher levels of wellbeing are more sociable and energetic, more charitable and cooperative and better liked by others. They are more likely to get married and to stay married and to have more social support. They also show more flexibility and ingenuity in their thinking and are more productive in their jobs. They tend to be better leaders and negotiators and earn more money. They are more likely to be resilient in the face of hardship, have stronger immune systems, be physically healthier and live longer.

What responsibility do schools have in enhancing student wellbeing?

Most teachers recognise that, if a student is disengaged, depressed, angry or sad, or has difficulties in making friends, then these factors will affect their capacity to succeed academically. The developing focus on student wellbeing as a factor that affects student learning is shaping schools' initiatives for developing more satisfied, healthier and more productive young people who flourish as human beings. This focus aligns with the Melbourne Declaration on Educational Goals for Young Australians[5], which states that:

> Schools play a vital role in promoting the intellectual, physical, social, emotional, moral, spiritual and aesthetic development and wellbeing of young Australians…

This Declaration outlines the responsibility of educators for the development of successful learners, confident individuals and active and informed citizens as defined below.

- *Successful learners* not only have the essential skills of literacy and numeracy, but also are seen as creative and resourceful individuals with a capacity to think critically, to analyse information and to solve problems. They also have the capacity to learn and plan, to collaborate, to communicate ideas and to work independently.
- *Confident individuals* are able to make rational and informed decisions, to be optimistic and have a sense of wellbeing, to accept responsibility for their own lives and to demonstrate a respect for others.
- *Active and informed citizens* act with moral and ethical integrity and develop into responsible local and global citizens.

These national educational goals for young Australians provide the direction and underpin the development of the Australian curriculum. The Australian curriculum's general capabilities are expected to be taught in all curriculum areas to all students[6]. These capabilities are not only traditional literacy and numeracy skills, but also the skills of social-emotional learning. The general capabilities are literacy, numeracy, ICT, thinking skills, creativity, self-management, teamwork, intercultural understanding, ethical behaviour and social competence.

Student wellbeing also underpins other national educational frameworks, such as the Revised National Safe Schools Framework; the National Framework in Values Education; the Healthy Schools model adopted by Mindmatter and Kidsmatter; The National Youth Strategy for Young Australians; and the National Family–School Partnerships.

What is student wellbeing?

A clear definition of student wellbeing and how it can be enhanced is critical to guide school policy and practices. Different professional disciplines take different perspectives on wellbeing. The clinical and health perspective tends to focus on wellbeing as the absence of negative conditions such as depression, anxiety or substance abuse. Contemporary psychologists tend to talk about wellbeing in terms of satisfaction with life[7,8]. Sociologists and community workers tend to focus on wellbeing in terms of the social processes in young people's lives and how that affects the individual[9].

The *Bounce Back!* program takes an educational perspective that focuses on what student wellbeing means in the social context of schools.

We define optimal (i.e. desirable levels of) student wellbeing as a sustainable emotional state characterised by:
- positive relationships at school
- predominantly positive feelings and attitudes
- resilience
- self-optimisation (making the most of your strengths)
- high levels of satisfaction with learning experiences[10].

More simply, student wellbeing could be described as a student's satisfaction with their quality of life at school.

The degree to which a student demonstrates effective academic, social and emotional functioning in their school community is an indicator of their wellbeing at school.

Bounce Back! takes a multi-faceted approach to how schools can build and implement the protective processes that help students feel safe, supported and connected to their school, teachers and peers. It also provides nine curriculum units (see **Classroom Resources**) for teaching students the skills, values and understandings that underpin wellbeing and resilience.

What is resilience?

There are many different definitions of resilience but all refer to the capacity of the individual to overcome odds and demonstrate the personal strengths needed to cope with some kind of hardship or adversity. Benard[11] suggests resilience is a set of qualities or protective mechanisms that give rise to successful adaptation despite high risk factors during the course of development.

This program defines resilience as the ability to cope and 'bounce back' after encountering negative events, difficult situations or adversity and to return to almost the same level of emotional wellbeing. It is also the capacity to respond adaptively to difficult circumstances and still thrive.

The concept of being able to 'bounce back' is very concrete for young people and is easily learned, even by very young children. However, telling children to 'bounce back' should not convey that it is easy to do, nor should it minimise the effort, sadness and pain that it sometimes takes to overcome a serious setback or great adversity.

Resilience is more than dealing with adversity

Students and young people can also apply the attitudes and skills of 'bouncing back' to everyday challenges such as not giving up on a difficult task, adapting to a step family, resolving a fall-out with a friend, coping better with not getting into a sporting team, moving to a new house or school, and so on. Being resilient also involves seeking new experiences and opportunities and taking risks. Risk-taking is likely to mean some setbacks and rejections but it also creates more opportunities for successes and greater self-confidence.

The emergence of the constructs of wellbeing and resilience

Over the past ten years there has been a gradual shift in both research and school practice away from the concept of student welfare and towards the concept of student wellbeing and resilience. This trend is evident in the emergence of the disciplines of Positive Psychology and Positive Education[12-14]. Positive Psychology is the psychology of what makes life worth living. It comes from the conviction that empowering people to develop positive mindsets and to live rewarding and happy lives is just as important as psychology's traditional focus on repairing their weaknesses and healing their pathologies. Positive Psychology, as outlined by its founder Martin Seligman[15], is the study of:

- positive subjective experiences (positive emotions)
- positive individual traits (positive character)
- positive institutions that enable positive experiences and traits
- positive relationships.

'Positive Education' applies the principles of Positive Psychology to the school context and focuses on the strategies for fostering student wellbeing and resilience and building communities of learners than thrive and flourish.

The construct of resilience emerged from the work of researchers who undertook longitudinal developmental studies of children at risk. This research showed that, despite encountering many life stressors as they grew up, some children survived and even thrived[16-17]. The wellbeing and resilience research has shifted the focus from children who are casualties of these risk factors to children who manage to bounce back from stress, trauma and risk. Focusing on wellbeing and resilience constitutes a dramatic shift in perspective from a deficit model of young people at risk to a model that focuses on the personal and environmental strengths that help young people overcome risk.

The protective processes and resources that promote student wellbeing and resilience

Young people spend six or more hours a day at school. Apart from families, schools are the most important socialising agents that provide access to a positive environment that promotes resilience. Schools can provide key people who show they care, a challenging curriculum, support for learning, and opportunities for meaningful participation. School connectedness is particularly important for those students who are not connected to highly resilient families. Schools can also teach students the protective personal skills that will help them bounce back when they experience hardships, frustrations and difficult times.

So what are the key components of environments that foster student wellbeing and resilience, and how can we recognise who is and is not resilient? The table on the next page provides a summary of research outcomes related to the protective environments, as well as the protective personal skills that lead to wellbeing and resilience in young people.

The section following the table shows how *Bounce Back!* can help schools to set up many of these environmental protective processes and teach protective personal skills.

Key components of protective environments and personal skills

Environments that promote wellbeing, resilience and academic success	Personal skills and attitudes for wellbeing and academic success
School connectedness A sense of belonging to a good school Meaningful participation and contribution Opportunities for strengths to be affirmed Opportunities for taking initiative Supportive, inclusive school culture Physical and psychological safety at school Strong school rules about bullying and violence **Peer connectedness** Classroom cohesion and sense of belonging Cooperative learning activities Circle Time Peer support strategies Pro-social peer groups **Teacher connectedness** Limited number of teachers Teacher knowledge of students Teacher warmth and availability High expectations, academic support and differentiated curriculum Cooperative and pro-social classroom culture Clear, consistent boundaries **Positive family–school links** Family involvement with school programs Strong teacher–family relationships **Family connectedness** Expression of warmth and affection Good communication and shared activities Positive approach to solving family problems Family loyalty, affirmation and support Individual responsibilities Pro-social and shared family values Warm relationship with at least one parent **One caring adult outside the family** Availability and interest in student Expresses unconditional positive regard **Community connectedness** Awareness of and access to support services Community service learning Involvement in pro-social clubs and teams Community norms against anti-social behaviour Strong cultural identity and pride **Spirituality or religious involvement** Participation in spiritual communities	**Helpful and positive thinking skills and attitudes** Optimistic thinking Having a sense of purpose and future Normalising instead of personalising Evidence-based thinking Using humour appropriately **Skills and beliefs related to resourcefulness and adaptivity** Having an orientation towards success Skills for setting, planning and achieving realistic goals Decision-making skills Problem-solving skills Creativity, flexibility and adaptivity Holding a belief that effort will pay off Organisational skills Skills to enable adaptive distancing from distressing and unalterable situations **Social and emotional skills (SEL)** Having a belief that relationships matter Social skills for getting on with peers Friendship skills Conflict management skills Help-seeking skills and preparedness to self-disclose Skills for recognising and managing own emotions Skills for reading, predicting and responding empathically to others' emotions **Sense of personal competence, self-knowledge, meaning and purpose** A pro-social personal value system Feeling competent in several areas of one's life Courage Realistic and positive self-knowledge of strengths and limitations Skills of self-reflection Age-appropriate level of independence Self-discipline—skills for delaying gratification and managing impulses Having a sense of meaning and purpose

Environments that promote student wellbeing and resilience

School connectedness
'School connectedness' has become an educational buzz word. It simply means the extent to which students feel they belong to a school that accepts, protects and cares about them, affirms them as people with positive qualities, and provides them with meaningful and satisfying learning experiences. School, above all other social institutions, provides unique opportunities for young people to form relationships and meet and work with peers and caring professional adults on a daily basis. School can offer young people hope and pathways for their future. Being connected to school is linked to increased student engagement and participation in school[18]; higher levels of academic achievement[19-20]; completing school[21]; and increases in positive behaviour and less disruptive or anti-social behaviour[22-24]. School connectedness is also linked to lower rates of health risk behaviour and mental health problems[20,21,23]. In order to enhance school connectedness for every student, there needs to be a clearly stated vision shared by the whole school community that can readily be translated into the school's structures and everyday practices. Such a vision needs to incorporate the following features.

- **Supportive school culture:** a culture of safety and care in which all students feel supported and included. There are clear and consistently enforced rules and procedures regarding agression and bullying, and infringements are dealt with quickly and firmly.
- **Positive relationships:** the establishment of a pro-social and collaborative school culture that is based on positive respectful relationships, cooperation, negotiation and the effective resolution of conflict.
- **Strengths-based approaches:** identifying, engaging and developing individual and school community strengths. Individual student or staff strengths can be defined as intellectual and character strengths.
- **Differentiated curriculum:** the provision of differentiated and relevant learning activities that actively engage students and give them a sense of satisfying participation and worthwhile outcomes. The Multiple Intelligences/Bloom Revised Taxonomy planning matrix for curriculum differentiation[25] has been used by thousands of teachers (both nationally and internationally) for that purpose.
- **Academic support for students who are struggling with the curriculum:** teachers are willing to adapt their curriculum, their teaching and their use of technology to effectively include all students in learning.
- **Fostering student commitment and pride in the school:** this used to be known as 'school spirit'. Students are committed to caring for and supporting other students in their school community and contributing to the school's positive reputation.
- **Fostering a sense of meaning and purpose:** a sense of meaning is gained when students are involved in a task or activity that has a positive impact on others, not just themselves. A sense of purpose is defined as having a sense of direction involving a worthwhile task or activity. Finding meaning and purpose is a core developmental task for all young people, especially adolescents. Students can gain a sense of meaning and purpose through helping others within the class, the school or the community, for example, through peer support programs, cross-age initiatives such as musical/drama productions, anti-bullying campaigns and community service learning.
- **Student participation:** students are given opportunities to take initiative. This means they are given the chance to set their own goals (both academic and enterprise goals), start things up, stay engaged over time and stick with their plan until completion. Teaching initiative skills also involves helping students learn how to handle the inevitable failures, mistakes and obstacles they will experience along the way[26]. Typical school experiences do not provide much opportunity for students to learn initiative skills, despite their importance to coping with life in the 21st century.

Actively engaging students in meaningful projects and helping them gain a sense of meaning and purpose is embedded in all the *Bounce Back!* curriculum units. The 'STAR! (Success)' unit (see **Classroom Resources**) focuses on students identifying, using and enhancing their strengths, and the diverse range of teaching strategies ensures a differentiated curriculum approach. The whole focus of the program is on developing a supportive classroom and school culture.

Peer connectedness
For most young people, one of the major reasons for coming to school is their desire to socially and emotionally connect with their peers. They look forward to seeing their friends, and enjoy belonging to both a friendship group and the larger peer group. Schools can establish the kind of social structures that enhance the development of such relationships and foster a sense of acceptance, belonging and fitting in. Such structures include cooperative learning groups, Circle Time, class meetings, classroom committees and peer support groups, which are all included in the *Bounce Back!* curriculum units (see **Classroom Resources**).

Many cooperative learning strategies are provided in Chapter 7: Teaching strategies in Bounce Back! (see page 89). In **Classroom Resources** all the curriculum units provide many engaging activities to connect peers with each other and develop their social competence. The classroom units on 'Core values' and 'Relationships' specifically teach pro-social values and social competence. All the classroom units incorporate learning activities that facilitate students getting to know each other through the sharing of perceptions and experiences related to the topics covered.

Teacher connectedness
Promoting positive relationships at school has been identified by many researchers as a core component for improving student wellbeing and engagement in learning. The quality of teaching and the teacher–student relationship, above all else, makes the most significant difference to student learning outcomes[27,28]. Feeling connected to their teachers helps students not only to experience more successful learning outcomes, but also to become more resilient[11] and to stay at school rather than drop out. Yet a number of research studies have indicated that students today do not feel closely connected to many of their teachers, especially in secondary schools[29,30]. Often students' perceptions of their low levels of teacher connectedness come as a surprise to their teachers.

Schools can empower teachers to establish positive and close relationships with their students in a number of ways. They can limit the number of teachers that students come into contact with; they can make time for teachers to get to know their students well through pastoral care and personal development programs; they can arrange for one teacher (who does not teach the students) to act as a mentor and confidante through a vertical tutoring system; they can make sure teachers have time to meet with those students who need more academic support or personal time; they can provide opportunities for professional development in areas such as differentiating the curriculum, personal development, resilience and student counselling; and they can 'power up' their student wellbeing and support services. Teachers can also take up the challenges of becoming more connected to their students and creating a pro-social and resilient classroom culture. They can do this by modelling resilient attitudes and skills, establishing a collaborative classroom climate, communicating warmth and positive expectations, adopting classroom practices that affirm student strengths, using positive behaviour strategies, respecting and acknowledging the value of individual differences, and by taking the time to get to know their students as people, not just pupils.

In Chapter 5: School environments for student wellbeing and resilience (see page 62), there are suggestions for ways in which teachers can become more connected to their students. As they teach the BOUNCE BACK! acronym, teachers are very likely to gain a deeper understanding of the core components of resilience and become more resilient themselves[31]. Becoming more resilient enables most teachers to more effectively model resilience skills and attitudes, and to become more skilled at counselling students by referring to their common understandings from the BOUNCE BACK! acronym.

As well, all classroom units of work at the three levels contain classroom-friendly learning activities that directly and indirectly create greater teacher–student connectedness.

Positive family–school links

Students are more likely to become more resilient, to learn more effectively and to complete school when the family and the school work together to give the same messages[32-34]. Online resources at www.pearsonplaces.com.au/bounceback.aspx provide information about resilience for parents.

Family connectedness

A high level of family connectedness is one of the most important of all the protective environmental resources[35-40]. Young people who feel they are supported by their families, have parents who set and enforce rules in their homes, and feel respected for their individuality while belonging to a cohesive and stable family are likely to be resilient[38]. All families face challenges at different times. In some families those challenges relate to the typical developmental stages of their children, and their relationship with partners. In others they relate to death, illness, marital separation, financial hardship, job loss, mental illness, alcohol and substance abuse or other kinds of adversity.

Family connectedness is the extent to which young people feel a sense of involvement and acceptance in their family, and the degree to which they feel close to their parents and siblings. It also relates to the extent to which families communicate effectively with each other, spend time with each other in shared activities, express and enact loyalty and commitment to each other, solve family problems and pull together in the face of adversity. All families have strengths that can be accessed in difficult times. Of course, many families need additional support and care, but a useful starting point is to help a family in need to understand and develop the strengths they already have and then help them to learn more of the skills that underpin resilience.

One caring adult outside the family

Resilience research has shown that having one adult in their life who is not a parent, but who is accessible and caring towards them and believes in them, is a highly significant protective factor for young people[11]. The adult may be a part of the extended family, such as an older sibling, a grandparent or an aunt, uncle or cousin. They may be a family friend, a youth worker or a teacher. Benard talks about the 'turnaround teacher' who can give young people the courage and confidence to cope in difficult circumstances. Caring about a young person means seeing the possibilities in them and having a sense of concern and compassion for their wellbeing. It means looking beyond their often negative and challenging words and actions and seeing their underlying feelings of anger, pain, fear, insecurity and confusion[11]. Caring also means being a sympathetic confidante for their distress and worries by carefully listening to and believing their story, and by showing interest, respect and empathy[39].

Community connectedness

Community connectedness means positive participation in the life of the wider local community and willingness to access community resources. Schools, churches, youth clubs, sports clubs and other community institutions can provide an infrastructure for young people's connection with their community. Opportunities for positive youth community involvement, such as participation in sports teams, art and drama groups and membership of pro-social youth groups, has been identified as one of the most prevalent protective factors in enhancing youth wellbeing[36]. The other two major protective factors in this study were core values and family connectedness.

Chapter 2
Wellbeing and resilience

It is salutary to note that informal rather than formal community connections often are more powerful. When asked who helped them to succeed against the odds, resilient young people in the longitudinal study by Werner and Smith[40] overwhelmingly gave credit to members of their extended family (grandparents, siblings, aunts or uncles), neighbours and teachers, and mentors in voluntary community associations such as YMCA, YWCA or church groups. Young people sought support from these informal community networks and valued this kind of support more often than the services of formal community organisations, mental health professionals and social workers.

Being connected to people in one's community has been shown to correlate strongly with self-confidence, having a feeling of control over one's life, not being involved with anti-social groups, and having higher educational aspirations and achievement[26]. However, it is not clear how much this correlation reflects the fact that those young people who are likely to seek access to the community in the first place are also more likely to have high levels of parental support, high ability and high socio-economic status.

Schools are in an excellent position to help young people connect with their local community. This focus can be work in different ways. Some schools become full-service schools where the school collaborates with community agencies and programs to met students' needs. Full-service schools can provide non-fragmented services through the collaboration of professionals in schools with health, family and welfare professionals. Other schools provide community education programs or after-school care, or invite the community to make use of school facilities, such as the gym, after hours. Access to community facilities such as TAFE education can give young people a second chance, and some schools provide early facilitated pathways to these resources for those students who are less likely to want to pursue university qualifications[39].

Community connectedness for young people includes their family's connections to their cultural or ethnic group. Different cultures provide different cultural resources to deal with crises. In Western culture, these might involve legal assistance and counselling and schools can help young people to access these community services. In some ethnic minority cultures, dealing with crises might include accessing a strong network of support within the community. Strong identity with one's culture can be a source of pride and positive self-esteem for young people. Schools have long understood the value of acknowledging and celebrating the different ethnic groups that make up the school community. Schools with religious affiliations often have strong connections to the local religious community, providing a sense of continuity and belonging for many students.

Community service learning is another strategy schools are adopting to build stronger school–community connections. Service learning integrates meaningful community service with student instruction and reflection to help students learn skills such as being resourceful, showing initiative and setting goals, and developing pro-social values and social skills. Such active and meaningful community engagement enhances young people's sense of wellbeing[41,42]. Community-based projects are most successful when students believe in what they are doing, have opportunities to make real decisions, are heard, have the skills to see the task through and do it well and work with others to be part of something bigger than just themselves[43]. Some schools have set up student action teams that work in partnership with local or state agencies, including the government. Student Action Teams (SATs) are 'teams of students who, as part of their school curriculum, adopt a community issue that they care passionately about, research it, decide what needs to be changed or improved and take action to achieve that'[44]. The 'STAR! (Success)' unit (see **Classroom Resources**) provides opportunities for students to develop initiative and collaboration skills. Schools can consider encouraging the local community to become involved in the *Bounce Back!* program, especially the policing community, welfare agencies, scouts and guides communities and sporting groups.

Spirituality and religious life

> I think that the very purpose in life is to seek happiness. ...Whether one believes in religion or not...we are all seeking something better in life. So, I think, the very motion of our life is toward happiness. (Tenzin Gyatso, the Dalai Lama, 1998)

Spirituality refers to the human tendency to search for meaning in life through self-transcendence or the need to relate to something greater than oneself. Religion refers to a spiritual search that is connected to formal religious institutions. Engagement in an active spiritual life makes it likely that an individual will be more resilient and be less likely to be involved in anti-social behaviour, to abuse drugs and alcohol, to divorce or self-harm. People with spiritual faith report higher levels of happiness and life satisfaction[45], are more likely to be physically healthier and live longer[46] and are more likely to retain or recover emotional wellbeing after suffering divorce, unemployment, serious illness or bereavement than people without such faith[47,48].

Many explanations can be offered for the connection between spiritual involvement and resilience. For example:

- Communities with shared spiritual values usually provide social support and connection for members, as well as a sense of belonging and affirmation. Many religions offer unconditional love and acceptance.
- For many people, a spiritual faith provides a sense of purpose, and satisfies a basic human need of wanting our lives to have some kind of meaning[45]. Seligman[8] has argued that loss of meaning and a sense of purpose contributes to today's high levels of depression among young people.
- Many religions offer people a sense of hope, often through prayer, when facing adversity, as well as answers to some of life's deepest questions[45].
- The principles and beliefs associated with many religions encourage an acceptance of, and stoicism in the face of, things that can't be changed.
- Some religions encourage the practice of deep self-reflection and the facing of truth and pain with courage.

Bounce Back! does not directly address spirituality. Those schools with religious affiliations will undoubtedly already have such learning experiences and strategies in place. However, the values addressed in the 'Core values' unit (see **Classroom Resources**) have been derived from those that underpin most religions, whether they be, for example, Christian, Buddhist, Muslim or Jewish. These values focus on integrity and self-respect, fairness and justice, support, care for others, compassion, acceptance of differences, cooperation, friendliness and respect for the rights of others. Of course, these pro-social core values are not held only by people with religious beliefs. Many people who are not affiliated with any religion, and would consider themselves to be agnostic or atheist, also hold and live by these values.

Personal skills and attitudes for wellbeing and academic success

The second component of *Bounce Back's* multi-faceted approach to student wellbeing and resilience is the explicit teaching of personal coping skills. The theory and research that underpin these skills is explored in depth in the next chapter.

Helpful and positive thinking skills and attitudes

Optimistic thinking
Optimistic thinking involves looking on the bright side of situations. There are four components to optimism:

- positivity, which involves focusing on the good things, but also finding the positives in negative situations, however small
- mastery, which involves feeling some sense of competence and control over one's life

- expecting good things to happen based on past successes
- explanatory style, which involves believing that bad situations are temporary, acknowledging that bad situations are usually not all your fault, and believing that bad situations are specific, don't affect everything else or necessarily flow over into all aspects of your life.

Having a sense of purpose and future
This means believing that things are more likely to turn out well than not, and having goals to aim for.

Normalising
Normalising means recognising that things that are happening in your life happen to lots of other people too. In contrast, personalising is when you think something that is relatively normal only happens to you, not others. Over time, personalising results in a negative self-perception, i.e. a belief that you are jinxed, doomed or inadequate.

Helpful thinking
Many people become unnecessarily distressed because they distort the picture and do not see a situation as it really is. Others have unhelpful and irrational beliefs. These beliefs are not helpful in regards to feeling emotionally in charge of yourself and achieving the outcomes you desire.

On the other hand, helpful thinking is both rational (i.e. reflects how things really are rather than how they should be or you would like them to be) and helps you feel emotionally in control. Helpful thinking also involves being open-minded and flexible in how you interpret situations and acknowledging that how you think affects how you feel and how you behave. It is also based on the assumption that negative emotions, though powerful, can be managed.

Using humour
Using humour appropriately has been linked to wellbeing and resilience as well as to social success. Humour helps to keep things in perspective. When we find a small thing to laugh about in a dark situation, we realise that it probably isn't the total disaster it seemed to be at first, and there is a glimmer of hope.

The classroom units on 'Looking on the bright side', 'STAR! (Success)', 'Humour' and 'People bouncing back' (see **Classroom Resources**) provide activities to teach all the skills and beliefs outlined above which are helpful and optimistic.

Skills and beliefs related to resourcefulness and adaptivity
Being resourceful and adaptable means being able to set, plan and achieve realistic goals, being well-organised, understanding that success depends largely on knowing your own strengths and limitations and on hard work, and persisting in the face of obstacles. It's about being able to adapt to change and understanding that change is a normal part of life. Being adaptable also means having the capacity to 'adaptively distance' oneself from distressing and unalterable situations when appropriate rather than constantly immersing oneself in the situation and thinking about it all the time.

Social–emotional learning skills (SEL)
Social–emotional learning skills are social skills for getting along with others, friendship skills, conflict management and help-seeking skills, and the emotional skills of recognising and managing one's own feelings and being empathic.

Sense of personal competence, self-knowledge, meaning and purpose
Personal competence involves:
- believing that you are a decent person because you have a set of pro-social values that you try to live by

- having enough self-confidence in your ability to achieve and perform in a number of different areas to enable you to take risks such as the risk of failing
- being able to act courageously when the need arises
- having a sense of age-appropriate independence
- being able to manage your own impulses and be reasonably self-disciplined.

Good self-knowledge involves:
- knowing your strengths and limitations using evidence rather than wishful thinking. achieving this requires self-reflection and reality testing.

Having a sense of meaning and purpose means:
- being able to use your self-knowledge to engage in tasks that are worthwhile, purposeful, productive or meaningful (i.e. they have an impact on others as well as yourself).

In summary

Student wellbeing and resilience are inextricably linked to student learning, and the goal of enhancing student wellbeing underpins many current educational policies. All definitions of resilience incorporate some reference to an individual's ability to overcome odds and to demonstrate personal strengths to cope with challenges, hardship or adversity. The construct of resilience emerged from longitudinal studies of children at risk. This research has prompted a paradigm shift from studying risk factors to looking at protective factors. A multi-faceted approach that incorporates ways to build environments that foster resilience, as well as teaches the personal coping skills of resilience, has a much greater chance of success than a program that addresses only one set of factors.

The environmental protective factors that foster wellbeing and resilience in young people include feeling connected to your school, positive family–school links, feeling connected to peers, feeling cared for and supported by your teachers in a pro-social classroom climate, having a sense of belonging and worth in your family, having one caring adult outside the family for support, being involved in community life, and being part of a spiritual community.

A second category of protective resources are the personal skills and beliefs that enable young people to cope more effectively. These personal skills include knowing how to think helpfully and optimistically, having skills for resourcefulness and adaptivity, demonstrating competence in social skills that help with relationship building and self-disclosure, being emotionally literate, and having a sense of personal competence, meaning and purpose.

A successful wellbeing and resilience program endeavours to increase the number of environmental and personal protective resources for all students. Such a program goes beyond simply describing 'what' the protective factors are and moves to a focus on 'how'. A focus on 'how' provides practical steps that professionals, teachers and families can take to foster wellbeing and resilience in young people today. A focus on 'how' acknowledges the dynamic nature of wellbeing and resilience instead of the static position taken by simply describing protective factors. *Bounce Back!* provides practical guidelines on the actions educators can take to build resilient classrooms and schools and teach the personal coping skills that help students develop a sense of wellbeing and resilience.

References

1. *Collaborative for Academic, Social and Emotional Learning*, 2010 [cited 18/1/10], available from www.casel.org
2. Zins, J.E., et al. (eds) 2004, *Building Academic Success on Social and Emotional Learning: What Does the Research Say?*, Teachers College Press, New York.
3. *Better outcomes for disengaged young people: Initial scoping, analysis and policy review*, 2005, Department of Premier and Cabinent, DESCS SA Government.
4. Lyubomirsky, S., King, L. & Diener, E. 2005, 'The benefits of frequent positive affect: Does happiness lead to success?', *Psychological Bulletin*, vol. 131, no. 6, pp. 803–855.
5. *National Declaration on Educational Goals for Young Australians*, 2008, Ministerial Council on Education, Employment, Training and Youth Affairs, Australia.
6. *The Shape of the Australian Curriculum*, 2009, National Curriculum Board http://www.acara.edu.au, Commonwealth of Australia.
7. Kahnemann, D., Diener, E. & Schwartz, N. 1999, *Well-Being: The Foundations of Hedonic Psychology*, Russell Sage Foundation, New York.
8. Seligman, M.E.P. 2002, *Authentic Happiness*, Free Press, New York.
9. Bourke, L. & Geldens, P.M. 2007, 'What does wellbeing mean? Perspectives of wellbeing among young people and youth workers in rural Victoria', *Youth Studies Australia*, vol. 6, no. 1, pp. 41–49.
10. Noble, T., et al. 2008, *A Scoping Study on Student Wellbeing*, Australian Government Department of Education, Employment & Workplace Relations.
11. Benard, B. 2004, *Resiliency: What We Have Learned*, WestEd, San Francisco.
12. Gable, S. & Haidt, J. 2005, 'What (and why) is positive psychology?', *Review of General Psychology*, vol. 9, no. 2, pp. 103–110.
13. Noble, T. & McGrath, H. 2008, 'Positive educational practices framework: A tool for facilitating the work of educational psychologists in promoting pupil wellbeing', *Educational and Child Psychology*, vol. 25, no. 2, pp. 119–134.
14. Seligman, M.E.P. May 2008, in 'Seminar at Happiness and its Causes Conference', Sydney.
15. Seligman, M.E.P. 2007, 'Coaching and positive psychology', *Australian Psychologist*, vol. 42, no. 4, pp. 266–267.
16. Silva, P. & Stanton W. (eds) 1996, *From Child to Adult: The Dunedin Multidisciplinary Health and Development Study*, Oxford University Press, Auckland, New Zealand.
17. Werner, E. & Smith, R. 1992, *Overcoming the Odds: High Risk Children from Birth to Adulthood*, Cornell University Press, New York.
18. Osterman, K. 2000, 'Students' need for belonging in the school community', *Review of Educational Research*, vol. 70, no. 3, pp. 323–367.
19. Lee, V.E., et al. 1999, *Social Support, Academic Press, and Student Achievement: A View From the Middle Grades in Chicago*, Chicago Annenberg Challenge, Chicago.
20. Catalano, R.F., et al. June 2003, 'The importance of bonding to school for healthy development: Findings from the Social Development Research Group', in *Wingspread Conference on School Connectedness*, Racine, Wisconsin.
21. Bond, L., et al. 2007, 'Social and school connectedness in early secondary school as predictors of late teenage substance use, mental health, and academic outcomes', *Journal of Adolescent Health*, vol. 40, no. 357, pp. 9–18.
22. Marzano, R.J., Marzano, J.S. & Pickering, D. 2003, *Classroom Management that Works: Research-based Strategies for Every Teacher*, Association for Supervision and Curriculum Development, Alexandria, Virginia.
23. Lonczak, H.S., et al. 2002, 'The effects of the Seattle Social Development Project: Behavior, pregnancy, birth, and sexually transmitted disease outcomes by age 21', *Archives of Pediatric Adolescent Health*, vol. 156, pp. 438–447.
24. Wilson, D. & Elliott, D. June 2003, 'The interface of school climate and school connectedness: An exploratory review and study', in *Wingspread Conference on School Connectedness*, Racine, Wisconsin.
25. McGrath, H. & Noble, T. 2005, *Eight ways at once. Book One: Multiple Intelligences + Bloom's Revised Taxonomy = 200 differentiated classroom strategies*, Pearson Education, Sydney.
26. Larson, R.W. 2000, 'Toward a psychology of positive youth development', *American Psychologist*, vol. 55, no. 1, pp. 170–183.
27. Hattie, J. 2009, *Visible Learning: A Synthesis of Over 800 Meta-analyses Relating to Achievement*, Routledge, London.
28. Rowe, K. 2001, 'Keynote Address', in 'Educating Boys in the Middle Years of Schooling Symposium', St Ignatius School, Riverview.
29. Trent, F. 2001, 'Aliens in the classroom or: The classroom as an alien place?' in 'Association of Independent Schools, NSW Sex, Drugs & Rock 'N Roll Conference', New South Wales.

30. Fuller, A., McGraw, K. & Goodyear, M. 1998, *The Mind of Youth Resilience: A Connect Project*, Victorian Department of Education, Victoria.
31. McGrath, H. & Anders, E. 2000, 'The Bounce Back! Program' in *Turning the tide in schools drug education project*, Victorian Department of Education.
32. Black, R. 2007, 'Crossing the bridge: overcoming entrenched disadvantage through student-centred learning' [cited 16/6/08], available from www.educationfoundation.org.au
33. Redding, S., et al. 2004, The Effects of Comprehensive Parent Engagement on Student Learning Outcomes, www.adi.org/solidfoundation/resources/Harvard.pdf.
34. Reschly, A.L. & Christenson, S.L. 2009, 'Parents as essential partners for fostering students' learning outcomes' in *Handbook of Positive Psychology in Schools*, Gilman, R., Huebner, E.S. & Furlong, M. (eds), Routledge, New York.
35. Suldo, S. 2009, 'Parent-child relationships' in *Handbook of Positive Psychology in Schools*, Gilman, R., Huebner, E.S. & Furlong, M. (eds), Routledge, New York.
36. Bond, L., et al. 2000, *Improving the Lives of Young Victorians in Our Community–A Survey of Risk and Protective Factors*, Centre for Adolescent Health, available from www.dhs.vic.gov.au/commcar, Melbourne.
37. Masten, A.S., et al. 1999, 'Competence in the context of adversity: Pathways to resilience and maladaptation from childhood to late adolescence', *Development & Psychopathology*, vol. 11, no. 1, Winter, pp. 143–169.
38. Werner, E.E. 1993, 'Risk, resilience and recovery: Perspectives from the Kauai longitudinal study', *Development and Psychopathology*, vol. 5, pp. 503–515.
39. Benard, B. & Slade, S. 2009, 'Listening to students: Moving from resilience research to youth development practice and school connectedness' in Gilman, R., Huebner, E.S. & Furlong, M. (eds), *Handbook of Positive Psychology in Schools*, Routledge, New York.
40. Werner, E.E. & Smith, R.S. 1993, *Overcoming the Odds: High Risk Children from Birth to Adulthood*, Cornell University Press, Ithaca, New York.
41. Oishi, S., et al. 1999, 'Value as a moderator in subjective wellbeing', *Journal of Personality*, vol. 67, no. 1, pp. 157–164.
42. Shinn, M. & Toohey, S.M. 2003, 'Community contexts of human welfare', *Annual Review of Psychology*, vol. 54, pp. 427–259.
43. Wierenga, A., et al. 2003, *Sharing a New Story: Young People in Decision-making*, Australian Youth Resource Centre, University of Melbourne for Foundation for Young Australians, Melbourne.
44. Holdsworth, R. 2006, *Student Action Teams: Implementing productive practices in primary and secondary school classrooms*, Connect, Melbourne.
45. Myers, D.G. 2000, 'The funds, friends and faith of happy people', *American Psychologist*, vol. 55, no. 1, pp. 56–67.
46. George, L., K., et al. 2000, 'Spirituality and health: What we know, what we need to know', *Journal of Social and Clinical Psychology*, vol. 19, no. 1, pp. 102–116.
47. McIntosh, D.N., Silver, R.C. & Wortman, C.B. 1993, 'Religion's role in adjustment to a negative life event: Coping with the loss of a child', *Journal of Personality and Social Psychology*, vol. 65, pp. 812–821.
48. Ellison, C.G. 1991, 'Religious involvement and subjective wellbeing', *Journal of Health and Social Behaviour*, vol. 32, pp. 80–99.

Chapter 3

Personal coping skills for wellbeing and resilience

Student wellbeing and resilience are complex concepts. Resilience is the possession of personal skills and protective factors to cope in difficult times. ***Bounce Back!*** takes a multi-faceted approach in reviewing the protective factors that schools can access to help a child or young person be resilient and enhance their sense of wellbeing, as well the personal skills of resilience that can be taught through the curriculum units. This chapter looks at the personal coping skills that can help young people develop a sense of wellbeing where they are generally positive, happy and resilient, have good relationships with family and friends, and are satisfied with their learning experiences at school.

We cannot protect young people from the stress of all difficult life events, but we can help them to develop the personal skills and assets necessary to cope with these events.

Everyday and major stressors

Learning personal coping skills can help students to better manage everyday stressors as well as major stressors. Everyday stressors are the typical things that students face as they proceed through developmental stages. They include changes in routine, social disappointments and the challenges involved in starting school, changing school or advancing from one grade to another. Whether these everyday events are stressful will depend on the student's personal coping skills and their home and school environment. Major stressors or risk factors are events such as family trauma or severe bullying (see table next page). At these times, young people will typically need extra support to develop and employ resilient attitudes and skills.

The personal coping skills, assets and attitudes that contribute to wellbeing and resilience are helpful and optimistic thinking, being resourceful and adaptive, being able to normalise setbacks instead of personalising them, social-emotional learning skills, help-seeking, using humour in a helpful way, engaging one's strengths and gaining a sense of meaning and purpose through meaningful participation in class, school and community activities.

Optimistic thinking

Optimism is a general belief that good rather than bad things will generally occur in your life. It's a tendency to expect positive outcomes, to look on the bright side of things and to think optimistically about the future (within the bounds of reality). Conversely, pessimism is expecting failure, anticipating bad outcomes or a tendency to take a gloomy view of things.

Optimism can play a vital role in helping students cope with setbacks or new situations. From the 'expectancy' perspective, optimism is having a disposition or tendency to expect things to work out, to be forward looking and proactive and to have the confidence to persevere when faced with adversity[1]. From the 'explanatory style' perspective, it refers to the different ways in which an optimist or pessimist explains the cause of events to themselves[2,3].

Everyday and major stressors

Everyday stressors	Major stressors
Preschool (1–4 years) Birth of sibling Adjustment to childcare Transition to preschool Separation from attachment figures **Primary school age (5–12 years)** Transition to school Competition with peers Peer relationships Peer teasing Peer pressure (e.g. to follow a fad or do something they don't want to do) Sibling reputation pressures Homework Poor academic outcomes Conflict with the teacher Disappointments connected with sport or other extracurricular activities Class presentation Worry about tests Time pressures (balancing schoolwork demands and extracurricular or home demands) Child–parent conflicts Early puberty **Adolescence (13–19 years)** Hormonal changes Growth changes Physical appearance Peer pressure Heightened sexuality Issues of independence and freedom Relationship issues Increased responsibility for self in school Career and university choices Transition to work Part-time work Gender role issues Romantic partnership issues	**Death** Parent Sibling Close relative Close friend Favourite pet **Serious illness or disability** Self Parent Sibling Close relative Close friend **Other extraordinary trauma** War Fire or flood Legal problems Sexual and/or physical abuse and/or neglect Robbery or assault **Parental issues** Divorce Remarriage Job loss, job start Child witnessing abuse/violence Mental illness Alcohol/drug abuse Being jailed **Change in** Standard of living School Residence Number of people living in home Parental contact (e.g. parent working long hours/shift work or loss of contact) **Being bullied** Physical Verbal Social exclusion Cyberbullying

Optimistic thinking has been linked to:
- maintaining high levels of wellbeing during stress
- taking risks in the belief that you have a good chance of getting the outcome you want
- persevering when things become difficult or after failure
- the use of adaptive strategies such as effective problem solving, obtaining social support, and looking for any positives in stressful situations
- feeling confident and presenting in a confident way
- being successful in academic, athletic and vocational endeavours
- being popular
- having good health, engaging in health-promoting behaviour
- living longer and being more physically healthy.

People who tend towards pessimism often feel down and helpless. Everything seems too hard to fix and too overwhelming. They tend to look on the worst side of things and to feel a sense of hopelessness and despair. Pessimism is linked to:
- a greater risk of being depressed
- maladaptive strategies such as avoiding or denying problems, or giving up without even trying
- failing because they haven't persisted or taken risks
- not doing as well in academic, athletic and vocational endeavours as their strengths would predict
- being socially isolated
- getting sick more often and being more vulnerable to infection.

Reivich[4] indicates that our optimism or pessimism becomes a habit by the end of primary school—and like any habit, the longer we practise it, the harder it is to change. It is important to teach children from an early age to think optimistically.

Expecting good things to happen
Building up an expectation that good things can happen is linked to feeling confident and in control of your life and having a sense of personal competence or mastery. Mastery is usually attained through the successful achievement of goals over time and hence the positive expectation that you can repeat the process. Conveying positive but realistic expectations to students and encouraging them to persevere can also help them to develop optimistic thinking. Persevering and being successful, especially when a task is challenging, promotes optimism and self-efficacy. Helping students to find the positive features of difficult situations, however small, also enhances optimism. Another term for this is 'positive tracking'.

Explaining why bad things happen
Our 'explanatory style' is the way we explain to ourselves why events happen to us. This determines how energised/optimistic or how helpless/pessimistic we become when we encounter everyday setbacks as well as momentous defeats. There are three dimensions to our explanatory style for adversity.

Explanatory style for negative events

Pessimistic explanatory style	Optimistic explanatory style
1. because of me	1. not just me
2. always	2. not always
3. everything	3. not everything

1. **The first dimension: Personal**—how much we think a negative situation has happened because of our personal attributes:
   - *Because of me:* The pessimistic style stresses that negative events happen mostly because of our own defects, stupidity, unworthiness or because we are jinxed and attract bad luck.
   - *Not just me:* The optimistic style stresses that negative events have many different causes, including circumstances outside one's control, bad luck and the behaviour of other people.
2. **The second dimension: Permanent**—how permanent we think a negative situation will be:
   - *Always:* The pessimistic style stresses the ongoing and long-lasting nature of negative situations.
   - *Not always:* The optimistic style stresses that a negative event is probably not going to last very long or it is a 'one-off'.

3. **The third dimension: Pervasive**—How much we think this one negative situation pervades other parts of our life:
   - *Everything:* The pessimistic style stresses that a negative event spoils everything.
   - *Not everything:* The optimistic style stresses that a negative event is specific and just affects that one relevant part of our life.

The pessimistic explanatory style for negative events leads to having little sense of control and a loss of hope. On the other hand, the optimistic explanatory style leads to a stronger sense of power over one's life and a belief that the future can be bright even if the present seems bleak.

The table below compares two students who are both feeling socially isolated a month after starting at a new school. One uses a pessimistic explanatory style for why they are having difficulties making friends, while the other uses an optimistic explanatory style.

Explanatory style for a negative event

Pessimistic explanatory style for a negative situation (feeling isolated at a new school)	Optimistic explanatory style for a negative situation (feeling isolated at a new school)
Because of me Everyone has a friend except me. Nobody likes me because I'm not cool and because I'm not a good reader.	**Not just me** I wish I had a friend at my new school. But I remember when my cousin started at a new school—she found it hard to make friends too. Mum is going to ask the teacher for help.
Always I'm never going to make friends.	**Not always** It's hard being new at school but soon things will get better.
Everything I hate it that we moved. I don't like my teacher or my new school or the kids in my class. I hate everything!	**Not everything** I haven't made any friends at school yet. But I've made friends with the kids next door so that's good, and I'm having a good time with the cricket team.

Explaining why good things happen

Explanatory style for explaining good events is just the opposite. Again, there are the three dimensions:
1. How much we think the good event is a result of our personal characteristics and behaviour:
   - *Not me:* The pessimistic explanatory style stresses that there are many possible reasons for a good event that are not related to their personal characteristics or their hard work or effort. Their success instead might be due to good luck, accidental circumstances or favourable treatment.
   - *Because of me:* The optimistic style stresses taking credit for a good event, i.e. believing that the good event happened mostly because of their abilities and the hard work and effort they put in.
2. How permanent or how long we think the benefits of a good event will last:
   - *Temporary:* The pessimistic explanatory style stresses that a good event is likely to be short-lived or it is a 'one-off'.
   - *Ongoing:* The optimistic style stresses the ongoing and long-lasting nature of good situations.
3. How pervasive or how much we think the good event will affect other parts of our life:
   - *Just this:* The pessimistic explanatory style stresses that a good event is specific and just affects that one relevant part of our life. There is no carry-over effect.
   - *Other things:* The optimistic style stresses that good events can have a positive effect on many parts of our lives.

Chapter 3
Personal coping skills for
wellbeing and resilience

The table below shows an example of two students who both do well in reading to the class. One uses a pessimistic explanatory style for why they did well and the other uses an optimistic explanatory style.

Explanatory style for a positive event

Pessimistic explanatory style for a good event (doing well at reading)	Optimistic explanatory style for a good event (doing well at reading)
Not just me I wasn't the only kid who read well. Other kids read well too. The teacher gave me an easy book to read.	**Because of me** I read well in class today because I have been doing lots of reading at home to get better.
Temporary Sometimes I make lots of mistakes when I read in class. I'll probably read badly next time.	**Ongoing** I'm getting better and better at reading because I've worked hard.
Just this I read well today but my other schoolwork isn't very good.	**Other things too** I really like reading in class. My schoolwork is really improving and so is my netball.

The BOUNCE BACK! acronym (see Chapter 4: Teaching the BOUNCE BACK! acronym, page 53) contains statements to build students' optimism and challenge negative thinking and a pessimistic explanatory style for bad events. It focuses on:
◎ understanding that bad events are temporary
◎ understanding that one bad event doesn't have to spoil your whole life
◎ not personalising bad events and normalising instead, i.e. accepting that some things that happen to us happen to nearly everyone—they're pretty normal
◎ not over-emphasising your own faults and blaming yourself completely
◎ identifying the bit you might be responsible for and what you can learn from your own actions or mistakes so you can avoid doing the same thing again
◎ learning from other people's contributions to what happened so you get a better idea of what to be careful about next time
◎ accepting that there are some random factors over which we don't have control. These factors usually are described as bad luck or random or unfortunate circumstances.

In **Classroom Resources**, there are activities in the 'Looking on the bright side' unit that focus on changing a pessimistic explanatory style for bad events.

Pessimistic thinking about bad events is a significant risk factor for anxiety and depression. Not surprisingly, young children who develop a pessimistic style at an early age are most likely to get depressed and stay depressed[3].

Changing students' explanatory style from pessimistic to optimistic is seen as an inoculation against mental illness and a protective factor in the development of wellbeing and resilience[5,6]. Programs designed to change students' explanatory style from pessimistic to optimistic have been more successful with young people from ten years old to early adolescence than with older adolescents. Evaluations of these programs have shown that students were significantly less depressed and their classroom behaviour significantly improved immediately after the program, and at a six-month and two-year follow-up[7,8]. However, it is never too early or too late to learn more effective ways of coping. We can start teaching very young children to be more optimistic, so that over time it becomes a well-established habit. We can also help older students to learn more optimistic thinking, even if the gains are a bit smaller.

A cautionary note
Being overly optimistic can be counter-productive if it is too unrealistic. Constant striving for control over events without the human or material resources to achieve a goal, or without

39

seeing real obstacles, can lead to a sense of helplessness and depression. We all face objective limits to what we can change or achieve no matter how hard we try.

Self-efficacy

Explanatory style is also linked to self-efficacy. Young people who habitually blame themselves whenever things go wrong and don't give themselves credit for the good things that happen in their life are more likely to have low self-efficacy. Self-efficacy is having confidence in your ability to solve a particular problem or perform a specific task.

Those who don't overly blame themselves when things go wrong feel less guilt or shame when bad events happen because they also take into account the behaviour of others or adverse circumstances. They like themselves better and therefore are less likely to feel disempowered by a setback. When good things happen in their lives, their self-confidence increases. They tend to 'pat themselves on the back' privately whenever anything they do, however small, is successful. They feel empowered because they believe that their own efforts have made the difference. Greater self-efficacy in an aspect of one's life leads to greater effort and persistence in the face of setbacks. A student with high self-efficacy in relation to a task will also set higher goals, be less afraid of making a mistake or failing and will look for new strategies when old ones fail, i.e. be more optimistic. But if self-efficacy is low for a task or situation, a student might avoid the task altogether or give up easily when problems arise.

The BOUNCE BACK! statements aim to increase young people's self-efficacy by encouraging them to understand the links between how they think about events and outcomes and how they feel and act. The 'STAR! (Success)' unit in **Classroom Resources** aims to increase students' self-knowledge and self-management by learning skills in planning goals, monitoring progress and evaluating performance. The focus is on developing a mindset for success that focuses on effort, not ability[9].

In ***Bounce Back!***, the focus is on developing high self-efficacy rather than high self-esteem. The reason for this is that the 'self-esteem movement' of the past three decades hasn't been successful. With good intentions, many parents and educators have fallen into the trap of making children feel good about themselves, even if they have not demonstrated mastery or competence or put in effort. Many classroom activities were simply 'feel good' activities such as 'I like Nick because he has nice brown eyes' or 'You are special and unique and there is no-one just like you'. Although enjoyed by students, such activities do not really bolster self-esteem and self-confidence or change behaviour. What does change behaviour is when students develop a greater sense of mastery and competence in areas of importance such as reading, maths and friendship skills, and then develop self-confidence and an expectation of further success.

Hope and goal setting

Hope is linked to optimism. Hope is expecting the best in the future and working to achieve it. It is associated with coping and academic success, and is a pathway to wellbeing. Academic hope is a better predictor of university success than high school academic results and SATs (standardised achievement test scores)[10]. Hope is powerful in good or bad times and provides the energy and motivation to plan and achieve goals. Hope initially develops from trusting relationships with others, especially in early childhood. Young people who fail to develop a sense of trust in early childhood may continue to mistrust people. A trust in others means that a person with 'high-hope' is more likely to seek help from others when a goal is blocked than those with 'low-hope'.

Hope is defined by Lopez[10] as goal-directed thinking, feeling and behaving that involves being able to:
1. clearly conceptualise and define goals (goals thinking)—*I want to go from here to there*

2. articulate ways to achieve their goals (pathways thinking)—*I know many ways to get from here to there*
3. initiate and sustain motivation for using the strategies to achieve their goal, based on a self-belief in their ability to do so (positive self-talk)—*I think I can get from here to there*).

The 'STAR! (Success)' unit in **Classroom Resources** incorporates the components of goal setting and goal pathways to help young people be more hopeful and to achieve more.

Luck

> I'm a great believer in luck, and I find the harder I work the luckier I get.
> (President Thomas Jefferson)

Is there such a thing as good luck? Many believe that you make your own luck. People's perceptions of whether or not they are 'lucky' are also linked to optimism. Dr Richard Wiseman, a British psychologist, conducted research in which he and his colleagues studied hundreds of people who believed that they had been very lucky in their lives. The results of their study revealed that people are not 'born lucky'. Instead, 'lucky' people are, without realising it, using four basic principles to create good fortune in their lives[11]:

1. **Maximise chance opportunities:** Lucky people create, notice and act on chance opportunities by networking and being open to new experiences.
2. **Listen to and act on hunches:** Lucky people listen to their intuition and gut feelings and act on the ones that seem right. In addition, they try to focus on their own thinking and clear their mind of other thoughts in order to reflect on their ideas.
3. **Expect good fortune:** Lucky people believe that their future can be full of good fortune. These expectations can become self-fulfilling prophecies by helping them to persist in the face of failure, and shape their interactions with others in a positive way.
4. **Turn bad events and situations into good ones:** Lucky people use resilience strategies to cope with misfortune. For example, they imagine how things could have been worse, and they do not obsessively dwell on the misfortune. They find whatever positives they can in a big negative picture and try to convert mistakes into something more positive such as useful learning experiences.

The 'Looking on the bright side' unit in **Classroom Resources** incorporates these key messages about the luck factor.

Help-seeking and self-disclosure

Seeking help and talking to others encourages young people to disclose their thoughts, feelings, past experiences and future plans. In this way they can gain support, get a reality check, clarify their thoughts and feelings, and learn to be comfortable with intimacy. Self-disclosure in friendships forges close bonds and trust. Of course, there are also some risks attached to self-disclosure and/or asking for help. There is a chance that a person will feel stigmatised, they may feel rejected or betrayed if the person they talk to doesn't keep their confidences or follow through for them, or they may get negative feedback about themselves that is hard to deal with. It is also possible that help won't be given in the way they expected.

A further problem is that excessively discussing problems and dwelling on the associated negative feelings with friends can, in some cases, increase anxiety and depression. These findings have been found for girls but not for boys[12,13]. This gender difference may be because boys self-disclose less than girls. These results suggest the importance of encouraging young people, when seeking support from friends and self-disclosing, to learn to cross-check their perceptions with others and focus on helping each other learn constructive ways of coping rather than simply dwelling or 'wallowing' in their problems.

Helpful and rational thinking

Helpful and rational thinking derives from the original cognitive behaviour therapy model (CBT), which was developed by Aaron Beck[14]. CBT is based on the understanding that how you think affects how you feel, which in turn influences how you behave. In particular, rational thinking is drawn from the rational emotive therapy (RET) model developed by Albert Ellis[15-19] from the original CBT model. CBT is based on the assumption that strong feelings such as anxiety, depression and anger are exaggerated and, in some cases, caused by our own thoughts and beliefs. CBT is a practical, action-oriented approach to coping with problems and enhancing personal growth. It has become recognised throughout the world as a highly successful form of treatment for depression, anxiety and anger. Distortions in our thinking play a key role in causing and maintaining low coping skills. What we think about a negative event can exaggerate our emotional and behavioural reactions.

The CBT model emphasises the use of tactics to help people to change their thinking, feelings and behaviour. These tactics are all based on the assumption that unhelpful thinking can be identified and helpful thinking can be substituted. The tactics are:

1. Challenging unhelpful and irrational beliefs such as:
   - Unrealistic expectations of self or others (*I must be perfect and never make any mistakes*)
   - *You can't help the feelings you have. There is nothing you can do about them. They just happen.*
   - Catastrophising (*If something CAN go wrong, then it definitely WILL go wrong. The worst outcome is inevitable so I had better try to cope with it in advance. It is the end of the world if something negative happens.*)
   - Mind-reading (*I can guess what they're thinking about me*)
   - Overgeneralising (*If something bad has happened to me once, it will happen again*).
2. Encouraging 'reality-checking' by talking to other people in order to understand how others see the situation and checking the 'evidence' and facts that supposedly support conclusions.
3. Accepting those things that cannot be changed because they are not under one's control.

Helpful thinking has the following features:
- It is evidence-based and encourages checking your facts and/or cross-checking with others to get a second opinion.
- It involves being open-minded and flexible in your thinking and looking for other ways to solve a problem when blocked.
- It acknowledges that how you think affects how you feel and how you behave and that negative emotions, though powerful, can be managed.
- It doesn't involve irrational generalising from 'once' to 'all the time'.
- It doesn't involve trying to mind-read.
- It involves considering alternative explanations rather than jumping to conclusions.
- It results in self-soothing and a stronger sense of self-confidence in dealing with problems.

Normalising

Normalising, instead of personalising, is an indirect aspect of optimism. Normalising means recognising that something that happens in your life also happens to lots of other people, or is typical of a set of circumstances or a stage of development. In contrast, personalising is when you think something that is relatively normal happens only to you, not others, and that it happens *because* you are who you are. If we personalise, we say, 'That occurred to me because I am me, so there is nothing I can do about it because it will undoubtedly happen again because I will always be me'. When we personalise, we automatically think, 'What's wrong with me?' or 'Why me?' If we normalise, we automatically think, 'What's wrong here?' and ask, 'Is this an out-of-the-ordinary event or the kind of thing that happens quite frequently to other people?' In normalising, we say, 'That happened to me because it is one of those things that happen to many people in their lifetime, not just me. If others can deal with it, so can I'. Over time, young people who personalise everyday difficulties develop a pessimistic explanatory style and a negative self-perception where they think they are jinxed, doomed or inadequate.

Young people need to be shown how to normalise many of the changes in their behaviours, roles and relationships that are due to developmental 'everyday' stressors. We can probably remember from our own experience, wondering if what we were experiencing as we proceeded through childhood and adolescence was 'normal' or typical. Challenges to our wellbeing can occur at any time due to illness, accidents, loss or trauma, but there are also everyday stressors at different developmental stages when everyone is likely to experience some anxiety and uncertainty. Many of these are listed in the everyday/major stressors chart on page 36. Young people need to understand that others are also likely to be experiencing the same kinds of feelings and it is normal at these turning points to experience some anxiety. Sharing their concerns with others helps with this 'normative' process.

It is also important that those working with young people clearly understand the developmental stages and characteristics of each stage of childhood development. Without this understanding, there is a risk of over-reacting or under-reacting to young people's problematic symptoms. Understanding the characteristics of young people's thinking at each stage of development and in response to everyday stressors helps teachers and others working with young people to normalise their experiences for them. Normalising, if it is done sensitively and not dismissively, does not trivialise or devalue young people's anxiety, but rather helps them to see that other young people are also experiencing similar feelings. This helps them to respond more constructively and optimistically to the situation.

Young people also need to be taught how to normalise and manage emotional states. Without being patronising or trivialising their feelings, those working with young people can encourage them to understand that it is normal and appropriate to temporarily feel sad, anxious, worried or disappointed when they experience hardship, loss, sadness, disappointments, reversals, setbacks and bad times. In fact, such feelings are useful in that they can motivate problem solving and empathy for others. An important message is that others survive difficult or bad events in their lives and they can too.

Using humour

Humour can be a useful tool for resilience as we are less likely to succumb to feelings of depression and helplessness if we are able to find something funny, even if only small, in the situation that is troubling us. Lefcourt[20] has argued that humour is a characteristic that is useful to our species, helping us as we attempt to live in what are often very difficult circumstances. Humour may also have evolved as an antidote to anger and aggression, allowing humans to live together without engaging in continuous conflict. When a major world crisis or tragedy occurs, a spate of jokes about it soon emerges. These jokes can help people to manage the stress or anxiety provoked by the tragedy.

The degree to which a person uses humour can tell us a lot about their resilience and coping style. For example:
- Those who use humour under stress are more likely to have a strong sense of their own personal control and feel less helpless. Teaching people to use humour as a coping strategy has been shown to increase their sense of having greater control and power over their own life.
- Students who are perceived as having a good sense of humour also tend to be more assertive and feel more in control of things in their life[20].
- A poor sense of humour is associated with an avoidance style of coping and a degree of passive acceptance of the negative effects that accompany stressful experiences[20].

Humour has positive benefits for physical health and wellbeing. Research indicates that people who laugh more and are able to look on the funny side of life have healthier immune systems than others. A good laugh also increases our heart rate, helps us breathe more deeply and stretches many different muscles in our face and upper body. One researcher estimated that a good laugh produces an increase in heart rate that is equivalent to ten minutes on a rowing machine or fifteen minutes on an exercise bike[21]. Laughter does indeed positively affect the body, mind and spirit.

Humour is a healthy way of putting a little 'distance' between one's self and the problem, a way of standing off and looking at the problem with a different perspective. Comic actor Robin Williams once described humour as 'optimism in action'. Humour can create hope by encouraging us to reframe and redefine a negative situation as a little bit more positive. Laughter throws a bit of light onto an otherwise dark and bleak situation.

Humour also helps in accepting life's imperfections, inevitabilities, difficulties, frustrations and disappointments. It helps us to accept what we cannot control, such as death, the behaviour of other people, others' incompetence, ageing, physical limitations and illness. Jokes and funny throwaway lines can also communicate messages that help us to understand what is normal and typical. In knowing that others share some of the same feelings, perceptions and troubles, we may feel more empowered to deal with these troubles.

There are many social benefits from using humour. For example:
- It can create a sense of community and closeness. We all benefit from closeness to others when we encounter difficulties in our lives. Social support moderates the impact of stressful experiences. Sharing a joke and laughing at similar things together not only gives the message that we are enjoying each other's company but also helps us to develop strong bonds with others and creates group solidarity.
- People who use humour, especially self-deprecating humour, often draw other people towards them. Being able to laugh at our own foibles and at aspects of our own crises tends to attract support from others. Other people may interpret self-directed humour in the face of adversity as a sign of courage.
- Humour can be a way of showing affection. Being able to gently and humorously 'stir' each other can be a sign of friendship and the strength of the relationship.
- Students with a good sense of humour are more popular and socially competent. They are also well liked by teachers as long as the humour is not disruptive and 'silly and immature'.

Humour can also decrease tension in social contexts. For example:
- Laughter and having fun together can break down barriers if people feel nervous or don't know each other well and can help create a sense of safety.
- Humour can be an ice-breaker and communicate care and support if people are fearful of the unknown, for example, in hospitals, medical staff often make light-hearted remarks in the face of a serious medical situation. The humour can be easily terminated when more seriousness is needed.
- Used wisely, humour can 'short circuit' a hostile exchange and allow people to 'back off' and change to a more positive and conciliatory direction.
- Humour can help to make the 'undiscussable' discussable. People can feel more able to talk about their feelings and difficult situations if there is an element of humour to lighten the discussion.

There are two significant gender differences in the use and appreciation of humour. The first difference is that girls and women use and appreciate more self-directed humour, while boys and men initiate and appreciate more other-directed and hostile humour. Secondly, boys are more likely to use humour to decrease the intimacy of a situation, whereas girls are more likely to use it to increase the intimacy level.

There are also some 'downsides' to humour. Exploitative and attacking humour allows others to be entertained by another's distress. However, while hostile humour may create a sense of cohesion in the 'in-group' that shares its animosity towards other groups or individuals, there is also a negative aspect to it. Group members soon become suspicious of each other, fearing that they will become the next targets of ridicule[20]. If humour is used to trivialise a serious situation and deny the reality of associated feelings, it may reduce efforts to deal with it. It can encourage disengagement from problem solving and avoidance of problem confrontations.

The 'Humour' unit in **Classroom Resources** includes a Giggle Gym that builds in humour sessions to create a classroom environment that is fun to belong to, and activities to teach messages about using humour in a resilient and helpful way. The 'Humour' unit also explores what makes something funny.

Social and emotional skills

The Collaborative for Academic, Social and Emotional Learning (CASEL) has identified five core competencies for school-based social and emotional learning (SEL)[22]. All five competencies are taught in *Bounce Back!* as shown in the following table.

Key area of social and emotional learning (SEL)	Bounce Back! units that focus on this SEL competency
Self-awareness and self-knowledge • Accurately assessing one's own feelings, interests, values and strengths • Understanding one's own thinking and learning processes • Maintaining a well-grounded sense of self-confidence	Emotions STAR! (Success) Core values Looking on the bright side
Self-management • Coping resiliently with difficult and challenging situations • Regulating one's emotions to handle stress, control impulses and persist in overcoming obstacles • Setting and monitoring progress towards personal and academic goals • Expressing emotions appropriately	Emotions People bouncing back Looking on the bright side Humour Courage STAR! (Success) Relationships
Social awareness • Being able to take the perspective of others and empathise with them • Recognising and appreciating individual and group differences	Emotions Relationships Core values People bouncing back
Relationship skills • Establishing and maintaining healthy and rewarding relationships based on cooperation, inclusion and respect • Resisting inappropriate social pressure • Preventing, managing and resolving interpersonal conflict • Seeking help when needed	Relationships No bullying People bouncing back Core values
Responsible decision-making • Making decisions based on consideration of ethical standards, safety concerns, appropriate social norms, respect for others and likely consequences of actions • Applying decision-making skills to academic and social situations • Contributing to the wellbeing of one's school and community (which contributes to a sense of meaning and purpose)	Core values STAR! (Success)

Empathy

Empathy underpins social-emotional learning and moral development. Students who 'share' or 'understand' someone else's distress that is a result of their own anti-social behaviour are more likely to stop and not do it again. High levels of empathy are linked to pro-social behaviour, while low levels of empathy are linked to anti-social behaviour including bullying, aggression and criminal activities. Being able to empathise is part of being resilient. Empathy has three components: cognitive, affective and action.

1. **The cognitive component**
    - Identifying how someone is feeling at an intellectual level by reading their expressions and behaviour. Drawing on one's own experiences can enhance this.
    - 'Putting yourself in someone else's shoes' to try to understand their perspective or point of view.
2. **The affective (emotional) component**
    - This is the capacity to emotionally experience the feelings of another. Affective empathy can also be defined as experiencing a vicarious emotional response to the perceived emotional experience of another. This could be a real person or a fictional character. The empathic person 'mirrors' the emotions and behaviour of another person as though they were doing it rather than just watching it.
3. **The action component**
    - The action component could also be termed 'empathic concern' and involves responding to the perceived distress of another with words or actions of kindness or support.

Having well-developed empathic skills helps students to:

- engage in more pro-social behaviours and avoid anti-social behaviours such as bullying. They use their empathy and pro-social values as a guide to how to behave decently towards other people (e.g. *How will that person feel if I steal their pen/say something nasty?*).
- be less likely to tolerate bullying behaviour on the part of others. They are also more likely to refuse to take part in bullying and more likely to act to prevent it or extend their support to the student being mistreated.
- be less judgmental and more accepting, show more kindness and support and therefore have more positive relationships.
- handle conflict more effectively, as they are more likely to try to see both sides of a situation.
- develop a capacity for ethical thinking. As students encounter more sophisticated issues and ideas, they need to recognise that there are legitimate viewpoints apart from their own. Good thinkers can hold two opposing ideas in their mind at once. They can also clearly state the view they don't agree with as well as the one they do agree with.
- develop a sense of social justice and concern for others in the broader community.
- not personalise other people's behaviour. If they can see why a person may be behaving towards them in a particular way, they are less likely to see that behaviour as a direct personal attack.
- have better friendships and support networks. Students who show that they are trying to understand another's point of view and their feelings are more likely to be liked and sought out, and others are more likely to respond to them by showing them the same sensitivity and concern.

Empathy underpins all the core values and is critical to developing the social-emotional skills discussed in the 'Relationships' unit in **Classroom Resources**.

Self-knowledge

A converging message from many areas of Psychology and Education, and especially from the Positive Psychology movement, is that a strengths-based approach is important for the promotion of student wellbeing and academic engagement. Researchers in CASEL explain that:

> ...there is no good alternative to a strengths-based approach to working with children. It involves a) establishing positive relationships with children based on their assets and their potential contributions as resources to their schools and b) finding naturally occurring contexts in which they can enact positive roles for which they must learn skills to be successful.[23] (p. 305).

A strength is defined as a natural capacity for behaving, thinking and feeling in a way that promotes successful goal achievement[24]. When students work with their strengths they tend to learn more readily, perform at a higher level, are more motivated and confident, and have a stronger sense of satisfaction, mastery and competence. Opportunities to identify and sometimes work with their strengths are especially important for students who are not academically strong[25]. Students who are given feedback on their strengths are significantly more likely to feel highly engaged and to be more productive than those who only receive feedback on their weaknesses. Results for the strengths-based feedback groups (compared to control groups with no feedback) included increases in grade point average, attendance and self-confidence[26,27].

The 'STAR! (Success)' unit in **Classroom Resources** incorporates two models for identifying and engaging students' strengths. One model is Howard Gardner's model of multiple intelligences for intellectual strengths (or abilities)[28] and the other is Peterson and Seligman's VIA model for character strengths[29].

Bounce Back! uses two approaches for engaging students' strengths: building up strengths and building upon strengths.

1. *Building up a strength* is identifying a strength that requires more work, such as a student's language skills (intellectual strength) or a student's skills at persevering or being braver (character strengths).
2. *Building upon a strength* is creating opportunities for students to use and develop their intellectual or character strengths, e.g. extending a student's artistic ability (intellectual) or their leadership skills (character).

Intellectual strengths/abilities

Howard Gardner's[28] model of multiple intelligences (MI) has been widely adopted in schools since its publication more than twenty years ago and identifies eight intelligences: linguistic, logical-mathematical, visual-spatial, bodily-kinesthetic, naturalist, musical, interpersonal (people) and intrapersonal (self).

Kornhaber[30] evaluated outcomes in forty-one schools that had been using MI theory for curriculum differentiation for at least three years and found significant benefits of the MI approach in terms of improvements in student engagement and learning, in student behaviour and in parent participation. There were particular benefits for students with learning difficulties, who demonstrated greater effort in learning, more motivation and improved learning outcomes. MI theory is the only theory of intelligence that incorporates interpersonal (understanding others) and intrapersonal (understanding self) intelligences. Using MI theory as a framework for curriculum differentiation thereby encourages teachers to embed tasks that develop students' skills in these social-emotional domains as well as the more traditional academic domains.

The use of MI theory for curriculum differentiation has been shown to build positive learning communities based on collective strengths in which students value and celebrate their differences and for students who struggle with learning to achieve more academic success[25,30-32]. Our MI/Bloom Matrix in *Eight Ways at Once* has been widely used in Australian schools for curriculum differentiation[31,32]. Teachers' use of the matrix in two primary schools over eighteen months was shown to increase their sense of professional competency in effectively catering for diverse students' learning needs and developed their competencies in helping their students to set goals and make meaningful choices about their learning tasks and products[25,31,32].

Character strengths and values

The model of character strengths that has become popular in Positive Psychology/Positive Education was developed by Peterson and Seligman[29]. They believe that character strengths are foundational to the human experience. Their model incorporates twenty-four character strengths organised in six categories, as shown in the following table.

Wisdom and knowledge	Justice
• Creativity • Curiosity • Judgment and open-mindedness • Love of learning • Perspective	• Teamwork • Fairness • Leadership
Courage	**Temperance**
• Bravery • Perseverance • Honest • Zest	• Forgiveness and mercy • Modesty and humility • Prudence • Self-regulation
Humanity	**Transcendence**
• Love • Kindness • Social intelligence	• Appreciation of beauty and excellence • Gratitude • Hope (optimism) • Humour • Religiousness and spirituality

A person's top three to five strengths are called their 'signature strengths'. A signature strength is defined as an important character trait that defines one's essence of being. Signature strengths are seen as so central to a person's psychological identity that suppressing or ignoring them would seem unnatural and very difficult. The five character strengths for adults that appear to be most highly related to life satisfaction are hope, zest, gratitude, curiosity and love[33]. An interesting staff-building activity is to ask all staff to complete the survey available on www.viacharacter.org and then share how they have used one of their signature strengths at school. A version for students from 10 to 17 years of age is also on the same website.

The character strengths of love, gratitude and hope have been shown to predict academic achievement in both middle school and college students[34]. Effective teachers (judged by the gains of their students on standardised tests) are those high in social intelligence, zest and humour[34]. Popular students as identified by teacher ratings are more likely to score highly on justice strengths (such as leadership and fairness) and temperance strengths (such as self-regulation, prudence and forgiveness).

All these character strengths are a focus in *Bounce Back!* Students are encouraged to identify and use their character strengths in the 'STAR! (Success)' unit and the activities in each curriculum unit can create age-appropriate opportunities to *build up* or *build upon* their different strengths.

Experiencing 'psychological' flow by using one's strengths

Students experience 'psychological flow' when they are so immersed in an activity that hours pass like minutes, their mind is totally focused and they are completely absorbed in what they are doing. Athletes call it 'being in the zone'. The state of flow occurs when students encounter a challenging task that tests their skills but they have the skills and strengths or capacities to meet this challenge. So both the challenge and the skills really stretch them. If the challenge exceeds their skills they become anxious. If their skills exceed the challenge of the task, they are likely to be bored. Csikzentmihalyi et al[35] investigated the phenomenon of flow by interviewing thousands of people from many different walks of life, including large cohorts of teenagers. He concluded that flow is a universal experience that has the following characteristics:

- clarity of goals and immediate feedback on progress, e.g. in a competitive game students know what they've got to achieve and whether they are winning or losing
- complete concentration on what they are doing at the present time
- actions and awareness are merged, e.g. a student is immersed in an art project and the process of painting becomes almost automatic
- losing self-consciousness is a common experience but after each flow experience, their self-confidence is strengthened
- sense of control over what they are doing and not worrying about failure
- time passes more quickly than expected
- activities are intrinsically rewarding.

Activities that lead to a flow experience depend on the individual but include sport, dancing, involvement in the creative arts and other hobbies, socialising, studying, reading and working. In fact, most daily activities can lead to flow as long as the task is sufficiently complex to activate the high challenge-high skill criterion. Providing opportunities for students to identify and use their strengths in challenging tasks is much more likely to create optimal learning experiences than using passive teacher-controlled tasks such as passively watching DVDs, completing worksheets or listening to 'lectures'.

A sense of meaning and purpose

A critical component of wellbeing is the belief that there is purpose and meaning in one's life. Meaningful participation in school- and community-based activities helps students to gain a sense of meaning and purpose. The kinds of activities that are most likely to create a sense of meaning and purpose for students are those that have an impact on other people, not just themselves. According to Seligman[36] (p. 260):

> …a meaningful life is one that joins with something larger than we are—and the larger that something is, the more meaning our lives have'. He states that life is given meaning when we use our signature strengths every day 'to forward knowledge, power or goodness.

A lack of meaning in life is associated with poor psychological functioning, while positive life meaning is associated with strong spiritual beliefs, membership of pro-social groups, dedication (e.g. to a cause), life values and clear goals. The importance of acting in accord with one's pro-social values and having a sense of meaning is illustrated by a longitudinal study that followed high school students into late adulthood at a time interval of over fifty years[37]. The students were first interviewed in the 1930s and then every ten years until the late 1990s. The results of the study indicated that 'giving' adolescents became both psychologically and physically healthier adults. This study lends support to the notion that 'it is good to be good' and there is a lifelong benefit for young people who begin being altruistic in their teens. These benefits of altruism accrue across the entire lifespan. Other comprehensive research documents the positive effects of community service on students' academic performance as well as their social-emotional learning skills and civic responsibility[38-40].

Student participation and voice is a recognised feature of high performing schools and has a positive effect on learning in the classroom and their engagement in school[41]. When students investigate issues of real concern to them and when they can take action to bring about change both in their school and in the community, this helps them to have a sense of meaning and purpose[42,43].

Being resourceful and adaptable

Being resourceful means:
- Solving problems by identifying and using the resources available to you, and using them creatively.
- Having an orientation towards success, which is a belief that you can achieve by your own efforts if you work hard and persist in the face of obstacles. This has been called the success or growth mindset[9]. A growth mindset is firstly believing that your ability can be increased and then working hard and spending more time and effort in gaining mastery in a subject rather than giving up. In contrast, a fixed mindset is thinking, 'I'm not smart enough' or 'I can't do maths', and just giving up when faced with difficulties or when mistakes are made.
- Being able to set, plan and achieve realistic goals and being able to organise yourself. Such skills result in a sense of optimism as well as higher levels of self-esteem and self-efficacy (the belief that you can do it).
- Holding the belief that it is important and helpful to be flexible when the need arises, rather than be restricted to a narrow set of options for dealing with problems.
- Understanding that change is a normal part of life (e.g. changing teachers, classes or school) changing friends, and being able to adapt to change.

Being able to 'adaptively distance' yourself from distressing and unalterable situations can mean:
- Not blaming yourself for things that you aren't responsible for, such as your parents' difficulties.
- Accepting that there are some things that can't be easily changed, such as having a sibling with a chronic illness or an alcoholic parent.
- Finding a therapeutic place where you can go when things are at their worst, such as a quiet and beautiful scenic spot where you feel more able to think clearly.
- Engaging in a challenging mental distraction such as working on a non-emotional task or project or making plans or lists.
- Thought stopping, where you 'blink' to get rid of distressing thoughts and then move into an exploration of a memory of a special and happy time.
- Moving temporarily away from the people who are part of the difficult situation. One example would be going to another room when your siblings are arguing. Adaptive distancing is *not* the same as using substances such as drugs and alcohol, which merely offer the illusion that there is no situation to be dealt with or accommodated.

In summary

This chapter reviews the personal coping skills, assets and attitudes that underpin the *Bounce Back!* program. The coping skills that contribute to wellbeing and resilience are helpful and optimistic thinking, being able to normalise setbacks instead of personalising, social-emotional learning skills, help seeking, using humour in a helpful way, self-knowledge and gaining a sense of meaning and purpose through meaningful participation in class, school and community activities, and being resourceful and adaptable.

References

1. Carver, C.S. & Scheier, M.E. 1999, 'Optimism' in *Coping. The Psychology of What Works*, Snyder C.R. (ed.), Oxford University Press, New York, pp. 182–204.
2. Seligman, M.E.P., et al. 1995, *The Optimistic Child*, Houghton Mifflin, New York.
3. Seligman, M.E.P. 1992, *Learned Optimism*, Random House, Sydney.
4. Reivich, K. 2005, 'Optimism lecture' in *Authentic Happiness Coaching*, University of Pennsylvania.
5. Peterson, C. 2000, 'The future of optimism', *American Psychologist*, vol. 55, no. 1, pp. 44–55.
6. Seligman, M.E.P. 1995, *The Optimistic Child*, Random House, Sydney.
7. Gilham, J.E., et al. 1995, 'Preventing depressive symptoms in schoolchildren: Two year follow-up', *Psychological Science*, vol. 6, no. 6, pp. 343–351.
8. Gillham, J. & Reivich, K. 2004, 'Cultivating optimism in childhood and adolescence', *The ANNALS of the American Academy of Political and Social Science*, vol. 591, pp. 146–163.
9. Dweck, C.S. 2006, *Mindset. The New Psychology of Success*, Random House, New York.
10. Lopez, S.J., et al. 2009, 'Measuring and promoting hope in schoolchildren', in *Promoting Wellness in Children and Youth: Handbook of Positive Psychology in the Schools*, R. Gilman, Huebner, E.S. & Furlong, M. (eds), Lawrence Erlbaum, Mahwah, New Jersey.
11. Wiseman, R. 2004, *The Luck Factor*, Arrow Books, London.
12. Rose, A.J. 2002, 'Co-rumination in the friendships of girls and boys', *Child Development*, vol. 73, no. 6, pp. 1830–1843.
13. Rose, A.J., Carlson, W. & Waller, E.M. 2007, 'Prospective associations of co-rumination with friendship and emotional adjustment: Considering the socioemotional trade-offs of co-rumination', *Developmental Psychology*, vol. 43, no. 4, pp. 1019–1031.
14. Beck, A.T. 1979, *Cognitive Therepy and the Emotional Disorders*, Penguin Books, New York.
15. Burns, D. 1980, *Feeling Good: The New Mood Therapy*, Avon Books, New York.
16. Clark, D. & Beck, A. 1999, *Scientific Foundations of Cognitive Theory of Depression*, John Wiley, New York.
17. Ellis, A. 1988, *How to Stubbornly Refuse to Make Yourself Miserable about Anything. Yes, Anything!*, Pan Macmillan, Sydney.
18. Ellis, A., et al. 1997, *Stress Counselling: A Rational Emotive Behaviour Approach*, Cassell, London.
19. Ellis, A. & Dryden, W. 1987, *The Practice of Rational Emotive Therapy*, Springer, New York.
20. Lefcourt, H.M. 2001, *Humor: The Psychology of Living Buoyantly*, Plenum Publishers, New York.
21. Wiseman, R. 2009, *Laugh Lab* [cited 18/1/10], available from www.laughlab.co.uk/
22. *Collaborative for Academic, Social and Emotional Learning*, 2010 [cited 18/1/10], available from www.casel.org
23. Elias, J.E., et al. 2003, 'Implementation, sustainability, and scaling up of social-emotional and academic innovations in public schools', *School Psychology Review*, vol. 32.
24. Linley, P.A. & Harrington, S. 2006, 'Playing to your strengths', *The Psychologist*, vol. 19, pp. 86–89.
25. Noble, T. 2004, 'Integrating the Revised Bloom's Taxonomy with Multiple Intelligences: A planning tool for curriculum differentiation', *Teachers College Record*, vol. 106, no. 1, pp. 193–211.
26. Harter, J.K. 1998, 'Gage Park High School research study' cited in Daly, A.J. & Chrispeels, J. 2005, 'From problem to possibility: Leadership for implementing and deepening the process of effective schools', *Journal for Effective Schools*, vol. 4, no. 1, pp. 7–25.
27. Williamson, J. 2002, 'Assessing student strengths: Academic performance and persistence of first-time college students' cited in Daly, A.J. & Chrispeels, J. 2005, 'From problem to possibility: Leadership for implementing and deepening the process of effective schools', *Journal for Effective Schools*, vol. 4, no. 1, p. 7–25.
28. Gardner, H. 1999, *Intelligence Reframed: Multiple Intelligences in the Twenty-First Century*, Basic Books, New York.
29. Peterson, C. & Seligman, M. 2004, *Character Strengths*, Oxford University Press, New York.
30. Kornhaber, M., Fierros, E. & Veenema, S. 2003, *Multiple Intelligences: Best ideas from research and practice*, Allyn & Bacon.
31. McGrath, H. & Noble, T. 2005, *Eight Ways at Once. Book One: Multiple Intelligences + Bloom's Revised Taxonomy = 200 differentiated classroom strategies*, Pearson Education, Sydney.
32. McGrath, H. & Noble, T. 2005, *Eight Ways at Once. Book Two: Units of work based on Multiple Intelligences + Bloom's Revised Taxonomy*, Pearson Education, Sydney.
33. Park, N., Peterson, C. & Seligman, M.E.P. 2004, 'Strengths of character and wellbeing', *Journal of Social & Clinical Psychology*, vol. 23, pp. 603–619.

34. Park, N. & Peterson, C. 2009, 'Strengths of character in schools' in *Handbook of Positive Psychology in Schools*, Gilman, R., Huebner, E.S. & Furlong, M.J. (eds), Routledge, New York.
35. Csikszentmihalyi, M., Rathunde, K. & Whalen, S. 1993, *Talented Teenagers*, Cambridge University Press, Cambridge, United Kingdom.
36. Seligman, M.E.P. 2002, *Authentic Happiness*, Free Press, New York.
37. Wink, P., et al. 2007, 'Religiousness, spiritual seeking, and personality. Findings from a longitudinal study', *Journal of Personality*, vol. 75, no. 5, p. 1051.
38. Billig, S. 2004, 'Using Evidence to Make the Case for Service–Learning as an Academic Achievement Intervention in K–12 Schools' [cited 24/6/08], Research Summary, available from www.service-learningpartnership.org/site/DocServer/caseforsl.doc?docID=106
39. Eyler, J. & Giles, D. 1999, *Where's the Learning in Service-Learning?*, Jossey-Bass, San Francisco.
40. Astin, A.W., Sax, L.J. & Avalos, J. 1999, 'Long-Term Effects of Volunteerism During the Undergraduate Years', *Review of Higher Education*, vol. 22, no. 2, pp. 187–202.
41. Black, R. 2007, 'Crossing the bridge: overcoming entrenched disadvantage through student-centred learning' [cited 16/6/08], available from www.educationfoundation.org.au
42. Holdsworth, R. 2002, 'Student action teams: What do we learn?' in *Role of Schools in Crime Prevention Conference*, Melbourne.
43. Chapman, J., Cahill, S. & Holdsworth, R. 2007, 'Student action teams, values education and quality teaching and learning', in *Values Education and Quality Teaching: The Double Helix Effect*, Lovat, T.J. & Toomey, R. (eds), David Barlow Publishing, Sydney, pp. 28–48.

Chapter 4

Teaching the BOUNCE BACK! acronym

The BOUNCE BACK! acronym acts as a kind of 'coat-hanger' for the program. This chapter firstly provides guidelines for teaching the acronym, then each coping statement of the acronym is introduced and the key principles that underpin each statement are explained. The major focus of the *Bounce Back!* program is on helping students to understand the coping statements so they can apply and use them in difficult times. The BOUNCE BACK! and BOUNCE! acronyms are available online as e-tools for the IWB and as printable BLMs (see **Years K–2: BLM 2.1** and **Years 3 & 4: BLM 2.2**). The BLMs can also be displayed on an IWB, data show and so on.

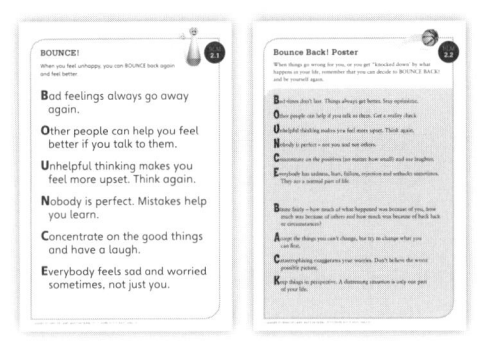

Guidelines for teaching the acronym

The coping statements should be learned so they can be used by students when needed. The following ideas will help students to understand and learn the acronym.

- Repeating and revisiting the acronym over many years helps students to master and easily remember the coping statements, especially at the time of difficulty.
- Involving parents in the program provides opportunities for the acronym to be reinforced and discussed at home as well as at school. See www.pearsonplaces.com.au/bounceback.aspx for ideas for involving parents in BOUNCE BACK! and for information sheets that can be sent home to parents.
- Three levels of delivery are outlined below. More class time can be spent on levels 1 and 2 and less time at level 3.
  - Level 1: Students focus on the statements and what they mean.
  - Level 2: Students focus on the ideas and concepts as applied to others such as family, friends, puppet or cartoon characters, characters in the news, books and films, and so on. This allows the concepts to be 'one step removed'.
  - Level 3: Students focus on the ideas and concepts as applied to themselves.
- Provide a classroom climate of safety and trust during all discussions and activities (see Chapter 7: Teaching strategies in Bounce Back!, page 84, for more details as to how to achieve this).
- Encourage students to refer to the coping statements in the acronym when they are trying to support their friends and classmates.
- Refer to BOUNCE BACK! coping statements when there is a playground or classroom problem or situation.
- Wherever possible, link the program to other areas of the curriculum, e.g. Social

53

Studies and the Environment, Science and Technology, English, Health and Personal Development, Protective Behaviours, and Religious Education.

The key principles in BOUNCE! and BOUNCE BACK!

The BOUNCE! (Years K–2) and BOUNCE BACK! (Years 3 & 4, 5–8) acronyms are formed by the key principles underpinning the coping statements. BOUNCE! consists of simpler versions of the first six BOUNCE BACK! statements for lower primary students. It is still important to talk to young children about 'bouncing back'.

Bad times don't last. Things always get better. Stay optimistic.
Other people can help if you talk to them. Get a reality check.
Unhelpful thinking makes you feel more upset. Think again.
Nobody is perfect—not you and not others.
Concentrate on the positives (no matter how small) and use laughter.
Everybody experiences sadness, hurt, failure, rejection and setbacks sometimes, not just you. They are a normal part of life. Try not to personalise them.

Blame fairly. How much of what happened was due to you, to others and to bad luck or circumstances?
Accept what can't be changed (but try to change what you can change first).
Catastrophising exaggerates your worries. Don't believe the worst possible picture.
Keep things in perspective. It's only part of your life.

Bad times don't last. Things always get better. Stay optimistic.
- Bad times and unpleasant feelings are (nearly) always temporary. Things in your life will get better so don't give up. It is important to stay optimistic and hopeful.
- Sometimes it takes a while for a difficult situation to improve, but it does always improve.
- Sometimes the situation may not improve (e.g. if someone is dying) but your feelings about it will improve if you work on them.
- When things are really bad, just try to get through one day at a time.
- In BOUNCE! (Years K–2), this statement is: *Bad feelings always go away again*.

Other people can help if you talk to them. Get a reality check.
- Nothing is so awful that you can't talk about it to someone you trust. Things will be easier if you share your worries but it takes courage to do so.
- Everyone needs someone to talk to now and then. Talking to someone about what is troubling you is a sign of strength, not weakness.
- Talking about what is worrying you to someone you trust means they can give you support. If you don't talk to them they won't know that you need help.
- Talking to other people allows you to 'cross-check' your ideas and perceptions with them. In this way you can see if they see the situation in the same way as you.
- If you talk to someone you trust you can get a 'reality check' because they will tell you if they think you are not being realistic. Maybe you are getting the facts wrong or you don't have all the facts you need. Maybe you are seeing things in a distorted way.
- In BOUNCE! (Years K–2), this statement is: *Other people can help you feel better if you talk to them*.

Unhelpful thinking makes you feel more upset. Think again.
- Our thoughts strongly influence our feelings and actions. Changing how we think helps us to manage how we feel.
- Unhelpful thinking involves thinking things such as:
  - 'Everybody must like me' (there is no-one who is liked by everybody)
  - 'I must never make a mistake' (everyone needs to make mistakes to learn things)

Chapter 4
Teaching the BOUNCE BACK! acronym

- – 'I must never lose' (everyone has to lose sometimes)
- – 'Bad things always happens to me' (they don't, but you are probably only noticing the bad things that happen to you and not noticing the good things that also happen to you).
- ◉ Don't mistake your feelings for facts. Just because you feel self-conscious doesn't mean people are looking at you. Sometimes you need to do a 'reality check'.
- ◉ Use low-key words for your feelings and they will stay more easily under control. For example, say to yourself: 'I am annoyed' rather than 'I am furious', or 'It is unpleasant and I don't like it' rather than 'It is a disaster and I can't stand it'.
- ◉ In BOUNCE! (Years K–2), this statement is the same.

Nobody is perfect—not you and not others.
- ◉ There is no such thing as a perfect person. We all have flaws. Perfection is not an option but improvement and striving for high standards *are* options.
- ◉ You're not perfect so don't be too hard on yourself when something doesn't turn out as well as you had hoped. Judge yourself by effort and be kind to yourself.
- ◉ Others (including parents, teachers, brothers, sisters and friends) are not perfect so don't have unreasonable expectations of them.
- ◉ Mistakes are part of learning. We all have to make mistakes to get better at things.
- ◉ In BOUNCE! (Years K–2), this statement is: *Nobody is perfect. Mistakes help you learn.*

Concentrate on the positives (no matter how small) and use laughter.
- ◉ Finding something positive in a difficult situation, no matter how small, helps you to hang on and feel a bit more hopeful.
- ◉ Feeling more hopeful helps you to feel better and cope better.
- ◉ Finding something funny in a difficult situation, even if it is only a small thing, will make you feel better able to cope. Laugher helps to relieve stress and worry.
- ◉ In BOUNCE! (Years K–2), this statement is: *Concentrate on the good things and have a laugh.*

Everybody experiences sadness, hurt, failure, rejection and setbacks sometimes, not just you. They are a normal part of life. Try not to personalise them.
- ◉ Bad things happen to everyone, even though you may think they happen only to you.
- ◉ Courage is needed when you feel sad or disappointed or when you fail at something.
- ◉ Personalising is thinking that when something bad happens it only happens to you. People who say 'I'm a jinx' or 'Bad things always happen to me' are personalising.
- ◉ Normalising is more helpful and realistic. This means accepting that bad things, such as rejection or failure or frustrations, happen to everyone now and again, not just you. Sometimes they seem to happen all at once! It's normal!
- ◉ In BOUNCE! (Years K–2), this statement is: *Everybody feels sad and worried sometimes, not just you.*

Blame fairly. How much of what happened was due to you, to others and to bad luck or circumstances?
- ◉ Don't just blame yourself when bad things happen—consider how much of what happened was due to your own behaviour, how much was due to what other people did and how much was due to bad luck or circumstances (such as being in the wrong place at the wrong time or random events).
- ◉ When something bad happens, try to do a pie chart showing:
  - – How much me?
  - – How much others?
  - – How much bad luck and circumstances?

55

Accept what can't be changed (but try to change what you can change first).
- ◎ You can try to change the things that you have some control over. For example, if you are worried about schoolwork there are lots of things you can do to improve your skills, such as asking parents or your teacher for help, making a plan and practising the skills. If you have had a fight with a friend you can try to talk with them about what is troubling you.
- ◎ Some things you are worrying about may be other people's worries, like Mum and Dad's worries, not yours. It is not helpful to worry about things that you have no control over or cannot change.
- ◎ Accepting what you can't change also means accepting other people for what they are, even if they don't measure up to what you would like. This does not mean you always like what they do, but you accept that they are who they are. You can't change them, but if you accept them they might be more able to change themselves.

Catastrophising exaggerates your worries. Don't believe the worst possible picture.
- ◎ Catastrophising means thinking about the worst possible thing that could happen and believing that it will happen. For example:
  - 'If I don't do well in this project the whole year will be ruined'
  - 'If I go skiing I'll probably make a fool of myself'
- ◎ Catastrophising makes you feel worried and miserable. You probably won't feel like doing anything because you expect the worst.

Keep things in perspective. It's only part of your life.
- ◎ If you don't keep things in perspective you get upset over very little things and make mountains out of molehills. You forget about the good bits and see only the bad bits.
- ◎ When something happens, some ways to help you to keep things in perspective are to ask yourself:
  - 'Does this really matter? Am I getting upset over very little?'
  - 'On a scale from 1 to 10, how important is this to me really?'
  - 'How much of my life has this really affected?'
  - 'How many parts of my life are still exactly the same and still as good as they were?'
  - 'Is it really the end of the world?'

Different ways to use the BOUNCE BACK! acronym

- ◎ Use the acronym as the basis of on-the-spot counselling and behaviour management.
- ◎ Display the acronym as a poster in the classroom so that students and teachers can regularly refer to it, both privately and in class discussions.
- ◎ Place an enlarged copy of the acronym somewhere in the staffroom so that teachers can work on their own coping skills and become more positive models.
- ◎ Create a new visual of the poster each year so that it doesn't become 'stale' and get ignored. Involve students in making posters using different fonts and graphics.
- ◎ Consider having the acronym in the school diary (if there is one).
- ◎ Display posters made by students of the various acronyms (e.g. BOUNCE!, BOUNCE BACK! and STAR!) in classrooms and corridors.
- ◎ Ensure that parents are also aware of the acronym and its coping messages. Provide them with copies of the acronym and ask them to continue the conversation at home.

Using the BOUNCE BACK! critical question prompts

Use the BOUNCE BACK! prompts (page 96) to continually link the program to the mainstream content of the classroom. These questions can be used in discussions on books, films, news items, biographies, historical events and global issues, and also with what happens on a day-to-day basis.

For example, if you were discussing a news story about someone saving a child from a burning car you could ask: 'Who was the bravest person here? How do we know that? What might have helped them to be brave?' If you were discussing a story that you were reading to the class you might ask: 'Where was this character using optimistic thinking? What evidence do we have that they were still able to stay hopeful? How did the main character make their plan to try to achieve their goal? What problems did they have to deal with along the way to enable them to persist?'

How the BOUNCE BACK! acronym addresses specific emotional and behavioural patterns

Each of the BOUNCE BACK! coping statements incorporates positive thinking/self-talk, which is an antidote to the development of specific dysfunctional emotional and behavioural patterns such as anxiety, depression, impulsiveness and aggression. The following table illustrates these links, e.g. the first statement 'Bad times don't last. Things always get better. Stay optimistic' is a helpful message and will help students who are prone to depression and anxiety.

Coping statement	Emotional/behavioural pattern
B	Depression
O	Anxiety, depression, impulsiveness
U	Anxiety, depression, aggression, impulsiveness
N	Anxiety, depression, aggression
C	Anxiety, depression
E	Anxiety, depression, aggression
B	Depression, aggression
A	Anxiety, depression and aggression
C	Anxiety
K	Depression, aggression

Myths and realities about resilience

The construct of resilience has become very popular. When a construct is popularised, there is a risk of it becoming over-simplified. The following section outlines some of the myths and realities related to the term 'resilience'. The realities draw on the resilience research literature. The complexity of the construct highlights the complexity of the task in enhancing young people's wellbeing and helping them to become more resilient.

Myth 1: *The best way to prevent problems for young people is to focus on what 'causes' the problems (the risk factors) and on the group of young people who seem to have the most risk characteristics.*

Reality: The majority of 'high risk' children and adolescents do not develop anticipated problem behaviours, such as abuse of illicit drugs. There is not a simple direct correlation between the risk factors in young people's lives and their problems. Also, it is not easy for teachers to prevent or change risk factors. A more effective approach is a holistic one that maximises as many protective factors as possible to help young people cope more successfully with the risk factors in their lives. However, this does not deny the need to create environments in which children and adolescents do not suffer abuse, neglect, bullying, violence and poverty.

Myth 2: *Young people will never be able to escape the cycles of violence, poverty or failure that have characterised the lives of their parents, family or community members.*

Reality: Fundamental to the concept of resilience is the capacity to bounce back in the face of adversity. This capacity may be linked to a positive change in a person's environment and/or the learning of new coping skills. All people have the capacity for positive change and for the development of personal coping skills that will help them to be more resilient. For some young people from difficult home environments, school and peer connectedness and finding a teacher who cares can play a crucial role in helping them develop some resilience to cope with the complexities of their lives. For others, learning the personal skills such as how to set and work towards goals can give them a sense of purpose and future. This can help them to distance themselves from events in their lives that are distressing and can not be changed. A combination of many processes provides more protection than one or two.

Myth 3: Resilience is an inborn characteristic. You either have it or you don't.
Reality: It is evident from research that some children are genetically predisposed to be less resilient and some to be more resilient. The Australian temperament study[1] has demonstrated that some characteristics that are present at birth are still present in the teen years. Some of these characteristics are:
- being bored easily
- not adapting easily to new situations
- having intense emotional reactions to situations
- being hard to calm down and comfort
- being shy.

Some young people inherit a genetic predisposition towards anxiety, depression or forms of mental illness, even though these may not always be apparent in early life. Others are born with cognitive and/or behavioural disabilities (such as dyslexia, attention deficit disorder and learning difficulties) that make it harder for them to cope and develop protective resources. Some young children suffer from long-term damage to their developing brain and are more at risk of anxiety and depression as adults as a result of early abuse and neglect. Each risk factor creates an extra challenge for parents, teachers and others as they try to support and care for such young people.

Evidence suggests that children are born with differing predispositions to becoming resilient. However, a predisposition is not the same as 'inevitable'. Even with predispositions and disabilities, children can become more resilient if they are in protective environments and if they are taught resilient skills and attitudes. Resilience is best viewed as a developmental process rather than a fixed trait. Young people who may be predisposed towards being less resilient may be even more in need of programs such as ***Bounce Back!*** than their peers.

Myth 4: A resilient person will demonstrate resilient behaviours in all situations.
Reality: People can readily demonstrate some resilient capabilities in one context and not so readily in another. For example, a student may be uncooperative and unfriendly at school, but different when he is playing with his cousins. A teacher may demonstrate high self-confidence when teaching students but less self-confidence in speaking to a group of parents. In both these examples the different social contexts provide different levels of threat for the individual. Speaking publicly to a group of parents can be more threatening for teachers than talking to a group of students because they have had less opportunity to practise these skills. When the social context or environmental circumstances change, our resilience can also change. Skills learned in one context do not always apply in other situations because the new context may contain more threats or new/different circumstances. Resilience is a dynamic process that is highly influenced by not only the individual's personal coping skills but also their current social context.

Myth 5: Resilience can easily be observed in the behaviour of young people.
Reality: The multi-faceted nature of wellbeing and resilience, with its social, emotional and cognitive components, sometimes makes it difficult to 'see'. Some students can appear resilient, confident and 'cocky', but under stress or threat they go to pieces and do

'dumb' things. Others can seem fragile and non-adaptive, but cope well in very stressful circumstances.

Myth 6: *All professionals working with young people agree on what resilience is and how it is best developed.*

Reality: The concept of resilience has multiple meanings within and across different professional groups. For professionals working in the context of community/social welfare, the main focus in the development of resilience will most likely be enhancing protective environmental factors such as an individual or a family's access to community support agencies and building family strengths.

For professionals in psychology and counselling, the main focus will most likely be using counselling research to teach personal coping skills that can create resilience.

For teachers, the main focus will most likely be on enhancing both school-related protective factors and teaching personal coping skills of resilience at a whole-class level. Teachers at the same school can also hold different views on whether a particular student is resilient or not. One teacher may see acting-out, defiant behaviour as not coping, whereas another teacher may see the same behaviour as indicative of this student demonstrating resilient behaviour given their tough life.

The concept of a resilient person is socially constructed. Planning and implementing a wellbeing program that builds resilience requires an understanding of both the environmental protective factors and the personal coping skills and beliefs that are valued in a particular cultural and ethnic community.

Myth 7: *You need to identify all the risk factors in a young person's life before you can help them to be more resilient.*

Reality: A focus on only the risk factors runs the risk of negatively labelling young people and focusing on their problems rather than possible solutions. As one young survivor said: 'Abuse is what happened to me, not who I am.'[2] This person demonstrates survivor's pride, a term coined by Wolin and Wolin[3] to refer to the well-deserved feelings of accomplishment that result from withstanding the pressures of hardship. Survivors want their struggle to be recognised and honoured, not pitied, and they want to be seen as someone with strength, not as a victim.

A focus on problems can set up a cycle of failure. A cycle of failure leads to a sense of helplessness and a propensity to feel overwhelmed and to give up. It is more productive to engage in a talent search of a young person's strengths and reframe their ability to overcome some of their difficulties as proof of their adaptivity, strength, intelligence, insight, creativity and tenacity. A focus on solutions can set up a cycle of positive actions. A positive cycle can engender a sense of empowerment and hope.

Myth 8: *Resilience can easily be developed through simple social and educational interventions. A focus on one protective factor, such as improving social skills, will make a student resilient.*

Reality: Resilience is multi-dimensional and reflects the social context of a student's life as well as their personal coping skills. Teaching only one set of skills, such as increasing social competence, will have limited long-term effects if some of the other factors in a student's environment don't change. A multi-factored approach that includes environmental protective processes as well as personal skills is more likely to help young people develop resilience than a one-dimensional program. The earlier a program teaches the personal skills, the more likely it will help students learn life skills that foster resilience.

Myth 9: *Resilience solves all problems; if a young person is resilient, then they can survive anything.*

Reality: No one is invulnerable. No one completely escapes life's lessons and challenges. All of us have scars and every one of us has their breaking point. If the risk factors in a young person's life increase and their protective resources decrease, they can find themselves unable to cope either temporarily or for a longer period of time. Resilience is sometimes difficult to foster because of the multiple and complex interacting protective mechanisms and risk factors in children's lives.

Myth 10: Resilient children demonstrate the same kinds of personal coping skills at all ages.
Reality: Resilience is a developmental process, therefore children will experience different everyday stressors and demonstrate different coping skills at different ages. Everyday stressors are the typical kinds of stressors that young people face as they proceed through the developmental stages. A typical everyday stressor for a preschooler may be separation from their parents when starting preschool or school; for a primary school student it may be disappointments relating to sport or schoolwork or peer teasing; and for adolescents it may be maintaining part-time work as well as achieving at school. Any program designed to help young people successfully manage everyday stressors needs to be made age-appropriate and tailored to the students' cognitive, social-emotional and physical developmental stage.

Myth 11: Putting funds and energies into helping students to connect with their school, teachers and peers is enough to help all students develop resilience.
Reality: A focus on the environmental protective factors that schools can put into place can significantly help students feel more connected to their school, teachers and peers. Feeling connected in this way can improve the likelihood that students will complete school and have a sense of future. However, a multi-faceted approach that incorporates both the school environmental protective factors and the personal skills of wellbeing and resilience provides a much better chance for young people to manage difficult events both in the short and the long term.

Indicators for referring a student for professional help

Teachers are the 'first aid workers' in students' mental health and often feel concerned about the emotional or social wellbeing of an individual student but feel out of their depth in helping them. Under those circumstances it is best to refer the student for professional help. Here are some indicators.

- A student has no one in their life they feel they can easily access and talk to.
- There is a pattern of ongoing depressed mood, even in very young children.
- There is a pattern of ongoing social and emotional withdrawal, especially if the student has previously been more socially outgoing.
- The student has been bullied or socially rejected over a long period of time.
- The student appears to have a very limited understanding of social interaction and has problems forming bonds with other students. This may be an indicator of Asperger's Syndrome.
- The student has a history of difficulties with angry outbursts or marked problems with controlling impulses.
- Many absences from school with 'indefinite' reasons (e.g. tiredness, felt unwell). These are often indicators of anxiety and/or depression (and sometimes of being bullied).
- Frequent visits to sick bay, sometimes (but not always) in a dramatic way or in an agitated emotional state. This can be an early indicator of an anxiety predisposition and may lead to obsessive-compulsive disorder (OCD) and/or depression.
- Talking about suicide. There is no discernible pattern as to who will attempt suicide. Some who talk about it don't do it, and others who talk about it will do it. It should always be taken seriously.
- Marked change in a previous pattern without reason (e.g. no longer submitting homework, not going out with friends any more, discontinuing sporting involvement).
- A previous suicide attempt followed by a markedly buoyant mood within a month or two. The strongest predictor of a suicide attempt is a previous suicide attempt, even if there seems to have been a full recovery.

References

1. Prior, M. 1999, 'Resilience and coping: The role of individual temperament' in Frydenberg, E. (ed.), *Learning to Cope: Developing as a Person in Complex Societies,* Oxford University Press, Oxford, pp. 33–52.
2. Rubin in Davis, N.J. 1999, 'School Violence Prevention', Status of Research and Research Based Programs on Resilience, http://mentalhealth.org/schoolviolence
3. Wolin, S. & Wolin, S.J. 2010, 'Shaping a Brighter Future by Uncovering "Survivor's Pride"', accessed 2/2/10 www.projectresilience.com/article19.htm

Chapter 5

School environments for student wellbeing and resilience

Next to families, schools are the most likely place where students can learn personal coping skills and experience the environmental conditions that foster wellbeing and resilience. For students who are alienated from their families, school takes on even greater importance as a place that offers the conditions and opportunities in which to develop resilience.

There are many strategies and approaches that schools and teachers can adopt to create positive schools and classrooms where students feel valued, are engaged, feel a sense of belonging and can learn personal and social-emotional skills.

1. Enhancing school, peer and class connectedness

Many factors in students' lives are beyond the school's control or influence and that puts some limits on what can be achieved by teachers. However, teachers still have a crucial role to play in fostering student wellbeing. Creating positive, safe and engaging classrooms is a complex and challenging task but the outcome in terms of student wellbeing and resilience is worth the time and energy. School matters a great deal to students, and the benefits from satisfying school experiences can be surprisingly long-lasting. One of the key writers on resilience, Michael Rutter[1] (p. 8), has explained it thus:

> It is not high school achievement as such that seems to make a difference, rather, it is positive experiences of a kind that are pleasurable and rewarding and which help children develop a sense of their own worth together with the confidence that they can cope with life's challenges and can control what happens to them.

School, above all other social institutions, provides unique opportunities for students to connect on a daily basis with their peers and caring teachers. School connectedness is students' belief that adults in the school care about their learning as well as about them as individuals. A great number of studies over the past twenty years have confirmed that students' connectedness to school is the most significant factor in determining whether or not they complete school. For a high proportion of young people, being connected to their peers and having a sense of belonging to a friendship group is, at certain times, more relevant to their lives than feeling connected to their family[2]. Adolescent girls, in particular, are often more likely to seek peer support than family support when they are experiencing difficulties[3]. For young people who don't feel connected to their family, their school can play a critical role in fostering their resilience.

2. Teacher optimism about student academic achievement

Teachers' optimism about their ability to make a difference in their students' lives in their own classrooms correlates with higher student performance and greater academic success[4]. Such optimism can be contagious. One study[5] identified that teachers' shared or collective optimism in expecting their students to perform well academically was more important in influencing their academic achievement than the students' socio-economic status, other demographic data and previous achievement history. Another study found that when the teachers collectively raised their expectations of their students and made their students aware of this, and challenged them academically, they were consistently rewarded by improved student learning; students' confidence in their learning increased and their behaviour improved[6].

Teachers may not feel empowered to make a difference at the system level of whole-school change, but working with their students in their own classrooms is working in their circle of influence. Reflecting on the kinds of teaching practices that foster student wellbeing and resilience in their classroom means not only reviewing 'what' is taught but also 'how' it is taught.

High academic expectations, a challenging curriculum with support for learning

The significant effect of teachers' expectations on student achievement and student wellbeing has been supported by research over many years. As noted above, students whose teachers have positive expectations for them not only demonstrate higher rates of academic success[4,6,7], but higher self-efficacy, more optimism[8] and lower rates of problematic behaviours[6,7]. Having high but achievable expectations for students also lowers their alcohol and drug abuse[9]. Many students who are 'at risk' and low on resilience do not perform well academically. Providing academic support and communicating an expectation that they can be successful is critical to helping these students succeed at school. John Hattie's book *Visible Learning* has highlighted the most effective strategies for increasing achievement and is a useful resource for teachers to reflect on their practice[10].

Achievement motivation

Teachers can also help students develop a 'growth mindset', which involves:
- believing that your intelligence/ability is not fixed, but can be developed by investing time and effort
- seeing learning as a valuable goal to work towards, even though you initially make mistakes and the process requires hard work and an investment of time.

Having a growth mindset encourages students to view effort in a positive way and to feel they have the ability, through their own efforts, to learn and master new material. When they experience difficulties in a subject or task, they use more constructive, mastery-oriented explanations. Rather than saying 'I'm hopeless at reading' or 'I'm dumb, I can't do this', and then giving up, they explain their difficulty as due to lack of effort ('I need to work harder'), a lack of information or skill ('I need help with this') or not having the right strategies ('I need to learn my six times table first'). Students who have a growth mindset work harder, spend more time on learning and use more positive, effort-based strategies instead of giving up.

Dweck and Blackwell have investigated the impact of a growth mindset on student learning outcomes for more than twenty years[11,12]. They have found that students with a growth mindset achieved increases in mathematics grades over seventh and eighth grade. In contrast, students with equal measured ability who had a fixed mindset (i.e. they viewed their intelligence/ability as fixed and unchangeable) did not achieve this level of improvement. The impact of a growth mindset was apparent for students at all levels of ability. Their research also demonstrated that students with a growth mindset used more complex thinking strategies and meta-cognitive strategies (i.e. self-monitoring of their learning), which led to deeper processing and understanding of the curriculum. Teacher and parent feedback on student performance influences the development of a growth or fixed mindset. Telling students 'You did well on that test, you must be really smart' leads to a fixed mindset, whereas telling students 'You did well on that test, you must have worked really hard' focuses their attention on effort and builds a growth mindset. The idea that effort pays off in terms of learning, as well as the importance of having a growth mindset rather than a fixed mindset about their abilities, is taught in the 'STAR! (Success)' unit and also links to helpful and optimistic thinking taught in the 'People bouncing back' and 'Looking on the bright side' units.

Research on learning and the brain

Research on neuroplasticity (the malleability of the brain) over recent years aligns with the notion of a growth mindset. It is now understood that learning causes substantial changes in the human brain[13]. Thinking occurs in the brain through the chemical communication of nerve cells connected in a complex network. Learning causes the cells of the brain to develop new connections, and existing connections become stronger. Studies in neurophysiology, neuroanatomy and brain imaging have all shown that when people practise and learn new skills, the areas of the brain responsible for those skills become larger and denser with neural tissue and that other areas of the brain are activated when the individual performs related tasks. Thus, our brains have the capacity to develop throughout life, but only in response to the stimulation of challenge and learning. Teaching students about the malleability of the brain, providing challenging material, and motivating them to apply effort and take an active role in their learning contributes to a growth mindset and higher achievement[12].

Not repeating students

Over the past 75 years, a pool of research-based knowledge about the effects on students of repeating a year level has been accumulating[5,14-16]. There are now strong indications that there are neither academic nor social advantages for the majority of students who repeat a year of their schooling. In fact, there is a high probability of harmful effects. Large-scale meta-analyses have provided the most important information about the effects of year level repetition[10]. The conclusions from these studies are clear-cut and almost unanimous: repeating a year does not improve academic performance, social competency or general behaviour of students at either the primary or secondary level. On the contrary, it creates a self-concept characterised by a sense of failure and a negative attitude to school, and places students at risk of further failure, increased anti-social behaviour and dropping out of school.

Differentiation

Classrooms that communicate high expectations are also characterised by a curriculum that is differentiated so that all students can be appropriately intellectually challenged and developed. The importance of a differentiated curriculum to cater for student diversity is highlighted in current curriculum documents[17]. A differentiated curriculum instead of 'one size fits all' means that students can access multiple entry points into the curriculum and produce different learning products to demonstrate what they know and understand. Curriculum differentiation is defined as consistently using a variety of teaching approaches to vary curriculum content, learning processes and products, assessment and the learning environment in response to the readiness and interests of academically diverse students[18].

A relevant and differentiated curriculum can draw on:
◎ real-life topics that reflect the interests and lives of students
◎ a wide range of teaching strategies to actively engage different students in learning
◎ the revised Bloom's taxonomy to plan activities from simple to complex thinking[19]
◎ Howard Gardner's model of multiple intelligences (MI) to plan a greater range of teaching and learning strategies across different intellectual domains and more choice than a traditional curriculum[20-22]. The MI model is the only theory of intelligence that includes intrapersonal (self) and interpersonal (people) intelligences, so provides a useful

framework for a focus on social-emotional skills as well as academic skills. MI theory also offers a strengths-based approach to curriculum planning and implementation. Strengths-based engagement is seen as critical for student wellbeing and is strongly advocated by the Positive Psychology/Positive Education movement[23].

The curriculum planning matrix that integrates Gardner's eight intelligences with the six levels of thinking in the revised Bloom's taxonomy[21,22] helps teachers to differentiate assessment and teaching by creating up to 48 ways to approach the same unit of work. Teachers' use of the matrix has been shown to increase their professional competency and confidence in effectively catering for students' diverse abilities and in helping their students to set goals and make meaningful choices about their learning tasks and products[24]. It also gives students an opportunity to reflect on their relative intellectual strengths and limitations and to understand that, for them, some learning may require more effort and hard work than learning in other areas.

All students can benefit from a diversified curriculum but such a curriculum is particularly advantageous for students with learning difficulties and those students who are disengaged and more at risk of dropping out[24,25]. As Gardner[26] (p. 25) says:

> When a student isn't learning something, you don't make the assumption that the student is stupid—you make the assumption that you haven't found the right key. The more resources you have for finding the right key, the more likely you are to succeed.

Recognising students' strengths is a starting point in adapting teaching strategies to develop those strengths. This can most readily be achieved by using the MI model as a curriculum planning tool. Research shows that teachers (and classmates) often develop more positive expectations of students' learning abilities once less-academic students are able to demonstrate their areas of intellectual strength(s), using an MI[20,24] model. Gardner[27] (p. 580) perceives that MI is:

> …a hopeful and optimistic theory…one that says one can build on strengths and there are many ways to achieve…and to accomplish something meaningful in school and in the world beyond.

Student engagement
Students can be engaged, busy and having fun but not actually learning anything worthwhile. Students are more likely to be actively engaged in learning when working in their area of relative strength, and also when working at a task that is moderately challenging—not too hard and not too easy for them. Under these conditions they are more likely to experience 'psychological flow', which has been defined as a state of intense, focused concentration or absorption in an activity[28]. When students experience 'flow' they feel more competent, in control and alert. Engaging in activities that trigger 'flow' can also help students when things are difficult and when adaptive 'distancing' is helpful.

Sometimes, giving students choice in what task they do or how they demonstrate what they know and understand encourages them to set their own challenges, and therefore be more likely to experience 'flow'. Observing student engagement in different learning activities helps a teacher understand the student's relative strengths and weaknesses across the different types of intelligences. Encouraging students to reflect on their own level of engagement in the different activities also helps them to gain a better sense of themselves as learners.

3. Provision of opportunities for meaningful participation and taking initiative

Our society promotes the idea of young people taking responsibility and ownership, but studies have shown that boredom, disillusionment and loss of motivation to achieve are more characteristic of today's young people than in previous generations[29,30]. This was illustrated in an Australian study that ran focus groups with 1800 Year 9 and Year 11 boys[30]. The study discovered a strong link between student disengagement in learning and curriculum and pedagogy that was perceived by these students as 'boring, repetitive and irrelevant'. The study showed that this disengagement can set up a spiral of disaffection that is probably more destructive for students who are identified as low achievers or non-achievers at school.

When students have opportunities for meaningful participation and encouragement to develop and show initiative, they are more likely to:

◎ develop a strong sense of their own competence
◎ take greater responsibility for their own actions
◎ be more able to independently deal with boredom and hence engage in fewer self-harmful or anti-social activities.

There are three categories of initiative that students in schools can be encouraged to become involved in:

◎ the pursuit of a personal or group goal
◎ school or community service or volunteer work
◎ a response to a problem that has some personal or community relevance.

For students to develop initiative, as many of the following features as possible need to be present. Students need to be:

◎ intrinsically motivated to some extent in the project/plan
◎ moderately challenged (not too hard or too easy)
◎ given a relatively unstructured starting point that means they need to set goals, make plans and justify them to others
◎ required to do a lot of decision making and problem solving
◎ working within set guidelines
◎ likely to encounter obstacles and setbacks and then have to work on solving these problems
◎ working within their class, school or local community, not in isolation.

4. Positive teacher-student relationships

The quality of teaching, above all else, has been identified as the key factor in determining how well students learn[10,31,32]. In these studies, the quality of the teacher-student relationship has also been identified as one of the most important factors, above content and pedagogy, in influencing students' learning.

Teachers can build positive relationships with their students in a range of ways, including:

◎ using effective teaching strategies
◎ establishing a collaborative classroom climate
◎ being empathic, giving them a chance to be 'heard' and communicating warmth
◎ communicating high expectations about what they can achieve
◎ taking the time to get to know their students as people, not just students.

Many different research studies (e.g.[32-34]) are remarkably consistent in the picture they present of the teachers that students respond to most positively. These teachers:

◎ are relaxed, enjoy their day and are able to laugh, especially at their own mistakes
◎ use fun and humour as part of their teaching
◎ are fair and consistent in their discipline procedures
◎ listen to what their students have to say
◎ treat each student with respect and empathy and as an individual, greet them when they arrive and whenever the opportunity arises, using their name and making eye contact
◎ show that they are pleased to see them rather than only making contact when there is a problem
◎ remember students' details and preferences
◎ use active listening and restorative conversations (see page 69) as part of behaviour management

- develop many opportunities for student voice (e.g. they might negotiate some assignment details with students)
- take an interest in what students do outside class and school
- trust students with responsibilities
- are authentic; listen to students' stories but also tell their own stories in an honest, realistic way
- have high but realistic expectations of all students
- don't shout/yell or 'go on about things'
- don't give up on their students, or tell them they're no good and should leave school
- explain the work, make the work interesting, find interesting things to do and don't make their students feel small when they don't understand
- are enthusiastic about what they teach
- make their curriculum relevant to their students' lives by firstly finding out what happens in the lives of their students
- have an enthusiastic and experimental approach to trying out new teaching strategies while keeping learning outcomes in mind
- are easy to talk to and students feel they can go to them when they are in trouble
- encourage high levels of parental involvement with school but don't over-focus on family factors as explanations
- have different learning pathways for different students.

All these characteristics reflect the value that students place on their teachers' support and interpersonal commitment to them. Yet research demonstrates that most students, especially boys, are reluctant to discuss their problems with their teachers. They are more likely to perceive their teachers as sources of discipline rather than sources of support, especially in secondary settings[3].

Supporting less resilient students

There are three basic principles that teachers can follow in their work with young people who appear to be less resilient. These are:
- Be persistent and communicate to the student that there is someone who is not going to give up on them or allow them to be distracted from the importance of school and their own wellbeing.
- Provide continuity by making sure there is someone who knows the student's needs and is available across time.
- Ensure that there is consistency in the most important messages from all concerned adults in the student's life—do the work, attend classes, be on time, express frustration in a constructive manner, stay in school, consider the rights of others, talk to someone if you're upset.

Other adults can also take on this role of 'going the extra mile', but teachers and schools are well placed to provide these three elements of persistence, continuity and consistency[35].

5. Establishing peer support structures

Peer support systems involve students participating in activities that befriend, help, mentor and/or tutor other students. They contribute to social and emotional learning and the development of pro-social values such as respect, cooperation and compassion. Many educational writers have suggested that there is a desire on the part of most young people to care for and support younger peers and/or peers in distress, despite not feeling confident that they have the skills to do so[36]. Older students who act as peer supporters report improved confidence and social skills, a greater understanding of other people's feelings and behaviour, more open-mindedness and a stronger sense of responsibility. Younger students who receive peer support report that they had developed more skills in expressing their feelings, increased their sense of trust, felt safer and had a sense of being listened to.

Peer support structures also provide benefits to the school as a whole. A buddy system can strengthen school community and help to challenge stereotypes, misconceptions or fears that students hold about younger or older age groups. A buddy system can also help students to feel valued and supported, teach important social skills and create a caring ethos in the school[37]. It can create feelings of connectedness that enable both older and younger 'buddies' to bond more closely with their school within a psychologically safe environment, thereby increasing the likelihood of more positive school behaviour[37].

Peer support systems can be collapsed into four broad categories: befriending systems, conflict resolution systems (peer mediation) counselling-based systems (peer counselling) and peer tutoring.

1. In **befriending peer support**, students are asked to act as a short-term friend towards another student and offer support and contact. This is the easiest approach to implement in a school because it is not as structured and complex as the other forms of peer support[38]. Buddy systems are a form of befriending and, like most peer-led interventions, are very engaging[39], as students are involved in behaviours they would naturally enjoy with each other, such as spending time together, talking to one another, playing games, being recognised for their efforts and being actively involved[40].
2. In **conflict resolution peer support**, nominated or self-nominated students are trained to mediate disputes between peers. This is commonly called peer mediation.
3. In **peer-counselling support**, nominated or self-nominated students are trained to help students in distress (e.g. because they are being bullied) through the use of simple counselling skills such as listening, showing understanding and support, and helping with problem solving. Students receive some training in basic counselling skills and are available to talk through personal or school-related issues with other, often younger, students. The BOUNCE! and BOUNCE BACK! acronyms are a way of providing students with small 'c' counselling skills. They would also need:
   – good listening skills
   – an understanding and commitment to the principles of psychological safety.
4. In **peer tutoring support**, an older student both befriends a younger student and also works with them on a regular basis to learn and revise academic content. Hundreds of evaluations of cross-age tutoring studies indicate that it can contribute to positive academic gains and effective growth for both tutors and tutees[41,42].

Effective practices in the implementation of peer support

The following guidelines outline effective practices in the implementation of peer support[43].

- **Effective preparation:** A peer support program needs systematic planning. This includes making decisions about partnerships, designing activities, training the older students, informing the younger students about what is happening, and monitoring and evaluating the process. It also takes a lot of time in the initial stages to set up the program.
- **Commitment:** Teacher commitment is an important feature of successful peer support programs. They also require the commitment of senior staff, especially the principal[44]. Student commitment to being an older buddy is also crucial to a program's overall effectiveness. When older buddies did not attend sessions or were inconsistent in their involvement, the impact on the younger buddies was negative rather than positive[45].
- **The addition of peer tutoring:** Older buddies/mentors can be involved in teaching social skills, values or about bullying (as in a mentoring program) or academic content and thinking skills[42,46].
- **Effective pairing of younger and older students:** Younger students should be the same gender and similar in background to the older buddy or mentor[47].
- **Optimal age difference between buddies:** The age difference should be about three years.
- **Awareness within the school community:** Awareness of the school's peer support program by all students and staff has also been identified as a significant factor in program success[48]. Advance preparation of parents has also been shown as essential to a buddy program's acceptance[49].

◎ **Teacher buddying:** Teachers 'buddying up' with other colleagues to serve as role models for students can contribute to more effective peer support/buddy programs[50].

6. Positive behaviour management approaches

Student wellbeing is more likely to thrive in a school environment where there is a focus on positive behaviour management. Such an approach highlights prevention as well as intervention and aims to teach students appropriate skills.

School-wide Positive Behaviour Support

Many schools are implementing a whole-school approach to behaviour management called School-wide Positive Behaviour Support (SWPBS)[51]. This is an approach to behaviour management that aims to prevent and reduce anti-social and challenging behaviours by identifying what skills need to be taught and using positive intervention strategies[52]. Positive behaviour support is consistent with *Bounce Back's* multi-factored approach to wellbeing and resilience. The approach reviews the students' learning environment to remove identified factors that maintain inappropriate or unacceptable behaviours. The focus is also on teaching students social-emotional skills such as negotiating, conflict resolution and empathy, and academic skills, such as numeracy and literacy skills, based on students' needs. The aim is to engage them in more appropriate and pro-social behaviour. Positive consequences for pro-social behaviour are provided and negative consequences such as punishment are minimised, but not eliminated.

Restorative practices

Restorative practices have been implemented in many schools. These are consistent with the *Bounce Back!* program in that they focus on the importance of building positive relationships and teaching social-emotional learning skills, including empathy and conflict management. In this approach to behaviour management, 'restorative' means that when a student misbehaves, restoring relationships, repairing harm and learning perspective-taking and social responsibility are more important and effective than simply delivering punishment. Restorative practices include:
◎ *conference circles*, where students sit in a circle, and use the structured format of restorative conferencing to discuss and problem-solve an issue that has affected the whole class or specific members of the class
◎ *the restorative interview or conversation*, where the teacher uses the incident of misbehaviour as an educative opportunity for teaching empathy, consequential thinking and the importance of making amends in order to repair harm and relationships
◎ *the restorative conference*, which is more formal and used with more serious and ongoing misbehaviour. It usually involves senior staff and parents, as well as the students involved and those who have been harmed by the students' behaviour.

7. Developing safe and supportive school communities

Feeling safe at school is a basic human right and is essential for student wellbeing and resilience, as well as learning. One in six students reports being bullied[53] and one in ten reports being cyberbullied each term, mostly by nasty text messages and instant messaging[54]. At this stage, secondary students are more likely to be cyberbullied than primary students, but it is expected that primary aged students will increasingly engage in cyberbullying as they become more adept at using technology. The effects of not feeling safe are well documented. A meta-analytic review of 20 years of research found that being bullied at school was associated with outcomes such as depression, loneliness, anxiety, negative self-concept and poor peer relationships[55]. Students who bully others also don't fare well. Many studies have emphasised the link between bullying at school and later violent, anti-social and/or criminal behaviour[56,57].

The vision of the revised 2010 National Safe Schools Framework is that 'all Australian school communities are safe and supportive learning environments that promote student wellbeing'. The revised NSSF (which was developed by the authors and Erebis International) provides clear guidelines, definitions of terms and resources to help schools develop a safe, supportive and inclusive school community. The 'No bullying' unit in **Classroom Resources** explicitly teaches students the skills and understandings to minimise school bullying.

8. Focusing on teacher wellbeing

Teacher wellbeing, or how satisfied and positive teachers feel about the quality of their work life, also affects student wellbeing. It also encompasses resilience, as teaching is a very complex occupation with many personal and professional demands. The complexity of teaching ensures there will be setbacks and difficulties, and for teachers to thrive in the face of setbacks is a key element of their wellbeing. An interesting study that compared teachers' views of their work with other occupations was conducted in the United Kingdom[58]. This was an in-depth study with teachers in eight high schools as well as an online survey with more than 1000 teachers. The online survey compared teachers' responses to 300 other professional careers. The teachers reported that their daily work was:

- fulfilling because it gave them a sense of meaning and purpose and a sense of accomplishment through developing young people and making a difference in their lives
- exciting because it offered variety, enjoyment and interactions with many different people where every day was different
- satisfying because it enabled their self-development, as well as the pleasure from helping young people to develop both intellectually and emotionally
- enjoyable because of the varied positive interactions with and feedback from both young people and colleagues and the broader community.

This study clearly documents the positive emotions and sense of meaning and purpose many teachers experience in their work. It also indicates that focusing on the positives in the workplace, rather than dwelling on the negatives, is likely to enhance our sense of wellbeing and resilience.

Being positive and optimistic has been found to broaden one's cognitive and social-emotional resources and build positive organisations[59]. Experiencing positive emotions enhances our capacity for optimistic thinking, problem solving and decision making and leads to more flexible, innovative and creative solutions[60,61]. Positive emotions also have the ability to 'undo' the effects of stress and encourage both emotional and physical resilience[62]. The UK Foresight's 2008 Mental Capital and Wellbeing Project drew on the latest research from across the world to consider how to improve everyone's wellbeing throughout life[63]. The project concluded that a small improvement in wellbeing can help to decrease mental health problems and help people to flourish. It distilled the wellbeing research down to five ways to enhance wellbeing; the acronym CLANG (Connect, Learn, Active, Notice, Give) helps in remembering these five ways.

1. **Connect** with people around you and with colleagues, family and friends. Building these connections will support and enrich you every day.
2. **Learn:** Keep learning. Take on a different responsibility at work; set a challenge you will enjoy achieving. Learning new things at work or in the community will make you more confident as well as being fun.
3. **Active:** Be active, go for a walk, run, swim, cycle, dance or garden. Exercising makes you feel good. Find a physical activity that you enjoy and that suits your level of mobility and fitness.
4. **Notice:** Take notice. Be curious, catch sight of the beautiful and savour the moment. Be aware of the world around you and what you are feeling. Reflecting on your experiences will help you appreciate what matters to you.

5. **Give:** Do something caring or generous for a student, a friend, a colleague or a stranger. Thank someone, smile, volunteer your time. Seeing yourself and your happiness linked to the wider community can be very rewarding and creates connections with the people around you.

Experiencing a sense of wellbeing and being resilient means that when faced with new initiatives, you are more able to:

◉ maintain a high level of productivity and quality in your teaching as you manage change
◉ remain emotionally and physically healthy during periods of uncertainty
◉ rebound from any difficulties arising from change and challenge to be even stronger than before
◉ be flexible about how to proceed when blocked
◉ become more organised to avoid being overwhelmed with information
◉ be proactive in engaging in any new initiatives rather than running away from them.

Our research has found that teachers who taught the 'People bouncing back' unit in **Classroom Resources** reported higher personal and professional resilience[64]. This makes sense because in teaching skills and understandings, we develop a deep understanding of this content.

References

1. Rutter, M. 1991, 'Pathways from childhood to adult life', *Pastoral Care in Education*, vol. 63, pp. 384–399.
2. Fuller, A., McGraw, K. & Goodyear, M. 1998, *The Mind of Youth Resilience: A Connect Project*, Victorian Department of Education, Victoria.
3. Fischmann, S. & Cotterell, J.L. 2000, 'Coping styles and support sources of at-risk students', *The Australian Educational and Developmental Psychologist*, vol. 17, no. 2, pp. 58–69.
4. Hoy, W.K., Tarter, C.J. & Woolfolk Hoy, A. 2006, 'Academic optimism of schools: A force for student achievement', *American Educational Research Journal*, vol. 43, no. 3, pp. 425–446.
5. Holmes, C.T. & Matthews, K.M. 1984, 'The effects of non-promotion on elementary and junior high school pupils: A meta-analysis', *Review of Educational Research*, vol. 54, pp. 225–236.
6. Groundwater-Smith, S. & Kemmis, S. 2004, *Knowing makes the difference: Learnings from the NSW Priority Action Schools Program (PASP)*, NSW Department of Education and Training.
7. Rutter, M. et al. 1979, *Fifteen Thousand Hours. Secondary Schools and Their Effects on Children*, Harvard University Press, Cambridge.
8. Bandura, A. 1996, 'Exercise of personal and collective efficacy in changing societies', in *Self-efficacy in Changing Societies*, A. Bandura (ed.), Cambridge Press, New York, pp. 1–45.
9. Brook, J., Nomura, C. & Whealdon, K. 1994, 'A network of influences on adolescent drug involvement: Neighbourhood, school, peer and family', *Genetic, Social & General Psychology Monographs*, vol. 115, pp. 303–321.
10. Hattie, J. 2009, *Visible Learning*, Routledge, New York.
11. Dweck, C.S. 2006, *Mindset. The New Psychology of Success*, Random House, New York.
12. Blackwell, L., Trzesniewski, K. & Dweck, C. 2007, 'Implicit theories of intelligence predict achievement across an adolescent transition: a longitudinal study and an intervention', *Child Development*, vol. 78, no. 1, pp. 246–263.
13. Doidge, N. 2007, *The Brain that Changes Itself*, Viking, New York.
14. Holmes, C.T. 1989, 'Grade-level retention effects: A meta-analysis of research studies', in *Flunking Grades: Research and Policies on Retention*, Shepard L.A. & Smith, M.L. (eds), Falmer Press, London.
15. Jimerson, S.R. 2001, 'Meta-analysis of grade retention research: implications for practice in the 21st century', *School Psychology Review*, vol. 30, no. 3, pp. 420–437.
16. Shepard, L.A. & Smith, M.L. 1990, 'Synthesis of research on grade retention', *Educational Leadership*, vol. 47, no. 8, pp. 84–88.
17. *The Shape of the Australian Curriculum*, 2009, National Curriculum Board http://www.acara.edu.au, Commonwealth of Australia.
18. Tomlinson, C.A. & Cunningham Eidson, C. 2003, *Differentiation in Practice*, ASCD, Virginia.
19. Anderson, L. & Krathwohl, D. (eds) 2000, *A Taxonomy for Learning, Teaching and Assessing: A Revision of Bloom's Taxonomy of Educational Objectives*, Longman, New York.
20. Gardner, H. 1999, *Intelligence Reframed: Multiple Intelligences in the Twenty-First Century*, Basic Books, New York.

21. McGrath, H. & Noble, T. 2005, *Eight Ways at Once. Book One: Multiple Intelligences + Bloom's Revised Taxonomy = 200 differentiated classroom strategies*, Pearson Education, Sydney.
22. McGrath, H. & Noble, T. 2005, *Eight Ways at Once. Book Two: Units of Work Based on Multiple Intelligences + Bloom's Revised Taxonomy*, Pearson Education, Sydney.
23. Seligman, M. 2009, 'Positive psychology and positive education workshop notes', in *Mind & its Potential Conference*, Sydney.
24. Noble, T. 2004, 'Integrating the Revised Bloom's Taxonomy with Multiple Intelligences: A planning tool for curriculum differentiation', *Teachers College Record*, vol. 106, no. 1, pp. 193–211.
25. Kornhaber, M., Fierros, E. & Veenema, S. 2003, *Multiple Intelligences: Best Ideas from Research and Practice*, Allyn & Bacon, Needham, Massachusetts.
26. Noble, T. & Grant, M. 1997, 'An interview with Howard Gardner', *EQ Australia*, vol. 5, no. 1, pp. 24–26.
27. Gardner, H. 1994, 'Intelligences in theory and practice: A response to Elliot W. Eisner, Robert J. Sternberg and Henry M. Levin', *Teachers College Record*, vol. 95, no. 4, pp. 576–583.
28. Csikszentmihalyi, M., Rathunde, K. & Whalen, S. 1993, *Talented Teenagers*, Cambridge University Press, Cambridge, UK.
29. Larson, R.W. 2000, 'Toward a psychology of positive youth development', *American Psychologist*, vol. 55, no. 1, pp. 170–183.
30. Slade, M. & Trent, F. 2000, 'What the boys are saying: An examination of the views of boys about declining rates of achievement and retention', *International Journal of Education*, vol. 1, no. 3, pp. 201–229.
31. Rowe, K. 2004, 'In good hands? The importance of teacher quality', *Educare News*, vol. 149, pp. 4–14.
32. Trent, F. 2001, 'Aliens in the classroom or: The Classroom as an alien place?' in Association of Independent Schools, *NSW Sex, Drugs & Rock 'N Roll Conference*, NSW.
33. Ruddick, J., Day, J. & Wallace, G. 1997, 'Students' perspectives on school improvement', in *Rethinking Educational Change with Heart and Mind. The ASCD Yearbook*, Hargreaves, A. (ed.), ASCD: Alexandria, Virginia, pp. 73–91.
34. Dornbusch, S.M., Laird, J. & Crosnoe, B. 1999, 'Parental and school resources that assist adolescents in coping with negative peer influences', in *Learning to Cope: Developing as a Person in Complex Societies*, Frydenberg, F. (ed.), Oxford University Press, Oxford.
35. Christenson, S.L. & Carroll, E.B. 1999, 'Strengthening the family-school partnership through "Check and Connect"', in *Learning to Cope: Developing as a Person in Complex Societies*, Frydenberg, E. (ed.), Oxford University Press, Oxford.
36. Rigby, K. 1997, 'Peer relations at school and the health of adolescents', *Youth Studies Australia*, vol. 17, no. 1, pp. 13–17.
37. Battisch, V. et al. 2001, 'Effects of the child development project on students' drug use and other problem behaviors', *Journal of Primary Prevention*, vol. 21, pp. 75–99.
38. Gini, G. 2004, 'Bullying in Italian schools: An overview of intervention programmes', *School Psychology International*, vol. 25, no. 1, pp. 105–116.
39. Tindall, J.A. 1995, *Peer programs: An in-depth look at peer helping - Planning, implementation and administration*, Accelerated Development Inc., Bristol, Pennsylvania.
40. Topping, K.J. & Ehly, S. (eds) 1998, *Peer-assisted learning*, Erlbaum, Mahwah, New Jersey.
41. Kalkowski, P. 2001, 'Peer and cross-age tutoring', *Research you can use: School Improvement Research Series* [cited 1/2/05 February 1], available from http://www.nwrel.org/scpd/sirs/9/c018.html
42. Topping, K. & Bryce, A. 2004, 'Cross-age peer tutoring of reading and thinking: Influence on thinking skills', *Educational Psychology*, vol. 24, no. 5, pp. 595–621.
43. McGrath, H. & Stanley, M. 2006, 'Buddy systems: Peer support in action', in *Bullying Solutions; Evidence-based Approaches for Australian Schools*, McGrath, H. & Noble, T. (eds), Pearson Education, Sydney.
44. Baginsky, M.I. 2004, 'Peer support: Expectations and realities', *Pastoral care in education*, vol. 22, no. 1, pp. 3–9.
45. Karcher, M.J. 2005, 'The effects of developmental mentoring and high school mentors' attendance on their younger mentees' self-esteem, social skills, and connectedness', *Psychology in the Schools*, vol. 42, no. 1, pp. 65–78.
46. Gensemer, P. 2000, 'Effectiveness of cross-age and peer mentoring programs', *ERIC Document Reproduction Service*, No. ED438267.
47. Doneau, S. 1985, 'Soliciting in the classroom', in *The International Encyclopaedia of Education: research and studies*, Husen, T. & Postlethwaite, T. (eds), Pergamon Press, Oxford.
48. Schaps, E., Battistich, V. & Solomon, D. 1997, 'School as a caring community: A key to character education', in *The construction of children's character, Part II, 96th Yearbook of the National Society for the Study of Education*, Molnar, A. (ed.), University of Chicago Press, Chicago.

49. Tansy, M. & de Barona, M.S. 1996, 'Peer and cross-age tutoring programs', *Guidance & Counseling*, vol. 12, no. 1, pp. 21–25.
50. Youngerman, S. 1998, 'The power of cross-level partnerships', *Educational Leadership Abstracts*, vol. 56, no. 1, pp. 58–60.
51. Sugai, G. & Horner, R. 2002, 'The evolution of discipline practices: School-wide positive behavior supports', in *Behavior psychology in the schools: Innovations in evaluation, support, and consultation*, Luiselli, J.K. & Diament, C. (eds), The Haworth Press, New York.
52. Horner, R.H. et al. 2009, 'A randomized, wait-list controlled effectiveness trial assessing school-wide positive behavior support in elementary schools', *Journal of Positive Behavior Interventions*, vol. 11, pp. 133–144.
53. Rigby, K. 2001, *Stop the Bullying. A Handbook for Schools*, ACER, Melbourne.
54. Cross, D. et al. 2009, *Australian Covert Bullying Prevalence Study (ACBPS)*, Child Health Promotion Research Centre, Edith Cowan University, Perth.
55. Hawker, S.J. & Boulton, M. 2000, 'Twenty years research on peer victimisation and psychosocial maladjustment: A meta-analytic review of cross-sectional studies', *Journal of Child Psychology & Psychiatry*, vol. 41, no. 4, pp. 441–445.
56. Nansel, T.R. et al. 2003, 'Relationships between bullying and violence among US youth', *Archives of Pediatric Adolescent Medicine*, vol. 157, pp. 348–353.
57. Rigby, K. & Slee, P.T. 1999, 'Suicidal ideation among adolescent schoolchildren, Involvement in bully/victim problems and perceived low social support', *Suicide and Life-Threatening Behaviour*, vol. 29, pp. 119–130.
58. Morgan, S. 2006, 'Teachers' Experiences of Teaching', in *Positive Psychology Conference*, Braga, Portugal.
59. Fredrickson, B. & Joiner, T. 2002, 'Positive emotions trigger upward spirals toward emotional well-being', *Psychological Science*, vol. 13, pp. 172–175.
60. Isen, A.M. 2001, 'An influence of positive affect on decision making in complex situations: Theoretical issues with practical implications', *Journal of Consumer Psychology*, vol. 11, no. 2, pp. 75–85.
61. Isen, A.M. 2003, 'Positive affect, systematic cognitive processing, and behavior: Toward integration of affect, cognition, and motivation', in *Multi-level Issues in Organizational Behavior and Strategy*, Dansereau, F. & Yammarino, F.J. (eds), JAI/Elsevier Science, Oxford, UK, pp. 52–62.
62. Fredrickson, B. & Tugade, M. 2004, 'Resilient individuals use positive emotions to bounce back from negative emotional experiences', *Journal of Personality and Social Psychology*, vol. 86, no. 2, pp. 320–333.
63. *UK Foresight Mental Health Project*, 2008, Foresight Capital Mental Health.
64. McGrath, H. & Anders E. 2000, *The Bounce Back! Program*, in *Turning the tide in schools drug education project*, Victorian Department of Education.

Chapter 6

Implementation and maintenance of Bounce Back!

This chapter draws on the school change and leadership research literature to identify the key factors that facilitate success in the implementation and maintenance of a school-wide wellbeing and resilience program such as *Bounce Back!*

Effective leadership

The importance of articulating a shared vision for whole school wellbeing
An effective school leader, according to Leithwood, Seashore Louis, Anderson and Wahlstrom[1], develops a clear (but shared) vision for the direction their school should take, develops people and re-designs the organisation of their school to align with their school vision. School-wide wellbeing is a broad umbrella concept that allows school leadership to coordinate the protective school and classroom practices that connect the whole school community and to develop teachers' commitment to teaching the social–emotional skills and understandings that are linked to academic success. A leadership focus on school-wide wellbeing has the high probability of school community 'buy-in', given that many schools are grappling with discipline problems, bullying, high student absenteeism and lack of student engagement, to name just a few current concerns. Such a focus can synthesise and unify a number of school initiatives such as anti-bullying initiatives, drug and alcohol prevention programs, mental health initiatives, social skills training, positive behaviour management and restorative practices. A shared school vision creates a sense of commonality that permeates a school and gives coherence to diverse activities[2]. A shared vision provides a clear picture that the whole school community can articulate and 'carry in their heads and their hearts'[2] (p. 206).

Acknowledging that change is a people process
The importance of a leader's capacity to build positive relationships within their school community as part of the change process is highlighted in Hoerr's statement on school leadership[3] (p. 7):

> A leader sets the vision but doesn't stop there. A leader listens, understands, motivates, reinforces and makes the tough decisions. A leader passes out praise when things go well and takes responsibility and picks up the pieces when things fall apart. Leadership is about relationships.

School relationships were defined by principals as the most challenging aspect of their job in a study conducted for the NSW Department of Education[4]. The principals ranked the qualities of effective school leaders as follows.

1. **Self-management:** this included staying calm, keeping things in perspective and maintaining a sense of humour. It also included being resilient, learning from errors, being able to take a hard decision and wanting to achieve the best outcome.
2. **Relationship management:** this included dealing effectively with conflict situations, being able to empathise and work productively with people from a wide range of backgrounds, having a willingness to listen to different points of view before making decisions and contributing positively to team projects.
3. **Skills in being resourceful:** this included identifying priorities and being flexible, having a clear justified vision for the school and being able to organise and manage time effectively.

These skills are the social-emotional skills that underpin not only successful leadership but also staff and student wellbeing. They are also the skills that are taught in *Bounce Back!* The impact of the social-emotional competencies of a leader on the workplace culture is highlighted in a study of 3781 executives. Almost 70% of their employees' perceptions of the working climate were linked to the leader's social–emotional competency[5]. A focus on school-wide wellbeing draws the attention of all in the school community to practices that build positive relationships, e.g. in staff meetings, in classrooms and in parent–teacher meetings, and the core values that underpin these practices.

Developing strengths

A shared vision on school wellbeing also provides a positive framework for developing people's strengths and their engagement in the school community—teachers, students and parents. Developing people involves building the social and psychological capital of those within the school. The new field of Positive Psychology is the scientific study of the strengths and virtues that enable individuals and communities to thrive. This field is based on the belief that people want to cultivate what is best within themselves and to lead meaningful and fulfilling lives. According to Seligman[6], the founder of Positive Psychology, this is best achieved by using one's strengths in the service of others. A shared vision on school-wide wellbeing encourages school leaders to identify the strengths of different staff and students and provide opportunities for the development of these diverse strengths within the school.

Developing people through a focus on strengths also encourages leaders to plan ways to re-design school organisational structures and practices to maximise staff and students' diverse strengths and to build a collaborative school culture that values these strengths. A collaborative culture in schools driven by shared leadership based on valuing each other's strengths is inclusive and empowering and drives quality teaching and learning[7].

Development of a positive school culture

Recent research highlights the role of positive emotions in broadening people's capacity to learn and building an organisation's capacity to thrive[8]. Positive emotions enhance people's capacity for optimistic thinking, problem solving and decision making and lead to more flexible, innovative and creative solutions[9,10]. Positive emotions can also predict the success of an organisation. Losada and Heaphy[11] conducted content analyses of 60 team meetings for the number of positive versus negative statements made during their annual strategic planning sessions. The 20 flourishing teams made three positive statements to one negative statement and were rated highly in terms of positive emotions. In comparison, the 20 failing teams expressed a high number of negative statements and negative emotions.

A leader's positive emotions are contagious and predict the group or organisation's performance. Positive emotions also help people to be more resilient and recover more quickly after setbacks[12]. A focus on whole-school wellbeing draws leadership attention to strategies to build positive emotions and a positive school culture, which contribute to higher productivity, improved problem solving and better learning. As Fullan[13] (p. 226) has asserted:

> If we dig deeper into the roles of emotion and hope in interpersonal relationships, we will gain a lasting understanding of how to deal with change more constructively.

Specific leadership strategies for building positive emotions and positive relationships associated with a positive school 'spirit' or culture are outlined below. School spirit both reflects and builds school connectedness.

Students demonstrate school spirit when they make positive comments about their school to outsiders and proudly let other people know of their school's achievements and positive features. Their school spirit is also shown in their support for other students in the school in competitive situations such as sporting events and rock eisteddfods, when they honour and maintain the traditions and rules of the school, and when they publicly affirm a connection to the school, e.g. by wearing the correct school uniform. Their willingness to be involved in school-based projects and social activities, even if they are out of school time, is another way they affirm their school connectedness.

It takes time to develop school spirit and it is harder to create in students if their teachers don't feel a strong commitment and loyalty to the school. Teachers need to genuinely feel and model school commitment and pride. Here are some strategies to enhance school commitment and pride and develop a positive school culture.

Recognise and communicate staff and student successes
- Establish a system of recognition for achievements by students and teachers, e.g. publicise staff and student successes by putting the information on a bulletin board in a high traffic area (courses completed, teams coached, prizes won, etc.).
- Identify ways to better communicate the achievements of the school, its teachers and students to the community, e.g. on the school website, in newsletters and emails home.

Keep the school website up-to-date
A surprising number of people visit a school's website. Involve students in ideas for the website.

Promote the best things about your school
Involve the whole school community in identifying the positive features of students and staff. For example:
- Brainstorm 'The best things about our school' at a staff meeting or in class.
- Have a teacher profile and several student profiles once a week in the newsletter, on the school website or on a bulletin board.
- Have a teacher weblink on the school's website or on a photo board in the school, accompanied by each teacher's photo (about five teachers at a time), their qualifications, professional interests, recent professional development activities, professional goals for the year and so on. Change the photos regularly to maintain people's interest. Displaying photos of the teachers engaged with their students in their classrooms is a great way of hooking students' and parents' interest. Add a dialogue box that includes each teacher's favourite 'saying' (you may have to carry out a student survey to find out what this saying is).
- Encourage students to interview a teacher in the school newsletter. Different teachers can be profiled each week, accompanied by a photo. Some questions students can ask teachers are:
  - What do you like best about teaching?
  - What's one good thing about teaching at our school?
  - Why did you become a teacher?
  - Where did you train to become a teacher? What is one good memory you have about your training?
  - What is one of your professional goals for the future?
  - What's one thing you like to do to relax when you are away from school?
  - What is your favourite music, book, movie, sport?

Use appreciative inquiry questions
Positive questions about what's working for individuals in relation to a particular project or in a staff meeting facilitate positive conversations where people collaboratively create a new vision, name their idea and map out how it can come to fruition. Some examples:
- Begin meetings with positive questions: What's working? What are the positive outcomes? How do we know? What are we learning? What are we proud of? These questions build positive relationships and generate positive energy for innovation.
- Ask staff to share a story that demonstrates the caring atmosphere of the school, or to tell about a time at school when they really felt they made a difference in someone's life (student, colleague, group or class).
- Encourage staff and students to identify their personal (character) and multiple intelligences strengths. Ask each staff member to share a story of how they engaged one of their strengths in their teaching/work. They could also describe a highly engaging teaching experience and share what strengths contributed to its success. How can they apply these strengths in other teaching/learning experiences, in the service of others?

Encourage staff to appreciate each other
Encourage the use of the whiteboard in the staffroom to communicate messages of appreciation and encouragement between staff (e.g. 'Jan, thanks for doing my yard duty when I was unwell, Anne').

Display school-wide wellbeing messages
Display messages in the staffroom and school corridors such as 'Our school community cares about people'.

Encourage whole-school collaborative projects
Promote school engagement through whole-school activities such as musical performances, fundraising events and concerts. Allow time for students to make banners and rosettes for a sports carnival, and perhaps develop a school barracking chant.

Hold a student wellbeing drama day
Use drama as a tool to explore issues that underpin student wellbeing. The Catholic Education Office in Melbourne, for example, runs a Student Wellbeing Drama Day across all schools in the Melbourne diocese.

Hold a 'Celebrating our strengths' day
Organise a day when every student displays or performs according to one of their top intelligences using Gardner's multiple intelligences model. Invite parents.

Organise student school community teams
Involve students in the design, building or refurbishment of areas in the school environment that will enhance the quality of life for those in the school. For example:
- improving the appearance of a wall with artwork or developing an area for exhibiting student artwork
- building a barbecue and seating area (this is a good opportunity for students to demonstrate practical skills, and retired experts in the community are often very happy to help out)
- re-painting an area
- designing a new garden or landscaped area.

Identify opportunities for community service learning
Community service has several benefits. Firstly, it allows students an opportunity to feel proud of their school. Secondly, it develops a sense of social justice and responsibility.

Thirdly, it can allow some less-academic students to 'strut their stuff'. Fourthly, it allows students to be connected to the larger community. You could consider:
- gardening for a community project or for elderly people
- singing, performing or drawing for, visiting or reading to elderly citizens in aged-care facilities
- undertaking work for or with a local preschool.

Effective implementation

This section provides implementation guidelines and ideas based on what we've learned from some great schools about how to best implement *Bounce Back!* However, many schools are implementing it in diverse ways.

Consider having weekly dedicated curriculum time

Many schools have a *Bounce Back!* session each week (usually for one hour). In some schools, all classes undertake a similar aspect of the program during that time but at different levels, e.g. all teachers focus on the 'Emotions' unit and take a similar theme, such as Anger Management. In some schools, each teacher chooses the topic for their *Bounce Back!* lesson and there isn't necessarily any commonality with other classes.

Develop scope and sequence charts (see page 103)

Ideally, all of the key points in each unit of *Bounce Back!* are covered in every class every year. This ensures that the key points are revisited many times and makes it more likely that students will begin to think and act resiliently in both the short and long term. However, schools are very busy places and this may not be feasible in your school. Some schools alternate the units so that some are taught in one year and the rest in the next year. It is essential that all the teachers working at the same level collaboratively plan the activities and books that each class will use across the nine units. This saves children studying the same books for two or three years in a row.

Students can complete activities in the program in a Bounce Back! workbook

It is a good idea for all students to have their own *Bounce Back!* workbook in which to record their answers to activities, write *Bounce Back!* stories, keep a copy of their acronym and record their self-reflections on class activities.

Integrate Bounce Back! with a range of curriculum areas

Activities from a variety of *Bounce Back!* units can be included in English, Social Studies, Health and Personal Development, Maths, Science, Technology and Religious Education lessons. The units also draw on the visual and performing arts. *Bounce Back!* lessons can be followed up in many ways that link with different curriculum outcomes. For example:
- You might start with the Bob Graham book *Let's Get a Pup*. (English)
- Then you might follow up with a Circle Time activity and discussion on the core value of compassion. (Health and Personal Development/Pastoral Care)
- A cross-off word activity (make your own or ask students to make one in a small group) could be developed around the words in the book as a literacy activity in the next literacy block session. (English)
- A small-group project or talk on the work of the RSPCA or similar organisations might be a longer-term follow-up. (English/Social Studies)
- In a school that has Religious Education there could be a cross-reference to the story of the Good Samaritan.

Use Bounce Back! themes as a guide to selecting texts or books for the library

Most schools use the junior picture books, older picture books, poems and novels as part of their English curriculum. Some of the best books for teaching literacy are those that incorporate *Bounce Back!* themes such as courage, coping with adversity, relationships, conflict and emotions.

Revisit each unit's key concepts whenever possible
Revisiting the key points from each unit many times across different curriculum areas and situations makes it more likely that students will begin to think and act resiliently in both the short and long term.

Add a wellbeing/resilience dimension whenever you can
Look for the aspects of wellbeing and resilience that can be explored in everything that is taught and in any naturally occurring opportunity. For example: Coping Skills (from the 'People bouncing back' unit) can be linked with topics such as inventions or exploration; the 'Looking on the bright side' unit can be linked with medical and scientific breakthroughs; Managing Conflict can be linked with historical conflicts or media.

Use the 'Core values' unit with classroom and school rules
The 'Core values' unit can be used as the basis of classroom and school rules. Negotiate 'Our class vision' with students at the start of the year and focus on drawing out these values.

FAQs about implementing Bounce Back!

What is the best order for teaching the curriculum units?
If you are teaching all the units each year, we believe the best order is as follows:
1. Core values
2. People bouncing back
3. Courage
4. Looking on the bright side
5. Emotions
6. Relationships
7. Humour
8. No bullying
9. STAR! (Success)

The first five units follow each other logically and developmentally. However, the last four could really be taught in any order, depending on the needs of the school, class or an individual student within a class. The additional 'Elasticity' unit (www.pearsonplaces.com.au/bounceback.aspx) can be taught as an introduction to 'People bouncing back' or simply as a science and maths unit. If you decide to alternate some of the units, this is one possible good combination for lower primary:

	First year of school entry	Year One	Year Two
Core values		✓	✓
People bouncing back		✓	✓
Courage		✓	
Looking on the bright side	✓		✓
Emotions	✓		✓
Relationships	✓	✓	✓
Humour		✓	✓
No bullying	✓		✓
STAR! (Success)		✓	✓

Case studies of three schools implementing Bounce Back! in slightly different ways

School A (K–Year 7 school)
Students make their own *Bounce Back!* posters, which are displayed around the room all year. An enlarged *Bounce Back!* poster is displayed in the staff room, as well as posters about how the core values are reflected in the actions of the staff (e.g. the teachers are committed to showing respect to all students, parents and colleagues). An A4 sheet containing the BOUNCE BACK! acronym is sent home to all parents. Teachers are given a laminated sheet of the BOUNCE BACK! acronym and encouraged to refer to it at every opportunity.

Every class in the school has a weekly one-hour session on the same unit/theme from *Bounce Back!* For example, the unit might be 'Courage' and the theme might be 'Everyday courage'. Each year level uses different books and a different activity to work on developing everyday courage. A scope and sequence chart, developed by the classroom teachers, identifies the books and activities that are used at each year level with each unit and theme.

School B (K–Year 6 school)
The school asks teachers on yard duty to carry a small laminated card containing the BOUNCE! acronym for K–2 students and the BOUNCE BACK! acronym for older students so they can refer to it when talking to students about playground issues.

Each year level in the school covers all the units every year and similar themes within each unit. However, the staff wanted to ensure that the students did not encounter repetition in the books and activities used. Therefore, teachers in each of the three year-level groupings that correspond to the three *Bounce Back!* **Classroom Resources** met several times and identified the books and activities that each year level would use for each unit and theme. The student wellbeing team also did a scope and sequence chart across the whole school to ensure there was minimal repetition of books and activities used.

- The 'Core values' and 'No bullying' units are included as part of RE/Pastoral Care.
- 'Elasticity' is covered as part of Science and Technology.
- Several units are covered as part of the school's language and literacy program, e.g. 'Looking on the bright side', 'Humour' and 'STAR! (Success)'.
- Aspects of the following are incorporated in Health: the BOUNCE BACK! acronym and the 'People bouncing back', 'Emotions', 'Relationships' and 'Courage' units.
- The activities related to goal setting—'STAR! (Success)' unit—are used throughout the year at every opportunity.
- Elements from all units are included in Society and Environment, e.g. Antarctica (Shackleton: 'People bouncing back', 'Looking on the bright side', 'Courage') and Inventions (Thomas Edison: 'STAR! (Success)').

School C (K–Year 8 school)
In the first three terms of the year, eight units from the program are systematically taught to all students during a weekly one-hour session called *'Bounce Back!'* Repetition of books and activities is minimised by a scope and sequence chart for each of the three year-level groupings. This is prepared by coordinators and given to classroom teachers for discussion. During the one-hour session, the key points and some key themes are covered. Specific books and topics are then picked up during the following week in Science, English, and Society and Environment. The units are implemented as follows:

- Term 1: 'Core values', 'STAR! (Success)', 'People bouncing back'
- Term 2: 'Emotions', 'No bullying', 'Relationships'
- Term 3: 'Looking on the bright side', 'Courage'
- 'Elasticity' and 'Humour' are alternated between year levels so that students are only taught them once every two years. However, 'Humour' is still presented and briefly discussed as a coping tool in 'People bouncing back'.

All the picture books and junior novels that are used in the program have a yellow smiley-face sticker on the front plastic cover and are kept in a separate resource cupboard in the staffroom with a teacher-borrowing book. The library has an additional copy of each picture book, as students often want to borrow a copy after it has been used in class.

Planning for sustainability

The following suggestions draw on our experience in working with schools that are successfully implementing *Bounce Back!* plus the work by CASEL[14,15] in researching hundreds of studies of school initiatives for factors that ensure successful and enduring implementation.

- Appoint a student wellbeing coordinator or team. The coordinator sets up a team of three to five people to drive the implementation of student wellbeing initiatives and resolve day-to-day problems. One of their responsibilities could be to develop the whole-school *Bounce Back!* scope and sequence chart (see example, page 103).
- Consistently support the student wellbeing team. Teachers' enthusiasm for the implementation of a wellbeing program has been found to be highly influenced by the active, engaged support and direction provided by the principal[16].
- Foster teachers' formal and informal professional development in student wellbeing, including the involvement of experts. It's often difficult for an individual school to fund formal professional development, so teaming up with other schools helps to defray costs. Informal professional development can include professional reading groups, or staff taking turns to teach the key concepts of a topic at a staff meeting, with suggestions for activities across the three levels. Teachers provide feedback on how the activities worked in their classes at the next staff meeting.
- Give student wellbeing initiatives high visibility in the school and in the local/parent community.
- Link student wellbeing initiatives to the national and state educational goals (see Chapter 2: Wellbeing and resilience, page 21).
- Share resources. For example, collate new activities or integrated ideas in an open-access resource file kept in the staff room or on the intranet. Have all the *Bounce Back!* literature books marked with sticky labels for levels and keep them in the staff room or in a separate section of library. A list of websites and CDs can also be part of the resource file.
- Create opportunities for staff to visit each other's classrooms to see how they are implementing *Bounce Back!*
- Network with other schools using the program or create opportunities to visit classes in other schools to see their program in action.
- Negotiate release time for collaborative team planning. Time for innovation is a perennial problem in schools. Translating a new program into classroom-friendly activities and checking that the new ideas mesh with curriculum outcomes takes considerable time. Often it is time that teachers simply don't have. There needs to be shared problem solving on the issue of providing more time for new programming.
- Provide opportunities in staff meetings for teachers to share program progress and successful ideas, lessons, strategies, activities and websites.
- Access community networks, especially for students who belong to minority ethnic and racial communities, to ensure that the program is context-sensitive and based on the reality of the settings in which your students live.
- Be aware of the implementation dip. When anyone first trials new teaching strategies or curriculum content, there is a risk they will initially feel less competent than they are comfortable with. If staff are encouraged to persevere, they will eventually feel more professionally competent than when they began the innovation[17].
- Prepare for the long haul and don't expect too much too soon. A new program such as *Bounce Back!* must be sustained for three to five years before it becomes a full part of the school. Ideally, *Bounce Back!* extends from one school grade to the next in a

sequential manner. Such coordination means that the key environmental and personal skills components of the program will need to be modelled, reinforced and practised over several years so that students revisit the key principles again and again as they move through year levels. This continuing exposure and 'mastery' means that the key resilience principles are more likely to become part of the students' behavioural repertoire. Teachers also benefit from this repetition. By teaching key concepts to students, they develop a deeper understanding of these concepts as applied to their own lives.

- Involve all stakeholders. Parents must be part of the program. One school formed a Parent Education Resource Committee (PERC). This committee was responsible for gathering data on the success of new school programs and practices and sharing that success with the whole school community. Their names and contact numbers were printed in the school newsletter and other parents were encouraged to call them. Because this parent team documented the progress of the new program, they became the best advocates for the innovation.
- Provide data that document progress and share successes with the whole school community. When schools and/or teachers are in a position to demonstrate some positive outcomes and benefits for students through their engagement with *Bounce Back!*, then even more widespread support can be gained. Because it is so important to gather data on student progress, there are resources on www.pearsonplaces.com.au/bounceback.aspx on ways to gather such data. Monitoring and documenting progress is not only critical to justifying the inclusion and continuation of the program, it can also provide a 'positive feedback loop' to sustain the implementation.

Successful implementation of *Bounce Back!* can lead to personal and professional growth for all involved. But being involved in a successful project can also lead to opportunities for staff promotion and that can mean a higher level of staff turnover than normal. The issue of staff loss needs to be addressed. As committed staff leave, there can be a 'cooling down' of a successful initiative. New teachers do not feel an ownership of the program and often are unsure of its history and how to implement it. Here are some ways to maintain everyone's energy for a successful ongoing program, to involve new staff, and to keep the program 'hot'.

- During the year, film and take photos of teachers using the program at many different age/stage levels. This can be used to introduce new staff to the program.
- Develop an induction manual for new staff that includes the school vision for the program, guidelines on how the school is implementing the program (e.g. scope and sequence charts) and a list of teachers who are happy to help or answer questions or to have visitors in their classrooms. Arrange for each new staff member to be mentored for a term as they plan for and teach the program.
- Collate collaboratively developed and shared resources and planning ideas in an open file in the staff room so that these resources do not leave when the teachers leave. Of course, they can make copies to take with them.
- Set up a mentoring or peer coaching arrangement between new teachers and teachers who are more experienced in the program.
- Provide each new teacher with a *Bounce Back!* book for their year level, literature and posters, plus access to the children's literature used in the program at their year level.

Seeking system support

Gaining system support for a new program can play a key role in its successful implementation. System support for wellbeing initiatives has been a significant factor in the success of school-wide wellbeing initiatives. For example, in South Australia, the Learner Wellbeing Framework has provided a vision, support and directions for all school systems (state, Catholic and independent). Similarly, the Student Wellbeing unit of the Melbourne Catholic Education Office (CEOM) has provided organisational support delivered through clusters of schools to build leadership and teacher capacity in the area of student wellbeing.

In summary

The challenge for leaders is to support their staff in implementing and then sustaining new programs such as *Bounce Back!*, while understanding and working within the inevitable processes of change that have been identified. This involves creating opportunities for teachers to collaborate, developing and maintaining a strong commitment to the school by both teachers and students, using a whole-school approach, and using planned strategies that will sustain and maintain the program over time and after staff losses. It also involves being realistic about the timeline for implementation, providing opportunities for staff to express concerns and solve problems related to the program, gaining system support and establishing collaborative partnerships with both the local and broader community. Leading change in this way also means recognising the need to manage the emotional and cognitive challenges for all involved in any new initiative.

References

1. Leithwood, K., et al. 2004, *How Leadership Influences Student Learning*, Wallace Foundation, New York.
2. Senge, P. 1990, *The Fifth Discipline: The Art and Practice of the Learning Organization*, Doubleday, New York.
3. Hoerr, T. 2006, *The Art of School Leadership*, ASCD, Alexandria, Virginia.
4. Scott, G. 2003, *Learning Principals: Leadership Capability and Learning Research*, Sydney Professional Support & Curriculum Directorate.
5. Goleman, D. 2000, 'Leadership that gets results', *Harvard Business Review*, pp. 78–90, accessed 8/3/2010, http://hbr.org/product/leadership-that-gets-results/an/R00204-HCB-ENG
6. Seligman, M.E.P. 2002, *Authentic Happiness*, Free Press, New York.
7. Bezzina, M., Burford, C. & Duignan, P. 2007, 'Leaders transforming learning and learners: Messages for leaders', in *Fourth International Conference on Educational Leadership*, Sydney.
8. Fredrickson, B. & Joiner, T. 2002, 'Positive emotions trigger upward spirals toward emotional well-being', *Psychological Science*, vol. 13, pp. 172–175.
9. Isen, A.M. 2001, 'An influence of positive affect on decision making in complex situations: Theoretical issues with practical implications', *Journal of Consumer Psychology*, vol. 11, no. 2, pp. 75–85.
10. Isen, A.M. 2003, 'Positive affect, systematic cognitive processing, and behavior: Toward integration of affect, cognition, and motivation', in *Multi-level Issues in Organizational Behavior and Strategy*, Dansereau F. & Yammarino, F.J. (eds), JAI/Elsevier Science, Oxford, United Kingdom, pp. 52–62.
11. Losada, M. & Heaphy, E. 2004, 'The role of positivity and connectivity in the performance of business teams', *American Behavioral Scientist*, vol. 47, no. 6, pp. 740–765.
12. Fredrickson, B. & Tugade, M. 2004, 'Resilient individuals use positive emotions to bounce back from negative emotional experiences', *Journal of Personality and Social Psychology*, vol. 86, no. 2, pp. 320–333.
13. Fullan, M. 1997, 'Emotion and hope: Constructive concepts for complex times' in *Rethinking Educational Change with Heart and Mind*, pp. 216–233, Association for Supervision and Curriculum Development, Alexandria, Virginia.
14. Elias, J.E., et al. 2003, 'Implementation, sustainability, and scaling up of social-emotional and academic innovations in public schools', *School Psychology Review*, vol. 32.
15. Collaborative for Academic, Social and Emotional Learning, n.d., 'The positive impact of social and emotional learning for Kindergarten to 8th grade', www.casel.org/downloads/PackardsES.pdf
16. Kam, C., Greenberg, M.T. & Walls, C. 2003, 'Examining the role of implementation quality in school-based prevention using the PATHS curriculum', *Prevention Science*, vol. 4, no. 1, pp. 55–63.
17. Fullan, M. 1996, 'Turning systemic thinking on its head', *Phi Delta Kappan*, vol. 77, no. 6, pp. 420–423.

Chapter 7

Teaching strategies in Bounce Back!

This chapter includes a description of all the teaching strategies used in the Years K–2 curriculum units in **Classroom Resources**. Because children in early childhood or lower primary classes are less skilled at working in groups, many of the cooperative learning strategies are simple pairs activities, then pairs sharing or whole-class cooperative activities. These strategies can also be used with content from any curriculum area.

There are three sections in the chapter:
- **Section A** outlines Circle Time, a strategy that is used in every unit, along with some guiding principles for helping students feel safe during Circle Time discussions.
- **Section B** outlines the core teaching strategies that have used in different units.
- **Section C** suggests ways to randomly organise students into pairs or groups.

Section A: Using Circle Time and creating psychological safety in class discussions

Circle Time is used in every *Bounce Back!* unit. It builds classroom community, positive relationships and teaches social-emotional learning.

What is Circle Time?
Circle Time is a planned and structured framework for whole-class discussion. Everyone has the opportunity to speak and be listened to. Everyone sits in a circle so they can see and hear everyone else and everyone is included in the Circle Time activities and discussion. Being in a circle means everyone is more engaged and distractions are less possible. Circle Time works best on chairs, although some teachers have younger students sitting on the floor in a circle.

What happens in Circle Time?
A typical Circle Time discussion in *Bounce Back!* follows this format:
- A reminder of the Circle Time rules (see over)
- A reminder about the talking prompt that you are using (see over); only the student who has this is allowed to speak
- An introductory game (optional), energiser or simulation
- An activity that introduces the topic for Circle Time (usually the reading of a relevant book)
- Students are invited to speak during the whole-class discussion in a variety of ways, for example:
  - Every student may be invited to speak around the circle
  - Selected students may be invited to speak
  - Students may be asked to volunteer to make a comment or answer a question

- Students may be asked to discuss in pairs and then one person in each pair is invited to explain what they agreed on.
◎ A final activity that closes the circle, for example, summarising the key messages from the class discussion or a sentence completion (*One thing I learned is…; One thing that surprised me was…; One thing that was new…; I feel…*)
◎ There is usually a follow-up group or individual activity after Circle Time.

The Circle Time rules
When everyone is sitting in the circle, begin the session by stating the rules.
1. Everyone has a turn and when one person is talking (i.e. the person who has the talking prompt), everyone else listens.
2. You may pass if you do not have anything to say (but the teacher may come back and ask you again when you have had a bit more time to think about what you want to say).
3. No put-downs are allowed during Circle Time.

Mixing students up in Circle Time
Students often sit in the circle next to their friend, so mixing them up to interact with different classmates can help to build class connectedness and maintain Circle Time energy. Some ideas for mixing them up include:
◎ Personal categories. Stand up and change places—
   - everyone who has blue eyes (brown eyes, green eyes)
   - everyone who has a sister (brother, pet)
   - everyone who can ride a bike (climb a tree, play a musical instrument)
   - everyone who has a birthday in…; whose name begins with…; likes swimming (football, doing jigsaws), etc.
◎ Given categories.
   - Number off everyone in circle, then even numbers change places.
   - Hand out 'category cards' (see page 93), then call one of the categories (e.g. everyone who is a country, change places). Other categories include seasons, flowers, colours, alphabet, shapes, animals, months and so on.

Talking prompts
Talking prompts remind students whose turn it is to speak, as only the person who holds the prompt is allowed to talk. The job of the other group members is to actively listen. Use novel talking prompts or work as a class to make an official 'class talking prompt'. Younger students love using small soft toys or other small toys. Older students like using wrap wristbands, soft balls or novelty balls. All ages like using a torch with cellophane over the light so it glows in a dim room. Use talking prompts in Circle Time and in cooperative group work if you feel that students are not having an equal say.

Helping students feel safe in Circle Time and other types of discussion
It is essential to create a classroom climate of safety so students feel that their self-disclosures and any differences in opinions, feelings, ideas or behaviour will be respected by their classmates. It is also important to help students learn about the kinds of personal information about themselves and others that are appropriate to share in class discussions. This climate of trust can only be built up over time and can easily be destroyed by insensitive comments or 'put-downs'. **Bounce Back!** does not have a strong focus on students sharing deeply personal information about themselves or people they know. The material is delivered at two levels of personal disclosure.

At the first level, students talk about their own ideas and opinions, give examples of concepts and processes, and talk about the concepts and ideas as applied to puppet characters, cartoon characters, book characters, people in the news and so on. For example:

- Can you think of an example of a situation in which someone (or someone your age) might feel worried?
- Why was Henry so sad?
- What do you think courage is?
- What are some good ways for the puppet to respond here?

At the second level, students talk about the ideas and concepts as applied to themselves and, perhaps, other people they know such as family or friends. For example:

- Can you think of a time when someone you know achieved a goal they set for themselves? What did they do to achieve it?
- What situations do you (or do students your age) find most scary?

Guidelines for helping students feel safe in class discussions

Here is a summary of the key points for creating a classroom environment that encourages students to feel safe and connected to their teacher and their classmates.

Teach the skills of 'listening well' and 'respectful disagreeing' before students start their discussion

These skills need to be taught beforehand and students need to be reminded to use them before each discussion-based activity or debrief. Here are some strategies to use.

- There are many activities in this book that give students the chance to learn and practise the skill of listening, for example 'Think–ink–pair–share' and 'Partner retell'. There are also listening activities in the 'Relationships' unit.
- Use a talking prompt such as a soft toy or ball that is held by the person talking and is a signal for others not to interrupt.
- Use talking tokens. If the same students tend to dominate the discussion, give each student two talking tokens and ask them to place one in front of them when they speak. They then have to wait until other students have used their talking tokens until they can speak again.
- 'Respectful disagreeing' involves encouraging students to first re-state what the other person said that they agree with, before stating their different opinion. For example, 'I can see what Emma means about parachuting being dangerous (*this is the bit that I can agree with*) because the parachute might fail, but I don't think it would be as dangerous as bungee jumping (*this is where I differ*)'.

Have a strongly enforced 'No put-downs' rule in place at all times

Remind students about the rule before any discussion and remember to enforce it in a non-humiliating way. Don't forget to include non-verbal put-downs in this category. This rule also relates to the core value of accepting differences in people (see 'Core values' unit) and not negatively judging others because they hold different values and ideas. There are more details on strategies for reducing put-downs in the 'No bullying' unit.

Paraphrase and clarify what students say when they make unclear comments

Often students make comments or ask questions that are not clear to other students or even perhaps to themselves. Initially, the language of feelings and relationships is not an easy one for many students. If this happens, re-state what they have said in a simpler or clearer way and check it with them.

Avoid tasks that require students to expose too much of their personal lives or feelings

A useful yardstick is to remember not to ask students to do or discuss anything you would not be comfortable doing or discussing yourself. You perhaps need to consider whether you are 'typical' before using yourself as the benchmark in this way. Do you think you are more disclosing or shyer than the norm?

Chapter 7
Teaching strategies in Bounce Back!

Understand that some students find it difficult to self-disclose, even at a relatively superficial level

The fact that a student finds it difficult to talk personally, even at a relatively superficial level, does not mean they are not interested in the topic, or that they are upset about it. They are probably still learning a lot even if they are not speaking much. Some students are just shyer than others, or they become more anxious when they are the centre of attention. Others fear peer disapproval. Here are some ideas to facilitate the inclusion of all students in the discussion.

- Remind students that having a different opinion is everyone's right. Even if they don't agree with what someone has said, they need to respect that person's right to differ.
- Give students the right to 'pass' on any question, but encourage them to try to contribute to the discussion where they can, and not to 'pass' too often.
- Use puppets, which allow issues and feelings to be presented and discussed 'one step removed'.
- Gently try to include reluctant speakers in the discussion but don't put them on the spot. For example, ask a few students (by using their names) if there is anything they would like to add. Include in this group some of those students who have already spoken and those who haven't, so you don't focus directly on the student who hasn't contributed.
- Structure some small-group or partner discussion tasks rather than always running whole-class discussions. Some students feel more uncomfortable being the centre of attention in a whole-class discussion, but feel less threatened by open-ended discussions in a small group. Encourage the group to 'own' everything that is said within the group and report back about what 'we talked about' rather than focusing on individual opinions or stories. It can be distressing for a student to hear a group member say, while reporting to the class, 'Josh told us about…'. This obviously depends a lot on the nature of the discussion. Also encourage everyone to sign any group product to enhance team interdependence and ownership.
- Provide students with less threatening alternatives when offering them opportunities to self-disclose. For example, you could ask or say either 'Tell about a time when you finished a friendship', or 'Why do you think friendships end?'.
- Invite students to describe a situation or likely emotions from the perspective of someone else or a character in a story or movie. The gap between describing the emotions felt by someone else and self-disclosing is not large and they will probably feel more comfortable expressing their own emotions with more practice. For example, you can say:
  – Does anyone have any suggestions to offer us about how a new student of your age might feel about being different in this way?
  – What sort of feelings would Zac be likely to have at this point in the story? Why might he feel that way?
- Remind students that they can choose to self-disclose at a relatively superficial level by giving less detail, simplifying a story or leaving out specific information and so on. It is not dishonest to do so under these circumstances.

Remember that some students feel anxious about finding a space in the discussion, so you need to find a way to 'let them in'

Some students feel anxious when they are competing for their turn to talk and perhaps find themselves interrupted or 'over-talked'. When there is a lull in the discussion, ask a general question such as 'Does anybody else have something to add?' Then scan the room, making specific but brief eye contact with those students whom you perceive as having not said much so far, but not pressuring them.

Understand that some students may be tempted to disclose too much

Occasionally, some students are energised by the opportunity to talk about a personal issue and they blurt out more than they should. At the time they may not think through the consequences of revealing too much about themselves, classmates, friends or family. Afterwards they may feel uncomfortable. This doesn't happen very often, but it might.

Here are some suggestions to minimise this possibility.
- Have a 'no names' rule in place most of the time. Remind students at the start of a discussion to be cautious about giving identifying details about the people they mention and stress the importance of protecting privacy. Instead they could say something like:
  – 'I know/knew someone who…'
  – 'I know of a situation where…'
  – 'A relative I know…'
- Before starting a class discussion, remind students that you will use 'protective interrupting' if you think they are saying something that is either too personal, only indirectly related to the topic or too complicated to be discussed in a whole-class discussion. Before the discussion say something like: 'Remember, sometimes it may be better to talk to me about some things that are worrying you after the lesson rather than discuss these things in class. If that happens I will say something like, "Excuse me Tom, can you and I talk about that later when we have more time?"'

Stress that you do not want anyone to feel that you have interrupted because you are not interested in what they are saying. Make a note about it and be sure to follow up later.

Always debrief students after any form of drama or role-play
Students can easily confuse how someone pretends to be in a role-play with how they really are. Using puppet drama can minimise this effect somewhat. You could also say something like: 'Welcome back Briony and Harry (their real names) and goodbye Jenny and Jake (their role-play names). Now, although we all know that this was just drama, sometimes our brains can mix up the actor with the role. Let's remember that Briony and Harry are not like Jenny and Jake, they were just acting like them. Harry, how did you feel about playing the role of Jake? How are you different from Jake? Briony, how did you feel about playing the role of Jenny? How are you different from Jenny?'

Ask all students to respect each other's confidentiality
Students need some expectation of confidentiality in discussions. You could say something like: 'Remember that anything that is said in this room should stay in this room.'

But you also need to point out to students that while you hope and expect that everyone will honour that rule, you cannot guarantee them confidentiality. Ask them to think about what might happen with any personal information they disclose and not to discuss anything about themselves or their family and friends they would not like others to talk about in out-of-class time.

Keep in mind that most boys are less practised at self-disclosure than girls
Asking boys to talk about their feelings about specific issues may run the risk of making some of them feel vulnerable and contradict their socialisation about not showing their feelings. So it's reasonable to expect that boys will sometimes feel uncomfortable with talking or writing about their feelings or openly declaring their fears, doubts, insecurities or affection to their classmates. They will often show that discomfort by 'being silly', misbehaving or cracking jokes. But don't make the mistake of thinking that they are not taking in what is being discussed, even if they appear to be dismissive and unengaged.

Boys are likely to have the same concerns about friendships, everyday courage and so on and the need for the relevant skills, but may have fewer opportunities to discuss or develop them in their peer life. You could say something like: 'We might talk about some slightly personal issues here, so please respect the importance of what we're talking about.'

Be aware of and show sensitivity to cultural differences
Western psychological therapeutic and counselling principles as well as Western educational principles and practices underpin the **Bounce Back!** program. Many of these principles are in accord with Eastern philosophies, such as some Buddhist principles. However, our society is so diverse in its ethnic and cultural make-up that sensitivity in choosing appropriate activities and adapting concepts may be needed in some classes, in order to take account of students' cultural differences in regard to language, values, background and experiences.

Section B: Core Years K–2 teaching strategies and games

Animal asks
A student's name is randomly chosen and this child chooses one of eight animals. Each animal corresponds to a question number (1–8) to be answered. Sometimes the prepared questions are specific to a topic; sometimes they are generic. The student answers the question and then randomly chooses another student to answer the question again or to summarise the first answer. This teacher e-tool is available on www.pearsonplaces.com.au/bounceback.aspx.

Bingo strips
Make a list of 15 words to be used in the game and revise them with students. Make one Bingo strip (i.e. five squares joined to each other in a row) for each student, with each strip containing a different combination of five words from the list. Make a separate card for each of the 15 words and place them in a container. Draw out one word at a time. Students cross off any word they have on their strip. The first student to cross off all five squares on their Bingo strip calls out 'BINGO!' and wins.

Cut-up sentences
This is a good activity to consolidate key messages. Write six short, theme-related sentences. Cut each sentence into individual words and place all the pieces of each cut-up sentence into a separate envelope. Make enough sets for each pair of students to have one set of all six sentences. Each pair reconstructs the six sentences. This e-game is available on www.pearsonplaces.com.au/bounceback.aspx.

Cross-offs
In this word game, students cross off categories of things to find the secret message. The secret message is a key teaching message for each *Bounce Back!* unit. This e-game is available on www.pearsonplaces.com.au/bounceback.aspx.

Freeze frame and rewind
This is a drama activity that helps students to understand issues or to empathise with people in particular situations.
1. Give groups a scenario to act out, e.g. a conflict situation or a scene from a story or to retell or make up a simple story.
2. At a vital point in the story, ask the actors to stop and freeze. This gives the participants and the audience time to reflect on what has happened, what effect this has had on the characters in the story, and what might happen next. Ask the students in the audience about their feelings, their actions and so on.
3. 'Rewind' allows students to rewind a scene and do it with a different ending.
4. This strategy can also be used with puppet plays.

Four corners
This activity is good for stimulating discussion.
1. Find four squares of different coloured paper (red/blue/green/yellow). Stick a different coloured square on the wall near each corner of the room.
2. Prepare a number of theme-related questions about personal preferences and experiences. Each should have four choices to select from. Here is an example:
    – Which thing would you find the scariest? The red corner—going to the dentist; the blue corner—riding a horse; the green corner—staying at a friend's house for the first time; the yellow corner—being lost in a crowd.
3. Ask students to go to the corner that best represents what they think. When they get there, they should discuss why they chose that corner. If there are more than three or four students in one corner, they should break into two groups.

Good fairy/bad fairy or Good wizard/bad wizard
This strategy helps students to understand that there are two ways of thinking about the same situation: a helpful, positive way and an unhelpful, negative way. It can be used as a puppet play or drama in conjunction with the freeze frame strategy.

It can be a small-group role-play with two or three actors plus a good fairy or wizard and a bad fairy or wizard. The group role-plays a scenario with the good fairy/wizard and bad fairy/wizard giving conflicting advice.

The good fairy or wizard whispers positive messages to the main character about choices they can make (e.g. 'Be brave because…', 'Be honest because…', 'Be strong because…').

The bad fairy or wizard whispers negative messages (e.g. 'Give up because…', 'Tell a lie because…', 'Just walk away and don't do anything because…').

Costumes help the students to clearly see and understand the roles of the good and bad fairy/wizard. The good fairy wears traditional fairy colours and sparkles and wings, the good wizard wears a sparkly cloak or wizard hat. The bad fairy or wizard wears black! Wooden wands can be painted and decorated from fabric or craft shops, or students can make their own.

If using this strategy with puppets, make puppets to look like a good fairy/wizard and bad fairy/wizard.

Inquiry-based learning
Inquiry-based learning is a student-centred or active learning approach that starts with asking students questions to raise their curiosity about a topic, then building on this to develop their information processing and problem-solving skills. The essence of inquiry-based learning is that students participate in the planning, development and evaluation of their projects and activities. The focus is on 'how they know' rather than on 'what they know'. For example:
- What do I want to know about this topic?
- What do I need to know?
- What do I know already? How do I know this?
- What kinds of resources might help?
- Where do I find them?
- How do I know that the information is accurate?
- Does this information help me to answer my question?
- How does this relate to what else I know?
- What parts are different to my answer?
- Does it raise new questions?
- What is the main point? What is the main thing to report about this topic?
- Who is my audience?
- How does this connect to other things we are learning?
- How will I present my findings? (e.g. slide show, demonstration, role-play, puppet show, class talk, poster)

Inside–outside circle
Students are organised into an inside and outside circle (facing each other) so each child has a partner. The outside circle (or inside circle) moves so students are randomly paired up with classmates to discuss issues.
1. Students form two concentric circles so each student has a partner. They face each other.
2. The teacher poses a question or issue.
3. One person in each pair answers and then they swap and the other person answers.
4. On a signal, the outer (or inner) circle moves two or three spaces and the process is repeated with a new partner and a new question.
5. Step 4 is repeated two or three more times.

Lightning writing

This strategy gets students quickly engaged in writing down all the things they can think of on a topic in a short time frame of one or two minutes.

1. Tell students they have only one minute to write down all the things they can think of on the topic, e.g. 'Write down what you think of when I say the word "success" (words and phrases)' or 'What do you think is meant by "bouncing back"?'
2. At the end of the specified time, ask different students to share their answers as a springboard for further teaching.

You could give the students sheets of paper already printed with an interesting border or graphics, plus the heading 'Lightning writing' with a lightning bolt.

Memory cards

This is a good activity to consolidate vocabulary. The memory cards are mixed up and placed face down. Students take turns to turn over one card and try to find its pair. The winner is the student who matches the most pairs. This e-game is available on www.pearsonplaces.com.au/bounceback.aspx.

Movers and shakers

This is a personal survey in which students give their responses by making specific movements rather than verbal answers.

1. Prepare about six Yes/No questions/statements and attach some movement options to each. For example:
   - Pretend to bounce a ball with your right hand if you play in a netball or basketball team.
   - Put your left hand on your hip if you have ever had a friend who has moved to another school.
   - Put your hands over your eyes if you have a night light on when you are sleeping.
2. Ask the whole class to stand up, leaving space to stand and move without bumping others.
3. Ask each question.

Paper plate quiz and People pie

This is one way to conduct a whole-class survey.

1. Prepare a paper plate for each student. One side has a smiley face with a big YES, the other side has a frowning face with a big NO. You could also have different colours, e.g. smiley face yellow, frowning face blue. A craft stick could be added for a handle.
2. Everyone sits in a circle with their paper plate.
3. Ask the whole class a question that requires a 'Yes' or 'No' answer, for example: 'Do you have a pet?' 'Have you ever grazed your knee and it got better?' The students show the 'Yes' or 'No' side of their plate in response. Alternatively, they could just raise their hand in response to a simple 'Yes/No' question.
4. For 'People pie', the students then move into a single circle, with all the 'Yes' people sitting together and all the 'No' people sitting together.
5. The teacher stands in the centre of the circle with a long piece of wool and passes it to the people at the ends of the YES section to make a visual pie graph. Count the number of people in each of the two categories.

Variation
- Students can predict how many will answer 'Yes' and 'No' before they respond.
- Students can use class data to draw up their own pie graphs after the activity.

Partner retell

Students first interview each other in pairs. Then in the follow-up whole-class discussion, they retell what their partner said. Before you start, tell the students they need to listen really well because they will be retelling what their partner said.

People scavenger hunt
Each student has a chart headed 'Find someone who', with a list of categories on it, e.g. has a cat/likes olives, etc. They talk to classmates to find someone different for each category and write each person's name against that category.

Reflections
In a whole-class context, students take turns to select and answer a reflective question about the topic. This e-tool is available on www.pearsonplaces.com.au/bounceback.aspx.

Round table
Students work in a small group at a table, looking for things in a specified category (e.g. in a magazine or on printed sheets) or grouping things into specific categories.
- Example A: Each group has a sheet of A3 paper. Each student cuts out and pastes onto the sheet one picture of someone feeling happy. In the next round, and with another A3 sheet of paper, they repeat the process with someone looking sad.
- Example B: Groups of three sit around a table. Each student has one A3 sheet, labelled with a different category (e.g. Happy, Sad, Angry). There is a set of pictures and glue sticks in the middle of the table. Each student finds a picture that fits the category on their sheet, pastes the picture on the sheet and passes the sheet clockwise to the next person. The students keep pasting and passing until all their pictures are used.

Secret word
Students work out the secret letter in each clue. They then form a word from all the letters. The secret word completes an important **Bounce Back!** message. This e-game is in many units and is available on www.pearsonplaces.com.au/bounceback.aspx.

Smiley ball
This is a good way to get students to answer questions:
1. Draw a smiley face on a medium-sized plastic ball.
2. Organise students in a circle on the floor (to roll the ball) or in chairs (to throw the ball).
3. Say a student's name, roll the ball to them and then ask them a question. They answer and then roll the ball back to you.
4. Keep going with students, repeating the question or asking different questions.
5. You could ask students to put their hands behind their back when they have had a turn.

Think–ink–pair–share (TIPS)
(Adapted from Lyman.[1]) Each student takes time to reflect on their answer to a question posed by the teacher and write down a few key words before they share their thoughts with a partner.

Whisper game
This is a listening activity. Write a different, theme-related word on each of eight cards. Create four identical sets of the eight cards. Three sets will be used by each of three teams of students. One set will be used by the teacher. Divide the class into three equal teams. Each team sits on the floor or in a line of chairs behind each other, facing the back of the room. The first player in each team faces the teacher. Place one set of well-shuffled cards at the back-wall end of each of the three teams. Select one card from your set and hold it up (or write it on the board) so that each of the front players (who are the only players facing you) can see it easily. They whisper the word down their line and the last player in their team has to pick out the same card from the pile in front of them, run to the teacher and give them the card they think is correct. The player who arrives first with the correct card earns three points for their team, the player who is second earns two points and the player who is third earns gets one point. Repeat this process with the player who delivered the card to the teacher then becoming the first player in each team who starts the 'whisper'.

Section C: Organising students into pairs and groups

The best approach in organising students into groups or pairs is 'random grouping'. This means that students are allocated to groups and 'mixed up' rather than choosing who they will work with. If you do this for 90% of the time then you can allow students to select their own work partners the rest of the time (but tell them that 'free choice' grouping will be disbanded if everyone hasn't been invited into a group within two minutes). Random grouping contributes to a more inclusive and positive classroom culture, characterised by a sense of connectedness as everyone gets to know and work with everyone else. Here are some ways of randomly organising pairs or groups of three for class of 24.

Name cards or craft sticks
Write everyone's first name on a card or craft stick (or ask them to do this with their own name). The teacher pulls out three from a container (or two for each pair).

Numbering off
Number each student from 1 to 8. Students with the same number go in the same group. If you have more than 24 students, choose the extra one or two to be 'wild cards' who can choose any group to go to. If you have more than 26, make extra groups.

Category cards
Make eight sets of three cards. Write a number from 1 to 3 on the back of each card in each set (to use for allocating roles). On the front of each card, paste or draw a picture or write a word related to a current theme. Students draw a card from a container and then find the other two students who have the same or a matching card. Sets could be made around:
- eight different animals
- eight different forms of transport (e.g. car, ship, truck, bicycle, bus, tram, plane, rickshaw)
- eight countries (students form groups with other students who have a fact about the same country, e.g. the name of the country, its main river, capital city, famous monument, language spoken)
- eight postcards (or old birthday or Christmas cards) or pictures from magazines turned into three-piece jigsaws
- eight sets of number facts that all have the same answer, e.g. one set of three cards could all have an answer of 10 (2 × 5, 5 + 5, 8 + 2)
- eight sets of playing cards that match on number, not suit
- eight sets of pictures or words that start with the same letter (e.g. cow, cup, cat, carrot) or the same letter combination (e.g. think, thank, throw).

Line-ups
Students line up in two lines either randomly or on the basis of a criterion such as the order of their name in the alphabet (first name or surname) or birthdays (month first, then day). Alternatively, you could ask each student to take a card (e.g. that has a word or a number written on it) and then ask them to line up in their allocated line in the correct order of the cards (i.e. alphabetical or from smallest to largest number). Then the first four in the line form a group, and then the next four and so on. You could also 'shuffle' the lines by asking the first two people in line 1 to go to the end of their line and the last two in line 2 to come to the front of their line. Then make groups based on two people from each line.

References
1. Lyman, F. 1987, 'Think-Pair-Share: An expanded teaching technique', *MAA-CIE Cooperative News*, vol. 1, pp. 1–2.

Chapter 8

Years K–2 resources

Section A: Books, films and songs

Most of the books in *Bounce Back!* are still in print. You will probably have a great many of them in your library already as we have drawn heavily on those books that are 'classics', are by highly respected authors and/or have been nominated for various children's book awards over the past two decades.

See www.pearsonplaces.com.au/bounceback.aspx for detailed information on the books referred to in each unit and how to obtain them. There is also information on how to find songs, lyrics and video clips.

Section B: Classroom resources

The following resources can be used to support the units and are referred to in **Classroom Resources**.

Bounce-backers

The bounce-backer comes back after being tipped over and becomes a great visual prompt for young students to remember that when they get knocked down or are feeling sad/low, they can bounce back!

For each student you will need:
- A hollow plastic playpen ball already cut in half. These can be bought cheaply in packs of 50 from discount shops or early childhood shops
- One craft stick for the body and extra craft sticks for the arms and legs
- Thick paper or cardboard to make a circle for the face
- Plasticine or play dough
- Markers, scissors, sticky tape and glue to share

Steps
- Students fill the half-ball with play dough or plasticine.
- They stick the craft stick in the middle, draw a face on the cardboard circle (or add their own photo of just their face or their whole body and then paste it onto the craft stick.
- They can make arms and legs from craft sticks and then draw and cut out clothes for the bounce-backer. Or print out photos of each student in school uniform for them to paste on their bounce-backer.

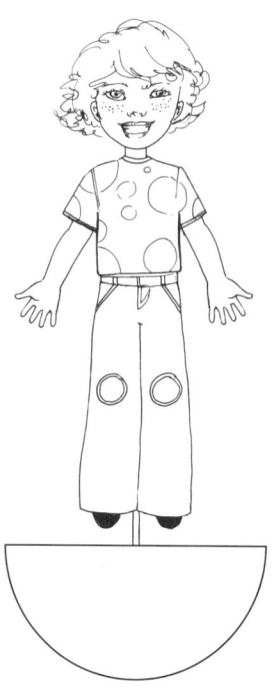

Chapter 8
Years K–2 resources

Variations and follow-ups
- A teacher or older peer buddy can fill the half-ball with plaster of Paris and, when half set, add the craft stick.
- An alternative is to stick a small wooden skewer in the centre of the ball with the pointy end up. When the plaster has set, they stick a table tennis ball or a small polystyrene ball (available from craft shops) onto the skewer. Then they draw eyes and mouth or use googly eyes.
- Add a costume to the bounce-backer. Draw a circle with a 21 cm diameter onto light card. Draw lines to divide the circle into thirds. Cut one of the lines to the centre of the circle. Draw and colour/paint the costume for the bounce-backer in one of the sections of the circle next to the cut line. Then make the circle into a cone shape by overlapping the paper until only the costume part of the cone can be seen.
- Understanding the motion of the bounce-backer. The bounce-backer comes back after being tipped over as its centre of gravity shifts. Comparisons can be made with seesaws.

Literature prompts

Picture books and simple novels are used throughout **Bounce Back!** as a starting point or to reinforce key messages. The following questions can be used to guide student reading and reflection on texts. They can be used for discussion in a whole class, a cooperative pair or a group. They can be used with activities such as 'Partner retell' (see page 91) and 'Think–ink–pair–share' (see page 92).

Prompts to help students understand the text:
- What do you already know about this topic?
- What do you think this book might be about? (after showing the cover)
- Who are the characters/people/animals?
- What happens?
- Where is it set?
- When did…happen?
- How/why did it happen?
- What happened in the beginning/middle/end?
- What does the cover/title tell us about the text?
- What does this picture tell you? How does it make you feel?
- What do you think might happen next? Why?

Prompts to help students to think critically about the text:
- What is this story about? How do we know?
- Who is in the story? Who is missing from the story? Who should/could be there?
- Who tells the story? What might another character say if they were asked?
- Do you like the story? Why? Why not?
- How could we change the ending of the story?
- What if a character did something different? How might the story be different?
- What characters do you like? What characters don't you like? Why?
- What clues do the words or pictures give us about how the characters are feeling?
- What do you think the writer wants the reader to think about?
- What does the author want us to believe about the world and the people in it? What suggests this to us? Does this 'fit' with what you believe about the world and about people? Why/why not?
- What is the message/moral in the book? What is the writer telling us? Do you agree with the author's message? What might you do differently now you have read this book?
- What might this character be thinking right now?
- Why did the story end in this way?
- What does the ending mean?
- How did the book make you feel? Is this a happy or sad book?

- In what ways is this book the same as/different to your favourite book?
- What if this book had no pictures?

Bounce Back! wellbeing prompts

These questions help students to understand the key *Bounce Back!* concepts when using the recommended literature. The *Bounce Back!* book prompts can be used with books, poems, songs and films in the program, or any other texts. Some questions will be more suitable for some books than others. Students can be given the questions as a basis for writing book reviews.

- Question focusing on predicting likelihood
  - How likely is it (was it) that what this person is (was) worried about what will (would) happen?
- Questions focusing on courage
  - Who showed courage in this story? What fear did they overcome?
  - What risks did they take? Were they thoughtful or foolhardy risks?
- Questions focusing on resourcefulness and goal setting
  - Where in the story did someone refuse to give up?
  - What plans did the characters in the book make?
  - Did anyone in this story learn from the mistakes they made?
  - Did the person work hard? What did they want to achieve? What goal did they set?
  - Did working hard help them be successful?
- Question focusing on 'Bad feelings and unhappy times always go away'
  - When did the character find out that their bad times don't last and things get better?
- Questions focusing on 'Other people can help you feel better if you talk to them'
  - Who did the character speak to when they were feeling sad, when they were worried, when they had a problem? How did speaking to someone help them to feel better?
- Questions focusing on 'Unhelpful thinking makes you more upset'
  - What feelings did the different people in this story have? (Stress accurate naming of the feeling and its intensity, as described in the 'Emotions' unit.)
  - Who was angry in the story? Was it helpful to be angry or not? What might have happened if they stayed calm and didn't get angry?
  - Did anyone in this story jump to conclusions without good evidence?
  - Did anyone in this story change the way they were thinking so that their thinking was more helpful (i.e. helped them not to exaggerate, to look for facts and to find a solution)?
- Questions focusing on 'Nobody is perfect. Mistakes can help you to learn'
  - How was this character 'not perfect'? What mistakes did they make? Is anyone perfect? When have you made a mistake? Did your mistake help you to learn?
- Questions focusing on 'Concentrate on the good things in an unhappy situation'
  - Did anyone in the story find something good in the bad situation? Did anyone look on the bright side?
- Questions focusing on 'Everybody feels sad and worried sometimes, not just you'
  - What were the difficult or hard times in the story? Do these things happen to everyone? Do you know other people your age who have had this sort of setback too?
- Questions focusing on 'Having a laugh helps you to feel better'
  - Did anyone in the story find something that was funny? Did laughing make them feel better? Did laughing make others feel better?
- Question focusing on 'Change happens a lot in everyone's life. It's normal'
  - What were some of the things that happened to the characters? In what way did these things change their life? Is it normal to have things change in your life?
- Questions focusing on 'Sometimes there is nothing you can do to change a situation and you just have to put up with it'
  - What happened to the character that they didn't like but they couldn't change?
  - In what ways did the character cope with the thing or things they couldn't change?

- Question focusing on 'One bad thing doesn't spoil everything else'
  - When one unhappy time happened for this character, what other things in their life were still OK?
- Questions on relationships
  - How did the character's relationship with others influence the story's outcomes?
  - Where did conflict occur and how was it dealt with?
- Questions focusing on emotions and empathy
  - How did this character feel? What words or pictures tell us how they felt? How did their feelings influence them to do what they did? Do you think this was a good thing to do? How would you feel if you were this character? Would you do what they did?

Class books

Class books can be made in shapes that reflect the contents (e.g. a heart shape for a book on families). Cut out cardboard to make the shaped covers. Then cut out a page for each student who is contributing to the book in exactly the same shape and size.

Digital photos of each student's page can be made and the photos inserted into Microsoft® Office PowerPoint® slides to make a digital class book.

Cube pattern

This cube pattern can be enlarged and made into a dice (e.g. a feelings dice) or suspended on a string as a cube to display information (e.g. six positive things in my life).

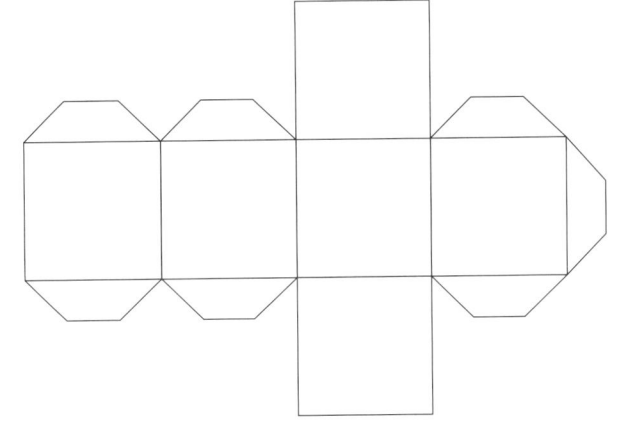

Digital stories

Students make a simple story using programs such as Microsoft® Office PowerPoint® and Kid Pix to add images to text. There is a lot of software available on the Internet to enable the addition of voiceovers, audio, captions and special effects.

Lift-up flaps and circles

Lift-up flaps and circles offer students a chance to invite classmates to interact with their work. They write a question on the front of the flap or circle (e.g. What animals cooperate with each other?). The answer is found when you lift up the flap to see what is written underneath (e.g. Meerkats).

Little flaps can be attached to a very large sheet of cardboard (along with those by other people) or to a bulletin board. To make a little flap, fold a small piece of card in two (like a place card or a small birthday card) and paste it onto cardboard, or attach it with a drawing pin (in the bottom part) to a bulletin board.

Big flaps sit on a bench or desk. To make a big flap, you will need:
- an empty shoe box with lid
- plastic document sleeves
- coloured cardboard
- a handle to lift up the top with, e.g. a champagne cork attached with a screw and washer underneath (optional)

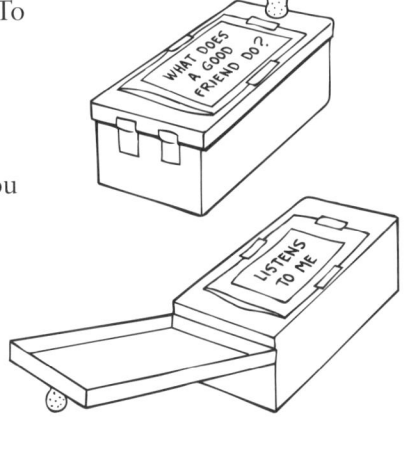

The question is written on a piece of cardboard, placed in the plastic sleeve and taped to the outside of the lid of the box. The lid sits on the box. The answer is written on another piece of card, placed in a plastic sleeve and attached to the inside bottom of the box. Add a handle to the lid. Using masking tape, attach the lid to the box at the opposite end to the handle.

Lift-up circles are attached to a very large sheet of cardboard (along with those of other people) or to a bulletin board. To make lift-up circles, make two identical cardboard circles. Write a question and an answer on each circle. Join them together and attach them with a split pin to the larger sheet of cardboard or with a drawing pin to the bulletin board. The top circle should be able to be swung to either side.

You can also have three sets of lift-up circles. The middle set contains a single circle with a question. The other two have different answers, one correct and one incorrect. On the bottom of the right answer is a smiley face and the words 'Well done! You are correct!' On the bottom of the wrong answer is a frowning face and the words 'Sorry, you are wrong. Try again.'

Flaps can also be made with a question on one PowerPoint slide and the answer on the next slide.

Students could work in groups of three to research a specific area of a topic such as 'Friendship'. Each group researches a different aspect of friendship. They present their project as a class flap display using all forms of flaps and lift-up circles. For example, 'Lift up the lid to find out how to be a good friend'.

Flipbook

For each student you will need:
- two A4 sheets of the same coloured paper or thin card
- three sheets of white A4 paper
- a hole puncher to share with other members of the class
- markers or crayons
- coloured wool

Steps
1. Fold the three sheets of white paper in half and cut along the fold to make six half sheets.
2. Place them together to make a book of six pages. These sheets of paper make the bottom half of the A4 book.
3. Use two A4 sheets of same-coloured paper to make the front and back cover of the book.
4. Use a hole puncher to make two holes in the top half and two holes in the bottom half of the book (the six half pages and two covers).
5. Use wool to tie the covers and pages together.
6. On the top half of the book (inside back cover), students write the main statement (e.g. 'I feel happy when …'). On each of the six sheets of the book they write and illustrate six endings that complete the main statement (e.g. Mum or Dad reads me a story; I visit my cousins; I ride my bike).

Fridge magnet frame

The fridge magnet is designed to serve as a memory jogger for key messages for the BOUNCE! and STAR! acronyms, or a prompt for goals they have set themselves.

For each student you will need:
- ruler
- coloured paper (for inserts)
- a piece of thick cardboard (150 cm x 100 cm) for the base of the frame
- paint and paintbrush/markers
- very small flat magnets (available at hardware stores and some newsagents or toy shops)
- PVA glue and scissors to share
- marker pen

Steps
1. Measure and draw a frame 1 cm from the edge of the cardboard.
2. Draw a second frame 1 cm inside the first frame you have just drawn.
3. Use a marker pen to draw a picture that extends into the outer frame (see picture at right).
4. Cut out the inside rectangle.
5. Glue a small magnet to each of the four corners.
6. Write the message on the coloured paper and insert it behind the frame.

Mobiles

A mobile is a sculpture with parts that move. Mobiles have two parts:
- the structure or base you hang things from
- the things you hang.

Bases can be made from skewers, a cork with two skewers inserted through it, bits of wood (cane, bamboo, driftwood, thin dowel, balsa wood), fine wire, cardboard, cardboard cylinders, drinking straws, string or fishing line.

Things to hang can be drawings, cards or cardboard shapes, things made out of paper, small boxes, tissue, papier-mache items, small toys and objects such as balls, wooden people (from craft shops), paper cut-out people, or small stones.

Puppets and masks

There are references to using puppets throughout the nine curriculum units. Here is a list of many different kinds of puppets. Masks can also be used instead of puppets.

Masks and stick puppets
Glue pictures of faces from magazines onto cardboard and add a craft stick to hold it with. You can use just eyes, or just the mouth or use the whole face. Cut out small eyeholes. Similarly, you could make paper plate masks to hold. Cut out eye holes and add wool for hair.

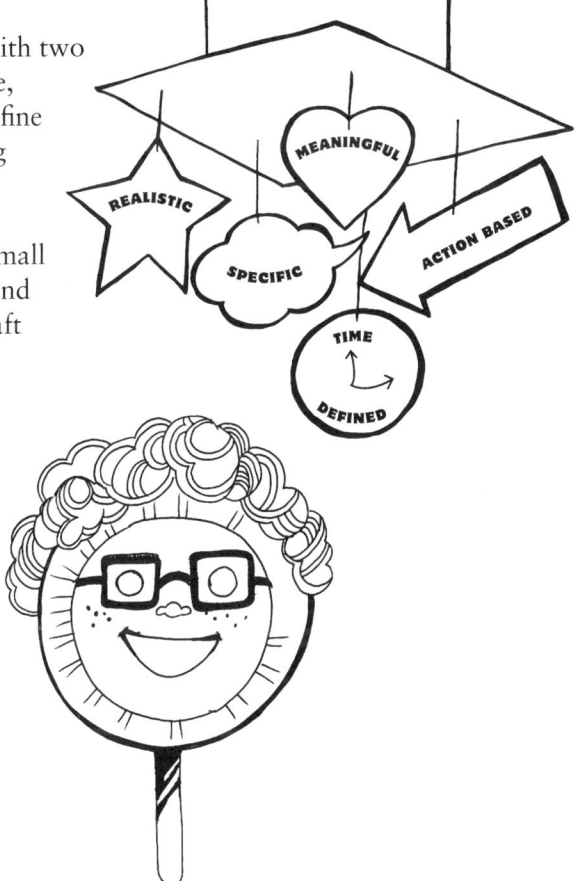

Finger puppets and hand strappers
Version 1: Use felt finger covers as illustrated.
Version 2: Make hand strappers by making a long paper watch with an animal shape or person's face in the position that the watch face would be. Strap them over the back of the hand and use fingers as legs.
Version 3: Cut out a circle on stiff card with two holes in the base for fingers. Students draw on the card or paste their drawings on the card as illustrated.

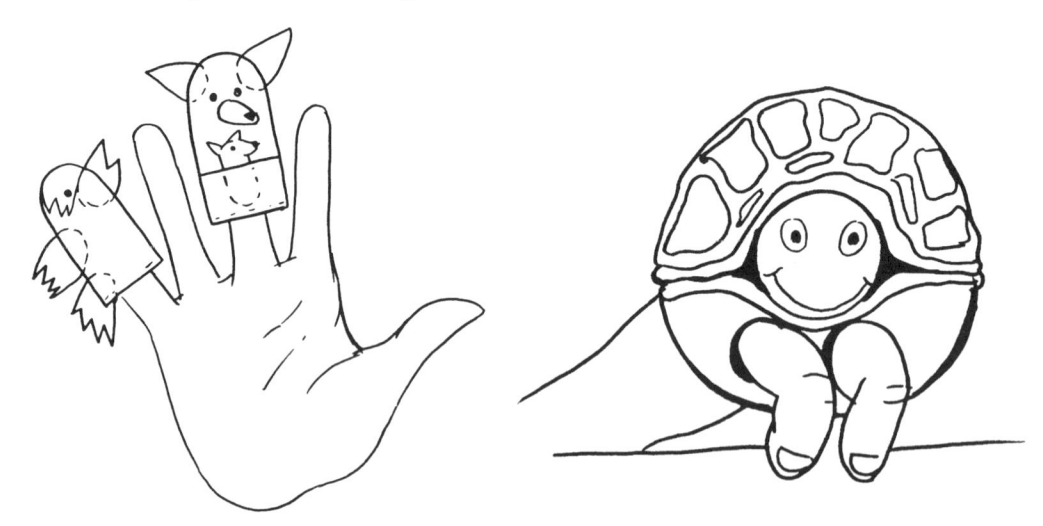

Balloon puppets
Add a balloon to a cardboard cylinder. Thread the string that ties the end of the balloon through the cylinder and tape to the side. Add a face and other features.

Brown paper bag puppets
Draw a face and hair on a paper bag. Stuff the bag with crumpled paper. Attach to a stick with a rubber band.

Glove puppets
Use a woollen or rubber glove. Staple an image onto the top of the glove. Or make the glove into an animal by stitching on fabric ears (e.g. furry fabric) and buttons for eyes. On a rubber glove you can draw features with a permanent pen. Add buttons for eyes.

Paper plate puppets
Add wool for hair, and draw in the face.

Paper spring puppets
Draw a body and then make legs and arms out of paper springs. To make the springs, students cut out two long strips of paper. Paste the paper at right angles to each other and then fold one on top of the other until all the paper is folded. Glue to the body of the puppet. Paste a long stick or craft sticks to the back of the puppet.

Self-photo puppets
Use photos of students' faces and glue them onto cardboard. Make a cardboard body. Add craft sticks or a wire coat-hanger (straightened and then doubled) for a handle.

Shadow puppets
Draw the shape of an animal or person on cardboard. Cut it out and make large eye holes. Straighten out a wire coat-hanger to make a long handle. Tape the puppet to the end of the handle. Wrap masking tape on the other end. Make a screen with a bed sheet hung over a rope. Put a light source such as a lamp between the puppet and the sheet.

Sock puppets
Cut a cardboard rectangle about 7 cm × 20 cm and fold it in half to form the inside of the mouth. Place the cardboard inside the sock and glue in place. Decorate the sock.

Split pin puppets on strings
Cut the shape of the character or animal from cardboard. Join legs, arms and head to the body with split pins. Add string to the head, arms and legs so that different parts of the puppet can move.

Soft toy/animal puppets
Use students' old soft toys or animals as puppets. Make a hole in the base and insert dowelling to serve as a handle.

Wooden spoon puppets/craft sticks
Draw features on the spoon or the top of a craft stick.

Wax-resist badges

You will need:
- wax crayons
- white card
- dark-coloured poster paint
- paintbrush
- scissors
- double-sided tape
- safety pins

Steps
1. Students draw a shape for the badge with wax crayons, e.g. a pot and sunflowers for 'Looking on the bright side', a funny face for 'Humour', a medal for 'STAR' or 'Everyday Courage'. They colour the drawing in bright colours.
2. Paint over the wax drawing with poster paint.
3. When the paint is dry, the crayon will shine through.
4. Cut out around the drawing to form the badge.
5. Turn the badge over.
6. Use a piece of double-sided tape to attach the safety pin.

Section C: An example of a Years K–2 scope and sequence chart

The following table shows how different lower primary classes can coordinate the teaching of the different *Bounce Back!* units. For further ideas see Chapter 6: Implementation and maintenance of Bounce Back! (page 74).

Chapter 8
Years K–2 resources

Sample scope and sequence chart: Bounce Back! Years K–2

Term	Unit	K/Prep (5 year olds)	Years 1/2 6–7 year olds (Even year)	Years 1/2 6–7 year olds (Odd year)
Term 1	Core values (Weeks 1–5) Link with negotiated class vision and school rules	Honesty Not cheating Being fair Being responsible · Choose two key books · Choose a consolidation activity	Caring about and supporting others (being kind) Teacher support Supporting people we don't know Family support Kindness to animals Cooperation · Choose two key books · Choose a consolidation activity	It's OK to be different Including others Being friendly Respect Self-respect · Choose two key books · Choose a consolidation activity
	People bouncing back (Weeks 6–10)	Everyone has unhappy times Change happens a lot Growing up and bouncing back Losing someone/pet you love Family changes 'We Can Bounce Back' song · Choose two key books · Choose a consolidation activity	Other people can help Learning from mistakes and problems Bouncing back from being sick or injured · Choose two key books · Choose a consolidation activity	Nobody is perfect Helpful thinking makes you feel better 'We Can Bounce Back' song · Choose two key books · Choose a consolidation activity
	Courage (Weeks –3)	Understanding fear Fear and courage are different for different people What is courage? · Choose two key books · Choose a consolidation activity	What is courage? Helping yourself be brave Being brave to help someone else The courage to be yourself When I first came to school · Choose two key books · Choose a consolidation activity	What is courage? Being foolish Being scared of the dark, dangerous animals or minibeasts Being brave about doctor and dentist Learning from mistakes Everyone has fears, even grown-ups · Choose two key books · Choose a consolidation activity
Term 2	Looking on the bright side (Weeks 4–6)	Looking on the bright side Positive tracking · Choose two key books · Choose a consolidation activity	Expressing gratitude and appreciation Bouncing back by thinking of positive memories · Choose two key books · Choose a consolidation activity	Being optimistic Symbols of hope · Choose two key books · Choose a consolidation activity
	Emotions (Weeks 7–10)	Everyone has feelings Changing bad mood into good mood Feelings happen inside our bodies Mixed feelings · Choose two key books · Choose a consolidation activity	How angry do you feel? Being the boss of your angry feelings Hands are not for hitting Do they really mean it? What to do when someone is angry with you · Choose two key books · Choose a consolidation activity	Everyone feels sad sometimes Don't be a worry bee Do you feel jealous? How do other people feel? What kind of surprise? · Choose two key books · Choose a consolidation activity

Handbook

103

Term 3	Relationships (Weeks 1–6)	Feeling shy and lonely Getting to know others What do children like about others? It's important to listen well when others talk Being noticed · Choose two key books · Choose a consolidation activity	Friendship Making new friends Being a good friend Friends can be different · Choose two key books · Choose a consolidation activity	Friendship and loyalty How to be a thoughtful friend Being separated from a friend Good and bad ways to disagree Apologising and being friends again · Choose two key books · Choose a consolidation activity
	No bullying (Weeks 7–10)	What is bullying? How it feels to be bullied Put-downs can lead to bullying · Choose two key books · Choose a consolidation activity	What is bullying? Bullying spoils things for all Think for yourself (1 and 2) · Choose two key books · Choose a consolidation activity	What is bullying? What can you do if bullied? What can you do to help someone being bullied? · Choose two key books · Choose a consolidation activity
Term 4	Humour (Weeks 1–3)	Humour is healthy Giggle Gym That's nonsense! What makes you laugh? · Choose several books · Choose a consolidation activity	Humour is healthy Giggle Gym Clowns and the circus Humour can be hurtful · Choose several books · Choose a consolidation activity	What makes you laugh? Giggle Gym (can be used throughout the year) Humour can be hurtful · Choose several books · Choose a consolidation activity
	STAR! (Success) (Weeks 4–6)	Being a STAR Stick with it and don't give up Think for yourself: how are you clever? Think for yourself: what kind of person are you trying to be? As I grow I get better · Choose two key books · Choose a consolidation activity	Being a STAR Always make a plan Remember to try hard, work hard · Choose two key books · Choose a consolidation activity	Being a STAR Solving problems Be the boss of yourself Be organised Using your strengths to help others · Choose two key books · Choose a consolidation activity